Handmade
Gifts

Handmade Gifts

DK

LONDON, NEW YORK, MELBOURNE, MUNICH, and DELHI

DK UK
Project Art Editor Gemma Fletcher
Project Editor Laura Palosuo
Designer Charlotte Johnson
Jacket Designer Rosie Levine
Pre-Production Producer Rebecca Fallowfield
Producer Ché Creasey
Photographer Dave King
Creative Technical Support Sonia Charbonnier
Managing Editor Penny Smith
Managing Art Editor Marianne Markham
Art Director Jane Bull
Publisher Mary Ling

DK US
US Senior Editor Shannon Beatty
US Editor Margaret Parrish
US Consultant Jennifer Wendell

DK INDIA
Senior Art Editor Ivy Roy
Art Editor Vikas Sachdeva
Assistant Art Editor Pallavi Kapur
Managing Art Editor Navidita Thapa
Pre-Production Manager Sunil Sharma
Production Manager Pankaj Sharma
Senior DTP Designer Jagtar Singh
DTP Designers Syed Md Farhan, Rajesh Singh
Adhikari, Rajdeep Singh

First American Edition, 2013

Published in the United States by DK Publishing

4th floor, 345 Hudson Street

New York, New York 10014

13 14 15 16 17 10 9 8 7 6 5 4 3 2 1
192398—Oct/2013

A catalog record for this book is available from
the Library of Congress.

ISBN 978-1-4654-0840-2

DK books are available at special discounts when
purchased in bulk for sales promotions, premiums,
fund-raising, or educational use. For details, contact: DK
Publishing Special Markets, 4th floor, 345 Hudson Street,
New York, New York 10014 or SpecialSales@dk.com.

Printed and bound by South China in China

Discover more at
www.dk.com

Contents

Introduction

Sometimes a box of chocolates or another pair of socks simply won't do. For a truly thoughtful present, making your own gifts is the way forward. You can create something beautiful, unique, and affordable, regardless of whether you have an hour or two to spend or an entire afternoon.

Every idea in *Handmade Gifts* is explained in step-by-step photographs so you can be sure that your gift will have a professional finish, and will be well worth the time you invest in making it. If the project requires a template, we include one so you know it will work. There are lots of ideas for how you can add your own twist, so you can make the gift that is exactly right for the person you have in mind.

We have included a range of gift ideas, each requiring different levels of skill and time—for example, you can crochet a beaded necklace or "cheat" with a knotted one. We hope you have a wonderful time making your gifts... and that you find time to make something for yourself!

For the home

Customized
pillow

Customize a plain pillow cover with appliqué fabric shapes, buttons, and decorative stitches to make a stylish or funky pillow at a low cost— a perfect gift for a new home or for a child's bedroom.

To make a blossom pillow you will need

Tools: washable ink pen • tracing paper • steam iron • dressmaker's scissors • sewing pins • sewing machine • sewing needle • cotton sewing threads *Materials:* iron-on interfacing • brown cotton fabric • white cotton fabric • pink floral cotton fabric • green felt • pillow cover • 8 small white buttons and 4 large white buttons

1

Enlarge the blossom pillow templates on p.226 to fit your pillow. Trace all the shapes except for the leaves onto iron-on interfacing.

2

Cut out the interfacing and iron each piece onto the chosen fabric for each: brown cotton for the bird and branch, white cotton for 12 petals, and pink floral cotton for 12 centers.

3

Carefully cut out all
the interfaced shapes.

4

Trace the leaf template onto paper and cut it out.
Use the template to trace and cut out six leaves
from the felt. There is no need to iron these onto
interfacing because felt will not fray.

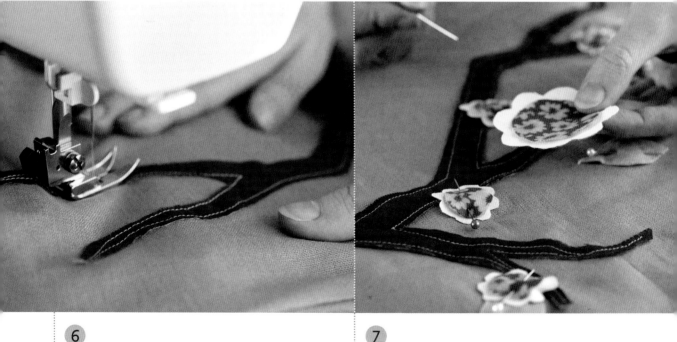

6

Machine sew the branch and bird onto
the pillow using a contrasting color of
cotton thread, carefully sewing about
1/8–1/4in (3–5mm) from the edges.

7

Match the large, white flowers with the large,
pink centers and the small, white flowers with
the small, pink centers. Place the flowers and
leaves onto the pillow and pin in position.

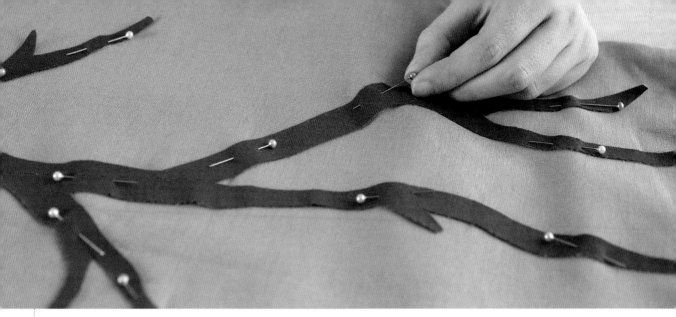

5

Place the pillow cover on a flat surface
and place the branch and bird in position.
Pin or use basting stitches to secure.

8

Tuck some of the leaves behind the flowers to
create a natural effect. Hand sew the leaves
on in a matching cotton down the centers,
using four or five backstitches to secure.

9

Sew large and small buttons into the centers
of the flowers, sewing through the pillow
cover to secure the flowers to the cover.

Castle pillow

Be as creative as you like with this castle. Start with the template on p.228 to create the basic shape. Use faux-leather fabric for the drawbridge and windows, and a favorite color for the flag. The prince and princess are made from felt scraps and are attached to the pillow by thin cord so they cannot be lost! You can make your own dolls, or add ready-made fabric dolls. Remember to make a few pockets in the design where you can place them.

} Tip: Use the templates on p.229 to make the dolls. Add yarn for hair and sew on faces.

Skull-and-crossbones pillow

A fun skull motif will appeal to children of all ages, particularly those with a love of pirates! Find the template for this project on p.227. Cut out the skull-and-crossbones shapes from black felt and baste into position on the pillow cover. Machine sew around the edge of the black shapes using white thread. Cut out eyes and teeth from white felt and sew them by hand into position onto the skull.

Guitar pillow

This is the perfect pillow for a teenager's room. Using the template on p.227, cut out the shapes for the guitar from black and white felt or faux-suede fabric. Baste and stitch the guitar body into place first using contrasting thread. Add the white inset section, sewing it on with white thread. Add the black details, again using contrast thread. Use white ribbon for the strings and sew into position. A drum or a section of piano keys would also look cool.

Personalized
journal

What better place to store notes and thoughts than in a handmade journal with a personalized cover? This technique demands precision—each stage is built on the previous one, so if you're slightly "off," the journal may look misshapen.

To make a journal you will need

Tools: bone folder • craft knife • pencil • metal ruler • self-healing cutting mat • needle

Materials: 6 sheets of heavy 11 x 17in white or cream paper • 1 sheet of decorative paper • white thread

1

Making sure that the grain is running vertically, fold each piece of white or cream 11 x 17in paper in half lengthwise and smooth the crease with the bone folder.

2

Starting from the inside of the folded sheet, cut along the fold with the knife, stopping at a point just over halfway along the fold.

3

Again, fold each sheet of paper in half lengthwise. Crease, then cut along the fold, stopping just after halfway. Fold each sheet in half again lengthwise, smoothing down the creases.

4

Assemble the folded sheets in a pile of "stacks." To make the cover, first fold the decorative paper in half along its width and press the crease down with the bone folder.

7

Use the ruler and the bone folder to crease the cover along the second pencil line you have just drawn. The area between the two creases will be the spine of your journal.

8

Measure the height of the cover and divide this distance into five equal sections. Mark each section on the spine, and then use a craft knife to cut a slit through each line.

5

Next, fold the paper lengthwise and smooth down the crease.

6

Open the cover and draw a line down this crease. Press down gently on the pile of stacks and measure the height of the pile. Then measure the same distance to one side of the crease. Draw a line.

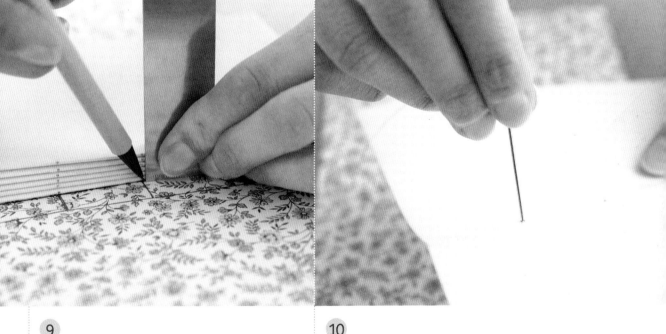

9

Use the ruler to draw lines on the pile of paper stacks to correspond with the slits in the cover.

10

Open up each paper segment and prick the needle through each mark. There should now be four evenly spaced holes in each paper segment. Thread the needle.

11

With one stack on top of the cover, push the needle through the first hole (hole A) and first slit (slit A) from the inside. Pass the thread around the top of the spine and tie a knot.

12

Pass the needle through the hole B from the inside and out through slit B. Run the thread along the spine and push the needle in through slit C and hole C to the inside.

15

Add a new stack and continue, securing pages and adding stacks. After the last stack, pass the needle around the top of the journal and below one of the stitches. Knot on the inside.

16

Fold the decorative paper back over the stack and smooth it down, creasing the fold with your finger.

13

Push the needle out through hole D and slit D. Looping the thread around the bottom of the spine, push the needle through just hole D again. Tighten the thread.

14

Add the next stack. Go through the first hole of the new stack (hole 2D) to the inside, then around the bottom of the spine and back through slit D and hole 2D. Continue, securing the second page like the first.

17

Now fold the paper under again to form the jacket. Repeat for the other side.

18

Cut through the edges of the pages of the first stack. Repeat for all the other stacks.

Dot-decorated
ceramics

Painting ceramics by hand can seem a bit daunting, but this dot-decorating method is virtually foolproof. Almost any line drawing can be turned into a dot painting, so once you have mastered the technique try out your own designs.

To make a dot-decorated vase you will need

Tools: scissors • ballpoint pen

Materials: ceramic vase • baby wipes or damp cloth • red transfer paper
• masking tape • black, food-safe ceramic pen or paint in a dispenser

1

Clean the vase to remove any loose dust or grease from the surface. Photocopy the vase template (see p.240) and reduce or enlarge it to fit.

2

Place a sheet of transfer paper behind the template and cut out the main dandelion motif. Then cut out the individual seeds.

3

Tape the dandelion template to the front of your vase, with the transfer paper underneath. Position the seeds around the template and on one adjoining side.

4

Use a ballpoint pen to trace the design onto the vase. Make solid lines across the dots, since these show up best.

7

Using the template as a guide, complete the design with dots. Keep the spacing of the dots even and work quickly to prevent the paint from pooling. Paint short, solid lines at the ends of the seeds and then fill in the dots.

5

Remove the template and check that the lines are visible. If not, wipe away the trace lines and repeat the process, pressing down more firmly.

6

Use a ceramic paint pen or paint in a dispenser to draw the stem of the dandelion in one continuous line.

8

Repeat Steps 4–7 to decorate the second side of the vase. Let the paint dry before repeating the whole process for the remaining two sides.

9

When the paint is completely dry, use a baby wipe or damp cloth to wipe off the trace lines. Follow the paint manufacturer's instructions to set the paint.

Mug and coaster set

Create this delicately patterned mug and coaster set
in exactly the same way as the vase (see pp.26–29),
using the mug and coaster template (see p.241). When
painting the dots, remember to work from left to right
(right to left if you're left-handed) across the pattern to
keep from smudging the dots you have already made.

Tip: Create a set of mugs using the same design in different colors. Make one for each family member.

Celebration bunting plate

As a general rule, it is not safe to eat food from hand-painted ceramics (make sure to check the label on your paints). The dot-decorating method can be used to create stunning display plates though, and this bunting plate is the perfect gift to mark a celebration. Use the template (see p.241) to transfer the pattern to the plate. Draw the black lines, let them dry, then work across the pattern, filling in the flags with colored dots.

Tip: Add a celebratory message or the recipient's name to the plate by painting a letter in each flag.

Mosaic
bowl

This calming, woodland-inspired mosaic bowl is created using the direct method, meaning that tiles are glued straight onto the object and then grouted. This will not produce a completely level surface, resulting in a tactile bowl.

· ·

To make a mosaic bowl you will need

Tools: tile nippers • rubber gloves • protective mask & goggles • grout spreader • sponge • lint-free cloth

Materials: wooden bowl • tesserae in different shades of green • flat-backed beads and 5mm millefiori beads • craft glue • mosaic grout (either premixed or made according to the manufacturer's instructions)

1

Draw a wavy line onto your bowl, about 1¾in (4.5cm) from the rim. Draw a second line roughly ⅝in (1.5cm) below this one. This will be the first accent line on your bowl.

2

Prepare your tiles by soaking or peeling off any backing sheets. Select the plain tiles and those for the accent lines, and place them in groups of the same color and type.

3

Cut tiles for the accent lines. Wearing goggles, hold the tile between thumb and forefinger and, positioning nippers at the edge, gently squeeze. Repeat to cut into quarters.

4

Arrange the tiles and embellishments between your wavy lines. Vary iridescent and matte tiles, as well as round and rectangular ones, to create a pattern.

7

Complete one line at a time, increasing or decreasing the shade and adding accent lines at regular intervals. When complete, let dry overnight.

8

Wearing rubber gloves and a mask, apply the grout generously to the mosaic, working in different directions. Make sure to grout around the outer edge of the bowl, too.

5

Move the pieces off the line, keeping their order. Add a dab of glue to the back of each piece and stick each one to your bowl, leaving even gaps in between.

6

For the lines of plain tiles, start with the lightest green tiles and cut them in half (see Step 3). Glue them on each side of the accent line, trimming them if necessary.

9

Using a damp sponge, carefully wipe away the excess grout. Let dry for 20 minutes, then, before the grout is hard, wipe gently again.

10

When the grout is completely dry, use a lint-free dry cloth to wipe away any residue and polish the tiles to a shine.

Owl jewelry box

You will need
Wooden box
Glazed and unglazed ceramic tiles
Glass pebbles and beads
White grout
Felt for bottom

This pretty jewelry box is made using the same technique as the mosaic bowl on pp.33–35. Start by drawing the design on the box (see template p.238) and then seal the box with watered-down craft glue. Start filling in the design, attaching the glass pebbles and whole tiles first. Cut the remaining tiles to size to complete the design. Finally, fill in the area around the design with randomly cut tiles—a technique known as crazy paving. Allow to dry and then grout the lid. Grout the box one side at a time, waiting for each side to dry before starting the next. Glue felt to the bottom to finish the box.

Flower garland mirror

You will need
Mirror with wide, flat, wooden frame
A selection of tiles and glass pebbles
White grout

Make this mirror in the same way as the mosaic bowl on pp.33–35. Draw on the design first (see template p.239) and seal the wooden frame with watered-down craft glue if necessary. Create the flowers first, starting with a glass pebble and using tile nippers to shape the petals. Next, make the leaf garlands. Fill in the gaps with crazy paving (see above), and use tile halves to fill in the outer edge of the border. Cover the mirror with masking tape to protect it when grouting. Grout the frame, making sure to create a straight edge around the mirror.

Round tea light holder

Ball-shaped, wooden tea light holder
Old crockery, broken into small pieces
Tiles and glass pebbles
White grout
Felt for the bottom

This tea light holder is made in the same way as the mosaic bowl (see pp.33–35), but using fragments of broken crockery. First, draw your design (see p.239) on the tea light holder and then seal it with watered-down craft glue. Glue down the glass pebbles first, and then use tile nippers to shape the crockery pieces into petals. Next, add any whole tiles. Finally, fill in the area around the design with more crockery pieces. Work a small area at a time. Some tiles may have to be held in place using tape until they dry. Grout, allow to dry, and attach felt to the bottom to finish.

Seaside coasters

You will need
MDF squares
Tiles in a variety of colors
Gray grout

These seaside-inspired coasters have been made out of squares of MDF, using the technique described for the mosaic bowl on pp.33–35. Using either the template from p.238 or your own design, first draw guidelines onto the coaster in pencil. Fill in the design first, shaping the tiles to fit. Try to keep the tiles fairly flat, since you will need to be able to rest a glass or mug on the coaster when finished. Next, fill in the background using square tiles, shaping them to fit as necessary. Again, try to keep the tiles as flat as possible. Grout the coasters, not forgetting the edges, to finish.

Ribbon-bound
photo album

This wonderful album is bound to become a family treasure. Use thick, acid-free cardboard for the pages to protect your photographs and thick, good-quality ribbon to ensure that the binding holds for years to come.

To make a ribbon-bound photo album you will need

Tools: craft knife • metal ruler • self-healing cutting mat • bookbinding needle

Materials: 11 x 17in sheets of heavy white or cream paper • 3 x 6in (15cm) lengths of ribbon • masking tape • 3 x 40in (1m) linen bookbinding thread • 2 sheets ¹⁄₁₆–¹⁄₈in (2–3mm) thick cardboard • 2 sheets decorative paper • glue • wax paper

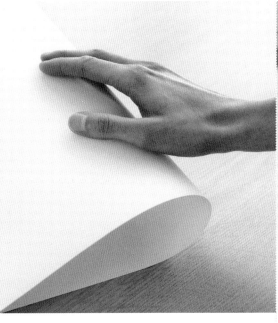

1

Find the grain of the paper by folding it over lengthwise and widthwise. The fold with least resistance tells you that the grain runs up and down.

2

With the grain running vertically, use the photo album template (see pp.236) to cut 18 rectangles to make 15 pages, two end papers, and one sewing template.

3

Transfer the hole markings to one sheet to use as your sewing template. One at a time, line up each of the 15 pages with the sewing template and pierce the needle through each mark.

4

Place one page at the edge of a table, the pierced side lined up with the table edge. Position the three lengths of ribbon between each set of holes and tape them to the edge of the table.

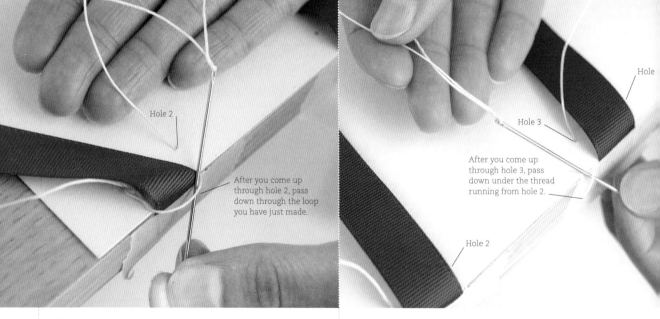

Hole 2

After you come up through hole 2, pass down through the loop you have just made.

Hole

Hole 3

After you come up through hole 3, pass down under the thread running from hole 2.

Hole 2

7

After you come up through the second hole, flip the ribbons over the paper. Pass down through the loop you have just made. Take care not to pull too tightly, keeping all the loops slightly loose.

8

Next, pass through hole 3, bottom to top, then under the thread running from hole 2. Pass through hole 4, bottom to top, and through the loop you have just made (see Step 7).

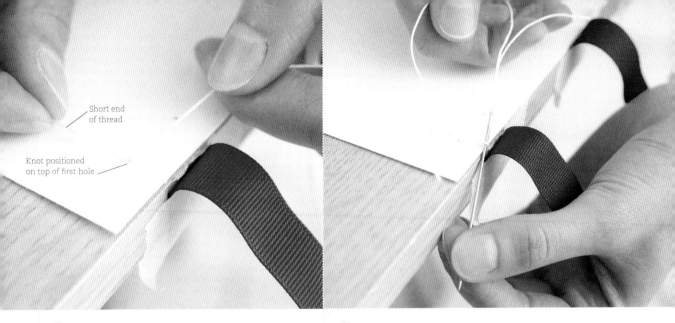

Short end
of thread

Knot positioned
on top of first hole

5

Flip the ribbons off the paper. Using a needle
and 40in (1m) thread, go through the first hole
from top to bottom. Loop around and tie a
double knot, positioning it on top of the hole.

6

Pass the needle underneath the loop you have
just made, right to left, and pull the thread
through. Pass under the ribbon and through
the second hole, going from underneath to top.

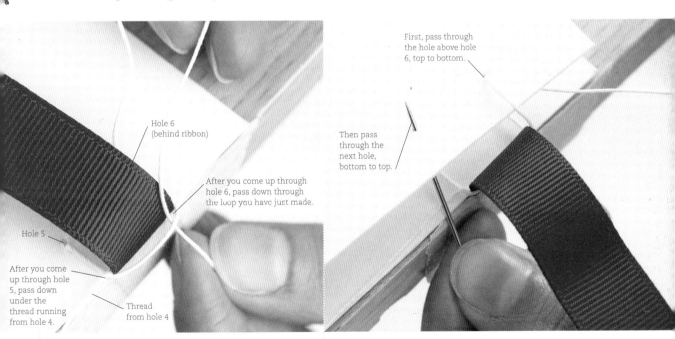

Hole 6
(behind ribbon)

After you come up through
hole 6, pass down through
the loop you have just made.

Hole 5

After you come
up through hole
5, pass down
under the
thread running
from hole 4.

Thread
from hole 4

First, pass through
the hole above hole
6, top to bottom.

Then pass
through the
next hole,
bottom to top.

9

Repeat for holes 5 and 6: pass up through
hole 5, bottom to top, and under the thread
running from hole 4; pass up through hole
6, and down through the loop.

10

Add the second page. Pass through the hole above
hole 6, top to bottom, across the ribbon, and come
up through the next hole. Repeat Steps 7–9 in
reverse, but don't go through the last loop.

11

After you come up through the last hole on the second page, pass down through the last loop as well as the loop below it. Add the next page, and pass through the first two holes as in Step 10.

12

Repeat Steps 7–11 for the remaining 13 pages, always passing through both the last loop and the loop below it, securing the loops together in bunches of two. When you run out of thread, attach more with a weaver's knot.

Mark the direction of the grain with an arrow.

14

Cut two cardboard covers, ⅛in (3mm) longer than the pages at the top, bottom, and one side. Cut two sheets of decorative paper, ¾in (2cm) longer on all sides than the boards. Spread glue on each board.

15

With the grain running vertically, place each board, glue side down, in the center of one sheet of paper. Trim each corner diagonally and glue the edges over the board.

13

With the book closed, push the needle underneath the first page. Open the first page and pull the thread through. Next, push the needle through the first hole on the second page. Turn the page, pull the thread through, and tie a knot on the other side of the second page. Cut the thread.

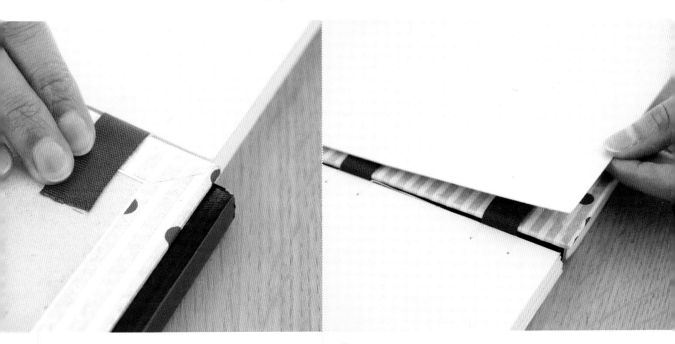

16

Place one cover on a book the same height as the stack of pages to hold it level and glue down the ribbon ends. Repeat for the other cover, trimming the ribbons if needed.

17

Glue the endpapers to the insides of each board to conceal the ribbons. Place wax paper between both covers and first pages. Weigh down the album and let it dry overnight.

Photo album variation

Once you have mastered the binding technique explained on pp.39–43, you can create endless variations of the album for different purposes and recipients. The nostalgic feel of this vintage-inspired album makes it the perfect place to store heirloom photographs. Cut the pages and covers in a landscape shape and use two sets of narrow ribbons to work the stitching around. Instead of sandwiching the ribbons between the covers and endpapers, glue them to the outside of the covers to create a look reminiscent of antique bookbindings.

Tip: Vary the colors of the pages, too. Use pink or blue for baby albums and black for black-and-white photographs.

Rollaway game board

This checkerboard has an integrated pocket for game pieces and it rolls up neatly, making it easy to store and ideal for travel. The patchwork top is cleverly made from fabric strips, saving you from having to piece each square separately.

To make a rollaway game board you will need

Tools: dressmaker's scissors • sewing machine • pins • iron

Materials: solid-colored fabric in brown and cream • decorative fabric in two different designs • thread • interfacing • 3cm button • thin ribbon • buttons in 2 colors to use as checkers

1

Use the chart in the Templates section (p.229) to measure and cut out the fabric pieces. Sew together one light and one dark strip with a ⅜in (1cm) seam allowance.

2

Sew a light strip to the other edge of the first dark strip. Add the remaining strips one at a time, alternating colors. Press all the seams open, forming a 12in (29cm) wide piece.

3

Mark lines across the strips every 2in (5cm). Cut along the lines to make eight bands. Pin the bands together, offsetting every other row by one square to make a checkerboard.

4

Sew the strips together with a ⅜in (1cm) seam allowance. Press open the seams. Trim off the extra squares on each side to create an 8 x 8 board, leaving the seam allowance.

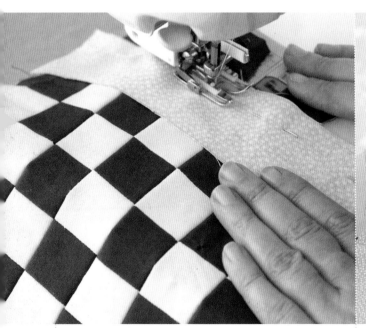

7

Place the two narrow strips of inner fabric at two opposite sides of the board, right side to right side. Pin, then sew with a ⅜in (1cm) seam allowance. Press the seams open.

8

Sew the two remaining inner fabric panels to the two remaining edges of the board with a ⅜in (1cm) seam allowance. Press the seams away from the board.

5

Apply interfacing to the wrong side of the 12 x 20in (30 x 50cm) piece of outer fabric and one of the 12 x 5¾in (30 x 14cm) pieces of inner fabric.

6

Fold over a ¼in (5mm) double hem at one end of the interfaced outer fabric and stitch. Do the same along one long edge of the inner fabric. These will form the pocket edges.

9

Place the right side of the outer fabric and the right side of the inner fabric together, making sure the pocket hems (see step 6) line up. Pin, then sew with ⅜in (1cm) seam allowance along three sides, leaving the pocket edges open.

10

Topstitch along the edge of the checkerboard closest
to the pocket edges to form a pocket with interfacing.
You can use the pocket to store the game pieces.

11

Sew a 3cm button in the middle of the outside
of the non-pocket end, approximately ⅝in
(1.5cm) from the edge. Thread a thin ribbon
through the buttonhole.

12

Tie a knot in the ribbon behind the button.
Wrap the ribbon around the rolled-up game,
securing the checkers inside. Secure the roll
by winding the ribbon around the button.

Jewelry

Beaded
necklace

There is such a wealth of beautiful beads to choose from, including ceramic, glass, enamel, and hand-painted. Design a unique piece of jewelry using this simple and versatile knot technique.

To make a beaded necklace you will need

Tools: scissors

Materials: spool of 1mm-wide, black, waxed cotton thread
• 5 large beads • 6 small beads

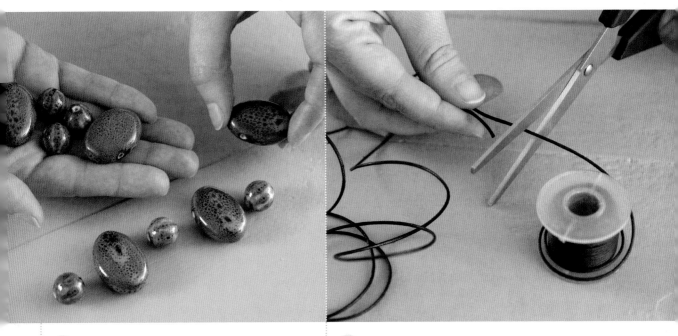

1

Choose beads with holes that are large enough to thread onto the waxed cotton thread. Plan out the order of your beads and lay them in order on the work surface.

2

Cut two lengths of waxed cotton thread roughly twice the length you want the necklace to be. You can tie the thread around your neck first to judge the length.

3

Lay the strands of waxed cotton thread together. Fold the two strands in half and tie a knot at this midpoint. This doesn't need to be very accurate because the threads will be trimmed later.

4

Take the middle bead from your design and thread it onto one of the strands from either side. Slide it down until it reaches the first knot.

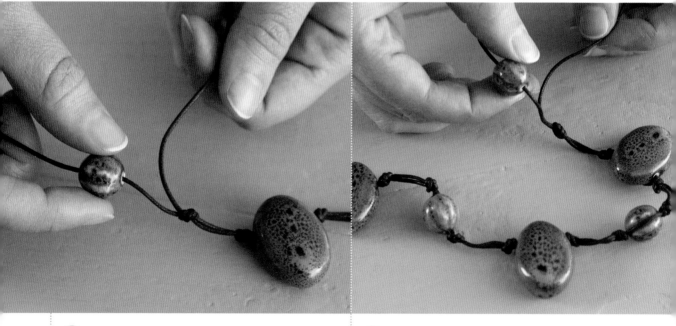

7

Take the next bead in your design and thread it onto one strand. Again, pass the other strand behind the bead, then take both strands and tie a knot to secure the bead in position.

8

Take the next bead from your design and thread and knot as before, leaving a ¾in (2cm) gap each time. Repeat until you have finished one side of the necklace, then thread and knot the other side.

5

Pass the other strand behind the bead and tie both strands together in a knot on the other side of the bead to secure the bead in position.

6

Leave a gap of approximately ¾in (2cm) and tie another knot with both threads together.

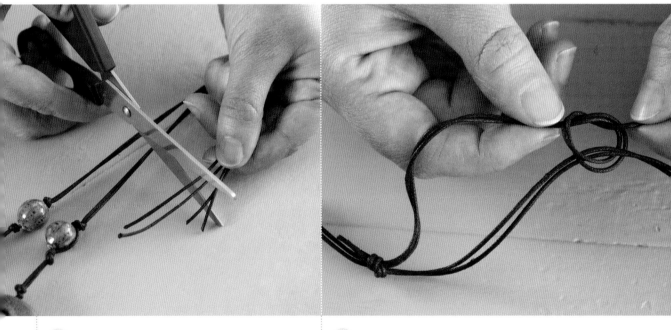

9

When you have threaded on your final bead, secure it with a knot. Place the ends of the necklace alongside each other and cut the strands of thread to the same length.

10

Knot one end of the necklace around the other end. Then knot the remaining loose end around the other end. You can now adjust the length of the necklace by sliding the knots.

Color variation

Once you have mastered the technique on pp.55–57, you can experiment with different bead colors and sizes. Keeping colors within the same palette works well, and you can introduce different sizes without your necklace becoming fussy.

Tip: Opaque and tinted beads from the same color palette work well together.

Painted beads

Hand-painted beads are expensive but making your own jewelry is a cost-effective way to showcase just a few handpicked beautiful beads. If using beads with a varied pattern, keep the size the same.

Tip: Use colored waxed cotton thread to match or contrast with your beads and help colors stand out.

Button-bead necklace

Flat button beads work well knotted together. This design knots the beads closely for a more formal look.

1. Tie a knot. Thread each strand through a bead as if sewing a button, passing through the bead from opposite sides.

2. Pull both strands tight and tie a knot to secure. Repeat with the next bead, tying them close together.

Tip: The knotting technique also works for flat or unusually shaped beads.

Make all of these pretty brooches in exactly the same way as the bird brooch on pp.61–63. Templates for the other shapes are given on p.237.

Embellished
felt brooches

It's hard to believe that scraps of fabric and felt, buttons, ribbon, and beads are all that are needed to make these whimsical brooches. Turn a brooch into a key ring or bag charm by attaching a split ring to the top with a ribbon.

To make a bird brooch you will need

Tools: pencil • dressmaker's scissors • iron • damp cloth *Materials:* double-sided fusible web • patterned fabric • 3 squares of felt in contrasting colors • 1 skein of stranded cotton embroidery thread • extra-heavy-weight sew-in interfacing • 35 seed beads • 1 black bead • 6in (15cm) narrow ribbon • 1 small button • sewing thread • pin back

1 Trace the bird template on p.237 onto the paper side of the fusible web. Cut around the bird and iron it, textured side down, onto the reverse of the patterned fabric. Cut out the bird.

2 Peel off the backing paper. Place the bird face side up on the first felt square. Cover with a damp cloth and iron for a few seconds until the bird is bonded to the felt.

61

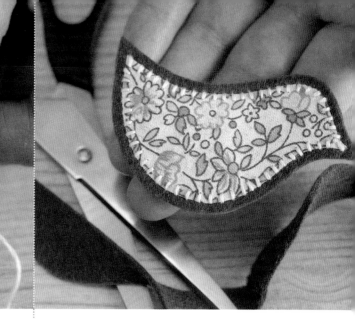

3

Using three strands of the cotton embroidery thread, sew around the bird shape using a topstitch.

4

Cut the felt around the the bird, leaving a felt border of approximately ⅛–¼in (3–5mm).

7

Using the wing template on p.237, cut a wing out of the first color of felt. Sew the wing onto the bird with the embroidery thread using a small running stitch.

8

Sew on the black bead for the eye. Cut the ribbon in half and sew on two small ribbon loops for the tail. Using the embroidery thread, sew on the button to cover the ends of the ribbon.

5

Place the bird onto the contrasting shade of felt with the interfacing underneath. Using sewing thread, sew on the seed beads, sewing through all three layers.

6

Carefully cut around the bird shape, again leaving a border of approximately ⅛–¼in (3–5mm). Make sure that you cut through both the contrasting felt and the interfacing.

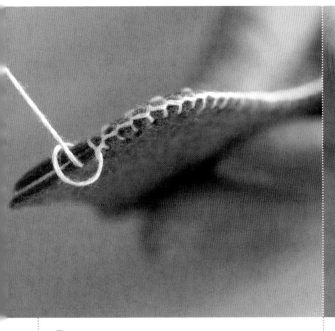

9

Using the brooch as a guide, cut an identical shape out of the last color of felt to use as the backing. Using the embroidery thread, attach the backing with a blanket stitch.

10

Using doubled sewing thread for strength, sew the pin back on the reverse side of the brooch. Make sure you only sew through the backing felt.

Silver clay
jewelry

Make beautiful silver jewelry items easily with silver clay. Available
from craft stores, silver clay is 99% silver. When fired with a kitchen torch,
the clay burns off, leaving behind a fully silver item.

For a silver leaf pendant you will need

Tools: Teflon mat or parchment paper • small rolling pin or piece of pipe • playing cards • craft knife • small straw • wet and dry
sandpaper (600 grit) or sanding pad (220 grit) • kitchen torch • firing brick or ceramic tile • timer • tweezers • soft wire brush
• 2 pairs of pliers *Materials:* oil (cooking spray is ideal) • ¼oz (7g) silver clay • real leaves or leaf skeletons • silver jump ring

1

Cut out a square of parchment paper or use
a Teflon mat. Prepare your work surface by
rubbing a small amount of oil over the paper
or mat, your hands, and the rolling pin.

2

Place two stacks of four playing cards,
each about 2in (5cm) away from each
other to act as rolling guides. Soften
the clay in your hands and roll it flat.

3

Lift up the rolled clay carefully and place a leaf underneath and on top of it as shown, making sure you line up the stems and tips of the leaves. Roll over the clay again to imprint both sides.

4

Carefully remove the leaves, and lay the clay on a cutting mat or cutting board. Using the craft knife and the template from pp.237, carefully cut a leaf shape from the clay.

7

Place the leaf on the firing brick or tile in a dimly lit, well ventilated room. Hold the torch 2in (5cm) from the clay and move the flame evenly over it. The leaf will start to glow a peachy orange color.

8

Once the leaf begins to glow, set the timer for two minutes. If the leaf turns bright red or shiny silver, it is too hot—move the flame away. Once fired, pick up the leaf with tweezers and quench it in water.

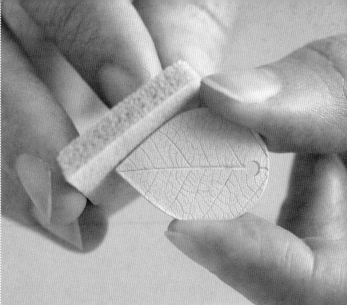

5

Using the straw, make a hole in the leaf about ¼in (5mm) from the top. This needs to be big enough for your jump ring, bearing in mind that the clay may shrink by up to 10% when fired.

6

Let the clay dry overnight, or, to speed up the process, use a hair dryer or put the clay in an oven at 300°F (150°C) for 10 minutes. Once dry, sand it very carefully to smooth the edges.

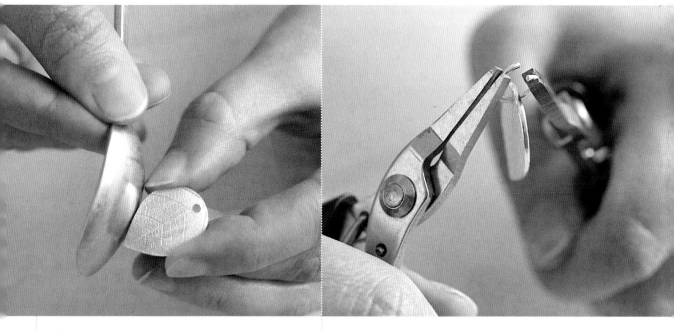

9

The leaf will now be a matte-white color, even though it is pure silver. Gently brush it with a soft wire brush to reveal the silver color. To achieve a high shine, rub with the back of a metal spoon.

10

Using two pairs of pliers, gently twist the ends of the jump ring away from each other. Thread it through the hole in your leaf, and then twist the jump ring closed.

Simple button cufflinks

A wide array of textured paper is available from most craft stores; a snakeskin pattern has been used to create these cufflinks made according to the same technique as the silver leaf pendant on pp.65–67 and using the template on p.237. To make, roll out and texture approximately ¾oz (20g) of silver clay. Carefully cut out two disks measuring ¾in (2cm) in diameter, and another two of ⅝in (1.5cm) in diameter. Pierce each of these disks twice using a toothpick (the holes should be positioned to resemble the holes in a button). Dry out and fire the clay as for the silver leaf pendant. Burnish for a high shine, then, using a needle and silver thread, sew the silver clay buttons onto a cufflink chain: ⅝–¾in (1.5–2cm) of chain with roughly ¼in (5mm) links is ideal. Tie off the thread, and use a tiny dot of superglue to ensure the end doesn't come loose.

Wallpaper earrings

Patterned wallpaper can be ideal for texturing metal clays, and the variety of designs available is huge. Make these earrings using the same technique as for the silver leaf pendant on pp.65–67, using ½oz (15g) of silver clay. Using the wallpaper, roll and texture your clay as before. Cut ovals from the clay approximately 1¼in (3cm) in length using the template on p.237 and pierce at the top with your straw. Dry out, and torch fire. Burnish for a high shine, and attach ear wires.

Leaf bracelet

This simple leaf bracelet requires approximately 1oz (25g) of silver clay. Roll and texture your clay as for the silver leaf pendant on pp.65–67. Then cut out seven pointed ellipses 1in (2.5cm) in length. Pierce each end of the ellipses with your straw. While the pieces of clay are still soft, lay them over a rolling pin to give them a curved shape. Let them dry, and then torch fire as before. Link the elements together using jump rings. Finally, attach a simple clasp.

Lace heart key ring

Fabrics, in particular lace, can be used to produce beautifully delicate patterns in metal clays. To make this heart key ring in the same way as the silver leaf pendant on pp.65–67, roll out approximately ⅜oz (10g) of silver clay. Texture it using lace, and then cut out a heart shape 1⅜in (3.5cm) in length using the template on p.237. Pierce the top of the heart with your straw. Dry out and fire the clay, then burnish to a high shine. Use a jump ring to attach the heart to a key ring and chain.

Crochet
necklace

This beautiful necklace is a great crochet project for beginners because it uses just one stitch—the chain stitch. For a quick lesson on how to make the stitch, turn to Crochet basics on p.244 before starting work on the necklace.

To make a crochet necklace you will need

Tools: B/1 (2mm) crochet hook • 10 steel (1mm) crochet hook (if needed) • darning needle

Materials: cotton yarn • approximately 15 beads in different sizes and shapes (make sure the holes are large enough for the beads to pass easily over at least a 10 steel [1mm] crochet hook)

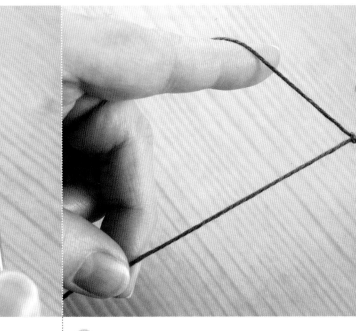

1

Make a slip knot by first crossing the yarn coming from the ball over itself to form a circle. Insert the B/1 (2mm) hook through the circle and pull the ball end through the circle. Tighten.

2

Pull both ends of the yarn firmly to tighten the slip knot around the shank of the hook, making sure that the knot is tight but not so tight that you can't move it along the hook.

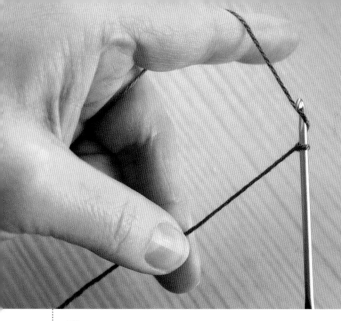

3

To begin the foundation chain, wrap the yarn from the ball around the hook. This action is called a "yarn over" (abbreviated yo). Use the lip of the hook to grip the yarn as shown.

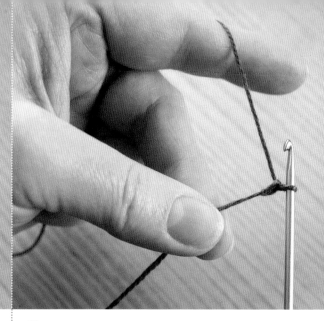

4

With the lip of the hook, pull the yarn through the loop on the shank of the hook and tighten it. This makes the first chain of your foundation chain (see p.244).

7

If you switched hooks in Step 6, switch back to the B/1 (2mm) hook. Yo. Grasp the yarn going to the ball with the lip of the hook (see Step 3).

8

Pull the yarn through the loop to secure the bead in place. Continue chaining and adding beads in this way until the necklace is the length you require.

5

Yo and draw a loop through the loop on the shank of the hook for the next chain. Continue making chains in this way, making a total of 10 to start.

6

Thread a bead onto the hook and insert it back through the loop (see inset). Pass the bead onto the loop, pulling the loop through it. If necessary, use a 10 steel (1mm) hook for this step.

9

Make a slip stitch (ss) (see p.245) in the first chain to join the necklace ends. Cut the yarn, leaving a tail. Pass the tail through the last loop and tighten to finish.

10

Using a darning needle, work both yarn tails through the chains on each side of the last ss to finish.

Découpage bangle

To make these stylish bangle bracelets, paper cutouts are glued down and varnished to create a smooth, shiny surface. Almost any paper can be used for this technique, making these bangles the ultimate custom-made gift.

To make a découpage bangle you will need

Tools: ruler • scissors • paintbrushes

Materials: bangle (wooden or plastic) • solid, colored, or patterned backing paper • craft glue • decorative paper motifs • white tack • craft paint • glitter (optional) • clear varnish

1

Measure the distance around the side of the bangle. Cut paper strips ⅝in (1.5cm) wide and long enough to wrap around the bangle. Cut enough strips to cover the bangle.

2

Spread glue all over the back of one paper strip, but don't soak it. Position the strip around the edge of the bangle so that the ends overlap on the inside. Remove any air.

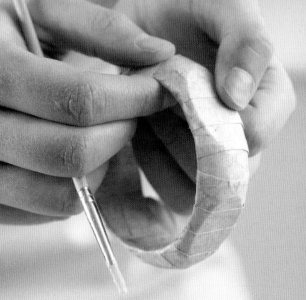

3

Continue adding strips, overlapping slightly with each previous strip, until you have covered the bangle completely with the backing paper.

4

When you have finished this stage, check that each strip of paper is glued down firmly. Smooth out any bumps or wrinkles, adding more glue as necessary.

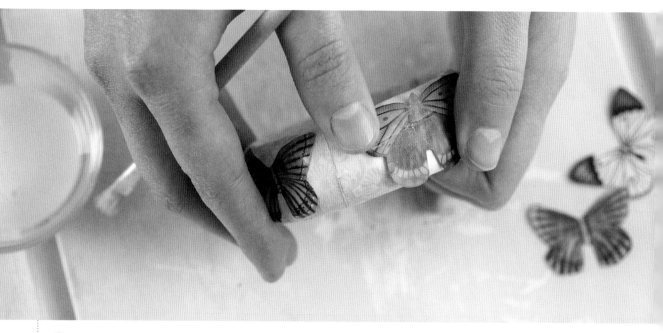

7

Glue the motifs onto the bangle. Take care when gluing down the motifs because they are likely to tear easily when wet with glue and will be difficult to reposition.

5

Cut another strip of the backing paper for the inside of the bangle. This will need to cover the entire inside surface for a neat finish. Glue in place and let dry.

6

Carefully cut out the motifs. Position them around the bangle using white tack, moving them around until you have decided on a design that works for you.

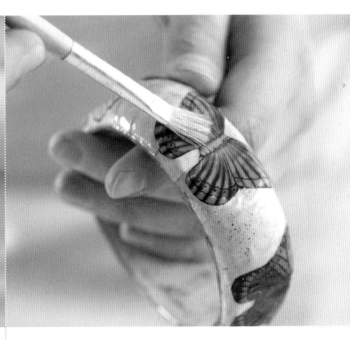

8

Paint a thin border around the top edge of the bangle; let dry. Turn the bangle around and paint the other edge. Add glitter, if desired, and let dry.

9

Varnish the bangle and let it dry for two to three days, turning occasionally. When hardened, repeat with a second coat. Let dry as before.

Crochet
flower pins

Jewelry

These pretty crochet flowers will brighten up any jacket or bag. They are more difficult to make than the crochet necklace (pp.70–73), but once you get the hang of it they are quick to create. Make them in a variety of colors, adding a statement button in the center for endless variations. You will need to know four different stitches to make these pins: chain stitch (ch), slip stitch (ss), single crochet (sc), and half double crochet (hdc). For a guide to these stitches, turn to Crochet basics on pp.244–245.

To make a crochet flower pin you will need

Tools: F/5 (4mm) crochet hook • sewing needle
Materials: cotton yarn • button • cotton sewing thread • pin back

1
Make a slip knot and tighten it (see Steps 1–2 on p.71).

2
To make the first chain (ch) (see p.244), first bring the yarn over the hook (yo).

3
Pull the yarn through the loop to make the first ch.

79

4

Work 5 more ch.

5

Ss (see p.245) into the first chain you made.

6

Tighten the ss to form a circle. Work 1 ch.

10

Work 6 ch.

11

Skip 2 sc and ss into next stitch to create first petal.

14

Work 7 half doubles (hdc) (see p.245) into first petal.

15

Work 1 sc into first petal to finish. Then ss into next ch to join.

16

Repeat Steps 13–15 for the other petals. Pull yarn through last loop to finish.

7

Work 1 sc (see p.244) into the center of the circle.

8

Continue working 14 more sc into the center of the circle.

9

Ss into the first sc to join the circle.

12

Repeat Steps 10–11 to create four more petals. Then ss into the first ch to finish round.

13

Work 1 sc into the center of the first petal.

17

Combine two flowers and add a button in the center.

18

Using sewing thread, sew a pin back to the back of the flower pin to complete it.

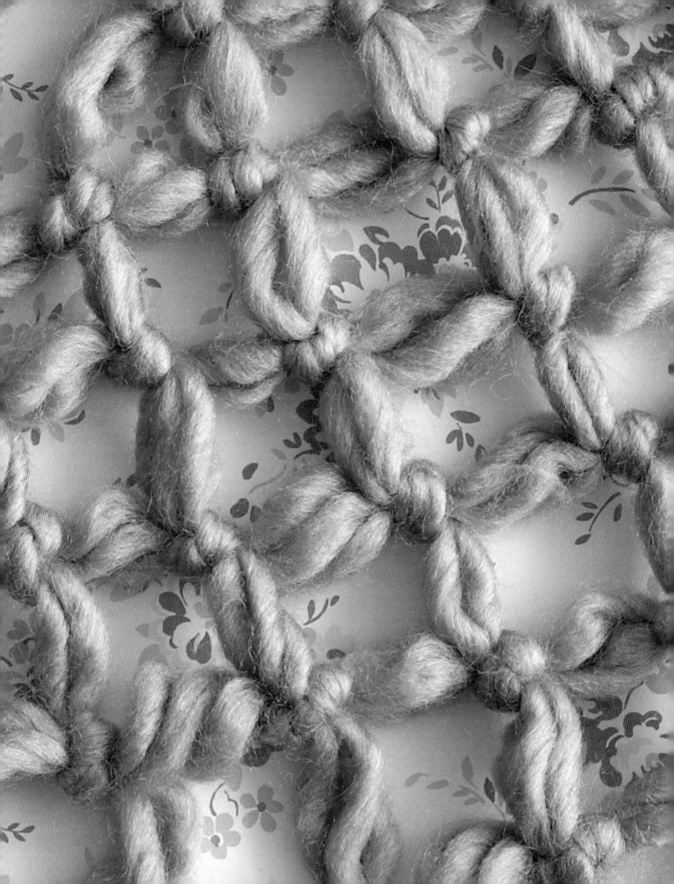

Bags and accessories

All of these bags are made in the same way as the wave-patterned bag on pp.85–87. Turn to pp.88–89 for further instructions, ideas, and inspiration.

Stenciled
bags

Turn plain canvas bags into unique and personal fashion statements with the use of paper stencils and fabric paint. Once you can stencil with confidence, why not try decorating a T-shirt or pillow cover?

To make the wave-patterned bag you will need

Tools: pencil • utility knife • cutting mat • iron • masking tape • plate or palette • sponge • hair dryer • paper towels

Materials: tracing paper • stencil paper or card stock • fabric bag • scrap paper or newspaper • fabric paint in two colors

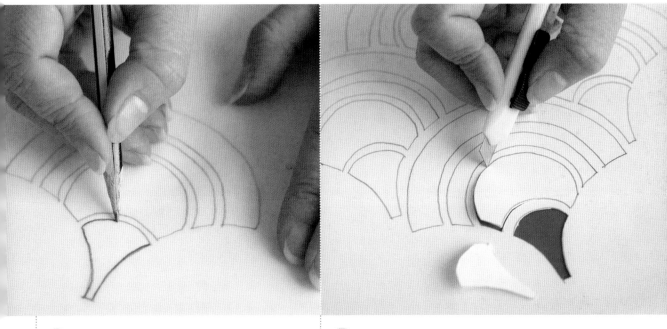

1

Trace the stencil template from pp.243 onto tracing paper. Transfer to card stock by flipping the tracing paper over and drawing over the lines while pressing down firmly.

2

Use a utility knife to cut the stencil shape out carefully. If making a repeat pattern, you can cut out the stencil shape a number of times on one sheet, making sure to leave a border of paper.

85

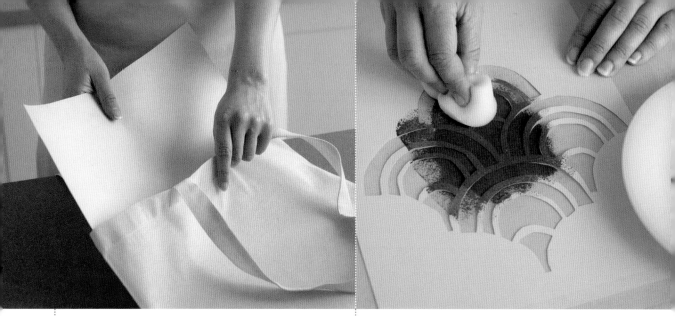

3

Prepare your fabric bag by ironing it, and line the inside with scrap paper or newspaper to stop any excess ink that may soak through the fabric from running through to the back of the bag.

4

Tape down the stencil. Pour some paint on a plate or palette. Dip a clean, dry sponge in the paint, dabbing off any excess. Then apply the paint with the sponge, starting from the center and working out.

6

Use paper towels to blot your stencil and let it dry. You can also prepare more stencils, allowing you to move on with the design while you wait for the first stencil to dry.

7

Once your stencil and fabric paint are dry, reposition your stencil on the bag. Repeat the application process as many times as desired, leaving a few gaps for the second color.

5

Remove your stencil and put it to one side to dry. Use a
hair dryer to dry the paint onto the fabric, making sure
you blow-dry the inside of your fabric bag as well as
the front so the paint doesn't dry to the lining paper.

8

Once you've stenciled all of the design
in one color and it has dried, apply the
second color in the same way as the first,
using a new stencil. Let dry overnight.

9

When the fabric paint has fully dried,
iron the fabric for a minute or two to fix
the paint to the material. You may wish
to use a cloth to protect your iron.

Fluttering butterflies

This bag has been stenciled in the same way as the wave-patterned bag on pp.85–87, using the templates on p.243. Butterflies of different shapes and sizes are positioned at slight angles on the same diagonal line, making it look like they are all fluttering in the same direction. Creating the same stencil in different sizes and overlapping some of the images also adds a sense of depth to the scene.

The same color paint has been used to create these butterflies, but you could try stenciling them in a variety of colors for a different look. Alternatively, wait for the design to dry and paint or stencil different colored markings on the butterflies.

Sewn bag

This large-scale design looks like thread that has been sewn onto the bag, attached to a needle that has also been pushed through the fabric. The look is achieved by creating gaps in the stencil design where the item or object would be obscured by the fabric. Follow the instructions on pp.85–87 to create this look, using the stencils on pp.242. Remember to cut separate stencils for different-colored elements.

Have fun playing with the blank canvas provided by the bag by thinking of other designs that could be interacting with it in some way. For example, you could stencil on a belt going through belt loops, or a ribbon "threaded" through the bag.

Repeated chevrons

This deceptively simple idea results in a striking design with an element of optical illusion. Using the template on pp.242, create a stencil, cutting several chevron shapes at equal distances from each other. Following the instructions for the wave-patterned bag on pp.85–87 and starting in the center of your bag, stencil the pattern onto the bag and dry it. Reposition the stencil so that it continues the chevron pattern as shown, pointing the chevrons the opposite way for every other column, and making sure to keep all the stenciled figures evenly spaced.

Any evenly spaced, repeated pattern makes a striking design, so try this with circles or triangles for a different look. You could also try varying the colors, either according to a pattern or randomly.

Pencil illusion

At first glance, it looks like these pencils are complete, but on closer inspection, you can see that only the tip and shaft of the pencil have been stenciled onto the bag. Your eye fills in the rest, completing the image with the background color. This is a great technique to use for stenciled designs, since it can be difficult to stencil very narrow lines or other details needed to complete an image. To make these pencils, use the stencil template on pp.242 and follow the instructions for the wave-patterned bag on pp.85–87.

Knotted scarf

Tempted by the balls of soft, luxurious yarn in your local craft store? You can make this cozy scarf without knowing how to knit; simply knot strands of yarn together to make this pretty macramé crisscross design.

To make a knotted scarf you will need

Tools: scissors • ⅜in (1cm)-thick polystyrene foam board (or use a corkboard) • sewing pins
Materials: 2 x balls 50g (88yd [80m]) super chunky yarn

1
Measure and cut the yarn into 18 lengths, each about 4yd (3.8m).

2
Arrange the lengths of yarn into six groups of three strands each. Wind the yarn into bunches and tie loosely, leaving a 20in (50cm) tail; this will make the strands easier to handle.

3

Take the first two bunches and tie them together with a double knot about 5in (12cm) from the top. Repeat with the other bunches, making three knotted sections.

4

Evenly space out the double bunches on a polystyrene foam board or corkboard. Secure them to the board with a pin through the center of each knot.

7

Repeat Step 5 to complete the next row of knots. Pin through the new knots to keep the scarf secure and to help space out the knots correctly.

8

Then repeat Step 6. Continue to tie knots in this way until you reach the end of the foam board. Unpin the knots and move the scarf up the board. Repin the last row and continue to knot.

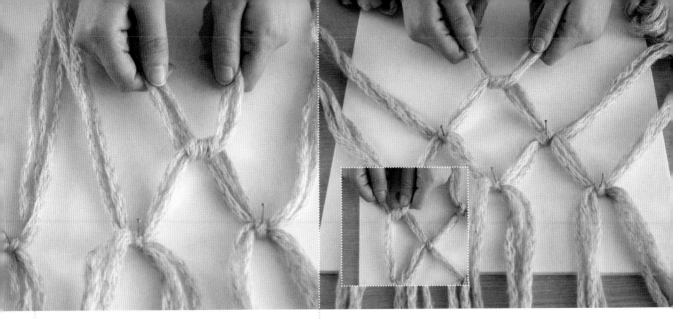

5

Working in bunches of two, knot together the second and third lengths from the left, about 2in (5cm) below the first knot. Repeat with the fourth and fifth lengths. Pin down.

6

Knot together the middle two lengths, again about 2in (5cm) below the previous knot. Then knot each of the sides, keeping the outermost length taut and making sure the side knots line up with the middle. Pin.

9

When you are about 5in (12cm) from the end of the yarn lengths, make a final three knots. Note that you will reach the end of the middle lengths sooner than the sides.

10

Cut all the strands to the same length, and the scarf is complete.

Close-weave scarf

Once you have mastered the technique on pp.91–93, you could reduce the space between the knots and increase the number of bunches for a tighter and thicker finish. This scarf is made with eight bunches of yarn, each made up of three strands.

◀

Tip: When using two colors, choose the same type of yarn for both so the texture and weight match.

Color-block scarf

Use different colors of yarn to add interest to your scarf. Start by pinning the bunches to the board in the order you want them. This scarf is made with eight bunches of yarn, each with two strands, and has two bunches of gray on each side of the four bunches of red.

Clasp-frame bag

Virtually any fabric can be turned into a stylish, retro-inspired bag or purse by using a clasp frame, available from craft stores and online retailers. Different sizes and styles of frame allow you to make bags for different purposes.

To make a clasp-frame clutch bag you will need

Tools: ruler • pencil • dressmaker's scissors • pins • sewing machine or needle

Materials: pattern paper • clasp frame • fabric for outer shell • lining fabric • felt • non-iron interfacing • cotton sewing thread • glue

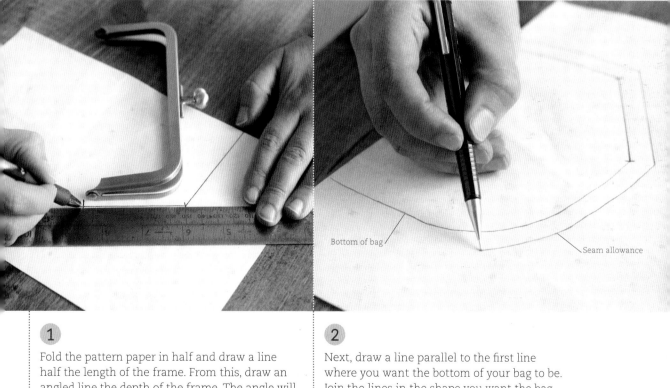

Bottom of bag

Seam allowance

1

Fold the pattern paper in half and draw a line half the length of the frame. From this, draw an angled line the depth of the frame. The angle will depend on how full you want the purse to be.

2

Next, draw a line parallel to the first line where you want the bottom of your bag to be. Join the lines in the shape you want the bag to be and add ½in (1cm) seam allowance.

97

3

Cut out the template from the folded paper. Unfold it and use it as a guide to cut out two pieces each of the outer fabric, lining fabric, felt, and interfacing.

4

Create two stacks. In the first, place the outer fabric pieces, right sides facing in, between the two felt pieces. In the second, sandwich the lining fabric, right sides facing, between two pieces of interfacing.

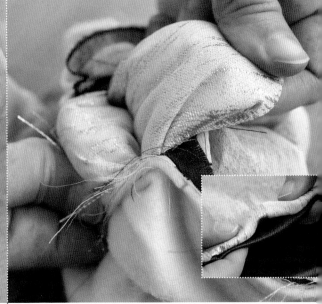

7

Sew around the top of the bag, stopping halfway down one of the long sides to leave a gap so the purse can be turned right side out. Trim the seams.

8

Turn the purse right side out, and iron it flat. Fold under the edges of the gap, pin it closed, and then topstitch around the top of the purse, closing the gap. This will make it easier to insert into the frame.

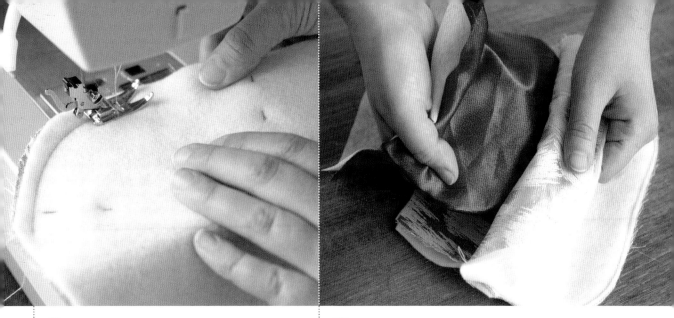

5

Pin each stack together. Sew around the curved pocket area of each of the stacks. Trim the seams.

6

Turn the lining piece right side out and place it inside the other piece, making sure it is as deep as it can go and matching up the side seams.

9

Put glue on the frame and along the top and the sides of the bag. Allow the glue to dry slightly before assembling the bag.

10

Ease the purse into the frame one side at a time, making sure that the fabric has been pushed right up into the gap. Use a small, flat tool to help, if necessary. Let dry for a few hours.

Clasp-frame purse

Perfect for loose change or for keeping your MP3 player safe and snug, this snappy little purse has been made using exactly the same technique as the clasp-frame clutch bag on pp.97–99. To create the small, almost-square shape, make sure that all sides of the unfolded template are roughly the same length.

Tip: Use contrasting colors for the outer shell and lining for a fresh, playful look.

Clasp-frame makeup bag

Use a large clasp frame to make the perfect bag for storing makeup or jewelry, in exactly the same way as the clasp-frame clutch bag on pp.97–99. Create a template for a fuller bag by drawing a wider angle for the second line in Step 1, and more room at the bottom by giving the side a steeper curve in Step 2.

Tip: Use fabric from old clothes to make a bag with true vintage appeal.

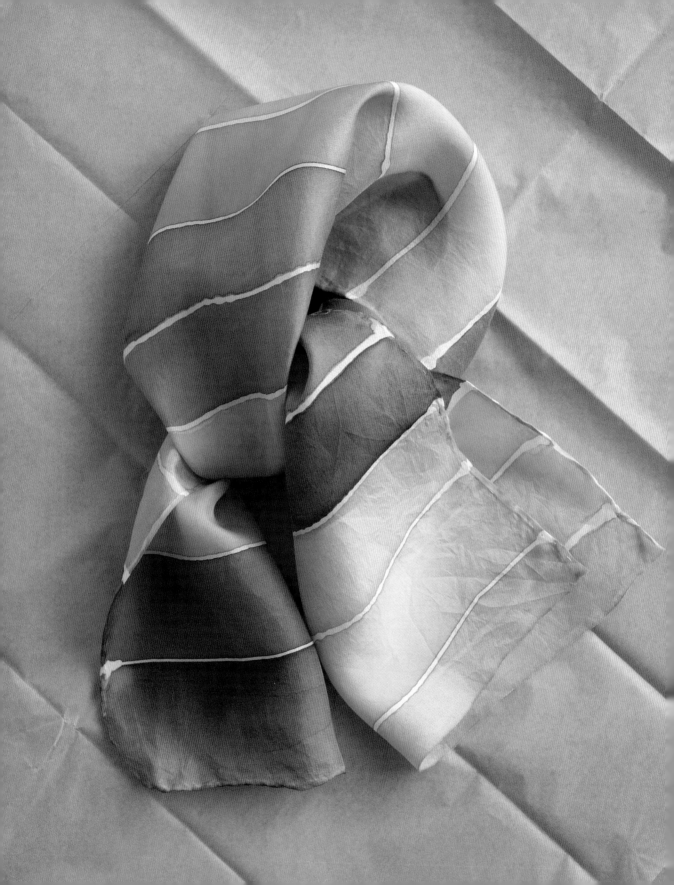

Painted
silk scarf

It is surprisingly easy to make this beautiful, striped silk scarf. For this method, the silk needs to be suspended in air while it is being painted. If you don't have a silk painting frame, you can suspend it across an old picture frame.

To make a painted silk scarf you will need

Tools: silk painting frame (or medium-sized picture frame) • masking tape • pencil • mixing dishes • square-edged paintbrush
Materials: ready-made silk scarf • tube of water-soluble resist • silk paints in your choice of colors

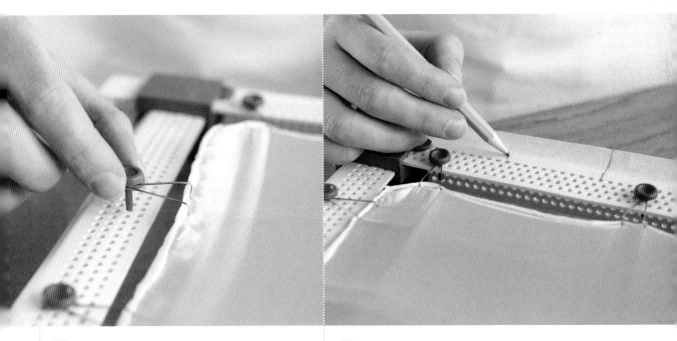

1
Fix the scarf to the silk painting frame. If you are using a picture frame, attach the scarf with masking tape and paint it in sections, moving it along as it dries.

2
Decide how you would like the white stripes on your scarf to be spaced. Stick masking tape down the side of the frame and draw a line for each stripe.

3

With a ruler as a guide, use water-soluble resist to draw a line at each marked interval. The resist will keep the paint colors in each section from running into each other. Make sure there are no breaks in the lines and that you continue each line all the way to the edge of the fabric (see inset).

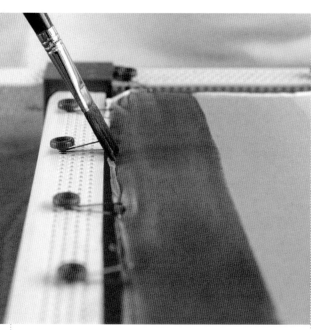

6

Starting with the left-most stripe (right-most if you're left-handed) and using a square-edged brush, paint the first section. Make sure you cover the scarf all the way to the edge.

7

Continue painting stripes in this way, switching colors and working across the scarf. Once finished, let the scarf dry.

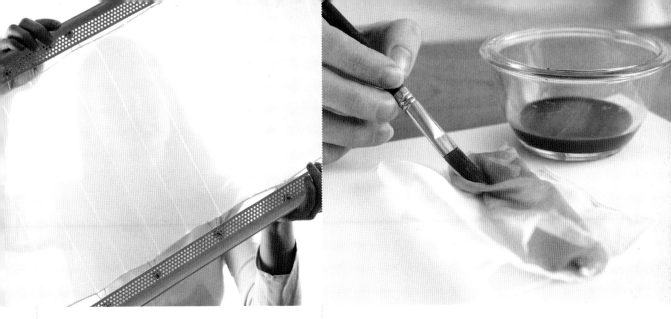

4

Let the water-soluble resist dry and then double-check that there are no breaks in the lines by holding the frame up to the light. Add more resist to any breaks and let dry.

5

Mix your colors. Combine a few drops of each silk color with 2 tablespoons of water and test the color on a silk scrap. Adjust the intensity of the colors until you're happy with them.

8

Once the scarf has dried completely, remove it from the frame and, following your paint-manufacturer's instructions, iron it on a silk setting to fix the paints.

9

Using a wool and silk detergent, hand wash the scarf to remove the resist residue. This will leave behind white lines in the scarf. Let the scarf dry, then iron again.

Make a sleeve for a device of any size by following the instructions for the tablet protector on pp.107–109. Choose the correct-sized button to finish.

Phone and tablet
protectors

Make a stylish and individual slipcase for a gadget-lover's phone, tablet, or laptop. These instructions are based on the individual device's measurements, and so can be used to make a cover for any make or model.

··

To make a tablet protector you will need

Tools: tape measure • dressmaker's scissors • iron • ruler • fabric marker • pins • sewing machine or needle
Materials: cotton fabric for the shell • lining fabric • fleece fabric • medium-weight, fusible, woven interfacing •
6in (15cm) round elastic • button • cotton sewing thread

1
Use a tape measure to measure around the length of the device. Divide this number by two, and then add 1¾in (4.5cm). Do the same for the width of the device.

2
Using the measurements from Step 1, draw and cut two rectangles from your chosen shell fabric. Then do the same for the lining fabric, fleece fabric, and fusible woven interfacing.

107

3

Iron one piece of fusible interfacing to the wrong side of each piece of shell fabric. With the wrong sides facing, lightly iron the lining fabric to the fleece fabric from the side of the lining.

4

Mark a sewing line ⅜in (1cm) from the edge along all four edges of one of the interfaced pieces, on the side of the interfacing. Do the same for one of the fleece and lining pieces, on the fleece side.

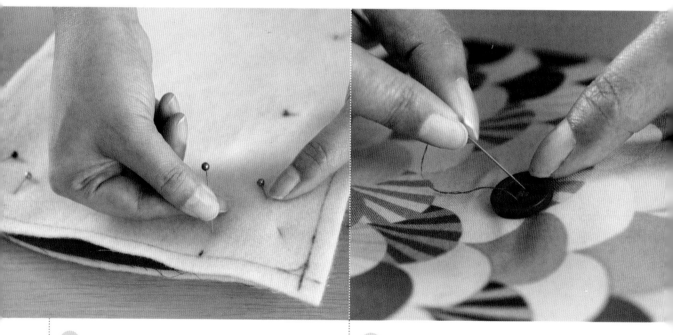

7

Pin the two padded lining pieces together, lining sides facing, marking a 4¾in (12cm) gap along the bottom edge. Sew as in Step 6, leaving a gap. Trim the seams and topstitch the edges.

8

Turn the shell right side out and press. Mark the center of the top sewing line, mark down 2in (5cm), and sew on the button. Turn wrong side out, add a sewing line to the other side, and mark its center for the elastic.

5

Round out the bottom corners of each of the pieces that you have drawn sewing lines on, using a button as a template and drawing around the button.

6

Pin the two interfaced pieces together, right sides facing and top edges matching. Sew down one side, across the bottom, and up the other side, along the line. Trim the seams and topstitch the edges.

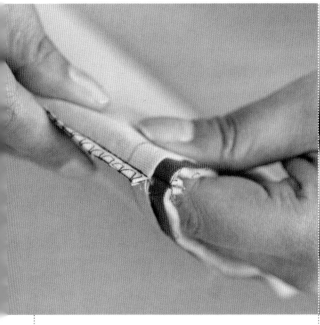

9

Turn the lining right side out. Slide it inside the outer piece. Insert the elastic loop between the two pieces as marked. Pin and sew around the sewing line, double-stitching over the elastic.

10

Trim the seam and topstitch the edges. Reach through the opening in the bottom lining to turn the cover right side out. Sew the gap in the lining closed by hand. Press the cover.

Pampering gifts

Each of these scented soaps has been made using the method on pp.113–115 and varying the ingredients. See pp.116–119 for variations of the soap recipe.

All natural
luxury soap

Handmade soaps make indulgent gifts, and using the melt-and-pour method they require no specialized skill to make. Create naturally scented and colored soaps using spices, dried fruits or flowers, essential oils, and soap colorant.

To make lemon soap you will need

Tools: gloves • heatproof bowl • pan • spatula • spoon • square mold • knife

Materials: 2lb (1kg) white melt-and-pour soap base • ¼–¾ teaspoon (1–3g) yellow soap colorant
• dried lemon peel granules • lemon essential oil • rubbing alcohol in a spray bottle • 9 dried lemon slices • plastic wrap

Makes
9 bars

1

Wearing gloves, chop the melt-and-pour soap into pieces and heat in a heatproof bowl over a pan of boiling water, stirring occasionally, until all lumps have melted.

2

Add the desired amount of colorant to the melted soap base and stir until the powder has mixed in and the color is evenly distributed.

113

3

Add the lemon peel granules a little at a time, stirring gently. Continue stirring until the granules are spread evenly throughout the soap mixture.

4

Just before you pour the soap mixture into the mold, slowly add the essential oil and stir gently until it is evenly distributed throughout.

7

Spray the almost-set layer again with rubbing alcohol. This will act as a glue and help it to bond to the next layer of soap.

8

Slowly pour the remaining mixture into the mold and add the dried lemon slices. You will need to act fast because the top layer will begin to set as soon as it is poured.

5

Pour approximately three-quarters of the mixture into the mold. Leave the remainder in the bowl over the hot water to keep it melted and warm.

6

Spray the mixture with rubbing alcohol to remove any bubbles. Let this first layer stand for 20–25 minutes, until it is almost set. It should be hard but warm.

9

Create a 3 x 3 pattern so that each bar of soap will contain a lemon slice. Spritz the surface with rubbing alcohol to remove any bubbles and let stand until hard.

10

Remove the soap from the mold and cut it with a knife into nine even squares. Wrap each square in plastic wrap to prevent it from attracting moisture.

Soap recipe variations

Make a variety of soaps by choosing different scent
and color combinations. All these soaps are made
in the same way as the lemon soap (see pp.113–115),
using 2lb (1kg) of white melt-and-pour soap base,
which yields nine square bars of soap.

A. *Bergamot soap*
¼–¾ teaspoon (1–3g) orange soap colorant
2¼ teaspoons (10g) bergamot essential oil
9 whole dried orange slices

B. *Rose soap*
2¼ teaspoons (10g) rose absolute diluted in 5% grapeseed oil
4oz (100g) rosebuds

C. *Cinnamon soap*
¼–¾ teaspoon (1–3g) caramel soap colorant
2¼ teaspoons (10g) cinnamon leaf essential oil
9 cinnamon sticks

D. *Camomile soap*
¼–¾ teaspoon (1–3g) dark green soap colorant
2¼ teaspoons (10g) camomile essential oil
1–1½oz (35g) dried camomile flowers

E. *Lavender soap*
¼–¾ teaspoon (1–3g) purple soap colorant
2¼ teaspoons (10g) English lavender essential oil
½oz (10g) dried lavender

F. *Vanilla soap*
¼–¾ teaspoon (1–3g) cream soap colorant
2¼ teaspoons (10g) vanilla essential oil
3 vanilla beans, cut in thirds (use seeds in the mixture)

G. *Juniper soap*
¼–¾ teaspoon (1–3g) pink soap colorant
2¼ teaspoons (10g) juniper essential oil
4oz (100g) juniper berries

H. *Sandalwood soap*
¼–¾ teaspoon (1–3g) light-brown soap colorant
2¼ teaspoons (10g) sandalwood fragrance
2oz (50g) blue poppy seeds

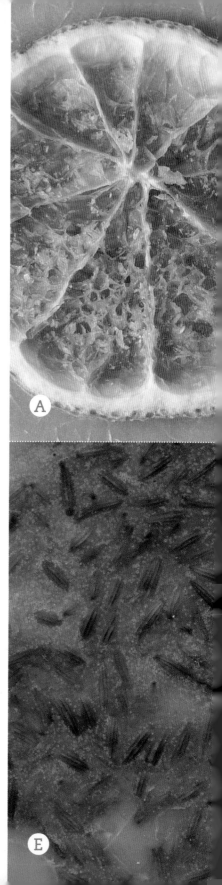

A

E

Juniper cake-slice soap

You will need
2lb (1kg) white melt-and-pour soap base
¼ teaspoon pink soap colorant
2¼ teaspoons (10g) juniper essential oil
4oz (100g) juniper berries

This soap cake is made like the lemon soap on pp.113–115, but in two stages. First, melt half the soap, adding the pink colorant and half the essential oil. Pour it into a round container and let it set, spritzing it with rubbing alcohol to get rid of any bubbles. Melt the second half of the soap, adding the remaining scent. Spritz the base again, then pour on the second layer of soap. Add the juniper berries to the top, spritzing it one final time to get rid of any remaining bubbles. Once set, remove from the mold and cut into slices.

Molded vanilla stars

You will need
2lb (1kg) white melt-and-pour soap base
¼–¾ teaspoon cream soap colorant
2¼ teaspoons (10g) vanilla essential oil
3 vanilla beans, cut in pieces

These vanilla-scented stars are made in the same way as the lemon soap (pp.113–115), but the mixture is poured into individual molds to set. Soap molds are sold in craft stores, or you can use silicone cake molds. Vanilla seeds are used instead of lemon peel granules as an exfoliant and for added scent. Vanilla beans can also be used to decorate the tops of the stars by placing them into the mold before the mixture is poured on top.

Cookie-cutter lavender hearts

You will need

2lb (1kg) white melt-and-pour soap base
¼–¾ teaspoon purple soap colorant
2¼ teaspoons (10g) lavender essential oil
¼oz (10g) dried lavender

These heart-shaped soaps are made using the same method and quantity of ingredients as the lemon soap on pp.113–115, swapping in the ingredients above. However, instead of cutting the soap into squares, they are cut with heart-shaped cookie cutters. The lavender buds will float to the top, creating an exfoliating layer.

See-through orange soap

You will need

2lb (1kg) clear melt-and-pour soap base
2¼ teaspoons (10g) bergamot essential oil
9 dried orange slices

Although made in the same way as the lemon soap on pp.113–115, using a clear soap base and adding a dried orange slice inside the soap gives these soaps a fresh look. Make them by first melting half of the clear soap base and adding half of the essential oil. Pour the mixture into a square mold, then add the orange slices evenly to the top. Allow this layer to set before melting the remaining half of the soap base and adding the remaining essential oil. Spritz the set layer with rubbing alcohol and add the melted soap mixture to the top. Spritz again to get rid of any bubbles and allow to set. Cut the soap into nine square bars.

Manicure roll

Use gorgeous Thai silk or pretty cotton for this manicure roll. Fill the pockets with nail-care essentials and add a couple of beautiful nail polishes to complete the gift. The recipient will feel very pampered!

To make a manicure roll you will need

Tools: dressmaker's scissors • steam iron • sewing machine • sewing pins

Materials: patterned silk-mix fabric • plain silk-mix lining fabric • iron-on interfacing • ribbon • bias tape • matching cotton sewing threads

1

Cut one 15 x 17in (38 x 43cm) piece each from the main patterned fabric, the lining fabric, and the iron-on interfacing.

2

Lay the main fabric right side down and place the interfacing on top. Iron to secure. Machine sew using zigzag stitch around the edge.

3

Using the zigzag setting, machine sew around the lining fabric to prevent fraying. Place the main and lining fabric together, right sides facing, and sew along the two long edges and one short edge.

4

Turn the fabric right side out. Fold the sides of the open seam inward. Press and pin. Topstitch along the edge to close.

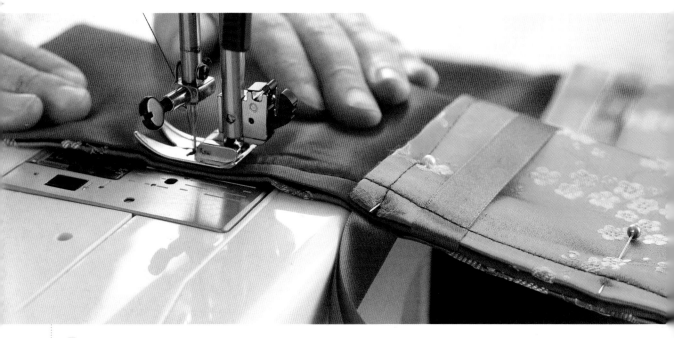

7

Starting from one of the bottom corners of the pocket, topstitch along the edge, securing the side of the pocket and the ribbon in place. Continue sewing up around the top of the flap and down the other side, securing the other side of the pocket.

5

Fold the topstitched edge over 4½in (11cm) from the bottom. Cut 16in (41cm) of ribbon and pin it across the pocket, folding and pinning the edges under the pocket.

6

Fold the rest of the ribbon in half and pin the end into the top left corner of the pocket, under the folded edge.

8

Choose how wide you would like the pocket divisions to be and mark them using bias tape. Pin the tape into position.

9

Machine sew the pockets, using the bias tape as a guideline. Remove the pins and tape and the manicure roll is ready to fold and tie up with the ribbon tie.

Container
candles

A homemade candle can be made into an extra special gift by putting it in a pretty teacup or a handy travel-sized can. Add color and fragrance to complement the container or the recipient.

To make a teacup candle you will need

Tools: double boiler (or large saucepan and heatproof bowl) • thermometer • heat-resistant mat or rack • metal spoon • 2 wooden skewers • 2 rubber bands *Materials:* teacup • soy wax flakes (1 cup of wax for every ½ cup of water the container holds, or the weight of wax in grams equal to the volume of water the container holds in ml) • wax dye • wick • wick sustainer

1

Boil water in the lower pan of a double boiler and add wax flakes to the top pan. Alternatively, use a heatproof bowl over a saucepan. Heat the wax, stirring occasionally.

2

When the wax has melted and reached a temperature of 160°F (70°C), take the pan off the heat and add a few drops of the dye to the wax. Stir until dissolved.

3

While the wax is heating, prepare the wick. Attach the wick sustainer (a metal tab) to a length of wick and place in the teacup. Secure the ends of the two skewers with rubber bands and insert the wick between them. Rest the skewers on the rim of the cup and pull the wick gently to ensure it is taut and centered in the cup.

4

Slowly pour the melted wax into the cup and tap it with a spoon to release air bubbles. Allow the candle to cool, add more wax if it has shrunk, then trim the wick when the candle has set.

Scented candles

There are two types of fragrance oil: candle fragrance oil (a synthetic blend) and essential/aromatherapy oil (extracted from plants and flowers, and 100% natural). Both types are stirred into the hot wax just before pouring. Try these different aromatherapy scents to enhance your mood:

A. *Pine or clove*
To increase energy

B. *Lavender or neroli*
To calm, soothe, and relax

C. *Jasmine or bergamot*
To uplift the mood and spirit

D. *Cinnamon or eucalyptus*
To promote concentration

E. *Sandalwood or lemon*
To relieve stress

Travel candles

Handy travel candles can be made in small cans or glass jars with lids.
Create them in the same way as the teacup candle (see pp.125–126).
If you are using different colors or scents, you will need to divide the
hot wax into batches before stirring in the dye or fragrance oil for each
can. After the candle has set, embellish or label the container as desired.
These candles have each been decorated with beads threaded on a wire
and a label made out of thick foil and embossed from the other side.

Layered candles

To make these layered candles, follow the instructions for making the teacup candle (see pp.125–126). Divide the melted wax into batches—one for each color you want—and stir in the dyes. With the wick in place, pour the first layer of colored wax into the glass, tap to release air bubbles, and allow to set. When it is solid to the touch, reheat the next batch of wax and pour in, and repeat for each layer. Leave for 24 hours until fully set.

Tip: Produce darker shades of the same color by increasing the quantity of dye used in each batch.

Candles in ramekins

Ramekins—small dishes that are most often used for individual dessert portions—are ideal for making a set of candles to give as a gift. The ramekins can be washed and reused as long as the candles have been made with soy wax flakes. (Alternatively, put them in a freezer for a few hours and the wax should drop out.) Use the method for making the teacup candle on pp.125–126.

Three-wick candle

This impressive three-wick candle can be created in the same way as the teacup candle (see pp.125–126), but you will need another set of skewers to hold the third wick (you should be able to get two wicks into the first set). Multi-wick candles give off more fragrance in addition to more light.

} Tip: Ceramic bowls or long, narrow plant containers can also be used for multi-wick candles.

Oilcloth
makeup bag

Fill this makeup bag with shredded tissue paper and cosmetics for the perfect pampering gift. The bag is made from oilcloth to make it water resistant, but you can use a sturdy cotton fabric or even quilted cotton for a different look.

To make an oilcloth makeup bag you will need

Tools: rotary cutter and mat (or dressmaker's scissors) • pins • sewing machine or needle

Materials: oilcloth • cotton lining fabric • 12in (30cm) zipper • cotton thread to match the lining fabric

1

Cut two pieces of your chosen outer fabric and two pieces of lining, each 8 x 12in (20 x 30cm). Cut two more pieces of lining fabric, each 3½ x 1in (9 x 2.5cm).

2

Fold over ¼in (5mm) of each end of the small lining strips. Fold one piece over the end of the zipper, pin in place, and sew across all layers. Repeat for the other end.

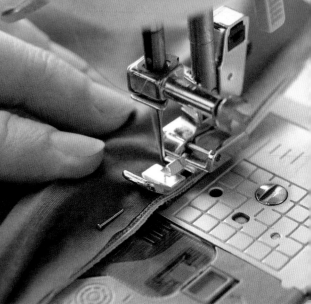

3

Layer one piece of outer fabric, facing up, with the zipper, facing down, and the lining, facing down. Pin. Then pin the other edge of the zipper to the other outer and lining pieces the same way.

4

Sew through all three layers along each side of the zipper, using a long stitch and the correct zipper foot for your machine. Make sure that you hold the layers not being sewn out of the way of the needle.

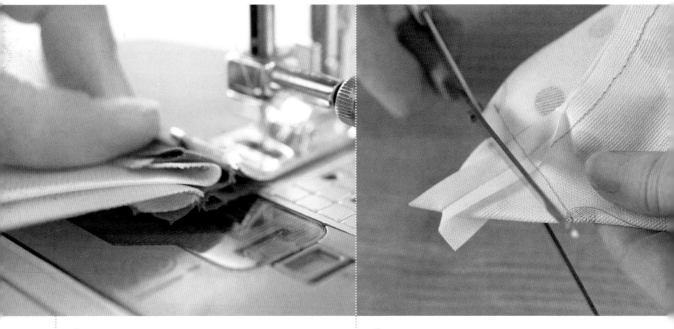

7

Make sure the zipper is three-quarters open. Sew around the edge of the lining and outer fabric, leaving a gap in the lining. When you get to the seams, flatten them to reduce bulk.

8

Shape all four corners by refolding each corner so that the seam is now in the middle of the new corner. Fold open the seam and sew across, 1¼in (3cm) up from the corner. Trim off the corner.

5

Use your finger to smooth along the line of the zipper, pushing the fabric out. If needed, you can iron the seams on a very low setting, from the lining side, protecting it with a dish towel.

6

Next, bring the right sides of the outer and lining pieces together. Pin the two lining pieces together, leaving a 4in (10cm) gap at the bottom edge. You don't need to pin the outer fabric.

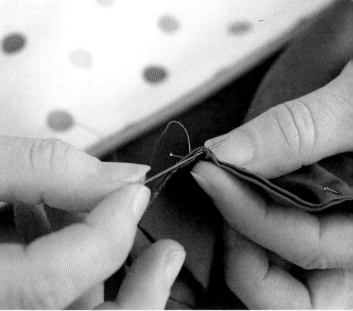

9

Reach through the gap in the lining to turn out the bag, pushing out the corners. If needed, iron on a very low setting from the inside, using a dish towel to protect the bag.

10

Finally, fold under the edges of the gap in the lining, and iron them so that they meet neatly. Then pin and sew the lining closed either by hand or machine.

Follow instructions on pp.135–137 to make the juniper bath bomb. Make a rose bath bomb the same way, but using rose essential oil and adding rose petals.

Fizzy bath bombs

Bath bombs are solid balls that fizz and bubble as they dissolve, adding scent and color to the bathwater. They make wonderful gifts and are surprisingly easy to make with ingredients that are readily available in most supermarkets.

To make a juniper bath bomb you will need

Tools: strainer • 1 medium-sized mixing bowl • 2 small mixing bowls • spoon • bath bomb mold

Materials: ¼ cup baking soda • ⅓ cup citric acid • ¼ teaspoon (1g) purple soap colorant • ½ teaspoon juniper essential oil • water in a spray bottle

Makes 1 bath bomb

1

Measure the baking soda and sift it into the larger mixing bowl.

2

Add the citric acid to the baking soda and mix well with your fingers until thoroughly combined.

135

 3

Split the mixture between the two smaller bowls. Add the colorant to the first bowl and mix well with a spoon or your fingers, ensuring that no lumps remain.

4

Add approximately half the fragrance to the first bowl and half to the second bowl. Mix each bowl well, again making sure that no lumps remain.

7

Add white mixture to the mold half, leaving a mound at the top. Repeat the process for the other mold half, this time starting with the white mixture.

8

Bring the two mold halves together, making sure that the two halves of the bath bomb are lined up exactly. Press the halves together.

5

Spray both bowls lightly with water and mix it in evenly with your fingers. Continue to spritz and mix until the mixture feels damp but not too moist.

6

Fill one of the mold halves halfway with the purple mixture. Gently press the mixture down into the mold with your fingers to remove any pockets of air.

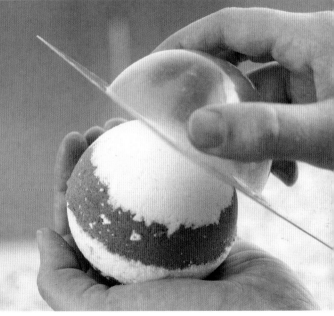

9

Leave the bath bomb to set for approximately five minutes. Try not to move it at all during this time because it can be very fragile before it is set.

10

Once set, first remove one of the mold halves. Then place your palm over the bath bomb and gently turn it over. Remove the other mold half.

Sweet dreams
eye mask

Sweet dreams are guaranteed with this eye mask, made using blackout fabric to ensure that no light passes through. You can also put a little dried lavender inside before you sew up the mask, to add a lovely scent when the mask is used.

To make an eye mask you will need

Tools: dressmaker's scissors • pins • sewing machine • needle • safety pin

Materials: patterned cotton fabric • cotton lining fabric • blackout fabric • cotton thread to match the bias tape and the main fabric • 20in (50cm) of ½in (15mm) bias tape in a matching color • 16in (40cm) of ½in (12mm) elastic

1
Photocopy or trace the eye mask template (see p.232). Cut one eye mask shape from the main fabric, one from the lining, and one from the blackout fabric.

2
Place the main fabric, right side up, on top of the blackout fabric. Place the lining fabric, right side down, on top of the main fabric. Pin all three layers together.

139

3

Sew around the edge, beginning and ending so that you leave a 2in (5cm) gap along the straight top edge. Reverse stitch at the beginning and end to secure the stitches.

4

Trim the seam allowance all around the mask to remove the excess fabric and neaten the edge. Then turn the mask right side out. Iron it flat.

7

Cut out a 2½ x 20in (6.5 x 50cm) piece of fabric for the casing. Fold the piece in half lengthwise, and fold the edges under again. Iron flat. Pin and sew the long edge closed.

8

Attach a safety pin to one end of the elastic and a large straight pin to the other to stop the end from slipping into the casing. Use the safety pin to push the elastic through.

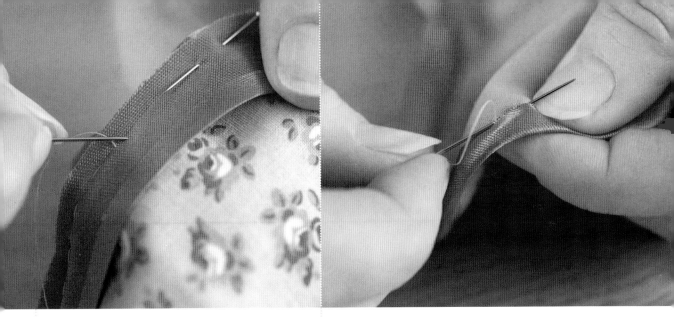

5

Open the bias tape and pin it onto the front of the mask, right side to right side, placing the pins on the fold line closest to the edge. Sew along the fold line using a running stitch.

6

When you reach the end of the bias, fold the short edge under and sew it over where you began for a neat finish. Fold the bias tape over to the back of the mask and slip stitch in place.

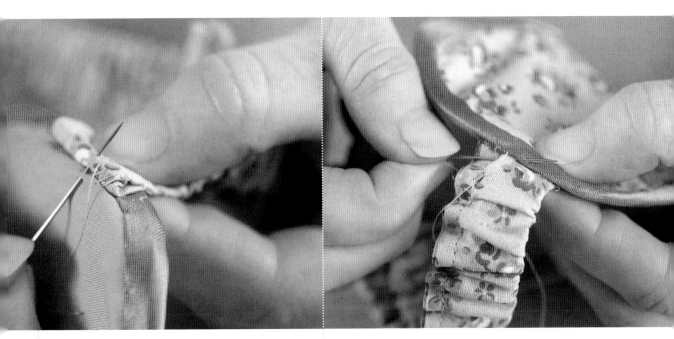

9

Once the elastic is all the way through, sew both ends of the elastic to the casing. Fold over the end of the strap to hide the raw edge, and hand sew to the back of the mask.

10

Flip the mask over, and sew along the edge where the elastic meets the bias edging. Repeat Steps 9–10 for the other end of the strap to finish the mask.

Pamper hamper

Surprise a friend in need of pampering with a hamper full of handmade, all-natural goodies. Any of the items in the Pampering section would make great hamper fillers. Our basket contains a set of all-natural luxury soaps (pp.112–117) packaged together in a box, a slice of juniper soap (p.118), a striped juniper bath bomb and a rose petal one (pp.134–137), an oilcloth makeup bag (pp.130–133), and a sweet dreams eye mask (pp.138–141). Round out the hamper with other inexpensive pampering items such as brushes, sponges, loofahs, and towels. You can even add bath salts in a glass jar. Wrap the hamper in cellophane and tie it with a ribbon or two for a truly luxurious handmade gift.

For pet lovers

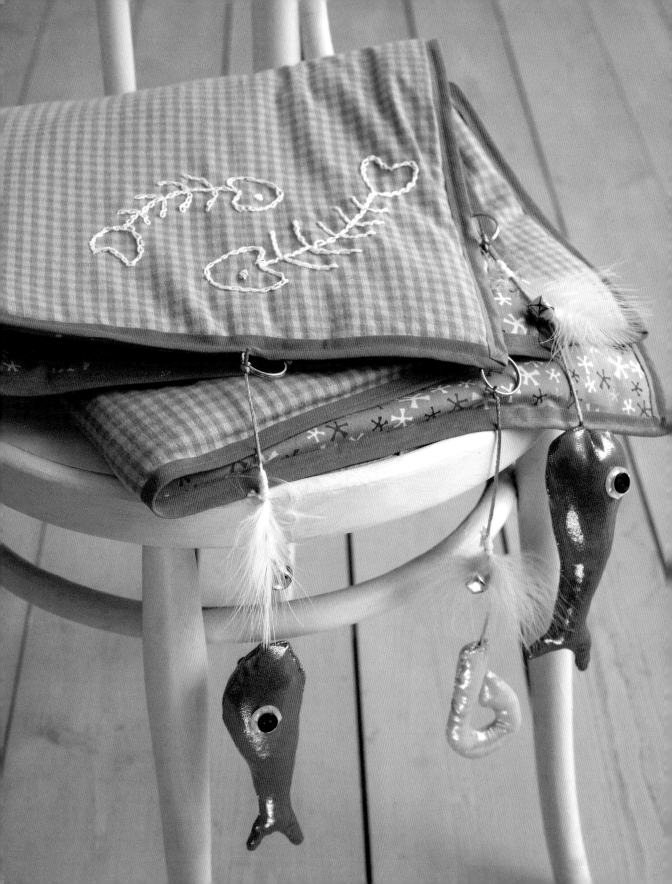

Cat's play mat

Here is a gift for the cat who has everything! This mat will keep your feline friend busy and would also make a luxurious lining for a cat basket, or it can be thrown over a favorite chair or sofa. For added appeal, fill the toys with catnip.

To make a cat's play mat you will need

Tools: scissors • sewing pins • sewing machine • sewing needle • embroidery hoop *Materials:* metallic fabric in orange and silver • thin cord • stuffing • cotton sewing threads • white and black buttons • small bells • feathers • white embroidery thread • batting • patterned cotton fabric • gingham fabric • orange bias tape • metal rings

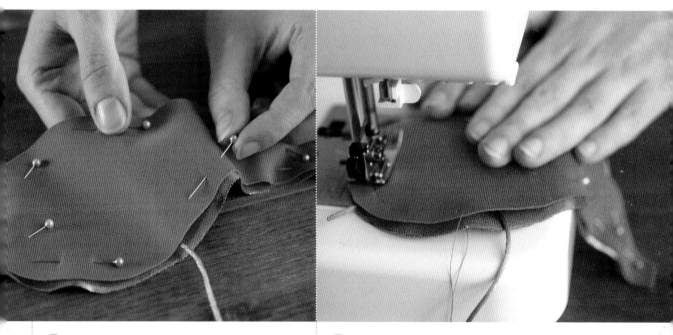

1 Using the template on p.233, cut out two sides for each fish from two pieces of orange fabric held right sides together. Pin. Pin the end of 8in (20cm) thin cord to the mouth as shown.

2 Machine sew around the edges, ¼in (5mm) from the edge, securing the cord at the mouth. Leave a ¾in (2cm) gap, allowing the rest of the cord to pass through the gap.

 3

Turn the fish right side out. You should have the long length of cord (the "fishing line") hanging from the mouth. Sew several times through the cord to make it secure.

4

Push stuffing into the fish and sew the opening shut using neat topstitching and matching thread. Repeat to make another fish. Make a fish hook in the same way, using the silver metallic fabric.

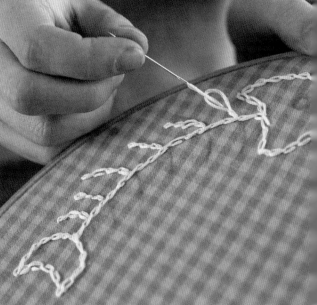

7

Cut a square of gingham fabric and a square of patterned fabric, each 27½ x 27½ in (70 x 70cm). Cut the batting so it is about ⅛in (3mm) smaller all the way around than the fabric squares.

8

Place the gingham fabric in the embroidery hoop and tighten. Use the template on p.233 to draw a pencil outline of a fish skeleton and use chain stitch and white embroidery thread to go over the design.

5

Sew a white and black button on both sides of each fish head. Make sure they are attached securely. Alternatively, embroider eyes using embroidery thread.

6

Thread and knot a bell to the fishing line about 2in (5cm) from the fish's mouth. Using embroidery thread, tightly bind a feather to the fishing line just above the bell.

9

Layer the fabrics—gingham, wadding, then patterned cotton—and pin together. Pin the bias tape around the edge and machine sew through it to sew the layers together.

10

Attach metal rings to two of the edges and one corner of the mat using cotton thread. Tie the fish and hook securely to the rings.

Catnip mice

Filled with catnip, these little mice make a delightful gift that a cat literally cannot resist. This is a great project for using up scraps and leftover pieces of material. Cotton fabrics work well, but you can also try tweed or leather.

To make a catnip mouse you will need

Tools: dressmaker's scissors • pencil • sewing pins • sewing machine • sewing needle

Materials: cotton fabric • felt fabric in two different colors • white wool yarn • batting
• cotton sewing thread • dried catnip (optional) • black embroidery thread

1

Using the template on p.231, cut out two main body pieces from two pieces of fabric held right sides together. Cut out the base and ears from colored felt.

2

Cut three lengths of yarn to twice as long as you would like the tail to be and knot them together. Knot the short ends around a pencil and make a braid to use for the tail.

3

Pin the body pieces together, right side to right side. Start sewing ⅜in (8mm) in from the bottom edge. Sew around the curve, stopping ⅜in (8mm) from the end.

4

Tie off the ends and trim the excess fabric to make the seam less bulky once the mouse is turned right side out.

7

Trim off the excess fabric in the seams and turn the mouse right side out, pushing the nose out with your finger. If necessary, use a needle to pull out the tip from the outside.

8

Push small amounts of batting into the mouse, ensuring that you fill the nose. When it is half stuffed, add dried catnip. Finish stuffing the mouse.

5

Pin the felt base to the long sides of the body pieces, so that the right side of each of the pieces is facing the felt base.

6

Starting from the back end (the slightly raised end) of the mouse, sew all the way around the sides, attaching the top layer to the base and stopping 1in (2.5cm) before the end.

9

Insert the tail underneath the back seam, pinning the seam closed. Using small stitches, carefully sew up the opening, securing the tail into position.

10

Bring one cut edge of the ear over the other so that the ear curves inward. Pin in place and sew down, repeating for the other side. Embroider two black eyes onto the mouse.

Dog biscuits

These homemade dog biscuits are sure to be a favorite treat! What's more, they are made from all natural ingredients, so they are good for your dog, and they contain parsley to help freshen his breath, too.

To make dog biscuits you will need

Tools: baking sheet • parchment paper • 2 mixing bowls • tablespoon • chopping knife • grater • wooden spoon • rolling pin • bone-shaped cookie cutter (or knife) • cooling rack *Ingredients:* chicken bouillon (cube or granules) • a large handful of parsley • 1 medium-sized carrot • 2½oz (75g) cheese • 1 tbsp olive oil • 1½ cups whole wheat flour • 1 cup oats • 1 tsp baking powder

1
Heat the oven to 350°F (180°C). Grease a baking sheet and line it with parchment paper.

2
Make double-strength chicken stock and let it cool. You can also use homemade stock.

155

3

Chop the parsley. Grate the carrot and cheese. You can use grated cheese from a package for this step if you prefer.

4

Mix the parsley, carrot, and cheese together in a bowl. Add the oil and combine well, until all the ingredients are coated.

7

Sprinkle some flour on the work surface and shape the dough into a flat disk with your hands. Using a rolling pin, roll out the dough to the desired thickness.

8

Use a cookie cutter (or knife) to cut shapes from the dough. Combine the scraps, roll again, and cut out more shapes until no dough remains.

5

In a separate bowl, combine the flour, oats, and baking powder. Mix them together well.

6

Combine the parsley, carrot, and cheese mixture with the flour mixture. Add the stock one tablespoon at a time to make the mixture moist. Knead with your hands to make a dough.

9

Bake for 25–30 minutes, until golden brown. Move to a wire rack and cool completely.

Simple silhouette

An even easier way to create an appliqué keepsake of your pet is to cut out a side-on silhouette from one fabric. Do this by enlarging a profile photograph on a photocopier to use as a template. You can make this floral pup using the template on p.231.

Appliqué
pet portrait

Use the appliqué technique to create a stunning portrait of a beloved pet, perfect for decorating a pillow or displaying in a frame. Use the cat template provided, or make your own from a favorite photograph.

To make an appliqué pet-portrait pillow cover you will need

Tools: iron • dressmaker's scissors • needle • pins • sewing machine

Materials: fusible web • black, gray, and white fabric • pillow cover
• contrasting thread for basting • blue, pink, and black felt • black and white thread

1 Resize the template (see p.230) to fit your pillow cover. Transfer the head piece on to the fusible web, and iron it on to the reverse side of your selected fabric.

2 Repeat the process for the back, chest, ear, and muzzle pieces. Then cut out each element. Note that the eyes and nose don't need to be faced.

3

Carefully peel off the backing paper from all the pieces with facing.

4

Assemble the pieces on the pillow cover. Make sure the head piece overlaps the chest piece and the back piece. Iron in place.

7

Pin, then baste the pieces, except the eyes and nose, in place on the pillow cover. Remove the pins.

8

Sew around the outside of each of the basted pieces about ¼in (5mm) from the edge, either by hand or with a sewing machine. Remove the basting thread.

5

Trace the eyes, nose, and pupils on to colored felt and cut them out.

6

Sew pupils on to the eye pieces using tiny backstitches and black thread.

9

Baste the eyes and nose on to the cat's face and sew around the edges of each piece. Remove the basting thread.

10

Using the image on p.158 as a guide, sew guidelines for the whiskers and eyelashes using basting thread. Sew over them using topstitch. Remove the basting threads.

Tartan dog jacket

Keep a favorite dog warm and cozy all winter long with this easy-to-make, fleece-lined jacket. You can adjust the pattern to make it in any size. It fastens with Velcro, making it easy to put on and take off.

To make a tartan dog jacket you will need
Tools: tracing paper • dressmaker's scissors • sewing pins • sewing machine
Materials: tartan plaid fabric • batting • interfacing • fleece fabric • cotton sewing threads
• Velcro • red grosgrain ribbon

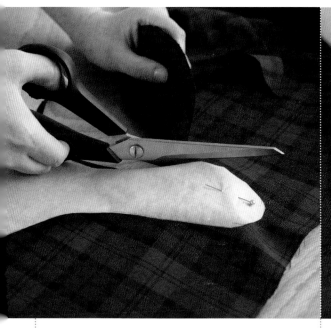

1
Using the template on pp.234–235, use tracing paper to make a pattern and adjust it to fit your dog. Cut out one jacket piece and one belly strap from each fabric.

2
Place the plaid fabric, right side out, on top of the batting and interfacing. Pin all three layers together.

3

Machine sew along the lines of the plaid fabric using a long stitch, first in one direction and then the other. This quilts the jacket.

6

Machine sew around the edges of the jacket, joining the upper and lining pieces. Neaten the edges with a zigzag stitch.

7

Pin the grosgrain ribbon around the jacket as shown. Machine sew around the ribbon to attach. Fold the other half of the ribbon over the edge, and topstitch or hand stitch to attach.

4

Pin Velcro onto the lining and the quilted upper at the points marked on the template. Sew the Velcro into place.

5

Pin the quilted upper and the fleece lining together, right sides out.

8

Make the belly strap in the same way as the jacket, attaching Velcro to the belly strap as indicated on the template. Pin the two sections as shown and sew together.

Edible gifts

Butter cookies

Deliciously light and crumbly butter cookies make a lovely gift on their own, but they are also a very versatile cookie base. Why not try icing them or adding chocolate and chopped nuts (see p.172) for a gourmet twist?

To make plain butter cookies you will need

Tools: large mixing bowl • wooden spoon • rolling pin • palette knife • round cookie cutter • nonstick baking sheets • wire cooling rack *Ingredients:* ½ cup granulated sugar • 1½ cups all-purpose flour, sifted, plus extra for dusting • 11 tbsp unsalted butter, softened and diced • 1 egg yolk • 1 tsp pure vanilla extract

Makes
30
cookies

1
Preheat the oven to 350°F (180°C). Put the sugar, flour, and butter into a large mixing bowl, or into the bowl of a food processor.

2
Rub together, or pulse blend, the ingredients until they look like fine bread crumbs.

3

Add the egg yolk and vanilla extract, and combine together until the mixture forms a dough.

6

Flour the dough and the work surface well, and roll the dough out to a thickness of about ¼in (5mm). Use a palette knife to move the dough to prevent it from sticking.

7

If the dough is too sticky to roll well, wrap it in plastic wrap and chill for 15 minutes, then try again.

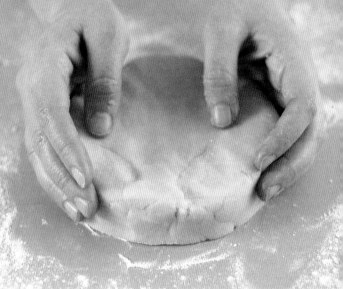

4

Turn the dough out onto a floured surface and knead it briefly until smooth.

5

Shape the dough into a round, flat disk with your hands.

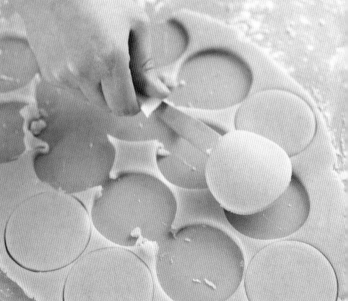

8

With the cookie cutter, cut out round cookies.

9

Transfer the cookies to the baking sheets with a palette knife. Reroll the dough scraps to ¼in (5mm) thick. Cut out cookies until all the dough is used up.

10

Bake in batches for 10–15 minutes until golden brown at the edges. Remove from the oven and let the cookies cool on the baking sheet until firm enough to handle.

11

Once firm enough, transfer the cookies to a wire rack. Allow to cool completely before serving. The cookies will keep well in an airtight container for five days.

Butter cookie variations

Add chocolate, raisins, and chopped nuts to the basic recipe to create butter cookies with a "wow" factor. Divide the dough into three parts after Step 3 and add the ingredients listed below to each batch. Add the raisins and chocolate directly to each batch of dough, roll, and cut out. Sprinkle the nuts and more chocolate chunks on top. Bake as directed and let cool. Pack them in a cookie tin or box up with tissue paper for a gourmet gift.

A. 1 tbsp chopped pistachio nuts and 1 tbsp white chocolate chunks

B. 2 tbsp raisins and 2 tbsp chopped hazelnuts

C. 3 tbsp dark chocolate chunks

Shortbread

Shortbread is a rich and crumbly type of butter cookie that is traditionally made into wedges but can also be shaped into cookies or fingers. The high butter content gives shortbread its crumbly, or "short," texture. This recipe makes eight wedges.

You will need

11 tbsp unsalted butter, softened, plus extra for greasing
⅓ cup granulated sugar, plus extra for sprinkling
1 cup all-purpose flour
5 tbsp cornstarch

1. Lightly grease a 7in (18cm) round cake pan with a removable bottom and line it with parchment paper.

2. Combine the softened butter and the sugar in a bowl, then cream together using an electric mixer for 2–3 minutes, or until very light and fluffy.

3. Sift the flour and cornstarch into the bowl and mix. Using your hands, bring the mixture together to form a dough, then place in the pan.

4. Press the dough into the pan using your hands, until it fills the pan and is smooth and even on top. Using a sharp knife, lightly score the shortbread into eight even wedges. Prick the shortbread all over with a fork, then cover it with plastic wrap and chill in the fridge for 1 hour.

5. Preheat the oven to 325°F (160°C). Bake the shortbread in the oven for 30–40 minutes, until lightly golden and firm

6. Score the wedges again using a sharp knife while the shortbread is still warm. Sprinkle a dusting of granulated sugar over the top and let cool completely. When cool, carefully remove from the pan. Break or cut the shortbread into wedges along the scored lines and serve. The shortbread will keep in an airtight container for five days.

Gingerbread men

These jolly gingerbread men are as much fun to make as they are to receive. Give them raisin faces and buttons or use colored icing to pipe on facial features, hair, clothes, and accessories. This recipe makes 16 gingerbread men (or ladies).

You will need
¼ cup molasses (not blackstrap)
1¾ cups all-purpose flour, plus extra
           for dusting
1 tsp baking soda
1½ tsp ground ginger
1½ tsp pumpkin pie spice
7 tbsp unsalted butter,
         softened and diced
¾ cup dark brown sugar
1 egg
raisins, to decorate

1   Preheat the oven to 375°F (190°C). Heat the molasses until it liquefies, then cool.

2   Sift the flour, baking soda, and spices into a bowl. Add the butter. Rub together with your fingertips until the mixture looks like bread crumbs. Add the sugar to the mixture and mix well with a wooden spoon.

3   Beat the egg into the cooled syrup with a fork until well blended. Make a well in the flour mixture. Pour in the syrup mix. Bring together to make a rough dough.

4   On a lightly floured work surface, knead the dough briefly until smooth. Flour the dough and the work surface well, and roll the dough out to ¼in (5mm) thick. Using a cookie cutter, cut out as many shapes as possible. Transfer to nonstick baking sheets. Mix the scraps of dough, roll again, and cut out more shapes until all the dough is used. Decorate the men with raisins, giving them eyes, a nose, and buttons down the front.

5   Bake for 10–12 minutes, until golden. Transfer to a wire rack to cool completely. These gingerbread men will keep in an airtight container for three days.

Spritzgebäck cookies

These delicate, buttery cookies are based on a classic German cookie traditionally served at Christmas. They're a clever twist on traditional butter cookies, and they make an indulgent gift. This recipe makes 45 cookies.

You will need
26 tbsp butter, softened
1 cup granulated sugar
a few drops of pure vanilla extract
pinch of salt
3 cups all-purpose flour, sifted
1¼ cups ground almonds
2 egg yolks, if needed
3½oz (100g) dark or milk chocolate

Special equipment:
Piping bag and star nozzle

1 Preheat the oven to 350°F (180°C). Line two or three baking sheets with parchment paper. Place the butter in a bowl and beat until smooth. Stir in the sugar, vanilla, and salt until the mixture is thick and the sugar has been absorbed. Gradually add two-thirds of the flour, stirring in a little at a time.

2 Add the rest of the flour and almonds, and knead the mixture to make a dough. Transfer the dough to a piping bag and squeeze 3in (7.5cm) lengths onto the baking sheets. Loosen the dough with two egg yolks, if necessary.

3 Bake for 12 minutes, or until golden, and transfer to a wire rack. Melt the chocolate in a bowl over a pan of simmering water. Dip one end of each cookie into the melted chocolate and return to the rack to set. The cookies will keep in an airtight container for two to three days.

Tip: If the dough is too stiff to be piped after adding the eggs, add milk, one tablespoon at a time, until it is loose enough.

Orange crunch cookies

These crunchy cookies have been given a tangy twist with orange zest. They can be decorated with orange-flavored icing for a more intense flavor or made plain for a more subtle taste. This recipe makes 20–24 cookies.

You will need
¾ cup self-rising flour
4 tbsp unsalted butter, diced,
        plus extra for greasing
⅓ cup dark brown sugar
½ egg yolk (beaten)
1 tbsp honey
1 tsp orange zest

For the icing
1¾ cups confectioner's sugar, sifted
3 tbsp fresh orange juice

Special equipment:
Piping bag and nozzle

1   Sift the flour into a bowl and rub the butter into the flour with your fingertips, until the mixture looks like bread crumbs. Using a table knife, stir the sugar, orange zest, honey, and egg into the flour and butter, until the mixture starts to come together in lumps.

2   Use your hands to bring the lumps together to form a smooth ball of dough. Briefly knead the dough and then lightly flour the work surface. Roll the dough into a log about 2in (5cm) in diameter and 4in (10cm) long. Wrap the log in plastic wrap and chill it for 1 hour 30 minutes, or until firm.

3   Preheat the oven to 350°F (180°C). Lightly grease two baking sheets with butter. Slice the log into 20–24 thin disks and place the cookies on the baking sheets. Bake for 7–9 minutes.

4   Remove the cookies from the oven and allow to set and cool. Beat the confectioner's sugar and orange juice together to form a smooth paste. Transfer the cookies to a cooling rack. Put the icing into a piping bag and then drizzle it over the cool cookies in a zigzag pattern. The cookies will keep in an airtight container for five to seven days.

Chocolate
truffles

Edible gifts

These chocolate truffles look so impressive that you'll be surprised to learn how easy they are to make. Coat them with cocoa and confectioner's sugar for a classic look, or use colorful toppings (see p.181) for a truly tempting box of treats.

To make cocoa- and sugar-coated chocolate truffles you will need

Tools: saucepan • bowl • whisk • teaspoon • tray • parchment paper • sieve • plate
Ingredients: ½ cup heavy cream • 2 tbsp dark rum, brandy, or sherry
• 9oz (250g) dark, white, or milk chocolate, melted • ¼ cup cocoa • ¼ cup confectioner's sugar

Makes
30
truffles

1
Place the cream in a saucepan, bring it to a boil to sterilize, then cool until lukewarm. Stir in the rum, brandy, or sherry, then add it to the cool, melted chocolate, stirring until blended.

2
Beat the mixture until light and fluffy, then chill for 2–3 hours, until it is firm enough to divide into portions.

3

Using a teaspoon, scoop out spoonfuls of the mixture and roll into neat balls. Place them on a tray lined with parchment paper, leaving plenty of space in between. Chill until firm; about one hour.

4

Sift the cocoa and confectioner's sugar together to create the coating.

5

One at a time, roll the chilled truffles in your hands to soften the outside slightly, then roll them in the cocoa and sugar mixture to coat.

Other coatings

To create a colorful box of truffles, divide the rolled balls into five batches after they have been chilled. Roll each truffle in your hands quickly to soften the outside slightly. Roll the first batch (around six truffles) in 2 tsp cocoa and 1 tsp confectioner's sugar. Roll each of the remaining batches of six in one of the toppings below.

A. 2 tbsp finely chopped pistachio nuts

B. 2 tbsp chocolate sprinkles

C. 2 tbsp dried strawberries, crushed and mixed with confectioner's sugar

D. 2 tbsp finely chopped hazelnuts

Colorful macarons

Light and delicate macarons make a truly sophisticated gift. To make a multicolored box, divide up the mixture and add different-colored food coloring to each batch. These macarons use fresh cream, so keep them chilled.

For pink macarons you will need

Tools: 2 baking sheets • parchment paper • 2 large mixing bowls • handheld electric mixer • piping bag • wire cooling rack • palette knife *Ingredients:* 2 large egg whites at room temperature • ⅓ cup granulated sugar • ½ cup ground almonds • ¾ cup confectioner's sugar • pink food coloring • ¼ cup heavy cream

Makes 20 macarons

1
Preheat the oven to 300°F (150°C). Line 2 baking sheets with parchment paper. Trace 20 x 1¼in (3cm) circles, leaving a good-sized gap between them. Turn the paper over.

2
In a large bowl, whisk the egg whites to stiff peaks using an electric mixer.

183

3

Add the granulated sugar a little at a time, whisking well between additions. The meringue mixture should be very stiff at this point.

4

Mix together the ground almonds and the confectioner's sugar. Gently fold in the almond mixture, a spoonful at a time, until just incorporated into the meringue mixture.

7

Bake in the middle of the oven for 18–20 minutes, until the surface is set firm. Leave for 15–20 minutes, then transfer to a wire rack to cool completely.

8

Pour the heavy cream into a bowl and add some more pink food coloring. Whisk the cream until it is thick and the color is evenly distributed.

5

Add a few drops of pink food coloring to the mixture, folding the mixture carefully, until just mixed in.

6

Transfer the macaron mixture to a piping bag. Using the guidelines, pipe the mixture into the center of each circle, allowing it to spread and fill out into an even, round shape.

9

Using a palette knife, add a blob of whipped cream to the center of one macaron half. Add the second half and sandwich gently. Serve immediately.

185

Creamy caramels

Set up a candy factory in your kitchen with this quick recipe for caramels. Sweet and rich, caramel is delicious plain, but you can also add nuts, raisins, and chocolate chunks (see p.189) for a variety of tasty treats.

To make creamy caramels you will need

Tools: 7in (18cm) shallow, nonstick square pan • medium heavy-bottomed saucepan • sugar thermometer • wooden spoon • knife *Ingredients:* 2 cups granulated sugar • 4 tbsp unsalted butter, diced • 6fl oz (170ml) can evaporated milk • ½ cup milk • ½ tsp pure vanilla extract

Makes 36 squares

1
Grease a 7in (18cm) shallow, nonstick square pan.

2
Pour the sugar, butter, and milks into a saucepan.

3

Gently heat the mixture, stirring with a wooden spoon until all the sugar has dissolved. Bring to a boil and simmer continuously for 20–25 minutes.

4

Use a candy thermometer to monitor the temperature of the mixture. Once it reaches 240°F (116°C), remove from the heat and add the vanilla extract.

5

Once off the heat, beat the mixture with a wooden spoon until it is thick and paler in color. Pour it into the prepared pan and let cool.

6

When cold, lift the caramels from the pan. Cut into small squares.

Variations

Create endless variations of the caramel recipe by mixing raisins, chocolate chips, nuts, or even marshmallows into the mixture after it has been thickened in Step 5. Some ideas to get you started are given below.

A. ½ cup raisins, chopped

B. 5½oz (155g) white chocolate chips

C. ⅓ cup cashew nuts mixed with 2 tbsp raisins

D. ⅔ cup pecan nuts, chopped

Flavored oils

Edible gifts

Homemade flavored oils make beautiful and useful gifts for anyone who loves to cook. Herb-flavored oils can be used to dress salads or as a base for marinades, while a few drops of chili oil add zing to pizza and pasta dishes.

To make chili oil you will need

Tools: knife • cutting board • sterilized glass bottle with stopper • pitcher or liquid measuring cup and funnel (optional)

Ingredients: 3½ cups light olive oil • 3½oz (100g) mix of red bird's eye chiles and regular red chiles

1
Slice the regular chiles in half with a knife, cutting all the way through the stem. Add the sliced chiles, whole bird's eye chiles, and any seeds to the sterilized bottle.

2
Fill up the bottle with 3½ cups olive oil and stopper it. The oil will keep for up to one month.

Basil oil

Fragrant basil oil makes a flavorful base for salad dressings, and it can be used to flavor sauces and soups. Bruising the leaves before you pour on the oil releases their delicate aroma.

You will need
3½ cups light olive oil
5oz (150g) basil

1 Heat the oil gently in a pan until it reaches 104°F (40°C).

2 Lightly bruise the basil and put it in a warm, sterilized jar or bottle. Pour the warm oil into the jar, then seal. The oil will be ready to use in three to four weeks.

Tip: Filter basil oil after three to four weeks to extend its shelf life. Rebottle the oil and seal the bottle before storing.

Garlic and rosemary oil

This traditionally flavored oil can be used as a base for marinades, or to lightly coat vegetables before they are roasted in the oven. The oil keeps for one month.

You will need

6 garlic cloves
3 stalks rosemary
3½ cups light olive oil

1   Crush the garlic cloves lightly. Place them in a sterilized jar or bottle with the stalks of rosemary.

2   Add oil to the bottle to cover the herbs, then seal.

Tip: Try combining rosemary with herbs such as thyme or cilantro for other exciting flavor combinations.

Gift wrap

Square
gift box

A gift box is the ideal way to present awkwardly shaped gifts. You can make this gift box exactly the required size by resizing the template. Use patterned card stock, or glue decorative paper to card stock before you create different looks.

To make a square gift box you will need

Tools: pencil • craft knife • cutting mat • ruler • blunt knife (or pair of scissors) • eraser

Materials: patterned card stock (or patterned paper glued onto card stock) • tracing paper • glue stick

1 Use a photocopier to resize the box stencil on p.199. Using tracing paper and a pencil, transfer the template onto patterned card stock (or glue patterned paper to the back of the card stock).

2 Use a craft knife and cutting mat to cut out the shape you have drawn. Make sure not to cut into the internal folding lines.

3

Once you have cut out the entire shape, score all the folding lines using a ruler and blunt knife, or one side of a pair of scissors. This will make the box easier to assemble.

4

Fold the sides inward along the scored lines, making sure that each crease is sharp. For a neat finish, erase the pencil lines along the creases inside the box.

5

Attach the three sides not adjacent to the lid to each other using the glue stick or double-sided tape on the outside of the flaps. Hold in place until set.

6

Fold in the flaps of the last remaining side, spread glue or attach tape to the patterned side of the flaps, and slot the side into place. Press the flaps down and hold in place until set.

Square gift box template

Please enlarge to the required
size on a photocopier

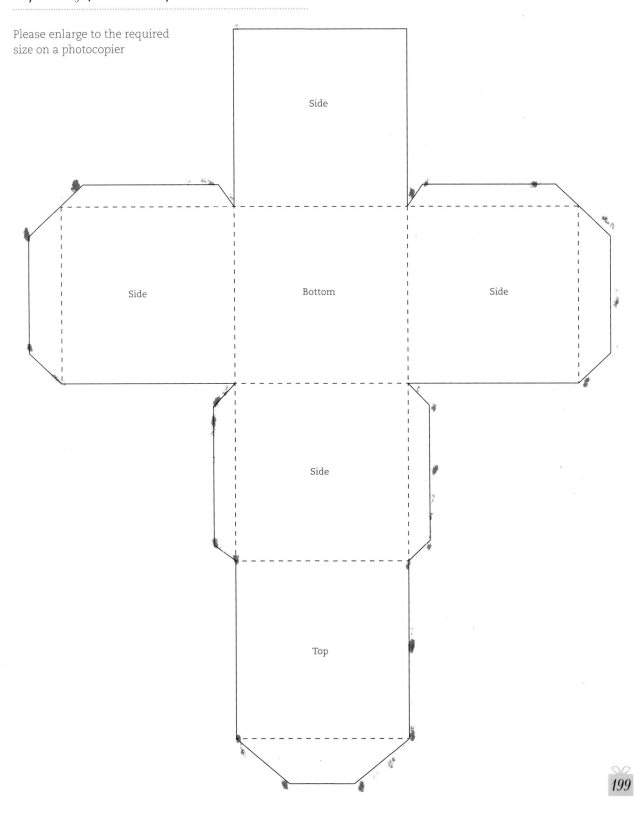

Side

Side

Bottom

Side

Side

Top

Decorating gift boxes

A few odds and ends (colored paper, ribbons, tissue paper, and buttons) can turn plain wrapped packages or dull boxes into beautiful, personalized gifts.

A. Gift tag and ribbon
Cut a luggage-label shape from white card stock. Punch a hole in the corner and thread through with ribbon. Tie this ribbon around the box and glue the ends at the base of the box. Tie another ribbon in a different color around the box.

B. Lots of dots
Layer sheets of tissue paper in different colors. Cut circles out of the sheets of tissue paper, cutting through all the layers. Using a needle and thread, sew a few small stitches through the center of each stack of circles to secure them and tie off at the back. Glue these to the box top.

C. Button bow
Cut out four rectangles in two colors of patterned card stock. Cut a triangle out of one end of each. Glue to the top of the box, layered on top of one another. Cut out a bow-tie shape from patterned card stock. Fold the sides of the bow-tie shape around and under to meet at the back. Glue this to the box and press down and glue in the middle to make the 3-D bow shape. Glue a button to the center of the bow.

D. Button band
Cut out a strip of patterned card stock long enough to wrap around the box. Sew on a variety of buttons using cream yarn. Wrap the strip around the box and glue at the bottom.

E. Floral wrap
Wrap a length of ribbon around the box and glue at the bottom. Cut out and glue another ribbon going the other way. Cut out flower shapes in different colors from tissue paper and layer on top of each other. Sew a few stitches to hold the flowers together. Glue the flowers on the box where the ribbons meet. Add a few extra smaller flowers, making them according to the same method.

F. Rosette
Cut two lengths of ribbon and point the ends by cutting out a triangle. Glue these to the top of the box. Using pinking shears, cut circles from patterned card stock and decorative papers. Cut each circle smaller as you go and stack them up to make the rossette shape. Thread a button through the circles to hold them together, then glue them on the box.

Tip: All these ideas can be used on larger packages and boxes. Or why not combine a few?

Jewelry case

This slim case makes the perfect gift box for jewelry and other small items likely to slip out of a looser box. Wrap your gift in tissue paper and close the box with a ribbon tied in a bow to ensure that it stays safe until opened.

To make a jewelry case you will need

Tools: pencil • craft knife • cutting mat • ruler • blunt knife (or pair of scissors) • eraser

Materials: card stock • tracing paper • tissue paper • glue stick

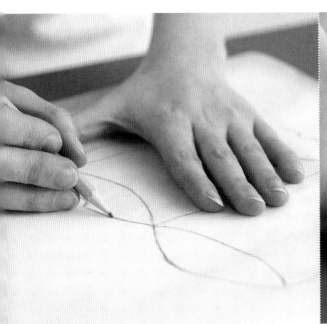

1
Use a photocopier to resize the template on p.204, if necessary. Transfer it onto a sheet of card stock using tracing paper and a pencil.

2
Flip the card stock over. Glue a sheet of tissue paper or decorative paper to the card stock, making sure that it is stuck down completely. You can also use patterned card stock.

203

3

Using a craft knife and a cutting mat, cut around the outside lines of the box. Make sure not to cut into the folding lines.

4

Using a ruler and one side of a pair of scissors, or a blunt knife, score along all the internal folding lines. You can erase the pencil lines at this point.

5

Fold the side flap up and spread glue on the patterned side. Fold the case in half and attach the flap to the inside of the opposite edge. Hold it in place until it sticks.

6

Choose one end to be the bottom of the case. Fold in the first flap along the curved line, and then the other. Fill the box and fold in the flaps at the other end to close.

Jewelry case template

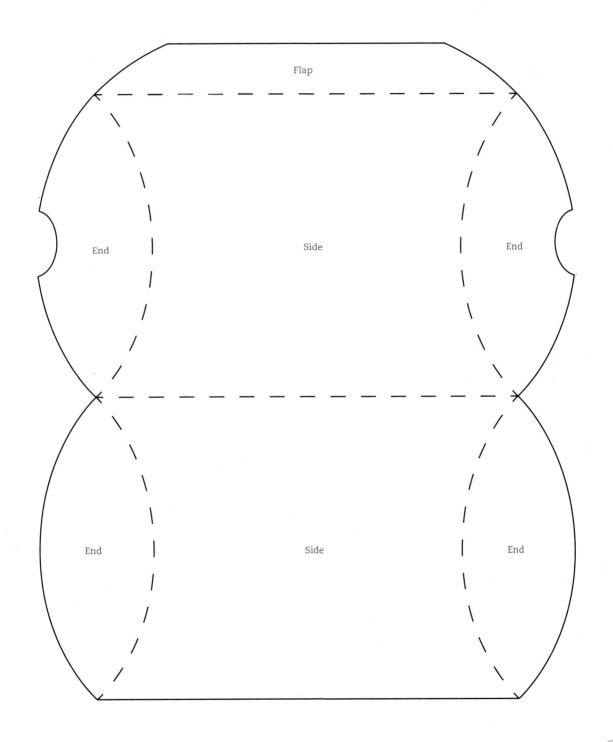

Flap

End

Side

End

End

Side

End

Pyramid
boxes

These small boxes are quick and easy to make, requiring no gluing at all.
They are the ideal size for a small gift, or to hold candy or party favors.
Personalize your boxes by using different colors and types of ribbon.

To make a pyramid box you will need

Tools: pencil • craft knife • cutting mat • blunt knife (or pair of scissors) • eraser • hole punch

Materials: patterned card stock (or patterned paper glued onto card stock) • tracing paper • ribbon

1

Use a photocopier to resize the template on p.209, if required. Using tracing paper and a pencil, transfer it onto a sheet of patterned card stock (or glue decorative paper to the card stock).

2

Using a craft knife and a cutting mat, cut around the outside of the box template. Make sure not to cut into the internal folding lines.

3

Lightly score along the fold lines using a ruler and a blunt knife (or one side of a pair of scissors).

4

Add a hole to the tip of each triangle using a hole punch. Try to keep them evenly spaced and make sure they are not too close to the edges in any direction.

5

For a neat finish, erase the fold lines. Fold each section and flap along the scored lines, making sure that each crease is sharp.

6

Assemble the pyramid box by folding in each side and tucking each flap into the center of the box. Fasten the box by threading a ribbon through the holes and tying a knot or bow.

Pyramid box template

Please enlarge to the required
size on a photocopier

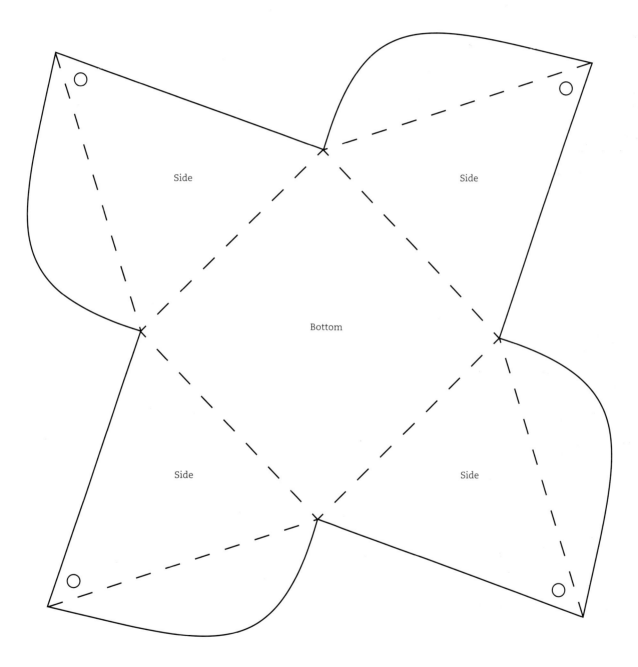

Side

Side

Bottom

Side

Side

Homemade
gift bags

Follow these simple instructions to turn any sheet of wrapping paper or gift wrap into a custom-made gift bag. For an even more personalized bag, use a sheet of paper printed with a message, or even a printout of a photograph.

To make a gift bag you will need

Tools: pencil • scissors • blunt knife (or pair of scissors) • glue stick • hole punch

Materials: tracing paper • wrapping paper or other printed or plain paper • card stock • ribbon

1
Resize the template from pp.214–215 to the required size on a photocopier. Using tracing paper and a pencil, transfer the template onto the wrong side of your chosen paper.

2
Cut out the bag shape along the outer lines. Make sure not to cut along any of the internal folding lines.

3

Score along the horizontal top and bottom folding lines, using a ruler and a blunt knife (or one side of a pair of scissors). Fold down the bottom and top flaps, making sure the creases are sharp.

4

Score along each of the vertical folding lines, going across the top and bottom flaps. Then fold the bag in along each of these lines in turn, again making sharp creases.

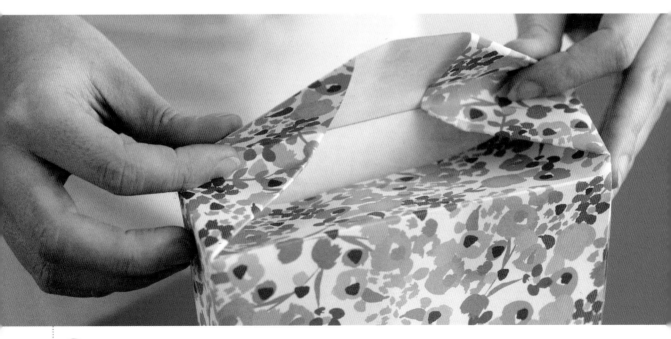

7

Fold the bottom of the bag as if you were wrapping a present. Fold one long side of the bottom tab in across the opening, creasing the sides sharply. Fold the sides in over the opening, again creasing sharply. Finally, fold in the remaining side to cover the opening, and glue or tape down the bottom.

5

Using a glue stick, spread glue evenly along the top flap. Smooth it down, holding it in place until it sticks. This will help the bag hold its shape.

6

Fold out the bottom flap. Spread glue along the outside of the side tab and attach it to the inside of the opposite end, all the way along its length. Glue the other side tab over the seam.

8

Cut out a piece of card stock the size of the base of the bag, and place it in the bottom of the bag. This will strengthen the bottom.

9

Using a two-hole punch (or a single-hole punch), punch two holes on each long side of the bag through the center of the reinforced top fold. Add ribbon for handles.

Gift bag template

Top

Bottom

JOIN

JOIN

Side
tab

215

Twist-top gift box

This ingenious gift box comes complete with its own closing mechanism—specially shaped flaps twist and lock together to hide your surprise inside. Wrap up homemade candy or jewelry in style for the perfect presentation.

To make a twist-top gift box you will need

Tools: pencil • craft knife • cutting mat • ruler • blunt knife (or pair of scissors)

Materials: card stock • tracing paper • decorative paper or wrapping paper • glue stick

1
Use a photocopier to resize the twist-top box template on pp.220–221, if required. Use tracing paper and a pencil to transfer the pattern onto a sheet of card stock.

2
Glue wrapping paper or decorative paper to the reverse of the card stock. Alternatively, use patterned card stock to make the box.

3

Using a craft knife and cutting mat, carefully cut around the pattern. First, cut along the outermost lines of the template.

4

Next, using the template on pp.220–221 as a guide, cut into the shape along the lines marked as cutting lines. Finally, remove the small shapes in the top as marked.

6

Fold all the scored lines as marked, making sure that all the creases are sharp. Assemble the body of the box by gluing both side flaps to the opposite side of the box.

5

Using a ruler and a blunt knife (or one side of a pair of scissors) score all the dashed lines from the wrong side of the card stock. Score the lines marked with dashes and dots from the right side of the card stock.

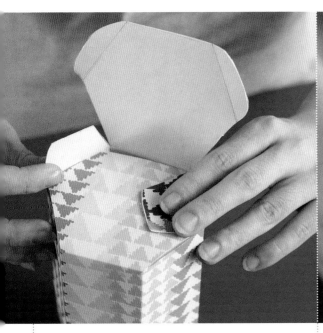

7

Assemble the base of the box by first folding in the piece marked Base 1. Next, fold down the two base flaps, and, finally, Base 2, tucking the attached flaps into the box.

8

Make sure that each of the creases made to the top part of the box is creased in the correct direction. Fill the box and push the flaps down and toward the center to seal it.

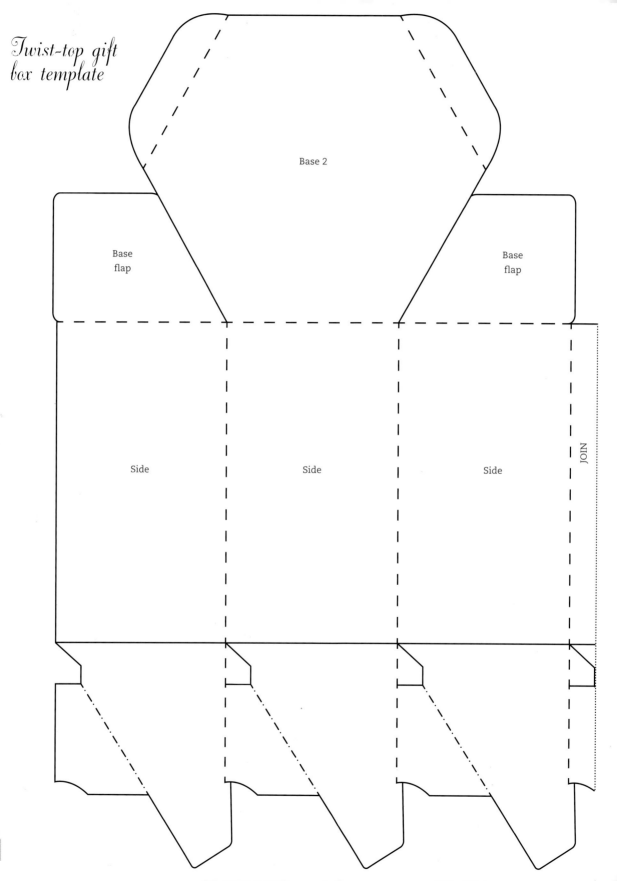

Twist-top gift box template

Base 2

Base flap

Base flap

Side

Side

Side

JOIN

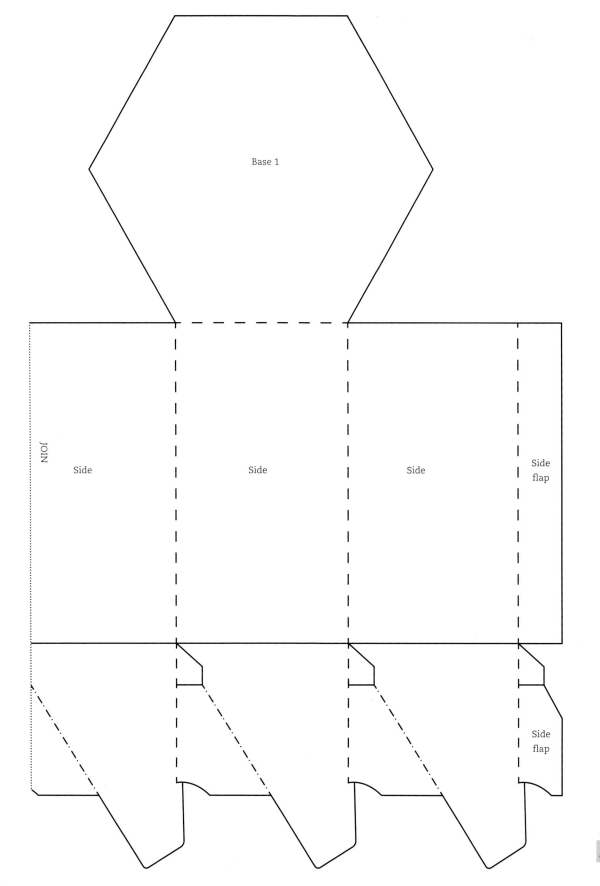

Base 1

JOIN

Side

Side

Side

Side
flap

Side
flap

Printed
gift wrap

Making your own gift wrap finishes off any gift with a personal touch. This stamped pattern of blocks of stripes is easy to create. Once you have mastered this technique, you can create your own unique shapes and patterns.

To make printed gift wrap you will need

Tools: scissors • glue

Materials: wood or balsa wood block • foam board • ink pad • sheets of white paper

1

To make a line stamp, start with a wooden block. Cut out strips of the desired width from foam board. Glue the strips to one side of a block and allow the glue to dry.

2

To make line-printed gift wrap, press the stamp on an ink pad and stamp in one corner of a sheet of paper. Continue stamping the paper, alternating the orientation of the stamp until the paper is filled.

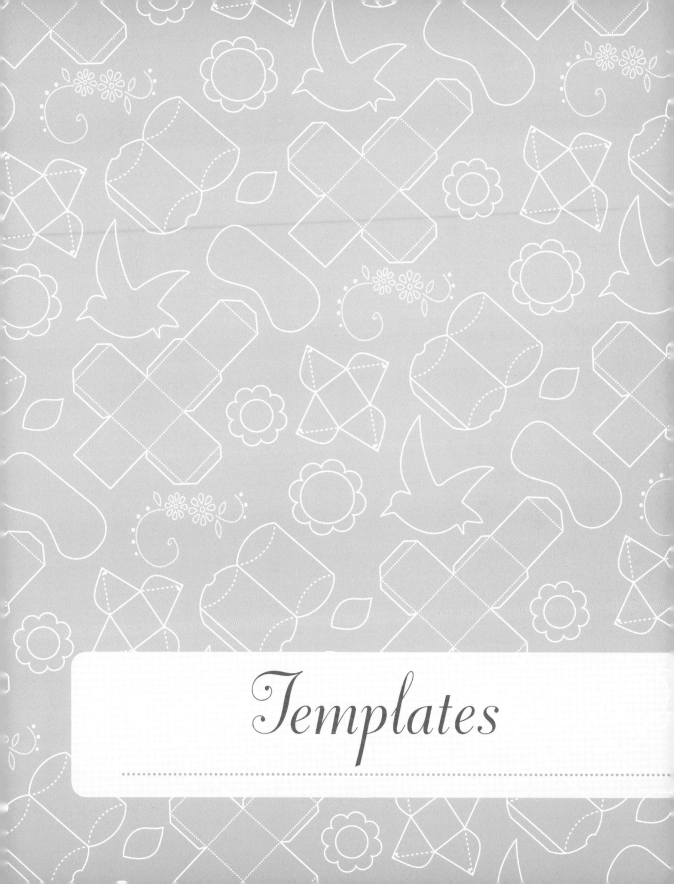

Templates

Blossom pillow (pp.14-17)

Please enlarge to the required
size on a photocopier

Bird
Cut 1

Large flower centers
Cut 4

Small flower centers
Cut 8

Branch
Cut 1

Large flowers
Cut 4

Small flowers
Cut 8

Leaf
Cut 6

Skull-and-crossbones pillow (p. 19)

Please enlarge to the required
size on a photocopier

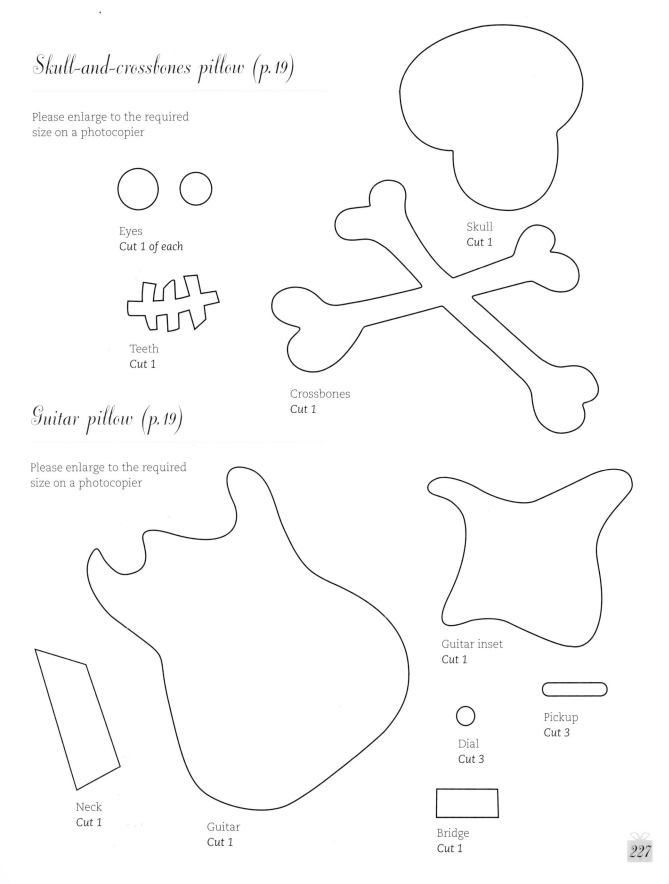

Eyes
Cut 1 of each

Teeth
Cut 1

Skull
Cut 1

Crossbones
Cut 1

Guitar pillow (p. 19)

Please enlarge to the required
size on a photocopier

Guitar inset
Cut 1

Dial
Cut 3

Pickup
Cut 3

Neck
Cut 1

Guitar
Cut 1

Bridge
Cut 1

Castle pillow (p.18)

Please enlarge to the required
size on a photocopier

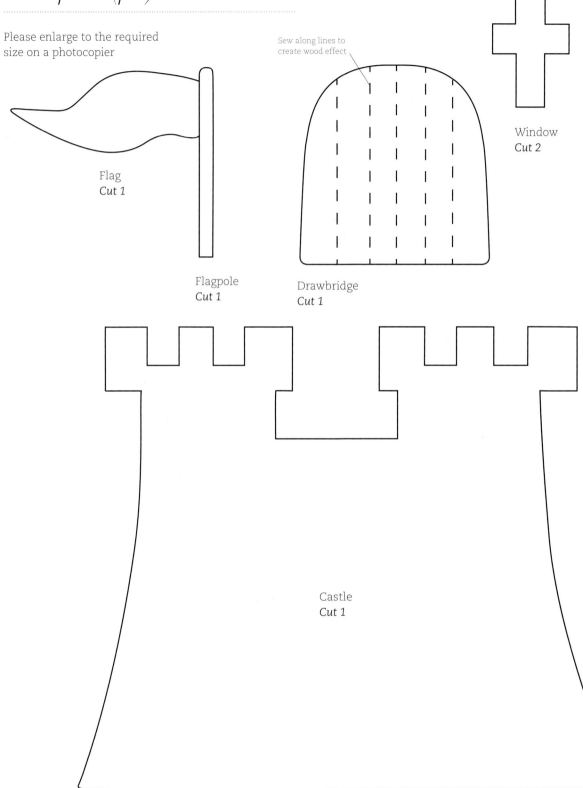

Flag
Cut 1

Flagpole
Cut 1

Sew along lines to
create wood effect

Drawbridge
Cut 1

Window
Cut 2

Castle
Cut 1

Castle pillow dolls (p. 18)

Please enlarge to the required
size on a photocopier

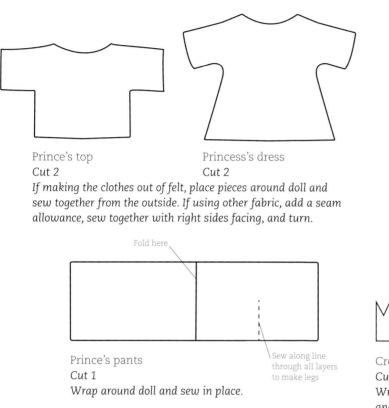

Prince's top
Cut 2
*If making the clothes out of felt, place pieces around doll and
sew together from the outside. If using other fabric, add a seam
allowance, sew together with right sides facing, and turn.*

Princess's dress
Cut 2

Body
Cut 2 for each doll.
*Sew together along
the edges, leaving a
gap. Turn, stuff, and
sew the gap closed.*

Fold here

Prince's pants
Cut 1
Wrap around doll and sew in place.

Sew along line
through all layers
to make legs

Crown
Cut 1 for each doll.
*Wrap around head
and sew in place.*

Rollaway game board (pp. 46-51)

Type of fabric	Cut	Measurements in in and cm
Board: dark fabric	x 5	2 x 16in (5 x 40cm)
Board: light fabric	x 5	2 x 16in (5 x 40cm)
Outer fabric	x 1	12 x 20in (30 x 50cm)
Inner fabric	x 2	12 x 5¾in (30 x 14cm)
Inner fabric	x 2	2 x 10¾in (5 x 27cm)
Interfacing	x 1	12 x 20in (30 x 50cm)
Interfacing	x 1	12 x 5¾in (30 x 14cm)

Appliqué pet portrait (pp. 159–161)

Please enlarge to the required
size on a photocopier

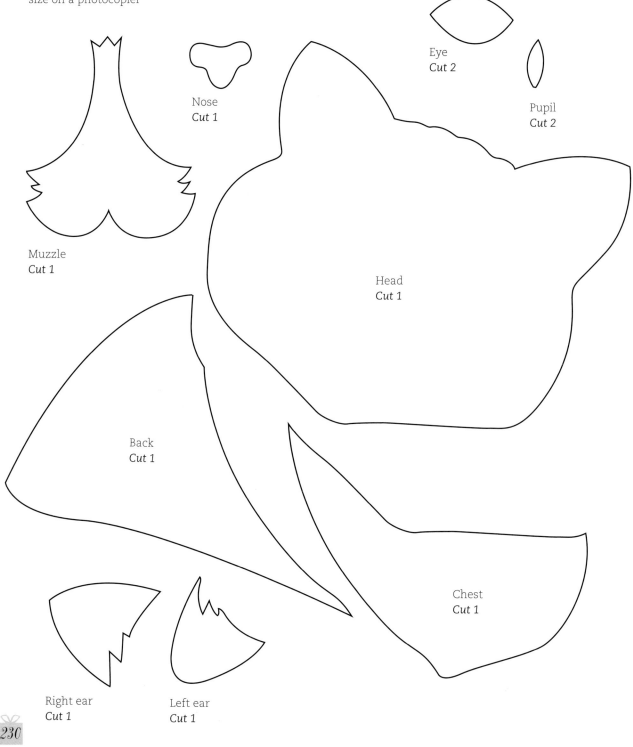

Nose
Cut 1

Eye
Cut 2

Pupil
Cut 2

Muzzle
Cut 1

Head
Cut 1

Back
Cut 1

Chest
Cut 1

Right ear
Cut 1

Left ear
Cut 1

Simple silhouette pet portrait (p.158)

Please enlarge to the required
size on a photocopier

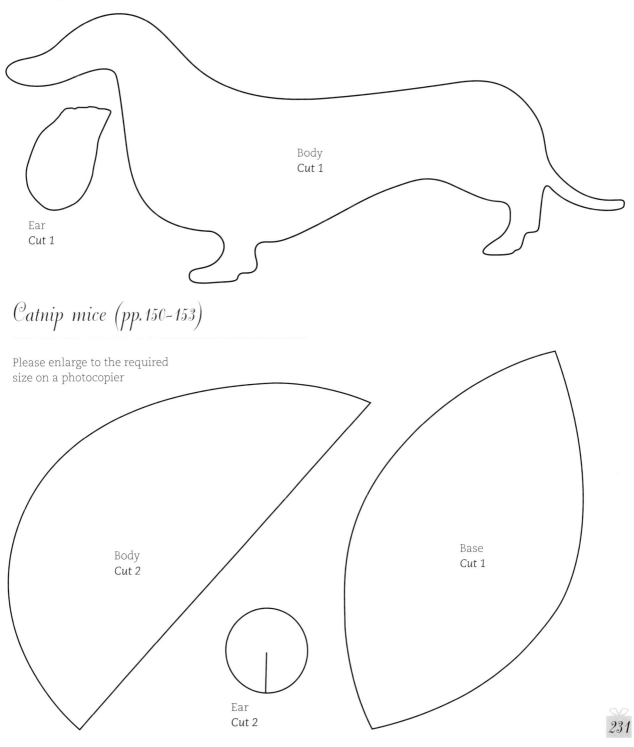

Body
Cut 1

Ear
Cut 1

Catnip mice (pp.150–153)

Please enlarge to the required
size on a photocopier

Body
Cut 2

Base
Cut 1

Ear
Cut 2

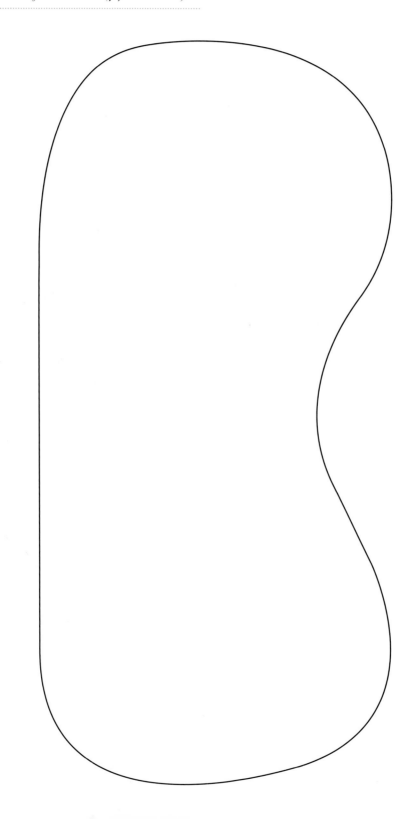

Cat's play mat (pp. 146–149)

Please enlarge to the required
size on a photocopier

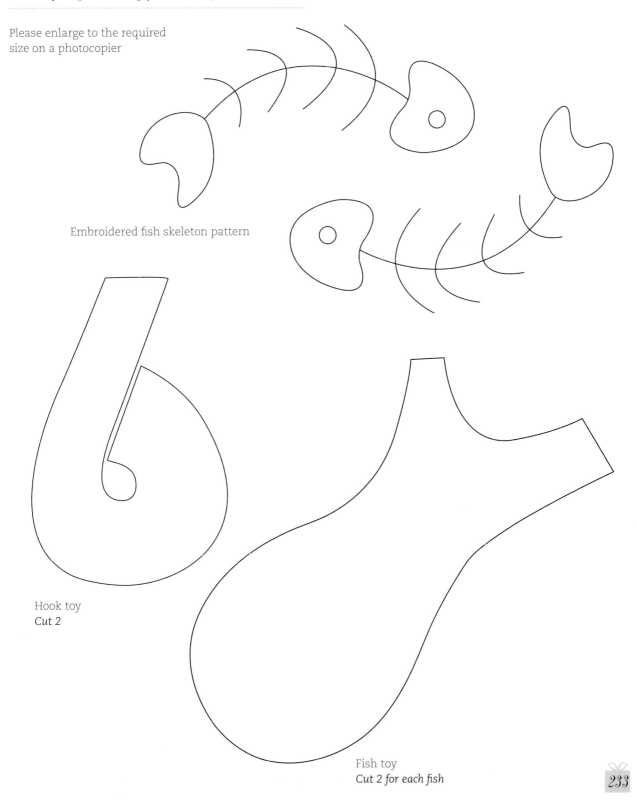

Embroidered fish skeleton pattern

Hook toy
Cut 2

Fish toy
Cut 2 for each fish

Tartan dog jacket (pp.162–165)

Please enlarge to the required
size on a photocopier

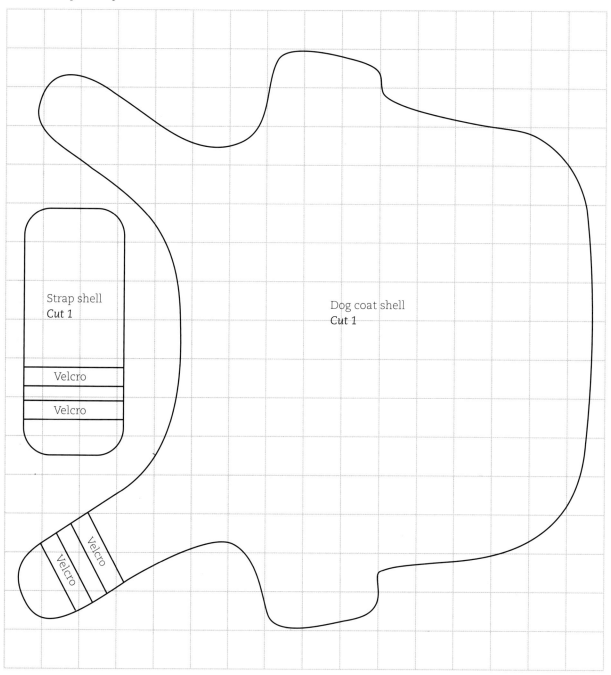

Strap shell
Cut 1

Dog coat shell
Cut 1

Velcro

Velcro

Velcro

Velcro

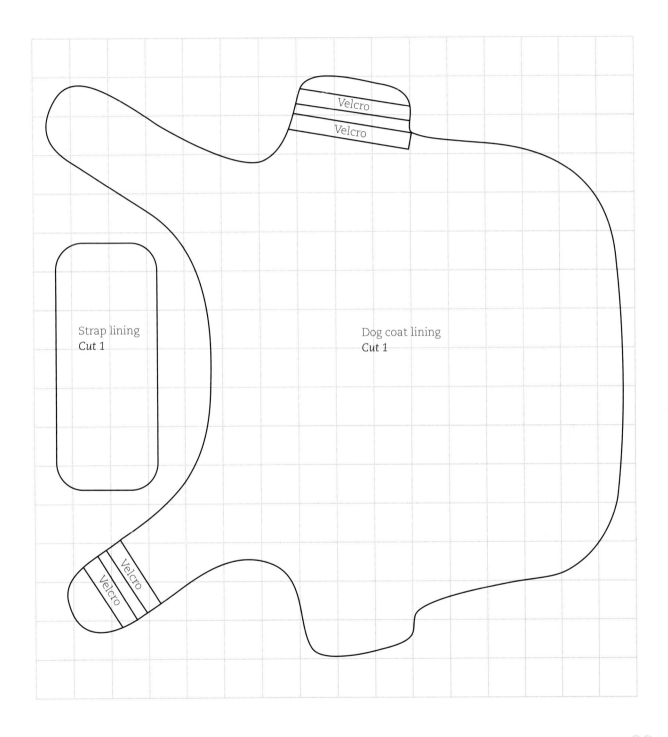

Velcro

Velcro

Strap lining
Cut 1

Dog coat lining
Cut 1

Velcro

Velcro

Ribbon-bound photo album (pp.38-43)

Please enlarge to the required
size on a photocopier

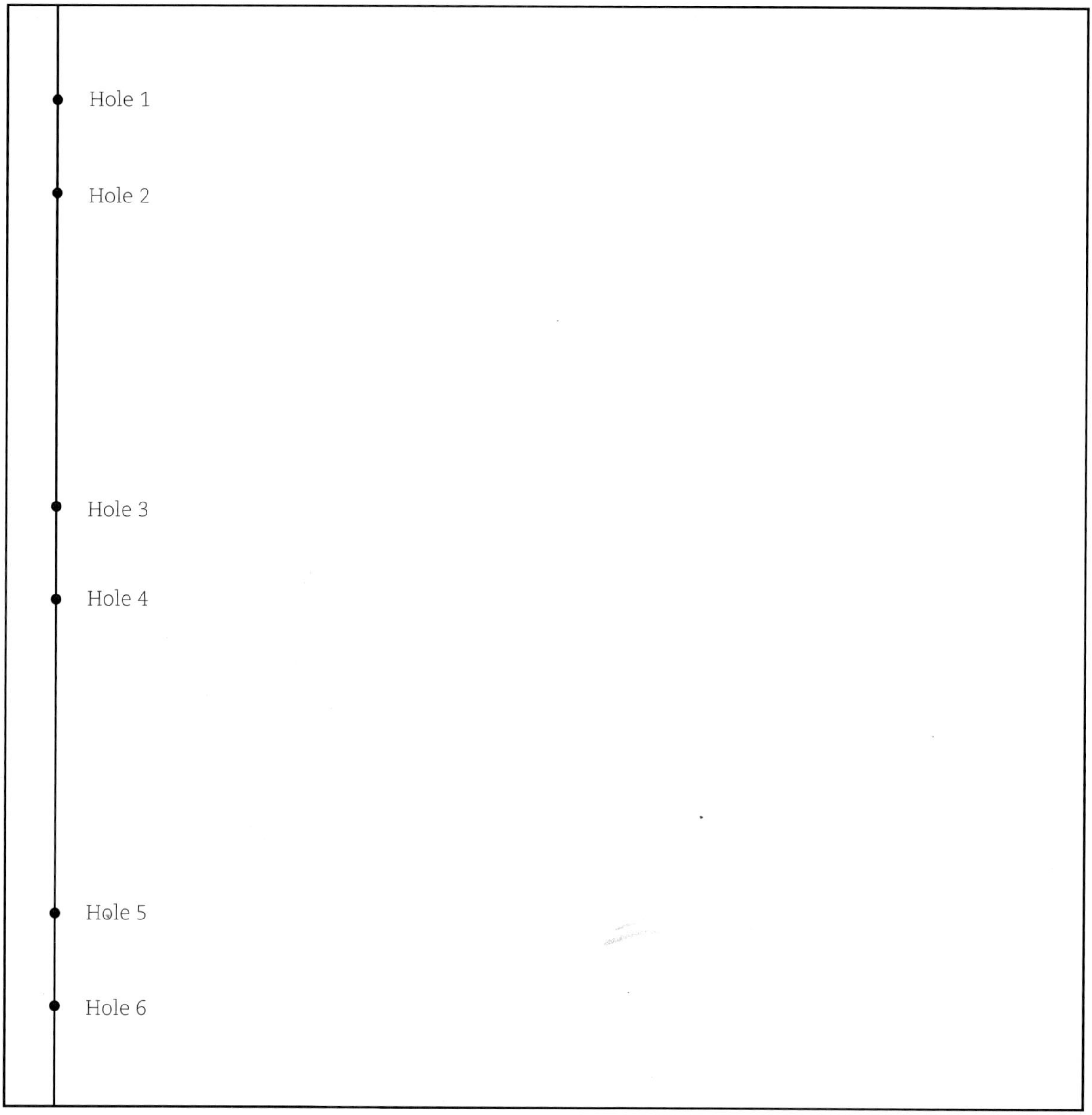

Hole 1

Hole 2

Hole 3

Hole 4

Hole 5

Hole 6

Silver clay jewelry (pp.64-69)

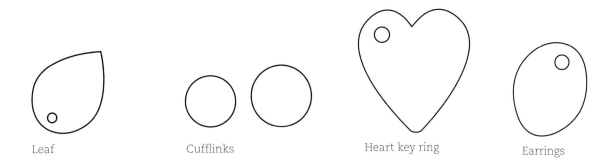

Leaf

Cufflinks

Heart key ring

Earrings

Embellished felt brooches (pp.60-63)

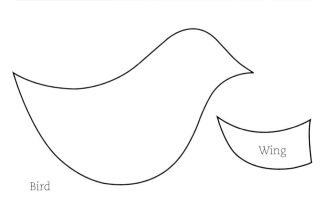

Bird

Wing

Heart

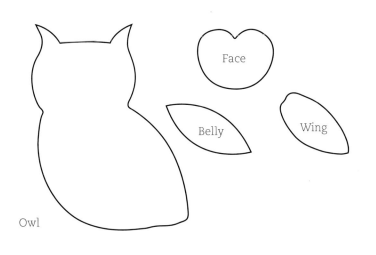

Owl

Face

Belly

Wing

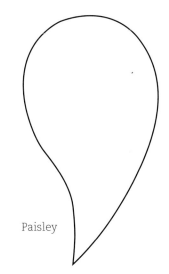

Paisley

Mosaic seaside coasters (p.37)

Mosaic owl jewelry box (p.36)

Top of box

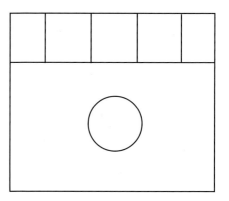

Side of box

Mosaic flower garland mirror (p.36)

Mosaic round tea light holder (p.37)

Dot-decorated vase (pp.26–29)

Please enlarge to the required
size on a photocopier

Dot-decorated mug and coaster set (p.30)

Dot-decorated bunting plate (p.31)

Please enlarge to the required
size on a photocopier

Stenciled bags (pp.84-89)

Please enlarge to the required
size on a photocopier

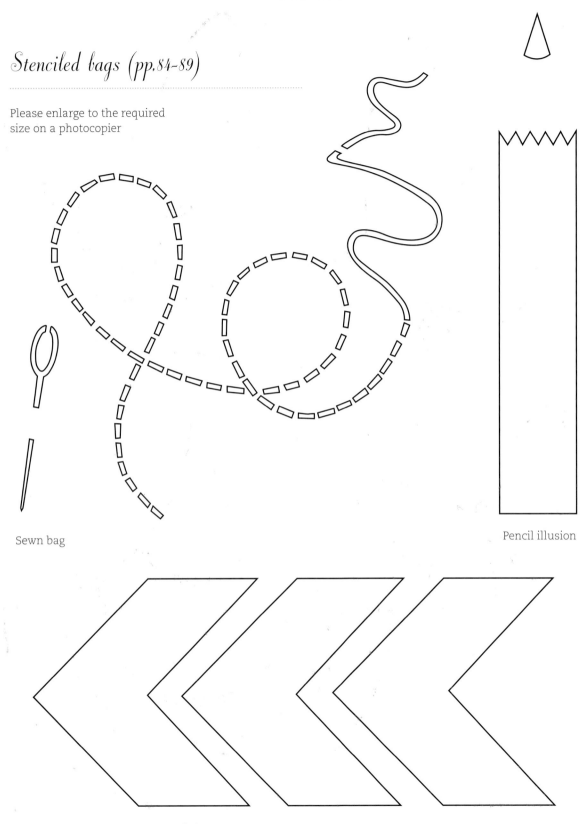

Sewn bag

Pencil illusion

Repeated chevrons

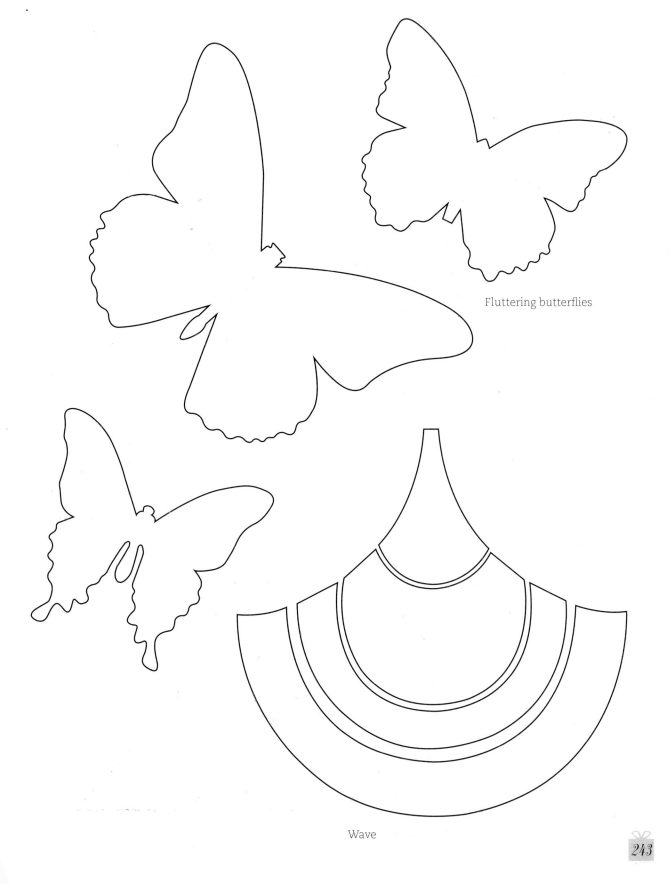

Fluttering butterflies

Wave

243

Crochet basics

Use this quick-reference guide to (re)familiarize yourself with four basic crochet stitches. These are adapted slightly to make the crochet projects in this book.

Chain stitch (ch)

1 Make a slip knot. Hold the slip knot firmly between finger and thumb.

2 Wrap the yarn over the hook (called "yarn over," or "yo") and catch it with the hook.

3 Pull the hook and yarn back through the stitch.

4 The chain stitch is complete. Repeat steps 2–4 to continue the chain. Count the "V" shapes to count the chains.

Single crochet (sc)

1 To make a row of single crochet, first work 1 ch. Push the hook into the center of the second stitch from the hook.

2 Wrap the yarn over the hook (yo).

3 Hook the yarn and pull through the first loop.

4 Bring the hook out. There are now two loops on the hook.

5 Wrap the yarn over the hook (yo). Hook the yarn and pull through both loops.

6 Now one loop is left on the hook. The single crochet stitch is complete. Repeat steps 1–5 to make the next stitch and continue until the end of the row.

Half double crochet (hdc)

1   To make a row of half double crochet, first work 2 ch. Wrap the yarn over the hook (yo).

2   Push the hook through the center "V" of the next stitch.

3   Wrap the yarn over the hook again.

4   Pull the yarn through the first loop. There are now three loops on the hook.

5   Wrap the yarn over the hook. Hook the yarn and pull it through all three loops.

6   Now one loop is left on the hook. This completes the half double stitch. Repeat steps 1–5 to make more half doubles.

Slip stitch (ss)

With one loop on the hook, hook into the next stitch, catch the yarn and pull the loop through the stitch and loop in one movement.

Pull the yarn through

One stitch left on the hook

Index

Acknowledgments

DK Publishing would like to thank US Culinary Consultant Kate Ramos; Kate Blinman for testing the recipes and for her assistance on the photo shoot; Ruth Jenkinson for additional photography; Becky Alexander, Christine Stroyan, and Katharine Goddard for editorial assistance; Angela Baynham for sense-checking; Katie Hardwicke for proofreading; and Marie Lorimer for indexing.

The authors

A skilled and dedicated team of crafters contributed their time and expertise to the making of this book. We hope you've been inspired by their talent and creativity.

Hannah Moore

Rollaway game board

Catnip mice

Appliqué pet portrait

Appliqué silhouette

Cat's play mat

Customized pillow

Guitar pillow

Skull-and-crossbones pillow

Castle pillow

Caroline Stamps

Sweet dreams eye mask

Oilcloth makeup bag

Kathryn Johnson

Embellished felt brooches

Isabel de Cordova

Travel candle

Layered candle

Candles in ramekins

Three-wick candle

The Oxford Soap Company

All natural luxury soaps

Molded vanilla stars

See-through orange soap

Cookie-cutter lavender hearts

Juniper cake-slice soap

Fizzy bath bombs

Ria Holland

Dot-decorated ceramics

Celebration bunting plate

Mug and coaster set

Paula Keogh

Manicure roll

Tartan dog jacket

Kate Davis

Silk scarf

Nicola Barter

Wave-patterned bag

Sewn bag

Pencil illusion bag

Repeated chevrons bag

Fluttering butterflies bag

Clara Smith

Silver leaf pendant

Simple button cufflinks

Leaf bracelet

Wallpaper earrings

Lace heart key ring

Gemma Fletcher

Dog biscuits

Knotted scarf

Color-block scarf

Close-weave scarf

Beaded necklace

Button-bead necklace

Glass-bead necklace

Painted beads

Victoria Read

Personlized journal

Ribbon-bound photo album

Portrait photo album

Glenda Fisher

Crochet flower pins

Belinda Nicholson

Découpage bangle

Claire Montgomerie

Crochet necklace

Lova Rajaonarimanana

Phone and tablet protectors

Karen Mitchell

Mosaic bowl

Flower garland mirror

Seaside coasters

Round tea light holder

Owl jewelry box

Charlotte Johnson

Pyramid boxes

Jewelry case

Homemade gift bags

Square gift box

Twist-top gift box

Carol Doherty

Clasp-frame bag

Clasp-frame purse

Clasp-frame makeup bag

Helen Fickling

Teacup candle

251

Place of Learning, Place of Dreams

Place of Learning, Place of Dreams

A HISTORY OF THE SEATTLE PUBLIC LIBRARY

JOHN DOUGLAS MARSHALL

A McLellan Book

University of Washington Press
SEATTLE AND LONDON

in association with the

Seattle Public Library Foundation

For Pam Gunther, in gratitude: Seattle, Netherlands,
Wickaninnish, Berlin, and Beyond

This book is published with the assistance of a grant from the
McLellan Endowed Series Fund, established through the generosity
of Mary McCleary McLellan and Mary McLellan Williams.

University of Washington Press
PO Box 50096, Seattle, WA 98145
www.washington.edu/uwpress

Library of Congress Cataloging-in-Publication Data
Marshall, John Douglas.
    Place of learning, place of dreams: a history of the Seattle
Public Library / John Douglas Marshall.
        p. cm.
    "A McLellan book."
    Includes bibliographical references and index.
    ISBN 0-295-98347-7 (alk. paper)
    1. Seattle Public Library—History. 2. Public libraries—
Washington (State)—Seattle—History. I. Title.
Z733.S442M37 2004
027.4'797'772—dc22   2003065750

The paper used in this publication meets the minimum re-
quirements of American National Standard for Information
Sciences—Permanence of Paper for Printed Library Materials,
ANSI Z39.48-1984.

Designed by Susan E. Kelly
Photographic research by Jodee Fenton
Color separations by iocolor, Seattle
Produced by Marquand Books, Inc., Seattle, www.marquand.com,
for the University of Washington Press

Printed and bound by CS Graphics Pte., Ltd., Singapore

Contents

Acknowledgments

WRITING A HISTORY of a public institution could be a nightmare assignment. Too many such organizations would demand history as fantasy, with only positive developments recounted, a white-wash reminiscent of Tom Sawyer's fence. The Seattle Public Library, to my relief, was a dream subject, a public institution that wanted its history told honestly, its struggles as well as its triumphs, its controversies too.

This history of The Seattle Public Library certainly could not have been written without the assistance of administrators and librarians at that remarkable institution. Two librarians did Herculean labors on behalf of this book, Susie Rennels and Jodee Fenton. Both read each chapter as soon as it was finished, checked its facts and observations, supported or debated its conclusions, and searched out reams of additional materials, no matter how obscure or elusive. These two people provided a crucial lifeline to me. Jodee was my prime library contact, and a better one is impossible for me to imagine. She was always upbeat about this project, engaged in every aspect of its planning and execution, utterly convinced that Seattle Public Library's story had to be told in a manner that was fair, honest, and, as warranted, critical. We started the project as strangers and finished as friends. Perhaps the best compliment I can pay to Jodee is that I find it difficult to imagine writing a future book without her alongside. She was indispensable. Also important were the dedicated people at the University of Washington Press, especially director Pat Soden, who always provided encouragement and wise counsel.

Editors and colleagues at the *Seattle Post-Intelligencer* were supportive of this project at the outset and that continued during the year of book writing when I also worked as book critic at the newspaper. I much appreciated the support of publisher Roger Oglesby, managing editor David McCumber, deputy managing editor Chris Beringer, and arts editor Duston Harvey, as well as fellow writers William Arnold, M. L. Lyke, Kathy Mulady, Phuong Cat Le, Regina Hackett, and Carol Smith. *Post-Intelligencer* librarians Lytton Smith and Mary Beth Edenholm were unfailingly helpful in unlocking the secrets of the newspaper's microfiche archive, which proved so important in creating this narrative. The *Post-Intelligencer* was *the* Seattle newspaper for many, many decades, which is why I was so pleased that the book's title ("place of learning, place of dreams") jumped off the page of a *Post-Intelligencer* editorial in 1901 and commanded that I borrow it in 2003. All thanks to an unknown *P-I* editorialist for helping solve a book writer's greatest quandary.

Friends also played an important role during the writing of this book. The willingness to listen to a tired writer's rantings is no small gift, whenever it is offered. I salute the assistance of Timothy Egan, Gary Luke, Kris Molesworth, Karen Willie, Skye Moody, Tina Kelley, Molly Billingsley, Katherine Wolfe, John Harper, Linda Hosek, Sam Howe Verhovek, Donna Stonecipher, and my brother and sister—S. L. A. Marshall III and Shannon Ruth Marshall. Richard Ford may have attained Pulitzer Prize heights in his literary career, but he voiced enthusiasm for this book during a Seattle visit when it was little more than an idea; that meant a great deal to me then and in the months afterward. David Halberstam's support was also heartening.

Trying to write a book in my "spare time" meant that those closest to me often had to make their own sacrifices as well, and they did so with a grace that was humbling to me. Schedules got changed, plans altered, yet they never wavered in their support. My daughter, Samantha, was the most insistent poser of that unavoidable question, "What page are you on now, Daddy?" My son, Thatcher, was always interested in this project, no matter what challenges and allures were offered by the start of high school. Both Samantha and Thatcher were vigilant observers during our frequent car trips past the Central Library site, checking to make sure that construction of the Rem Koolhaas building was not making greater progress than construction of the book manuscript. Thank goodness I finished first, or there would have been kid heck to pay.

My greatest debt of all is to Pam Gunther, who had never been involved with a book project before but proved to be an exemplary partner. Pam played many crucial roles during the writing of this book, including supporter, critic, editor, best friend, and enticing diversion (my favorite role). We embarked on this book journey only a few months after we first met, venturing into uncharted new territory for an uncertain new relationship. We persevered through its many challenges, and we were still together long after the book's last sentence was written.

Place of Learning, Place of Dreams

The Dawning of Koolhaas

THERE HAVE BEEN FIRE, flood, earthquake, and controversy over a graphic sex education book. There have been grand opening celebrations, severe budget cuts, epidemic quarantine, two Red scares two decades apart, books returned years overdue, battling board members, outreach programs galore, low staff salaries, answers to millions of research questions, and the first escalator ever to transport

ABOVE: Only a month before his Benaroya Hall presentation, Rem Koolhaas received the Pritzker Prize, architecture's highest honor, which added new luster to Seattle Public Library's daring selection of the Rotterdam-based architect.

OPPOSITE: Architect Rem Koolhaas of the Office for Metropolitan Architecture (OMA) is dwarfed by large screens with slide and video images during his May 2000 presentation before a large crowd at Benaroya Hall in Seattle. On the left screen is a *Time* magazine article that quotes a comment from a *Seattle Times* columnist castigating Koolhaas's design for Seattle Public Library's new Central Library.

patrons in an American library. There have been open shelves, 100th anniversary cake, union-organizing drives, victory reading contests, the swan song of the card catalog, library outposts in firehouses and pharmacies, and two head librarians resigning under fire. There have been award-winning restorations of historic buildings, a Seattle reading program copied around the globe, disruptive teens, Great Books, censorship fights, thousands of loyal members of the Friends group, and gifts from philanthropists Andrew Carnegie, Paul Allen, Bill and Melinda Gates, and a Seattle commercial fisherman named Henry Fransen who left a bequest of $10,012.85 with the hope that "in my small way, I may be able to repay the kindness shown to me by the employees of the Seattle Public Library."[1]

There have been all sorts of remarkable occurrences at the Seattle Public Library in its more than 100 years of history, but perhaps none is more remarkable than this moment. Here on a pleasant May afternoon in the year 2000, there is a crowd of 1,500 people gathered in the elegant confines of Seattle Symphony Orchestra's Benaroya Hall to listen to an architect discuss revised schematic plans for a new Central Library building. Here, in a Northwest city where architecture has seldom spawned more than passing yawns, there is scarcely a seat unoccupied on the main floor of this stunning new concert hall. An excited murmur ripples through the gathered throng until the first signs of the program's delayed start and then the murmur is replaced with an expectant hush.

Seattle librarian Deborah L. Jacobs emerges from backstage and takes her place at the podium, a harsh spotlight falling upon her head and shoulders. Three years earlier, she had arrived in Seattle from leading the library in Corvallis, Oregon, her move north a giant increase in responsibility after nearly two decades in the Willamette Valley college town. Jacobs, an ebullient campaigner for libraries, had spent countless hours devoted to winning passage of a huge library-building bond issue in Seattle that had been narrowly defeated once before at the polls. The revised bond issue carried the optimistic title "Libraries for All," what might have seemed public relations hype, except for the fact that it totaled $196.4 million and was the largest library bond ever submitted for voter approval in the United States. Its ambition was staggering—to double the space in the city's twenty-two branch libraries, including the building of five new branches, and also to construct a $159 million Central Library to replace a shopworn 1960 building that now had about as much appeal as an immigration processing center.

Campaign materials supported Seattle Public Library's "Libraries for All" bond issue, the largest such measure ever approved by American voters.

Jacobs had turned passage of the bond issue into a personal crusade. Other aspects of library service would always remain a priority: the librarian would still focus her disapproving gaze on what she considered inexcusable failings of "infrastructure"—every soiled computer keyboard, every stuck library door, every tattered volume on the shelves. The bond was not the library's imperfect present, but rather its bright shining hope for the future. So Jacobs crisscrossed the city with her boundless supply of energy and optimism and questions. Four nights a week, three months straight, the librarian attended neighborhood meetings, all spent listening to citizens, collecting ideas, and building support. She had used the same tireless approach in spurring approval for a landmark $7 million library levy in Corvallis, just one of several major accomplishments that had convinced *Library Journal* magazine to select Jacobs as its National Librarian of the Year in 1994.

Jacobs had still been unsure that the massive bond in Seattle would pass. After all, it defied conventional electoral wisdom and boldly sought $31 million more than the rejected 1994 library bond issue. "I was never confident," Jacobs recalled, "even though I knew we couldn't have run a better campaign."[2] Voters, though, left no doubt about their verdict: they approved the historic library bond issue by a historic margin, almost 3 to 1. Congratulatory bouquets filled her office after the resounding triumph at the polls, but Jacobs scarcely paused to sniff the flowers before plunging into implementation of the bond issue, including the complex public process of conducting an international search to select a notable architect for the new Central Library.

It was only fifteen hours ago that the forty-six-year-old librarian had finally allowed herself to pause and reflect on what had been accomplished. There had been a reception at the elegant Four Seasons Olympic Hotel where major library donors had gathered with the eventual winner of the architectural competition to design the new library. The plane bringing the architect was late at the airport, but that annoying delay could not diminish Jacobs's celebratory mood. "What I remember from that evening," she said later, "is really being able to step back and look at the project. I thought to myself, this is it—it's working. This is everything I had hoped for and dreamed."[3]

Jacobs's euphoria has hardly dissipated as she stands at the podium in Benaroya Hall. The architect himself had preferred a more intimate setting for his presentation, but he had gone along with the move to the main symphony hall when there was no better alternative to accommodate the expected crowd. The interest in him and the library project had continued to crescendo, with each successive event requiring the surprising move to a larger hall. Reserved-seat tickets could have been sold to these public meetings. This has become the irresistible chance to witness history and celebrity in Seattle.

Today's appearance carries an added urgency. It is the last time to see the architect and the revised building plans and scale models at such a large public forum before the library is built. The process had been much more preliminary back in December 1999 when he appeared in Benaroya's smaller Nordstrom recital hall for the unveiling of his first design for the library. Eleven public groups have since evaluated the plans, along with thirty-seven subgroups of library staff members, the sort of intense involvement that is characteristic of public process in Seattle—for better at times, but more often for worse. The library plans have been detailed, discussed, picked apart, put back together, critiqued, reviewed, revised, and then revised some more, with the goal of improving the project.

"As some of you know," Jacobs says in her introduction, "library board and staff presented the design team with a very detailed and complex building program that identified every single foot of the 355,000 square feet of our Central Library, as well as all the necessary and important adjacencies. We detailed in that the number of books, number of computers, number of staff, et cetera. And the building that you're being presented with today responds to 100 percent of that program that we gave the architects.... While the library might look the same superficially, there are many changes. And these changes are in direct response to your comments and your thoughts and the thoughts and comments from the library board and staff, the design commission, and just about anybody else in town who has access to e-mail, voice mail, the U.S. mail or sees me in the grocery store."[4]

Laughter ripples through the crowd at this mental image of the city librarian in the supermarket, perhaps trying to pick out a perfectly ripe mango and instead being interrupted by would-be architecture critics who want to pepper her with questions about this library design detail or that. The sudden laughter connects audience with speaker and further elevates the mood of Jacobs, who is feeling, at this moment, "absolutely on top of everything."[5]

That euphoria bubbles over into her final words from the podium: "I'm personally excited about this building. And as I study it more and more, I'm incredibly amazed at both the complexity and simplicity of it. And, as the librarian I am, I'm looking forward to providing incredible library service to all of you in this building. So, with that, I'm pleased to present, wherever he is, Rem Koolhaas."[6]

There is instant applause, loud, insistent. A year ago, there would have been scratched heads and maybe polite clapping at the mention of this name. Only the architects in a Seattle crowd would probably have known Rem Koolhaas, and maybe only the hippest of architects. But so much has changed since he won the library commission in May 1999. Then, he was the long shot, the outsider, the rising star with buzz among the cognoscenti but no major buildings yet built in the United States. If the hiring of Jacobs was a leap for the library's five trustees, a risk-taking chance on someone without the expected big-library credentials, then the hiring of Koolhaas and his Rotterdam-based Office for Metropolitan Architecture (OMA) was a bungee jump into a rocky chasm.

Seattle's stunning plunge suddenly seemed much less daring just a month before today's presentation.

THE
PRITZKER
ARCHITECTURE
PRIZE
2000

PRESENTED TO
REM KOOLHAAS

SPONSORED BY
THE HYATT FOUNDATION

Koolhaas had won the Pritzker Prize, international architecture's version of the Nobel Prize, conveying a $100,000 award and a host of headlines around the globe. Suddenly, the fifty-six-year-old former journalist from the Netherlands vaulted from cult figure to canonization, saluted in the Pritzker citation "for his bold, strident, thought-provoking architecture."[7] The chairman of the Pritzker jury, J. Carter Brown, spared few superlatives in making the prize announcement: "Rem Koolhaas is widely respected as one of the most gifted and original talents in world architecture today. The leader of a spectacularly irreverent generation of Dutch architects, his restless mind, conceptual brilliance, and ability to make a building sing have earned him a stellar place in the firmament of contemporary design."[8]

Koolhaas acknowledges the Benaroya applause with a businesslike "thank you very much, first slide, please," then moves smartly into his presentation. He has a restless stage presence, this tall, thin, balding figure in the elegant gray slacks and light gray short-sleeved shirt, his bare arms suggesting that he is not only designing the building, but might also lend a hand with some of

the construction labors. Koolhaas stands behind the lectern briefly, then moves to the side, his hands in his pants pockets, then gestures broadly with one arm, a laser pointer in his hand. The lights dim further and a series of slides begin to appear on a mammoth projection screen at the center of the stage. Even though his six-foot-five-inch figure is dwarfed by the slide images, Koolhaas is still a riveting presence with his distinctive, accented English and his air of unfettered self-assurance.

Koolhaas begins his presentation at a trot, with few pauses for breath and no glances at any notes. In the opening moments, he not only cautions the audience that the "somewhat revised" new design is "not the definitive building yet," but he also offers thoughts on the architectural context of downtown Seattle ("important, but, if I may say so, also fairly boring").[9]

Suddenly, a different sort of image appears on the screen, nothing at all to do with the library building. Whispers of recognition start to skitter through the crowd. "I think it's important," Koolhaas says, "also to explain that our application here was not innocent, and that we had been for a long time looking for an opportunity in America to make a major statement with a building. And that we felt, based on research, that perhaps Seattle offered the most interesting and promising possibilities. Because Seattle is a city which is hovering around a certain size. And it is clearly at a transitional moment when it has to decide to become a real city, or a real metropolis, or not. And I think what is interesting is that this is a decision that you can take, but, as this image illustrates, it is also a decision that is taken for you."[10]

The whispers of recognition in the crowd have now given way to some genuine laughter. Because still up on the screen, like some unavoidable nightmare, is a slide of the street turmoil from the 1999 World Trade Organization (WTO) debacle in Seattle. The slide shows a dozen police officers in riot gear, nightsticks at the ready, facing off against a small group of demonstrators. These familiar images instantly recall when the city's moment in the international spotlight turned into a watershed embarrassment of violent street unrest and schizophrenic police response, hard knuckled one day, hands off the next. The WTO slide stays on the screen longer than any of those that have preceded it, five seconds, ten seconds, half a minute. This calculated move is characteristic Koolhaas, bold, provocative, even shocking. Here is an architect from Europe who is designing one of Seattle's most important civic projects ever, and he is poking ironic fun at a disaster that most residents of Seattle would rather forget. This is clearly the kind of guest who feels no compunction about poking the host in the ribs, if it will prove his point.

"You will become a city," Koolhaas intones, "with all the splendors and miseries of that, and all the complications of that. Your previous ideal is coming to an end and you have to face the kind of responsibilities that come with being really urban. And one of those responsibilities is obviously to live with architecture."[11]

Koolhaas could be addressing his students at Harvard University's Graduate School of Design, where he has taught for five years. His Seattle presentation is reflecting his long-standing urge to be a social critic, as he demonstrated in writings that first catapulted him to wide notice. As Koolhaas has admitted, "In my own mind, I am as much a writer as an architect."[12]

Delirious New York was his debut in 1978. That book was a "retroactive manifesto" for Manhattan, a copiously illustrated analysis of New York City architecture, planning, and popular culture, and written with flair, humor, and panache.[13] Koolhaas comes off in *Delirious New York* as the cheeky but affectionate and knowing outsider. In a typical passage, he describes the signature Unisphere sculpture from the 1964 World's Fair as "the Globe again, but ghostlike and transparent, with no contents. Like charred pork chops, the continents cling desperately to the carcass of Manhattanism."[14]

S,M,L,XL, a massive catalog of the built and unbuilt projects of Koolhaas and OMA, followed in 1995, the projects grouped by size. It was Rem's Greatest Hits album and a worldwide hit itself, a $75 volume selling an astounding 150,000 copies in five years (versus 40,000 in more than two decades for *Delirious New York*). *S,M,L,XL* quickly became a quirky bible of architectural hip, opening with this enigmatic Koolhaas-ism: "Architecture is a hazardous mixture of omnipotence and impotence."[15] What Koolhaas and design cohort Bruce Mau of Toronto had really devised was an ingenious shelf buster of sly self-promotion, a six-pound, 1,334-page recap of OMA's history retold in stark photographs and razzle-dazzle graphics. Plus, there were Koolhaas writings and musings and even a glossary of favored Koolhaas terms ("cannibalize," "powercut," "space-time") running along the edges of pages and all defined in wry Rem-master manner: "Red—Red is the most joyful and dreadful thing in the physical universe; it is the fiercest note, it is the highest light, it is the place where the walls of this world of ours wear the thinnest and something beyond burns through."[16]

Koolhaas has brought this book approach to the new library project in Seattle. Two volumes have been compiled, a slim one setting forth the essence of OMA's design proposal for the library, and the other a coffee-table tome that includes selections from the three months of research that went into the design. Those selections ranged from the David Letterman–inspired lists of "10 bad things about Public Libraries" and "1 good thing about Public Libraries" ("the throng of people who constantly inhabit the library" appears on both lists[17]) to early Koolhaas design doodles and influential magazine articles. Much attention is devoted to an examination of the acute space problems that plagued the 1996 New Main Library in San Francisco, which led to the controversial discarding of 200,000 volumes and the forced resignation of librarian Kenneth Dowlin, an unabashed supporter of library high tech over library books. Both Koolhaas volumes for the Seattle library were enwrapped in covers featuring bold stripes of hyper-colors that can be seen from far across

The exhaustive research compiled by OMA for the Seattle library project resulted in books bearing this distinctive cover pattern, one that librarian Deborah Jacobs joked was worthy of a dress.

a room or even a boulevard. The distinctive covers prompted librarian Jacobs to joke at one public meeting, "I'm hoping to get a dress out of that pattern."[18]

The book storage problems encountered at San Francisco and other new libraries have had a profound impact on the Seattle design, as Koolhaas is soon telling the crowd at Benaroya. Libraries keep adding more books and more programs, resulting in an inevitable space crunch; at least they always have in the past.

"The territory for books extends at the expense of the public programs," Koolhaas stresses. "And so what you see—and the current [Seattle downtown] library is a heroic example of that—is that an avalanche of books compresses and pushes the public program to almost a residual condition. So, in terms of obvious mistakes to avoid, that erosion of the public [space] and the increase of books was clearly one that we felt was important to stop. Therefore, the library that we're going to be presenting is based on a different diagram. It's based on a diagram that dedicates a given proportion to the collection and the exhibition and exposure of books to readers, but then draws a border, a line around that quantity and stabilizes it.... One of the key activities that we have followed in the past six months is a very meticulous and scrupulous calculation, from many different sites, to make sure we are doing the right thing in terms of what the most plausible prediction was and is for the quantity of books [an additional 600,000 volumes, in the OMA research, over twenty years]."[19]

This programmatic evaluation has guided the entire Seattle library design process until, as the slides at Benaroya show, the entire program has been reduced to colorful bar graphs that allocate specific portions of square footage to five specific program areas or "platforms." They are underground parking, children's area and auditorium, multimedia and reference desk, books and reading, and administrative offices. Of course, in the cool Koolhaas world, some of these program areas carry distinctive monikers. Where library visitors first encounter a grand public space is "the living room." A mammoth air-terminal counter of reference librarians awaits them in "the mixing chamber."

Koolhaas continues his tour through what he terms "the experience of the building."[20] He shows how the building's irregular shape (horizontal blocks stacked atop one another but shifted out of alignment) and its eleven-story height provide angled views toward Elliott Bay, Mount Rainier, and Interstate 5. He pledges that the children's area is "without the kind of condescending childishness that many children's libraries have, where everything becomes funny, cute, and kind of relentlessly Disneyfied."[21] He touches on plans for the 275-seat auditorium.

Then, without a change in tone, pace, or emphasis, the architect moves on to what he describes as "the key to the building as whole."[22] This is—besides the building's stark mesh exterior skin—the most-mentioned feature in early commentaries and likely to be in later ones as well. For instead of dividing up the library's book collection into various rooms, the nonfiction collection will be in a continuous spiral that will display the entire Dewey Decimal System over three and a half floors. Linking the bookshelves is a gently sloping ramp, the ramp forming a promenade that may become known as Book Lovers' Lane in Seattle.

"You start at the top and you simply walk past the books," Koolhaas explains. "It has the advantage of exposing you to all the books, if you don't know what

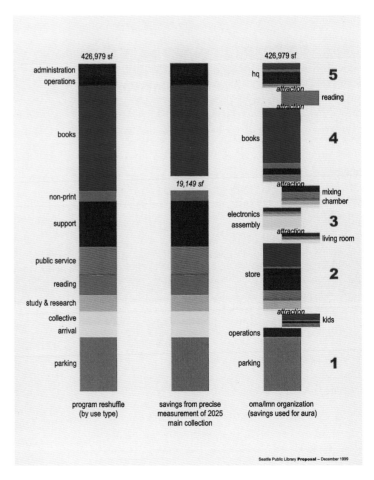

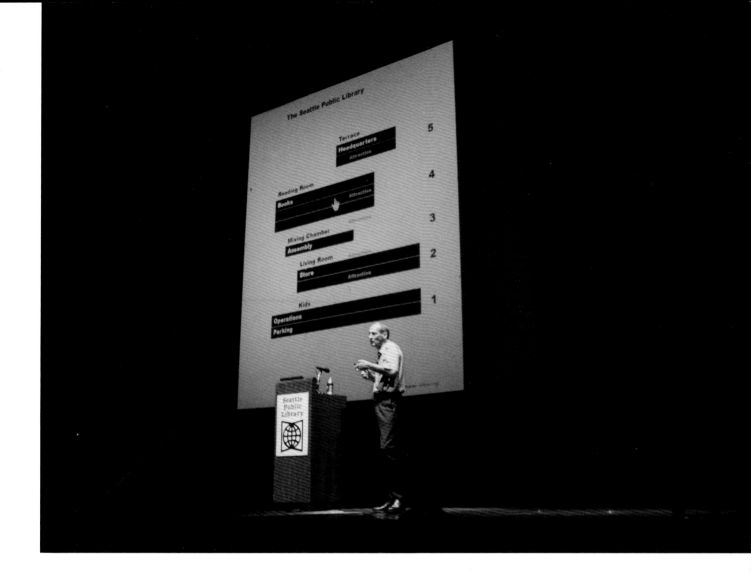

ABOVE: Koolhaas details how Seattle Public Library's programming influenced the design for the new Central Library.

LEFT: One of Koolhaas's slides shows how OMA's research into the programs of Seattle Public Library resulted in various "platforms" or portions of the new Central Library.

RIGHT: A simple diagram explains the design rationale behind the new Central Library's innovative book spiral for the nonfiction collection.

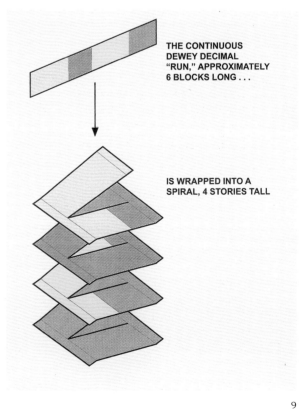

THE CONTINUOUS DEWEY DECIMAL "RUN," APPROXIMATELY 6 BLOCKS LONG . . .

IS WRAPPED INTO A SPIRAL, 4 STORIES TALL

9

you're looking for. And, of course, you can make any kind of shortcut if you do know what you're looking for. So, instead of an ordeal and instead of a problem of division, it really exploits the unique condition of the library—the concept of being comprehensive. And in that comprehensiveness, it creates almost random exposures and random moments of surprise ... in the discovery of books.... It's simply an idea that deals with the fundamental quality of a library, namely its comprehensiveness, and turns that into a virtue, rather than something that has to be undone—a configuration of the building itself."[23]

The logic of the design is persuasive. Passing through 500 feet of traditional flat floors in a library provides access to an estimated 1,400 bookcases, while traveling the same distance in the sloping spiral provides access to 2,500 bookcases. But such an innovative book ramp also seems destined for criticism, especially in these days of strict American laws about access for people with disabilities (laws that, in an earlier public presentation, Koolhaas had described as "incredibly stringent" and "draconian").[24] Criticism of the book ramp has indeed come since its unveiling, which led to the construction of a full-scale prototype section in a Seattle warehouse. It was road tested by architects, library staff members, trustees, and members of the public, some in wheelchairs of various designs, some on crutches. The book spiral mock-up passed its test drives and walk-throughs once people could see that the ramp itself was slanted slightly, and the book stacks at the sides of the spiral were the same horizontal display familiar from libraries everywhere.

The book spiral design proves persuasive, too, to an unprecedented participant in its review process—the federal government. Investigators from the Civil Rights Division of the U.S. Department of Justice later begin a "compliance review" of the ramp to determine whether it might violate the 1990 Americans with Disabilities Act. Detailed answers to inquiries and an evaluation of architectural plans demonstrate that people with wheelchairs could easily navigate the ramp without gathering momentum, let alone speed, and the federal investigation is called off. The deputy director of the department's Disability Rights Section announces termination of the investigation in a letter to Seattle Public Library that closes, "We appreciate your cooperation with this matter and wish the Library success as it begins construction of its innovative design."[25] Koolhaas has no way of knowing of the upcoming federal investigation, but he does foresee its questions. Twice in his presenta-

tion, the architect stresses that the ramp's slope is far below the legal minimum.

Koolhaas has entered the homestretch of his talk, although few in the audience can sense that by his pace. He continues to charge onward, the words flowing in run-on sentences that become run-on paragraphs, with many flashes of brilliance, a few detours into pedantry. Most in the crowd hang on Koolhaas's every word; their silence seems respectful, even awestruck. This is a bravura performance, Euro-smooth and ironic at times, but dazzling in its surety and worthy of its symphony hall setting. No orchestra maestro could play an audience better.

Then comes a true Koolhaas moment. He has been talking about the design process in Seattle and budget constraints on a public building and how that has necessitated adoption of various compromises. He sees that as an aesthetic virtue since it forces elimination of unnecessary elements of the structure and leads to a better building. This explanation is not just lip service to a client coming from the architect's mouth, since one of the key elements of Koolhaas's reputation is his proven ability to build within budgets, often for less money than competing firms.

These philosophical thoughts about design somehow propel Koolhaas into a triple axel on stage. Few in the audience see it coming, which only increases the sense of surprise. Up comes a slide that shows a page from a recent issue of *Time* magazine with a feature on Koolhaas and his work prompted by his Pritzker Prize. Two elements on the *Time* page stand out—one is the bold headline ("The Rem Movement"), the other is a passage circled in red where the architect's laser pointer now alights.

"This is kind of a funny thing," Koolhaas deadpans. "There has been an explosion of publicity and Seattle has gained an irrevocable place, almost like an urban myth, in my history. Because a key editorial writer here has been cited in every single one of the articles for saying, 'I have this feeling that Rem Koolhaas will wake up one night and realize, oops, he designed for Seattle the ugliest library building in the world.'"[26]

The laughter rolls through Benaroya once more, louder this time than at any other time during this presentation. Koolhaas lets out a little chuckle amid the crowd's guffaws, then takes a sip from a bottle of water before adding, "So I think that one achievement of these past twelve months has been the firm establishment of that myth. And we both have to live with it, probably ad infinitum."[27]

More laughter erupts. This focus on the "ugliest library building in the world" criticism by columnist Susan Nielsen of the *Seattle Times* is the flip side of Koolhaas's slide with the Seattle street scene from the WTO protests. It is Koolhaas casting his ironic glance on his own foibles, a way of using wry humor to lessen the sting of criticism and also to build rapport with the Seattle audience. We are both linked together, the architect suggests, by our embarrassments on the international stage.

Nielsen's two columns on the Koolhaas design (December 23, 1999; January 13, 2000) included that often-cited great line, but were otherwise unremarkable, shallow. They came from the shocked-by-the-new school of commentary, offering not much more depth or insight than a *Times* letter writer who thought Seattle would be better served by returning to the golden olden days of Andrew Carnegie ("Let's take the basic Carnegie Library design, a classic look, update it slightly and enlarge it").[28] Nielsen's columns were a glancing blow at best and were effectively countered in a well-reasoned op-ed piece in the *Times* by Matthew Stadler, a forty-one-year-old literary novelist who served on the fourteen-member advisory committee that evaluated library design proposals from the competing architects. Stadler was no unbiased bystander, but he did offer an eloquent defense of Koolhaas:

> It's discouraging that Nielsen's fear of the future keeps her from engaging with this curious, excitable designer. ... He's asking all the right questions, but apparently in a vocabulary Nielsen hates. Or maybe it's his accent. Spooked by the future, and by an architect who is excited about its possibilities, Nielsen has neglected to listen to anything Koolhaas says. Worse, she insults library patrons by casting us as both suspicious and ignorant of a design process that has been exemplary in its openness. Many of us have taken advantage of this vigorous, frank accessibility and have discovered there's an actual person designing this library—not a caricature. He is an engaged, curious and excitable designer, eager to make the best building for this time and place. We should pay him the courtesy of treating him as such, and treat library patrons as intelligent people seeking information and facts, not divisive harangue.[30]

Stadler's pro-Rem parry was much more in keeping with most of the Seattle response to Koolhaas and his radical library design. The city by Puget Sound seems in full swoon over the new Dutch master ("Make us cool, Rem," implored editorial columnist O. Casey Corr in the

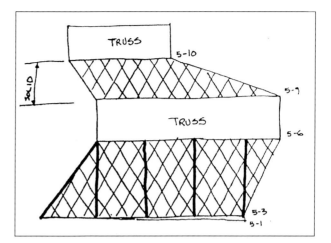

Early sketches in the OMA design process suggest the Central Library's distinctive patterned exterior, or "skin."

Seattle Times).[30] Koolhaas's iconoclastic magnetism has been increased by a memorable name that suggests "cool house" but, in Dutch, actually means "cabbage hare." Still, personal charisma can carry only so much favor for such a startling architectural design, even in the throes of public infatuation. Another important factor in the design's favor is how successful the architect has been in making the design seem as inevitable as the Seattle drizzle—its form so closely determined by library function that there seems no other logical option, a hallmark of OMA work. Or perhaps much of the support comes because, as Stadler mentioned, the library has been through an extensive public review process that has allowed many people to have a look at the building and perhaps offer a comment.

This public involvement has been so unlike what happened with the Experience Music Project, the rock museum financed by Microsoft billionaire Paul Allen. That was Seattle's first experience with large-scale avant-garde architecture, a daring series of "swoopy" metallic shapes from architect Frank Gehry of Los Angeles that seemed to be plunked down one day at the base of the Space Needle, a privately funded fait accompli. The boldness of Koolhaas's design for the library has been applauded on the mainstream editorial pages of both the *Seattle Times* and the *Seattle Post-Intelligencer*, as well as by many critics and commentators in their pages. Plus, the selection of Koolhaas has resulted in a deluge of praise for forward-thinking Seattle in publications around the globe and on the World Wide Web, a salve to the city's international wounds wrought by WTO. So Koolhaas's library is well on its way to winning the Seattle Establishment seal of

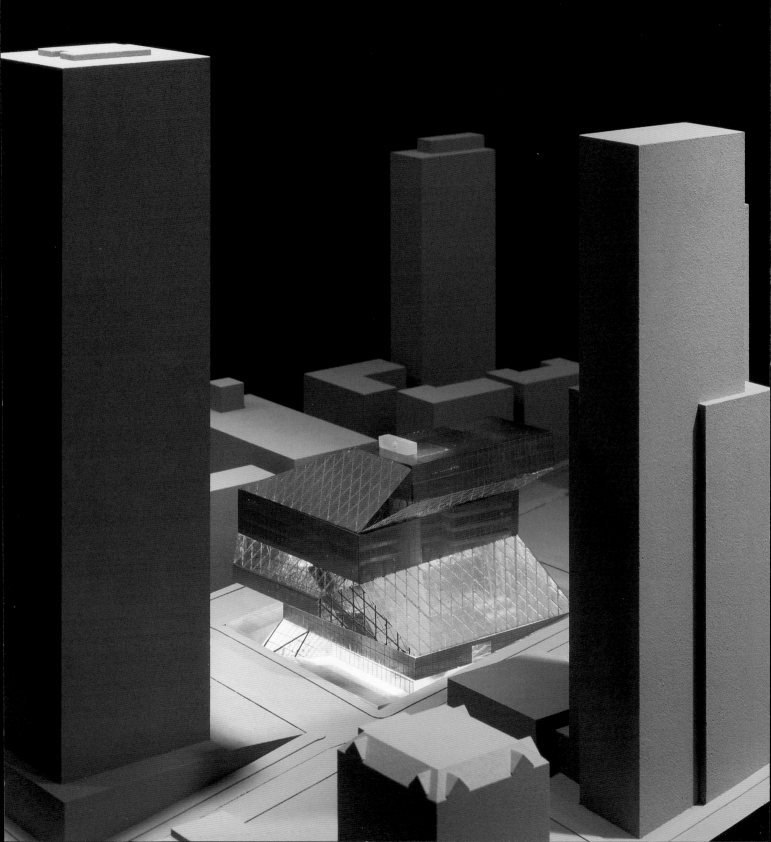

approval. The civic consensus seems to be: Isn't it time for a truly different public project for a change? And what better place for daring than a building dedicated to free expression?

Koolhaas strides smartly into his conclusion, as a series of slides provides a visual counterpoint to the architect's closing words:

> I want to end this presentation with a number of views of the building simply to give you a sense of the richness of the building, as you approach it from different sides. And also as it reacts to different exposures of the sun, or the absence of sun. Because the building is so faceted, whatever the climate is, it will create different reflections, different transparencies, different opacities. Sometimes when there is counter light, the entire thing becomes transparent and all you see will be activity [inside].
>
> Here are some elements of the building in the grayness of Seattle. It will always look totally different from whatever angle you see it, but it will always be, unmistakably, the library. And here, as we zoom out in a helicopter and recognize that in a sea of things that are more or less private, there is only one element that is undeniably public. Thank you.[31]

Resounding applause fills the hall, as Koolhaas steps briskly from the podium. The cascade of clapping continues for a time, then the huge crowd starts to disperse after the ninety-minute presentation. Many people move toward the Benaroya Hall exits, but others in the throng head straight for the stage. Some hope to trade a few words with the library's Euro star architect. Some want his autograph.

An OMA slide shows how the new Central Library's unusual shape should be instantly recognizable when approached along Seattle streets.

CHAPTER 2

Seeking a Library

THE STREETS IN THE LITTLE VILLAGE were dirt. The buildings were wood from trees skidded down the steep street to the edge of Elliott Bay and turned to lumber in the steam sawmill that had been the main industry in town since a handful of white settlers had arrived seventeen years before. More settlers were arriving all the time, lured by the promise of a new start in the Northwest, although

ABOVE: Pioneer Henry Yesler—whose roles in early Seattle included primary employer, mayor, and community Santa Claus—was a key figure in most efforts to improve civic life in his adopted home, including the early attempts to form a library.

OPPOSITE: Henry Yesler's mill on the waterfront was the economic engine that drove early Seattle, as is shown here in 1875, when it produced a thriving mercantile district along Mill Street that included (from left) a news and book depot, City Market, Pioneer Drug Store, and Seattle Bakery.

LEFT: Attorney James McNaught, a much-noticed newcomer with a gift for words, was elected president of the fledgling Seattle Library Association in 1868.

RIGHT: Sarah Burgert Yesler was elected as the Seattle Library Association's first librarian in 1868, an honorary position that recognized her growing community prominence and activism, despite a life marked by illness, hardship, and tragedy.

their numbers had only passed 500 recently. This village called Seattle, named to honor a friendly local Indian chief, was a raucous, rough-hewn settlement in 1868, but already a place with strivings.

Many of the leading citizens turned out on July 30 to attend a meeting in the community gathering place that had opened three years before at Front and Cherry streets. There were fifty residents in Yesler's Hall when the assembly was called to order, both men and women and including a half-dozen married couples, all drawn by the chance to make a statement together about what kind of community they were creating on the shore of Puget Sound. This was the organizational meeting for what they were calling the Seattle Library Association, a group dedicated to fostering "mental culture and social intercourse" based on the belief that "these objects can be obtained in no better way than by the establishment of a library."[1]

Those in attendance voted to set charter dues at $1.50 for gentlemen and $.50 for ladies. They chose a committee of five to draft the new group's constitution and bylaws. They scheduled regular Wednesday meetings. And they elected the library association's initial officers, seven in all. Their president was a recently arrived attorney in town named James McNaught, a young up-and-comer distinguished by his formal attire and his appetite for reading and culture. McNaught

had provided the oration at the recent Fourth of July gathering, his stirring words coming after the parade with the Seattle Brass Band but before the horse races commenced and sent a cloud of dust over the cheering crowd along Front Street (later First Avenue).

Those at the organizational meeting also selected Sarah Burgert Yesler to serve as the association's first librarian, an honorary position since the library had no books yet, but also recognition of Sarah Yesler's important role in Seattle. She was not just the wife of Henry L. Yesler, the successful entrepreneur whose name graced the community hall and the mill that was the lifeblood of the town. Sarah Yesler was a force in her own right, an energetic volunteer and budding social activist, an engaging woman without airs who was well liked, admired, and respected. Having Sarah Yesler as the first librarian told everyone in town that this fledgling library was a community enterprise with a definite future.

The *Weekly Intelligencer* certainly got that message. Seattle's most promising newspaper had been founded exactly a year before by Samuel L. Maxwell and had quickly established itself as a serious publication quite unlike the five other local papers that had preceded it in the past several years.[2] The *Weekly Intelligencer* took note of the library association's first meeting and weighed in with this assessment of its potential:

This busy 1873 ledger reflects the flourishing days of what was then called the Seattle Library and Reading Rooms.

of the Immediate Re-annexation of British Columbia to the United States."[4]

Ceremony added a note of seriousness, too, with the officers presiding over the events, passwords exchanged, and penalties levied for the revealing of any secrets. By October, the organization had spent $50 to install a stage, and that significant investment was followed some months later by the purchase of the popular reed organ known as a harmonium. The association bought its first books, the initial foundation of its new lending library, in April 1869, sending a $60 order to A. L. Bancroft & Company publishers.

But the association's impressive beginnings and grand plans gradually withered away. Attendance dropped, books disappeared. Cultural efforts proved hard to sustain in a frontier town so focused on the daily business of survival and growth. Still, the ideal of a library, its shining promise of "mental culture and social intercourse," did not expire. A resuscitation effort was mounted in 1872 when the library association was reorganized at a June meeting that elected new officers drawn again from the town's leading citizens.

Henry Yesler was selected as president this time, Sarah Yesler as treasurer. That two of the six officers came from the same modest frame house on Front Street was no coincidence. The Yeslers were Seattle's unofficial first couple, enthusiastic meeters and greeters and dancers but, most of all, doers. The revived library association held a strawberry ice cream social as its first fund-raiser, but when it came time to increase membership, there was no substitute for Sarah Yesler's energy and influence. By fall of 1872, the library association counted eighty members; half had been enrolled by the treasurer herself.

Sarah Yesler had that pitch-in spirit from the time of her arrival in Seattle. Henry Yesler had come to town first, leaving his wife behind in Ohio with their young son while the ambitious carpenter and millwright scouted opportunities out West, first in Oregon, then in California. He finally found what he was seeking in Washington State, arriving in the little community of Seattle in 1852 soon after the first white settlers. Yesler immediately convinced pioneers Carson Boren and Dr. David Maynard to adjust their property lines so that he could take over 320 acres of prime real estate in the town, including the site for his sawmill, backed by a $30,000 line of credit from a silent partner in the Midwest. Yesler's mill prospered from the time when some of its first lumber was used to construct the building to shelter its own machinery.

"Carried out, as it promises to be, in a proper manner, the Association will be the means of doing an immensity of good."[3]

That seemed to be where this new organization was headed in the following weeks and months. Increasing numbers of members did come to the association's fortnightly meetings, drawn to these social evenings by their lively mix of entertainments and rituals. There were readings and orations, songs, debates, dialogues, instrumental music, and lectures, including John Denny on "Seek for Knowledge and Treasure Up Wisdom" and Elwood Evans on "The Right, Propriety and Desirability

Sarah Yesler did not join her husband in Seattle for almost seven years, a difficult separation in miles, but also in experience. She had been just seventeen when she married her twenty-nine-year-old husband in Massillon, Ohio, on New Year's Eve, 1839. She gave birth to a daughter, who died after one short year of life, her name soon lost to others; she gave birth to a son, George, about a year later and raised him on her own from age six while her husband roamed the West, their marriage held together tenuously by letters that occasionally reached their intended recipient. "Two years is as long as I can think of staying alone," Sarah Yesler wrote to her husband early in their separation. "If you intend staying longer I think I must come out. Life is but short at most, and I think it is well to spend as much of it together as we can, and then I think it will be better for George."[5]

Sarah had to endure a disappointing wait three times that long before finally leaving their twelve-year-old behind with her relatives when she set out to join her husband, traveling from New York to San Francisco on two ocean steamers that traversed that great distance in just two weeks. The expectation was that George would join his parents in Seattle after a time, but he suddenly took ill and died within a year of his mother's departure. That sad, startling news finally arrived in Seattle weeks later on a mail steamer carrying a letter from her father. The death of her son plunged Sarah Yesler into a depression that became a recurring problem during the years in her new home.[6]

Sarah Yesler's life in Seattle was not without other personal stresses. She arrived to find that her husband was the father of a girl born to the daughter of one of the Duwamish Indian chiefs, Salmon Bay Curly, who had worked in the mill along with many of his brethren.[7] Sarah also discovered that her husband was already well established as one of Seattle's leading citizens, far beyond his station in Massillon, and that carried expectations for his wife as well. Yet Sarah Yesler quickly won her own notice, serving as hostess to the many boarders and guests drawn through the open door that Henry Yesler maintained at their home. Sarah Yesler also became involved in many community activities, including the first county fair, where she won a prize for flower arranging, and the first stirrings of the library and the suffragette movement, where she was elected as acting president of the Washington Woman Suffrage Association. The energy that Sarah Yesler once expended toward raising children was rededicated to this village on the edge of the wilderness where she and her husband finally created their life together.

Henry Yesler would have his critics a century later, those who said his main motivation in those early Seattle days was the lining of his own pockets. But his fellow citizens recognized Yesler's talents as one of Seattle's leaders, entrusting him with a series of elected positions, including mayor on two occasions, although he also lost two mayoral elections, including his first run in 1870 when his campaign slogan was "the Best Friend that Seattle has ever had." Yesler did play pivotal roles in the young town's life, helping resolve two grave crises that were three decades apart—the two-day attack by Indians in 1856 that became known as the Battle of Seattle and the mob hysteria over Chinese immigrants in 1886. Most of the time, Yesler was "the genial mill owner," a soft touch with money for the less fortunate who frequently sought him out, although he was contentious in his disputes with the city and not that rigorous in repaying his own debts.[8] The bearded fellow, often seen on the streets with his whittling knife and a stick of white pine, even served as Santa Claus during the town's holiday celebration in 1864. Yet Yesler was also a man with some mettle and vision, often in the forefront of most efforts to improve Seattle and its civic life, whether through his fair treatment of the natives who worked in his mill, or the building of the town's first primitive water supply system, or the community's effort to build its own railroad to Walla Walla after Seattle was spurned by the big-money railroads back East in favor of Portland and Tacoma.

The entire town of Seattle emptied out in a railroad-building effort on May Day in 1874, with people gathering on the banks of the Duwamish River, the women of the community providing the sumptuous noontime dinner and the men rolling up their sleeves to prepare the roadbed grading. A few afternoon speeches kicked off this remarkably optimistic undertaking. Henry Yesler was the third man called upon to provide suitable inspiration to the crowd from atop a wagon. He uttered just nine words, but nine words that summarized both his own character and the approach that he and his wife brought to so many of their efforts in Seattle. "It's time," Yesler stressed, "to quit fooling and go to work."[9]

The revived library association soon picked up momentum. Librarian Angus MacIntosh unveiled a plan to have programs every Saturday evening, including an inaugural series of seven lectures at Yesler's Hall. A public reading room was to follow next, its collection of reading materials greatly spurred when Dexter Horton, the town banker, proposed an 1872 version of a "challenge grant"—he would contribute $500 of his money for the purchase of books if a matching $1,000 could be raised from other people, as it indeed was.

The following summer, the library association boasted a collection of 278 volumes and more than thirty newspapers from around the country. Its receipts were $1,875.55 and its expenses were $342.75, such a flush balance sheet that more books were ordered and what was now called the Seattle Library and Reading Rooms moved into quarters on Front Street.[10] When the large order of new books arrived from San Francisco, handbills went up all over town announcing that the newly stocked reading room was now open Saturday and Sunday afternoons. By the fall of 1874, the book collection numbered 1,200 volumes and librarian John Webster was keeping the reading room open four evenings a week.

There seemed to be no stopping the library in Seattle until progress slowly ground to a halt once again, in part because of tough times. And what must have first seemed a brilliant maneuver to insure the library's success instead proved to be the cause of its demise. In 1877, the library moved into the second floor of the Stacy Building at First and Madison, sharing that space above a wholesale liquor store with the newly established Young Men's Christian Association of Seattle (YMCA), a decision based on the notion that the YMCA staff would be able to oversee the book collection and keep it open longer hours. But the move into a space with another organization robbed the library of its independent presence and its support. There was some inherent conflict between the roles of these two organizations on the second floor—one dedicated to providing reading material and social discourse for all citizens, the other dedicated to saving the souls of young men through Bible study and prayer meetings. It was probably inevitable that the growing activities of the Christian organization would take precedence in the shared space and that the book collection would begin to be viewed as just another of its programs. The once promising Seattle library withered away on the YMCA vine, losing members, losing money, losing community interest until it finally died in 1881, its last gasp being the donation of its 1,460 volumes to the Territorial University, which later became the University of Washington. And for seven years, seven years that saw the population jump from 4,570 to 19,116, Seattle was a town without a library for public use.

Leigh S. J. Hunt aimed to change that. The owner of the combined *Post-Intelligencer* had no way of knowing that what had happened with the Seattle library in the past had already established a pattern that would mark its future—each period of robust dreams and promise followed by a period of retrenchment and bust, the library's fate almost always determined by the health of the local economy. All the owner of the morning newspaper knew was that he believed in civic betterment in Seattle and that a public library was a worthy expression of that impulse. Yet the Indiana native's preference was to wield influence behind the scenes. That was his approach in the drive to build a steel mill across Lake Washington and turn the little community of Kirkland into "the Pittsburgh of the West." As C. T. Conover, his onetime city editor, wrote of Hunt: "He was a sphinx, but had an uncanny power over men and women and could get their financial support on any project he chose to suggest."[12]

Hunt hit upon a novel notion with the library organizing drive in 1888: he would leave it to the ladies. Babette Schwabacher Gatzert—wife of Bailey Gatzert, a former mayor and prominent Jewish businessman—was asked to convene a meeting of notable women in Seattle, with two dozen bringing their enthusiasm to the gathering in her home.

Conspicuous in her absence was Sarah Yesler, Gatzert's good friend and nearest neighbor. They were fellow founding members of Seattle's first charity organization, the Ladies Relief Society, until Sarah Yesler passed away the year before. She had continued her Seattle good works despite the bouts of melancholy, despite the financial problems that often ensnarled her husband and required her efforts at appeasing creditors as bankruptcy loomed, and despite the gossip that sometimes surrounded the Yeslers' spiritualist beliefs and their refusal to attend church. Even her own personal life sometimes prompted whispers, including her close friendship with a woman and her six-week treatment for an unnamed ailment in San Francisco. Sarah Yesler, daughter of Ohio pioneers, had a steadfastness in crisis, even refusing to turn over the Yeslers' Chinese cook, who had sought refuge in their home amid the growing anti-Chinese fervor in 1886. A band of angry men turned up at their door and demanded that she surrender their cook so that he could be put aboard a waiting boat for deportation, but she refused, saying, "I must stand by the law. This is my house and I will protect it."[13]

A year later, after only a few weeks of illness, Sarah Yesler's sudden death at age sixty-five cast such a pall over Seattle that all flags were lowered to half-staff, both in the city and the harbor, and all stores and businesses closed their doors during the hours of her funeral service. Sarah Yesler, the *Post-Intelligencer* said

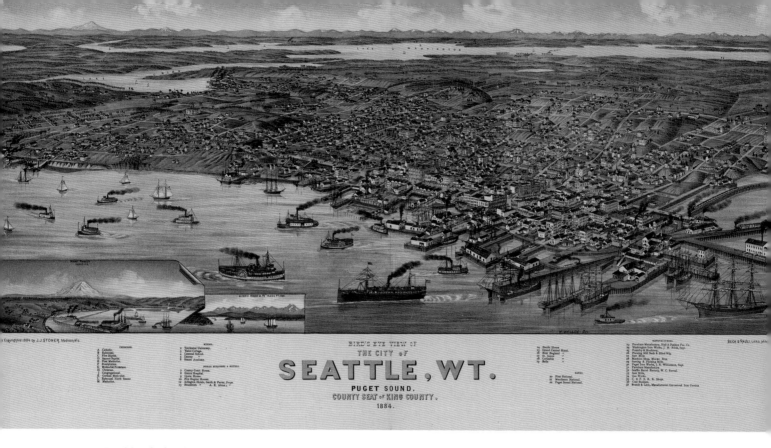

BIRD'S EYE VIEW OF
THE CITY OF

SEATTLE, WT.

PUGET SOUND.
COUNTY SEAT OF KING COUNTY.
1884.

By 1884, the brisk shipping trade had prompted the young city of Seattle to expand
from its original site beside Elliott Bay to the hills and lakes beyond.

in an editorial, "was as completely devoted to the city of her adoption as if it had been that of her birth and it is safe to say that no person within its borders was better known or more generally respected than she."[14]

The organizational meeting at the Gatzert home had the desired effect, with the formation of the Ladies Library Association, but with one result that Hunt had not anticipated. His wife, Jessie, was elected to head the group, perhaps in recognition of the $1,000 that the newspaper owner was providing as the association's first subscriber. His wife's office proved to be a little too prominent for the behind-the-scenes leader and she soon resigned in a meeting in their own home that selected Agnes McNaught as its new president. Jessie Hunt remained as a trustee of the Ladies Library Association and took an active role in the drive to solicit subscriptions.

Success bred success. New members readily signed up, although one who had been counted on for a membership instead offered a significant gift. Henry Yesler proposed donation of a small tract of land downtown for the location of a library. But the longtime library supporter, in the throes of grief over his wife's recent death and involved in contentious court proceedings over her lack of a will, imposed a series of restrictions on the gift of the triangular property bounded by Third

Avenue, Jefferson Street, and the former logging skid road now called Yesler Way.

Henry Yesler was no longer the familiar figure on the streets that he had once been. He usually remained ensconced in the massive new mansion that he had built at Third and James, a forty-room showplace of fine woods and handsome appointments, so huge that he and Sarah had decided to rent out rooms and suites for professional offices just months after moving into their new home in June 1886.

Yesler's stipulations on his property gift to the library showed the inflexibility of his advancing age. Some stipulations regarded financial matters, but others were operational, including the requirement that library books would never be selected on the basis of religious tenets. The seventy-eight-year-old Yesler also insisted that the Ladies Library Association be renamed the Yesler Library Association of Seattle and that the gift property (valued at $25,000) be deeded to male representatives of the organization, two stipulations that were followed. Still, the *Post-Intelligencer* had no hesitancy in describing Yesler's gift as "the most important and notable donation of private means to public uses ever made in this city, and it comes with special grace from the pioneer citizen who is honorably and popularly designated as the 'father of the city.'"[15]

Other money rolled in to the library association. An elegant library ball, held at the armory on April 25, 1889, was a singular success in a city that now boasted more than 20,000 residents. Tickets to the gala evening cost $1.50 for dinner and dancing and they raised a substantial $800. A benefit baseball game raised another $300, and an outing in Victoria, British Columbia, also was a fund-raising success. Plans advanced to construct a five-story library building, what would be familiar a century later in Seattle as a "mixed-use project," with a store on the ground floor, the library on the second, and rental offices occupying the three floors above. On May 25, 1889, the *Post-Intelligencer* carried a confident headline: "Yesler Public Library: Work on the Five-Story Building to Begin Shortly."[16]

Then disaster struck again. The Great Seattle Fire roared through the downtown business district on June 6, 1889, a conflagration so intense that the roar of its flames could be heard miles away and its cloud of dark smoke could be seen in Tacoma.[17] The huge task of rebuilding the sixty-four acres of devastation consumed the city for over a year, with modern buildings of brick and stone replacing wooden structures of pioneer days and many previous plans delayed, including those of the library association. Doubts grew about the Yesler gift site in the interim; it seemed too small for the library, and its triangular shape posed other problems. The association preferred to sell its donated property and use those proceeds to build elsewhere, but that idea was blocked by Yesler, who had scandalized the city with his marriage to Minnie Gagle, his twenty-two-year-old second cousin. The new Mrs. Yesler had moved into the mansion back in 1888 with her parents and younger sisters.

But public funding for the library finally arrived, with voter passage of the Freeholders' Charter on October 1, 1890. The library was designated as an official city department, governed by a library commission that had to include, in a bow to the Ladies Library Association, at least two women among its five members. The new charter mandated that the library receive 10 percent of the amount paid for city licenses and fines, the same budget devoted to the parks department. It was not a huge amount for a free public library by any means, but it promised to be regular as rain and library plans marched ahead.

The fifth floor of the flatiron Occidental Building in Pioneer Square was rented to house the public library.

Seattle Public Library, funded by the city for the first time, opened in 1891 on the fifth floor of the flatiron building that housed Hotel Seattle at the crossroads of Pioneer Square. The once elegant structure was demolished decades later and replaced by the infamous "sinking ship" parking garage.

A. J. Snoke, a former Ohio schoolteacher and small-town librarian, was hired to organize the new library. Books valued at $6,000 were ordered from Boston. The library itself opened in two stages in 1891. On April 8, a reading room was opened, with 142 periodicals set out on a collection of tables where a crowd of eager readers congregated from the outset. This date of April 8, 1891, would forever be celebrated as the founding of the Seattle Public Library, a historic moment for the city certainly, but a founding day that ignored twenty-three years of extraordinary library efforts in Seattle, all worthy of celebration and remembrance.

On December 1, 1891, the Seattle Public Library first opened for book borrowing from its Circulation Department. The time was 9:00 A.M. sharp, 6,000 books were carefully arranged via the Dewey Decimal System invented two decades previous, and Snoke stood ready to greet the library's first patron. The librarian did not have to wait long, as Arnold W. Conant soon walked in. The vice president of Mechanic's Mill and Lumber Company requested a copy of Mark Twain's *Innocents Abroad,* which Snoke retrieved from the shelves. The librarian handed a brand-new copy of Twain's 1869 bestseller to Conant, who departed down the stairs with the first book ever borrowed from the Seattle Public Library.

Just a month later, a nine-page annual report was compiled for this new city institution. The library commission reported that the library had received $19,276.57 from the city in its first fifteen months of operation, an average of $1,285.10 per month. Books borrowed since the opening totaled 2,243, with works of fiction accounting for more than half of that figure (1,423), followed by travel books (210) and works of literature (143). There were 142 periodicals in the reading room, including 13 daily newspapers and 76 weeklies, and the room was drawing 150 people per day to peruse its collection. The library had spent $9,226.43 on book purchases, $2,597.10 on labor and furnishings for its rented rooms, plus $2,486.71 on salaries. The Seattle Public Library ended its first fifteen months with a balance of $781.04.

The commission could not resist the urge to trumpet the library's accomplishments in the 1891 annual report. On the first page was this assessment of its brief history: "As library facilities may be ranked among the luxuries of civilized life, they are not usually found among the things first thought of and provided in the settlement of a new country. The absence of such facilities until a recent date in Seattle is not, therefore, an exception to the general rule. It is, however, an exception, and

A. J. Snoke, a scholarly Civil War veteran, served as Seattle's first official librarian and presented a copy of Mark Twain's *Innocents Abroad* to Arnold W. Conant, the library's first borrower, on December 1, 1891.

one of rare precedent, that a city which but a few years ago was a small hamlet on the westernmost border of civilization should, by one stroke of enterprise, place itself in the very front rank of the liberality of its provision for an institution of such sort."[18]

Librarian Snoke, a scholarly fellow with a thicket of beard that extended far down his chest, was forced to resign because of ill health less than a year after he had greeted Arnold Conant during the opening. The librarian's swift departure was a cruel blow to a man who had come to Seattle at age fifty-one, following dreams of a better life in the Northwest after three decades of teaching in the Midwest, including sixteen years in the small town of Princeton, Indiana, where he also led the library. Snoke, a veteran of the Civil War battle of Harper's Ferry, had spent a frustrating year looking for work in Seattle and trying to support his family amid many hardships, then finally secured the job as organizer of the new Seattle Public Library. Snoke never did library work again after his forced resignation. He returned to teaching and died eight years later.

Great promise was the order of the day for the library in 1892, with steady gains on all fronts. More than twice as many people were now crowding into the reading room, with all chairs often taken by the library's readers and others standing and waiting for a seat. The number of volumes in the collection increased from 6,541 to 8,549; the number of borrower cards grew from 944 to 3,633; and the year-end budget surplus soared to $3,727.90. These were heady days for Seattle Public Library, so heady that the library commission's annual report criticized its current home as "entirely inadequate" and raised for the first time the need for a new "permanent home." "The library is growing," the commissioners stressed, "and will continue to grow very rapidly."[19]

But December delivered a sad omen of difficult times ahead when the library lost one of its greatest supporters with the passing of Henry Yesler. The pioneering entrepreneur was nearly eighty-two when, as the newspaper headline put it, "the summons came."[20] Yesler's last words were in response to a nurse's offer of another spoonful of food at shortly past midnight. "No," Yesler said moments before he slipped into unconsciousness, "not any more."[21] Less fitting final words are difficult to imagine since the Maryland native had spent a lifetime saying "yes" and "more." As the *Post-Intelligencer* noted in an editorial, "In the death of Henry L. Yesler, Seattle loses a citizen whose name is written on every page of its history. He was among the leading spirits of Seattle, alike when it was a frontier settlement, a struggling village, a growing town and a great commercial city. While there are many who have done much in the work of building this city, it may be said with justice to all that no man has done more than Henry L. Yesler.... No man labored more than he for the welfare of this city. In every public movement he was among the foremost. In every business enterprise he bore his part."[22]

One of Yesler's last public acts that year came after the Women's Home Association had constructed a boarding house for working women and called it the Sarah B. Yesler Building. Yesler dispatched a letter to the association and requested "the privilege of furnishing it [the home] in a good, comfortable style, as a testimonial of my gratitude to the association in its selection of the name, and also as a token of my appreciation of the objects of the association."[23] Yesler's last public appearance in Seattle also was much in keeping with his character. On October 1, the aging millionaire demonstrated his vigor during a parade to the armory. He refused an offer to ride in the horse-drawn vehicle bearing officers of the organization sponsoring the parade and instead marched along the entire route with a torch in his hand. Yesler remarked to his marching companion: "Now, after I am gone, I want you to tell them that, though I was 82-years-old, I preferred marching in the ranks and carrying a torch to riding in a carriage at the head of the procession."[24]

Also gone in the following months was the rosy outlook that had marked the early years of the Seattle Public Library. The new year of 1893 did get off to a promising start on January 6 with the completion of the Great Northern Railway Company's 1,816-mile line from Saint Paul, Minnesota, to Seattle. The final spike, basic iron, was driven into the ground with alternate blows by two railroad superintendents at a point thirteen miles west of the summit of Stevens Pass. The nation's fifth

Money problems and rapid turnover at the top plagued the early days of Seattle Public Library, with its first four librarians, including John D. Atkinson, each serving no more than eighteen months.

Declining fortunes in 1894 prompted the short move to Seattle Public Library's second home, upstairs in the Collins Building at Second Avenue and James Street, but the library's finances continued to worsen and closure was narrowly averted on several occasions.

transcontinental line was celebrated with six shots from a revolver, a few blasts of locomotive whistles, and assorted whoops and hollers from a handful of railroad workers. The first freight train to travel the new route arrived in Seattle in February, with passenger service established several months later. Seattle, after two decades of disappointment, was no longer playing second railroad fiddle to Tacoma.

But May saw a national stock market crash and the onset of the "Great Panic of 1893," a depression that would grip the country for four years. The hard times arrived later in bustling Seattle than in many other places, but they did arrive and affected many lives and many institutions. Six of its street railway lines stopped operations, bank deposits plummeted, and eleven of Seattle's banks, more than half of its financial institutions, failed. The Seattle Public Library was not immune to the travails.

A move across Second Avenue to new quarters upstairs in the Collins Building at James Street may have masked the library's problems for a time, as did the new ladies' reading room, which was furnished "in perfect elegance and taste," thanks to an $827.85 donation by the Ladies Library Association.[25] City funding for the library dropped precipitously with the decline in licenses and fees and the library commissioners grappled repeatedly with the horrible prospect of having to close the library. Seattle's four newspapers stepped up during one acute financial crisis and staged a library benefit at the Opera House. The popular entertainment raised enough money to help the library avoid closure once again. At year's end, the public library's coffers held the paltry sum of $15.89.

It was a desperate time requiring desperate measures. In February 1895, the library commissioners reluctantly imposed a temporary fee for the use of the

Charles Wesley Smith's background included work in schools, real estate, and auditing, but he had no library training when he became Seattle's city librarian in 1895. Smith, an erudite gentleman, proved a quick study who soon provided crucial leadership, stability, and vision for the embattled library.

Seattle Public Library. The fee of $.10 per month or $1.00 per year did raise crucial income for the library, but it also had a much-feared impact—borrowers declined rapidly. The number of annual borrowers prior to the fee was 7,558; afterward, it was 2,090. The downward spiral continued. Library salaries were slashed, a cheaper library site was sought, and librarian John D. Atkinson resigned in September.

Into this maelstrom stepped Charles Wesley Smith. New librarians had been coming and going at Seattle Public Library with depressing regularity. Snoke's eighteen-month tenure was followed by that of Mrs. L. K. Harnett, who served for a year. Atkinson served eighteen months. There was no reason to suspect that Smith's tenure would be much longer. In truth, the library's current crisis seemed to suggest that Smith might serve a much shorter time. What the Seattle Public Library truly needed at this juncture was stability at the top, and that was the gift it received from Smith. He went on to outlast his predecessors and then some, staying at his post for a dozen critical years. The first

duty of the thirty-year-old librarian, though, was hardly an auspicious start to his tenure: he had to find cheaper quarters for the library and supervise its move there.

Like most of his predecessors, Smith had no formal library training when he became Seattle librarian. Yet the man with the distinctive handlebar mustache had already demonstrated a talent for adaptation and change from the days of his schooling. Smith had grown up as the son of a minister in upstate New York, graduated from a seminary academy, and had done course work at two of the finest schools in the East, Wesleyan College and Harvard University. He worked as a school principal and as a math instructor in various locales until 1889 when he headed west to Seattle, where he worked for four years in real estate. Then, he spent three years as auditor for West Street and North End Electric Railway Company. Smith had also won admittance to the state bar around the time that he became librarian. He was a person of obvious talent and drive.

Smith soon assumed the role of library evangelist. After only three months on the job, his writing in the library's 1895 annual report was confident and sure, full of rhetorical flourishes, well-reasoned arguments, and a goodly dose of sermonizing. He strenuously opposed funding the library with the uncertain revenue from city licenses, penalties, and fines, which he also opposed on philosophical grounds. "The city's highest interests," Smith wrote, "should not be mated to its lowest; the center of sweetness and light for the community should not have its benign influences limited by reckoning its sole revenue in terms of suffering and crime.... The public library is now recognized as an educational influence of the highest order. It is a member of the great trio of intellectual forces which shape the destinies of free people—the public school, the press and the library. The library is a necessary complement of the other two and, in some respects, may be the most important of all.... A large part of our population comes full-grown to our shores—in this State one-fourth are foreigners—to be assimilated into our national life. They must be educated to the status of freemen. For them, the schools are closed; but, in the public library, the wisdom and experiences of the ages is at command. It is the people's university; it is the storehouse of the 'medicine of the soul'; it is the 'friend and helper of all those who seek to live in the spirit.'"[26]

Smith argued, too, for an annual tax levy to support the library. And in those depressed times, times of library retrenchment and declining patronage, the librarian boldly devoted an entire section of the annual report to the urgent requirement for a new, fireproof

Annual rent savings of $1,400 prompted Seattle Public Library's 1896 move into its third home, upstairs in the Rialto Building at Second Avenue and Madison Street. Librarian Charles Wesley Smith inaugurated several innovations at this site, including the first book shelving open to public perusal in a library on the West Coast.

library building that could handle the library's needs for years to come. Smith was a person on a mission, undeterred by current circumstances. He reasoned, "Money spent upon a good public library and creditable housing for it is by no means wasted, looking at it from a purely material point of view. As an advertisement of the city's resources, culture and spirit, it will pay for itself many times over."[27]

The library's move into the Rialto Building at Second and Madison in February 1896 gave Smith the opportunity to demonstrate that he was not just good with words. The library's quarters on the second floor of the building provided more space but also an annual savings in rent of $1,400. That savings allowed the library to drop the temporary fee for its use and borrowers started to return in droves. The Seattle Public Library was finally on the mend. It also saw the first of Smith's innovations as he began to put his stamp on the institution with power that his predecessors had not been granted. A revision of the city charter turned the library commission into an advisory body (with women members no longer mandated) and gave control of the library to the librarian, even though Smith himself had preferred the previous form of governance.

Smith was a cost-conscious steward of the library but a firm believer in what later would become known as customer service. A separate children's department was established early in his tenure; adult borrowers were granted the right to check out two books, as long as only one was a work of fiction. In August, the library started its own bindery, an unusual department in a small library but one that Smith thought could prove advantageous since the library was often hampered by having to withdraw books from circulation that had been worn out by repeated usage. The new bindery, which cost less than $200 to assemble, sent refurbished books back to the shelves much more quickly.

Smith's greatest innovation in the Rialto space also involved the shelves. Seattle Public Library became the first library on the West Coast, and one of only sixty libraries in the country, to institute a radical change in library operations—opening its shelves to all borrowers. No longer would librarians stand guard over the collection, waiting at the circulation desk to retrieve books requested by library patrons. They would now have their own access to the collection and could browse at will. Smith argued eloquently for this radical change:

> The only use of a book is to be read and have its contents known. If it is hidden away on a dusty shelf, its very existence is unknown to the mass of men and it is only food for a worm. It is true, novels and other books in lighter vein circulate from hand to hand by the recommendation of neighbors and friends; but the only way an acquaintance with the more solid books can be gained is by seeing and handling them without any intervention. To many, it seems at first thought hazardous to permit the public to handle its own books, but with proper arrangements and ordinary precaution, such for instance as any bookseller exercises, I believe the real danger to be almost inappreciable. The system causes the staff some additional work to keep the books in order. But the fact remains that the first and great object of the public library is not the guarding of its contents, much less the complacency of its guardians; but the education of the people by having its books read. It may be added that the saving in the cost of serving the public by reason of each person's selecting his own books at the shelves is fully thirty three and one-third percent; this is, of course, far in excess of any possible losses to be incurred.[28]

The library's rebound continued, as the aftershocks of the Great Panic finally came to an abrupt halt in Seattle amid the boomtown frenzy of the Klondike Gold Rush in 1897. But the often itinerant Seattle Public Library was on the move again in 1898. The Rialto space had done what it was supposed to do, save money and allow a return to free operation. But as Smith observed, "The location has never been a pleasant one, nor has it afforded the city a dignified housing for its Library."[29] The next home for the library seemed fortuitous beyond belief, and also a most appropriate homage to the couple who played such a signal role in its early history. The Seattle Public Library was moving uptown to the Yesler mansion on Third Avenue, that architectural showplace now rented out by Yesler's estate. Smith could hardly contain his excitement: "For the first time in its history, the Library thereby gains a home of its own, independent of all other interests, and is left free to work out the problems of its mission in the community untrammeled by many of the difficulties it has heretofore labored under. For my part, I look forward to the coming year with high hopes for its success, and I shall be much surprised if its records do not show marked advances over the year just closed."[30]

Smith proved an accurate prognosticator. The librarian and his staff of fifteen threw open the doors of the Yesler mansion on January 12, 1899, and saw an immediate increase in patronage. Up the broad front steps the crowds came, passing under the two-sided sign emblazoned with Free Public Library and then entering a library with separate departments often housed in their own private rooms with glorious hardwood floors. Circulation and reference were now departments on their own, the bindery was in the kitchen, and the librarian had an office in one of the former bedrooms. There was also a children's area, as Smith had envisioned, "completely separated from the rest of the Library, well supplied with those soulful writings—books and periodicals—that go so far with children towards negation of the opinion that this world is a vale of tears. Here, in their own rooms, where they feel perfectly at home, yet where, you may be assured, they will behave themselves better than in any other spot on earth (because no other is so enjoyable), is the place to mold the habits of reading and form the tastes which shall fix their destiny."[31]

The move to the Yesler mansion was providing great dividends for the Seattle Public Library. Circulation continued to grow in 1899, reaching 137,941 volumes, an increase of 26 percent over the preceding year. All two hundred chairs in the library were often

Seattle Public Library's shoestring early days seemed to come to an end in 1899 with rental of the Yesler Mansion at Third Avenue and James Street. Library usage soared with its relocation into the city's most elegant structure, but librarian Charles Wesley Smith worried about the wooden mansion's susceptibility to fire.

filled and compliments about the work of the staff were frequently heard in its handsome rooms. The mansion's surrounding lawn and gardens were tended by the parks department and this pleasing landscape was enjoyed by library users and strollers and became a place of great civic pride. There must have been a great temptation to see the Yesler mansion as the library's salvation, a location to savor for many years to come, especially after all the previous moves and troubles.

Smith would not surrender to that temptation. He was a leader with relentless ambition and vision. The Seattle Public Library, in his mind, had risen to a level where it could be ranked "with the first half dozen public libraries west of the Mississippi River."[32]

Its income in 1900 was expected to exceed $20,000, courtesy of a recently enacted tax levy, and that level of financing would put it in the top twenty public libraries in the United States. But it was still deficient in the size of its collection (17,579 volumes), with book purchases always falling far below the amount being expended on rent. In the library's nine years as a public institution, it had spent $20,679.67 on its quarters and $13,806.48 on its collection. What that rent had purchased was a vagabond existence for the Seattle Public Library, with three moves in the past six years. This galled the librarian, who wanted nothing less than "this institution to be perfect of its kind."[33]

Critical to accomplishing that mission was the construction of its own library building, with space for growth as well. Smith had made that point in his first annual report in 1895 and was still beating that drum four years later. He envisioned the library as "a center of public comfort as well as of public education," a place that could continue to serve as "the poor man's club," but also could provide "a luncheon room for working girls." He wanted the library to be "a center of refining and cheering influences," with new programs, including an art gallery and a museum.[34] All this could be accomplished, the librarian firmly believed, only in its own building.

The lease on the Yesler mansion ran for another year and Smith could see the benefits of extending it a few years more. A stable home in pleasing quarters was something that Seattle Public Library had only begun to enjoy. But time was of the essence and the city should move ahead in purchasing a suitable property for a new library, the librarian urged. The Yesler mansion, despite its considerable advantages, had one serious drawback: it was constructed entirely of wood. Others could marvel at the well-appointed rooms in this architectural showplace, but the librarian could not ignore the fact that the Yesler mansion was a potential firetrap for a public institution filled with books and paper.

"A library is necessarily a great coward from fire," Smith wrote in the 1899 annual report. "Should this one be destroyed (and as it has always been situated, once a fire started destruction would be almost certain), not only would there be a visible cash loss of a large amount upon the property, but there would besides be an actual loss of prepared materials and stored-up labor for the future that is incapable of cash appraisal. The need of a library for a fire-proof building is as great as that of a hall of records."[35]

Until that fireproof library was finally built in Seattle, Smith could only hold his breath and hope for the best with the Yesler mansion. It had been such a wonderful improvement over the library's past quarters.

CHAPTER 3

From the Ashes

THE TELEPHONE CALL came around midnight, only minutes after librarian Charles Wesley Smith had retired for the night in his home on Beacon Hill. It was New Year's Eve, with 1900 turning into 1901, but Smith was in no mood to celebrate. He was exhausted from an entire day and evening spent conducting the annual inventory of the library's collection, which now stood at more than 30,000 volumes. Doing inventory was tedious and tiring work, but necessary. Smith was a scrupulous steward of the growing Seattle Public Library and he knew that accurate statistics helped measure its progress and buttress its case with city officials and the public.

ABOVE: Seattle firefighters struggle valiantly to stem the Yesler mansion fire, with brief hopes that it might be contained, before it flared up once again in a conflagration that spared few library assets except, by some miracle, the 3,000 volumes of the children's collection.

OPPOSITE: The Yesler mansion fire in the last hours of New Year's Eve, as 1900 became 1901, turned Seattle Public Library's elegant new home into a ghostly shell of charred rubble.

The telephone call at that late hour could be nothing good. At best, it could be a wrong number. At worst, it could be very bad news. Smith got up from bed and went to the telephone, his worries confirmed when the man's voice over the wire said that he was a reporter for the *Post-Intelligencer.*

"Is the library insured?" the reporter inquired.

"Is it," Smith responded, "on fire?"

"Is it insured?"

"Yes, it's insured. But is it on fire?"

"It is."[1]

Smith dropped the receiver, left it hanging by its cord as he rushed to throw on some clothes. Soon, the librarian and his seventeen-year-old stepson hurried down streets with remnants of snow, making their way toward the fierce red glow lighting downtown. They encountered a chaotic scene at the Yesler mansion, with fire crews furiously battling a ravenous blaze and groups of onlookers watching the drama and the destruction. There was some hope for the library in the first minutes after the fire had been discovered by a police clerk returning to the station after his nighttime meal. He sounded the alarm, and three fire engines and their crews quickly arrived on the scene and doused the most virulent flames on the side of the mansion. Smoke and steam soon replaced the flames, suggesting that the fire was being contained. One fire crew entered the building through a broken window and pulled a hose into the basement, where the fire seemed to have started near the hot-air furnace. Another fire crew broke down the mansion's back doors with their axes and positioned a hose on the main floor where they unleashed a torrent of water. But the fire soon flared up again, its intensity rekindled in the massive wooden structure.

As the *Post-Intelligencer* reported only hours later, "Window after window was lighted up as the fire progressed upward, and through the big sheets of plate glass, the curling wreaths of smoke and tongues of fire could be seen enveloping the long shelves of books. At three minutes past 1 o'clock, a huge column of fire shot through the center of the main roof, lighting up the hills a mile away and making the whole scene as bright as midday. A sigh that was almost a groan went up from the thousands of spectators who had gathered to watch the battle with the fire fiend. The library was clearly doomed."[2]

But the fire crews refused to quit their dangerous labors, even when one of their comrades was overcome by smoke and another fell through a hole on the main floor and landed upon a pile of burning books in the basement. Other firemen rushed to rescue him, pulling hard on his safety rope. Another crew battled their way past the gable over the front entrance, but the roof soon collapsed with a crash. Fire chief Gardner Kellogg had seen enough at the scene of the engulfed mansion and recalled his crews. "Make her burn as slowly as you can, boys!" Kellogg shouted amid the din. "You can't save her. Don't try to go inside!"[3]

Librarian Smith was not just an idle spectator as a decade of the library's work went up in flames. He and his stepson made several desperate forays into the burning mansion, focusing their efforts on the rescue of his personal papers and the library's records, including the charge cards that registered which books were checked out of the library and thus were safe from the fire. The two continued their frantic efforts, even after Smith injured his knee. "I guess we took some risk," he conceded years later.[4]

Dawn brought a depressing start to the New Year in Seattle. The once handsome Yesler mansion was a ghostly shell, many of its scorched exterior walls still standing in sad silhouette, but the roof now gone except for the soaring turret that was a signal feature of the building's front. Inside, there were piles of smoldering rubble, plus standing shelves filled with books, some little damaged, others reduced to char. Smith stayed at his post throughout the day, trying to bring some order out of the chaos, and was sometimes heartened by what he found. Miraculously, the entire children's collection of nearly 3,000 volumes had escaped almost unscathed. A few hundred adult volumes appeared in salvageable shape, including enduring classics by authors that included Louisa May Alcott, Honoré de Balzac, Charlotte Brontë, Anthony Trollope, and Jules Verne. The library's bookbinding machinery, a matter of great pride for the librarian, also suffered little damage.

Smith soon set up a temporary office in the undamaged outbuilding that had been the Yesler mansion's stable before being converted into the library's newspaper reading room for men. The librarian traipsed back and forth between the two buildings throughout the long, sad holiday, as crowds of gawkers showed up to see what the newspapers had reported. Police officers were soon guarding the rubble and preventing entry, except to those who had good reason to be admitted, including the librarian and reporters and photographers.

Smith found himself subjected to questions from the press throughout the trying day. Some concerned the library's operations in the aftermath of the fire, which Smith was happy to answer. Yes, all the library's charge cards had been saved, so there were accurate records of what books were on loan. No, this terrible event did not mean that extensions were going to be granted before those books must be returned; patrons should bring those books to this temporary office according to the proper schedule, or the usual fines would be assessed.

Press questions to the librarian about the fire itself proved peskier for Smith to answer, especially when they concerned its possible origins and the suspicions in some early reports that the fire might have been set intentionally, what was called "incendiarism" at the time.

"It is my belief that the fire started from the furnace in the east side of the basement—everything points to this," Smith told a reporter from the *Post-Intelligencer.*

The fire-decimated Seattle Public Library rebuilt its collection in temporary quarters on the main floor of the old Territorial University building at Fourth Avenue and Seneca Street. The university building was available because the college, destined to become the University of Washington, had moved to a new campus in the Montlake area.

> I do not believe there is anything to the incendiary theory. I notice the statement in the *Post-Intelligencer* that the doors to the library were found open. This is a mistake. The doors were firmly locked as usual when the building was closed Tuesday night. They must have been forced open by those first to enter the building last night.
>
> There is $14,800 in insurance on the library, all of which can be collected as the actual loss exceeds this amount. Of the insurance, $7,000 was placed only a few days before the fire.[5]

But the loss of the Seattle Public Library was much more than a matter of dollars and cents. It was the loss of a home away from home for many in Seattle, especially men who used it as a daily refuge from the siren song of Skid Road taverns and bars. What they would do now was much on the mind of the librarian. Smith continued, "The loss of the library will be keenly felt by the people who were in the habit of coming daily to the building and reading. During Thanksgiving week, our average daily attendance reached 2,000 and, last Saturday, 3,000 people visited the building. Nearly 300 men have been in the habit of passing their evenings reading in the library, and these will miss their old associations and companionship."[6]

The dire library situation prompted an emergency meeting that afternoon in the crowded city comptroller's office. Members of the city council and library commission met in a joint session to discuss both the library's immediate needs for a temporary home and its future needs for fireproof new quarters. The old

Territorial University became the prime focus in both cases, since the school's move to the Montlake area had left a mostly vacant main college building. That structure was seen as the library's temporary location, with later construction of a permanent library on the same property, perhaps in a new building that would also house city government and the police department. A three-man subcommittee of the council and commission was established to proceed with these urgent matters.

Things percolated along in the following days, with meetings and negotiations producing a lease for the main floor of the Territorial University building, a lease with a minimal monthly fee of just $25. Some progress on the public library's behalf was being made. Then, the 80,671 residents of Seattle awoke on the Sunday morning of January 6 and received a shock almost as dramatic as the devastating fire at the Yesler mansion.

Massive headlines in the *Post-Intelligencer* proclaimed: "ANDREW CARNEGIE GIVES $200,000 FOR LIBRARY BUILDING IN SEATTLE. Noted Philanthropist, Informed of Recent Calamity in This City and Commending the Pluck of Its People in Pledging Support for Maintenance, Sends New Year's Greetings and Makes Handsome Provision for Erection of Home for Public

The *Post-Intelligencer*'s dazzling scoop on Andrew Carnegie's donation to Seattle Public Library dominated the front page of the paper's edition on January 6, 1901.

Library."[7] It was a sweet, sweet scoop for the city's leading paper, a news coup of the rare sort that staggered both its competitors and its readers. Pioneering attorney John Leary, a former Seattle mayor who had combined the *Post* with the *Intelligencer* in 1881 during his brief ownership of the newspaper, was among those in Seattle startled when he picked up that Sunday edition. As Leary told a friend, "When I looked at the first page of the *Post-Intelligencer* this morning and saw the announcement about Mr. Carnegie giving a new public library building, I wondered if I could believe my eyes."[8]

The amazing account in the newspaper did stretch credulity. All that most residents knew was that Seattle had been taking admirable early steps in the aftermath of the library fire. But, behind the scenes, a whirlwind of secret activity had been taking place at the instigation of the *Post-Intelligencer* and its library-loving editor, Joseph G. Pyle. His affection for libraries had been fostered during two decades in Saint Paul, where he served for six years on that city's library commission. Then he

moved west to Seattle and transferred his enthusiasm to the public library in his new home.

"For the first months of my residence in this city, I spent a great part of every day in the library," Pyle told a public meeting after his newspaper's great scoop. "I had opportunity to observe the library and came to even more thoroughly appreciate the great work it was doing. The excellence of the selections of books upon the shelves was impressed upon me, and I came to realize the ability with which the institution was being managed. I then wished that the library had quarters worthy of the city, and in succeeding months, this wish came frequently back to me. I began inquiries six months ago as to the prospects for better provisions for the library in the future. The fire opened an opportunity, and it seemed that the time had come for a telling stroke."[9]

Pyle's first telegram to Andrew Carnegie was indeed "a telling stroke." Only a few hours after the fire had broken out, at a time when the charred ruins of the Yesler mansion were still smoking, Pyle dispatched this message to the famed philanthropist: "Seattle public library and its building totally destroyed by fire this morning. City authorities willing to purchase site and guarantee $50,000 annually for maintenance. Can you give Seattle a library building?"[10]

The appeal to Carnegie did not come out of the blue. "The World's Richest Man" had made a huge fortune in iron and steel, then announced his remarkable intention to divest himself of his fortune before his death. The favorite philanthropic focus for the Scotch-born millionaire was the construction of libraries, in recognition of their crucial influence on his early life. Carnegie had grown up amid hardscrabble poverty outside Pittsburgh but had gained access to the personal library of a wealthy resident who shared his volumes with townsfolk. The young Carnegie wrote a personal appeal requesting weekly admittance to the library of Colonel James Anderson, even though it had been limited to workingmen, and the grateful youth never forgot what Anderson's books had meant to him. "It was when reveling in those treasures that I resolved," Carnegie later wrote, "if wealth ever came to me, that it should be used to establish free libraries, that other poor boys might receive opportunities similar to those for which we were indebted to that noble man."[11]

By the time of his death in 1919, Carnegie had donated more than $56 million to construct 2,509 library buildings in 1,412 cities and towns in the United States.[12] That residents in Seattle would turn to Carnegie in the city's time of dire library crisis made absolute sense, since the name of Carnegie and new libraries were virtually synonymous. It made even more sense since entreaties to the industrialist on behalf of Seattle had begun years before, no doubt sparked by his personal visit to the city in 1892.

Carnegie and his extensive party had rolled into town that year aboard his luxurious Pullman railcar on a seven-week pleasure tour through the American West, his first visit to the Pacific Coast. The "King of the Vulcans" was often entertained at lavish banquets along the route, especially in California. His Seattle visit, which commenced on a Sunday evening, was more low-key, perhaps befitting the spirit of a town that was still so dedicated to rebuilding efforts after its great fire less than three years before. But the fifty-six-year-old industrialist proved to be a most energetic tourist, taking a bracing walk through downtown that evening, then spending most of the next morning in a whirlwind round of sightseeing. He rode in a car east to Lake Washington, where the parting of clouds provided a glimpse

of Mount Rainier that prompted Carnegie to stand and wave his hat in salute. He later rode a streetcar up Queen Anne Hill and remarked that, to his delight, the vista there reminded him of Edinburgh. By noon, Carnegie was on his way to his next stop in Tacoma, having left behind a series of verbal bouquets for Seattle. As the *Press-Times* proclaimed in a headline, "A Man of Millions, Andrew Carnegie Is Pleased with Seattle."[13]

Library supporters from Seattle had begun a tentative dance with Carnegie in 1899, led by librarian Smith, who corresponded with eastern friends of the industrialist and made them aware of the city's library needs. Direct contact with Carnegie was first established by Charles E. Shepard, who had recently left the library commission where there had been some discussions of enlisting Carnegie's support for a new library in Seattle. Shepard, a prominent attorney, journeyed east not long after leaving the library commission and delivered a personal letter to Carnegie's New York office. The philanthropist was vacationing at his Scottish summer home at Skibo Castle, but an encouraging response arrived at Shepard's office that fall. "Your letter has interested

Philanthropist Andrew Carnegie rescued Seattle Public Library after the Yesler mansion fire with a stunning donation of $200,000 to build a new downtown library.

Prominent attorney Charles E. Shepard played a crucial role in Seattle Public Library's secret overtures to Andrew Carnegie, which had begun even before the Yesler mansion fire.

Mr. Carnegie," wrote James Bertram, his secretary. "He gives money for a library building to cities sometimes which provide a suitable site and agree to maintain a library at a cost of, say, not less than $5,000 a year. In such cases, he has given $50,000 for the building. He asks me to say to you that he remembers his visit to busy Seattle with great pleasure, and it would give him much pleasure to donate the sum for the building upon the conditions quoted above."[14]

Things began to heat up between Seattle library supporters and Carnegie. The dance had moved on from its hesitant first steps to something approaching courtship. More letters were dispatched to New York, with the latest correspondence from Seattle coming in the middle of December. That packet included a letter from the library commission supporting Shepard's efforts and also saying that plans were progressing for a new library in Seattle, plus another letter from Shepard explaining that this matter was not yet public knowledge out of fear that it "would seriously affect the interests of the city in procuring a desirable site

at a reasonable price."[15] Shepard added that it would probably be several weeks before the library site was secured and then an outline of more detailed needs would be forthcoming.

But the Yesler mansion fire occurred before a site was procured, and Carnegie was suddenly confronted with a telegram from an insistent newspaper editor seeking an immediate pledge of library help for Seattle. That Carnegie would indeed assist Seattle was a foregone conclusion at this point—the previous dances had succeeded with their courting efforts—but this longtime proponent of self-improvement still had some questions that needed answers, even amid the sudden emergency across the continent.

Carnegie sent this wire back to the *Post-Intelligencer* editor: "Sorry indeed to hear of the library being destroyed. Seattle should build fireproof next time. Am disposed to give Seattle a suitable building if site and maintenance provided by city. Your wire says that city would expend $50,000 a year in maintenance, which may be an error in transmission. Refer you to correspondence with Mr. Shepard of library committee last year."[16]

Pyle wasted no time in firing back another telegram, assuring Carnegie that the $50,000 in maintenance was no mistake; this sizable sum was indeed what the city was pledging. Carnegie wired back that he was worried about not including Shepard in this new discussion. Shepard had just been reappointed to the library commission, probably in recognition of his developing relationship with Carnegie, and he moved to reassure the philanthropist in a telegram that was co-signed by two city council members and by editor Pyle ("we are working in harmony").[17] Still, Carnegie had one lingering question that had not been answered to his satisfaction, as he related in his next telegram: "What does a city of 80,000 inhabitants need of $50,000 annually to maintain a library? Seems to me that this is somewhat more than is necessary for the city to tax itself. Atlanta has more population, and I gave that city $125,000 for the building. Presume this would give you a building suitable for present needs, but site should have vacant ground for additions."[18]

Editor Pyle was not about to let some comparison with Atlanta decrease Seattle's chances with Carnegie. Too much was at stake now, so Pyle's next telegram was less courtship dance with Carnegie than knockout counterpunch against an Atlanta-size gift. The editor responded, "Increase in population from 1890 to 1900, Atlanta, 37 percent; Seattle, 88 percent. Seattle's population practically all white and all readers. Actual revenue for 1900 is $30,000. We would like to build fireproof and for the future as well as the present. In less than five years, a building costing $250,000 and maintenance of $50,000 will be none too large for our needs. Nothing from you or Shepard published yet. Can you say anything now for publication tomorrow?"[19]

Just in case Pyle's salvo was not sufficient, Shepard and librarian Smith dispatched their own telegram to Carnegie with supporting statistics. The final waltz was at hand. Only an hour or two passed before the *Post-Intelligencer* received a telegram from New York, which was displayed in a large box on the next day's front page:

> "J.G. Pyle, Editor Post Intelligencer, and Library Committee, Seattle, Wash.
>
> "I like your pluck offering fifty thousand dollars yearly for library purposes. You may build up to cost two hundred thousand, which I shall provide as needed.
>
> "We remember our visit to Seattle and kind reception with great pleasure, and are delighted to shake hands, as it were, over this matter.
>
> "Be sure to have spare grounds about building for additions, which Seattle's brilliant future will surely require.
>
> "Happy New Year to all her people.
>
> "Carnegie."[20]

There are moments that define a city, capture its character, foreshadow its future, and this is one of those moments for Seattle. The effort to secure a Carnegie library demonstrated that Seattle was a city of intense strivings, a city that yearned for a place on the national stage but was not going to be satisfied with the usual or the expected. What was good enough for cities like Atlanta was not good enough for Seattle. People had settled in this far northwest corner of the country enflamed with the notion that life would be better, then they endured far too many harsh challenges of wilderness, isolation, and weather in pursuit of those dreams. True, Seattle attracted more than its share of individualists, characters, and crackpots. This was where civilization ended, after all, the last big stop before the Pacific or even Alaska. But people in Seattle could pull together in crisis or tumult, as they had amid the Great Fire in 1889 and the Klondike Gold Rush in 1897. Let Atlanta be perfectly satisfied with its $125,000 library from Andrew Carnegie, but Seattle wanted something more, and said so. The self-made millionaire respected that brand of "pluck," so Carnegie committed to send $200,000 to Seattle, more than he had awarded for a library anyplace in America except six cities in his home state of Pennsyl-

vania and in Washington, D.C., all of which received just $50,000 more than the distant city in the Northwest.

Celebration ensued in Seattle. Hosannas were raised to praise the generosity of Carnegie and the daring of the *Post-Intelligencer*, hosannas that the newspaper was only too pleased to reprint in voluminous accounts, page after page. Much verbiage was expended in saluting this fortuitous start of the new century, one stunning week when Seattle had secured not only a new Carnegie library of prodigious size but also a $4 million national contract to build a great battleship called the *Nebraska* that was expected to reap thousands of new jobs.

The *Post-Intelligencer* hailed the twin windfall in an editorial: "The building of the battleship alone will bring hither from 4,000 to 6,000 additional people at once. Long before the Carnegie public library is open for its first distribution of books, we shall need all its facilities and more than all the revenue that has been pledged to it. It is the people's palace; the home, instructor, the place of learning and the place of dreams for all sorts and conditions of men. Upon what other institution, save the common schools, should we spend so liberally and so gladly?"[21]

Superlatives and thanks were the order of the day. Carnegie came to the rescue with "princely generosity," librarian Smith displayed "intelligence and energy," lawyer Shepard "paved the way," the *Post-Intelligencer* "seized the opportunity."[22] The Seattle City Council passed a resolution expressing gratitude to Carnegie, as did the Methodist Ministers Association.

Nowhere did the tide of thanks rise higher than in a special meeting two days later when most of Seattle's leaders in business and the professions packed into the assembly room of the Chamber of Commerce. The meeting was convened at 3:30 P.M., a prime hour to conduct daily business affairs, yet the room was so crowded that extra chairs had to be brought in and many leaders were left standing in the rear. Few seemed to mind, since this was a celebration of a historic moment in the life of the city. Rapt attention was broken only when a speaker mentioned the name of Andrew Carnegie, which then prompted an instant outpouring of applause.

Librarian Smith was the first speaker called to the podium by the chamber president. Smith's writings in the library's annual reports had displayed fine phrasemaking, impassioned pronouncements, and other stylistic flourishes, but his writings seemed a pale hint of what he summoned up before the town's leaders:

> I feel pride that in my position as librarian I am, to a certain extent, the keeper of the intelligence of the

community. Being at the head of so important a work has been a source of great gratification for me. In the conduct of that institution, my particular guiding star has been Andrew Carnegie, and I have taken steps with reference to our library being brought closer to that star. I little thought when the reporter called me up by telephone and asked how much insurance we carried and I stepped out of my door and saw the great red glow in the sky, that this great calamity was means to entrance upon a greater and stronger work, that my guiding star was to come to earth and be a pillar of fire to guide us into the promised land....

We are to be congratulated in every way upon this great gift, not alone for what it means to this city, the measure of which no man can tell, but for the high estimate that has been placed upon the future of this city by a shrewd businessman.[23]

Editor Pyle was next, with his perspective and gratitude, followed by Shepard, the third member of the triumvirate considered most responsible for securing Carnegie's great gift. The fifty-two-year-old attorney, a man of handsome and stylish mien, was a New York State native who had been educated at Yale, where he won several prizes in composition and rhetoric. He first practiced law with his brother in Fond du Lac, Wisconsin, and served there as a library commissioner and later as a state legislator. But ill health forced him to

The Seattle Public Library's board of trustees paid $100,000 in 1902 for the city block that would become the site of the new Carnegie library. The elegant mansion once owned by James McNaught (left) was moved north across the street and preparation soon began on the library site bounded by Third and Fourth avenues, Madison and Spring streets.

leave Wisconsin for more hospitable climes and he settled in Seattle in 1891. He soon became known in his new home not only for his mastery of the law but also for his service as a junior warden in the Episcopal Church, as well as for his love of literature and scholarship, his passion for walking and mountain climbing. There was nothing about Shepard and his accomplishments that suggested frivolity; he was a serious and high-minded man, much like Smith, his library compatriot.

So there is no indication that Shepard was joking when, in the midst of his speech, he leveled a startling accusation at the librarian:

> Mr. Carnegie has given us not only his money, but also his good advice. And the first point of his advice was to have a fireproof building. It was badly needed. There has been grave suspicion of incendiarism; and the library board thinks it knows the man. In crime we look for a motive and an opportunity. Now, we suspect that the man who had the strongest motive for a new library building has created the situation which brought about this gift. Mr. Smith, the librarian, has been complaining about his narrow quarters for a year. All the rest of us who have been in correspondence with Mr. Carnegie can prove an alibi.
>
> Mr. Smith was certainly at the fire a few minutes after it started, and it is a fair presumption that he was there a few minutes before. Mr. Chairman, this must not occur again. And I pledge you the word of the library board that we will put Mr. Carnegie's money into a fireproof building, and then we will put Mr. Smith into it, and keep him there just as long as he will stay![24]

There is no record of the assembled leaders gasping at Shepard's accusation against the librarian or indulging in some knowing laughter. There is no record of audience reaction whatsoever. Shepard continued his speech for another minute or so, but without mentioning Smith again. Two other speakers followed, with no mention of Shepard's charge, although the second speaker did conclude with a curious comment. Frank J. Barnard, superintendent of Seattle schools, talked at length about how important Seattle Public Library and its librarian had been to the schools in providing graded book lists for study by every class of students, and then the superintendent closed, "All honor to Mr. Carnegie, who makes it possible for Seattle Public Library to arise from its ashes greater than before. All honor to the man who applied the torch."[25] That comment was soon followed by the passing of a resolution of thanks for those most responsible for securing the Carnegie donation, with the resolution naming Shepard, Pyle,

Smith, and two city council members. Then the meeting was adjourned.

Shepard's accusation against Smith was reported in the next morning's *Post-Intelligencer* as part of its exhaustive coverage of the Chamber of Commerce meeting, although the accusation went unreported elsewhere. Smith went on to continue working as librarian for another six years, perhaps dogged at times by titillating rumor and innuendo about the Yesler mansion fire, the likelihood of his involvement seemingly increased by his own admission on that fateful morning—that the insurance on the mansion had been doubled only a few days before the fire. Shepard's accusation would shadow the librarian not only in the immediate aftermath of the fire but in a few histories published in subsequent decades. Yet a century later, the charge of arson against Smith seems specious. For the librarian to torch the library would have required him to abandon all that had been accomplished in the difficult first decade of Seattle Public Library, an act totally out of character for this zealous library evangelist. The librarian's motive for setting the fire, contrary to what Shepard asserted, seems murky at best. Smith was certainly aware that negotiations with Carnegie had reached an advanced stage, with a library gift for Seattle assured, so torching the library in order to replace it violated all common sense, especially at that propitious moment. The time for such a desperate act, if there ever was a time, had definitely passed.

The city and the library soon went back to business. Librarian Smith submerged himself in the move to the aging Territorial University building and the rebuilding of the library's ravished book collection. Within a month, Smith announced aggressive plans to spend $5,000 on new books, what he described as "all we can handle at once."[26] By the end of the year, 10,407 volumes had been purchased. Smith was so consumed by the challenging tasks at hand that his annual reports for 1900, 1901, and 1902 contain none of his effusive commentary, just a few short pages filled with statistics that chart the library's steady rebound from calamity.

But the days of community elation and harmony in the aftermath of the Yesler mansion fire were soon replaced by months and then years of discord. The library board and the city council battled for two years over the site for the new Carnegie library and whether it should be incorporated into a new city hall building or stand alone. The matter was finally settled in 1902 after the library board was expanded from five to seven members granted through a city charter amendment, and the Washington Supreme Court affirmed the board's jurisdiction over the library's governance and finances. The newly empowered library board soon decided to go it alone, proceeding with the purchase of a separate site for the library, the block bounded by Third and Fourth avenues, Madison and Spring streets. The board paid $100,000 in city funds for the site, which included the elegant Victorian mansion of James McNaught, the well-spoken attorney who had moved back East in 1890 when he became chief solicitor for the Northern Pacific Railroad. The McNaught mansion had become the first home for the Rainier Club in its formative years, then was converted to a rooming house. The gingerbread mansion was dragged directly across Spring Street to its new location on Fourth Avenue before the library site was cleared.

Selection of an architect for the Carnegie library became the next focus for the library board. Professor William R. Ware of Columbia University was hired as consulting architect and undertook a study of current library buildings in the United States, visiting many in hopes of drawing upon their best qualities for this new library in Seattle. Librarian Smith often accompanied Ware on his research treks, providing his own expertise and insights. The resulting architectural competition drew an impressive collection of proposals from thirty different firms, twenty from around the country and ten from within the state. The winning entry was an imposing 200-foot-long structure of classical design submitted by Peter J. Weber of Chicago, a German-born architect who had been one of ten prize winners in a competition to design the New York Public Library and who had also received honorable mention in the competition to design the state Capitol building in Olympia. Four months after the Seattle architect selection, librarian Smith still could scarcely contain his excitement over Weber's initial plans.

"The selected design . . . has received no word of adverse criticism as to its exterior," Smith wrote, "while the satisfactory arrangement of the interior was ensured in advance by the preparation of tentative interior sketches by those having practical knowledge of the work of the institution. Every feature of the interior has been carefully wrought out with a view to facility and economy of administration; and it is not only evident that our building, both as now designed and as enlarged by the future contemplated extensions, will be a thing of beauty architecturally, but I confidently predict it will be a joy forever to the future librarian, his staff and the public."[27]

Smith was a busy fellow and so was his growing staff of twenty-four. The year 1903 produced a series of

PERSPECTIVE VIEW

Architect Peter J. Weber of Chicago won the competition to design Seattle's new Carnegie library with a classical structure that triumphed over the entries from twenty-nine other firms, nineteen from around the country, ten from around the state.

signal accomplishments that enhanced Seattle Public Library at the time and also set the tone for its expansive future. The library's first fully functioning branch was opened, with the conversion of a reading room and delivery station in Fremont that soon boasted a collection of 1,000 volumes as well as daily deliveries of books and materials from the main library. Also continued in operation was a downtown reading room that was opened after the Yesler mansion fire to serve working people; this reading room in an old building at Fourth and Jefferson was the site of the library's much used collection of daily newspapers. Seattle Public Library's stature as a regional institution was greatly increased in 1903 when it was selected to be an official repository for U.S. government documents, the first such repository west of Denver and north of San Francisco. And 1903 also saw the addition to the staff of Josephine Taber, the first trained librarian hired for Seattle Public Library. The Ohio native, raised in a Quaker family, had graduated from Wellesley College and the New York State Library School and was working at the Carnegie Library in Pittsburgh when she was lured west with the promise of an annual salary of $900. Taber started in Seattle as the children's librarian, where she coordinated the circulation of 3,000 books to Seattle public schools, but soon rose to the position of superintendent of branches, where she provided twenty-seven straight years of service.

The greatest accomplishment of 1903, in Smith's estimation, was the rebuilding of the library's book col-lection. The year saw the acquisition of 17,208 volumes, the largest annual addition in the history of Seattle Public Library. Three years had passed since the disastrous library fire and Smith could now say with pride that all the destroyed volumes had been replaced with new editions. The library's overall collection of almost 40,000 volumes was now double the size that it had been when it had been engulfed in flames. This rapid growth in the collection was not without its critics, as Smith acknowledged in the 1903 annual report. But the librarian had his rationales for what he was doing and he outlined them in a spirited defense that can also be read as another indication that he had no part in starting the Yesler mansion fire. Smith wrote:

It has been suggested that it might have been wiser to have made fewer purchases of books, allowing our funds to accumulate for building or other purposes. Whoever has gone through the experience we have of seeing a good working library blotted out in a night and then been compelled in 30 days, with only a handful of books, to take up the work where it was dropped and keep it up under conditions already described, must feel the deepest sympathy with our desire to buy as many books as we could, as fast as we could. Though at first fully 50 percent of the inquiries must be met with the reply [of] "We have nothing," we have slowly and laboriously reduced this percentage of failure to fulfill our proper function in the community, until now it is the rare exception rather than the rule, that any inquirer must be turned away dis-

Josephine Taber, shown in a portrait from her days at Wellesley College, became Seattle Public Library's first trained librarian when she was hired in 1903 at an annual salary of $900. The Ohio native, who was raised as a Quaker, came to Seattle from the Carnegie Library in Pittsburgh.

CHARLES WESLEY SMITH   (291)

Mr. Smith is librarian of the Seattle public library, and is very proud of the new Carnegie library building now nearing completion.

Librarian Charles Wesley Smith came under scrutiny for his aggressive rebuilding of Seattle Public Library's book collection after the Yesler Mansion fire, but also provided skilled leadership in the move to the new Carnegie library, as was recognized by this caricature from the *Argus*.

appointed and dissatisfied. Much remains to be done and we must go on indefinitely buying more and more books to keep up with the people's legitimate demands; but a breathing space has been reached where we are no longer afraid or ashamed to see patrons coming to the building, as was the case for a long time.[28]

Seattle Public Library's transitional home in the aging Territorial University building was seen as a godsend in the aftermath of the Yesler fire, but it did not wear well in the subsequent years. By 1903, Smith was describing those quarters as "unlovely—almost squalid" and was moved to observe, "It is a constant marvel to me that we accomplish so much as we have been able to do in the last three years with so little murmuring from our public. Our patrons have indeed been long-suffering and kind, doubtless largely in the hope of the future model building, where all reasonable wishes ought to be gratified."[29]

Yet the progress toward the much anticipated Carnegie library continued to be fitful at best, plagued by

problems and delays. On March 1, 1904, construction bids were opened for the project with disappointing results. All five firms presented bids that considerably exceeded the $200,000 in Carnegie money, so the project had to be reevaluated and a series of cost savings instituted. The top floor of the building had to be left unfinished, and the building's exterior material went from costly marble or granite to less expensive sandstone from Tenino, Washington. The rear of the building along Fifth Avenue, site of expected future extensions, would be functional brick. These necessary changes did bring the winning bid from the Seattle contracting firm of Cawsey & Carney down to $196,400, a considerable relief until it was recognized that the amount still meant the library would have no money for furnishings.

To the rescue came the Reverend J. P. Derwent Llwyd, the forty-two-year-old chairman of the library board's building committee. The rector of Saint Mark's Episcopal Church had arrived in Seattle in 1897 and quickly established a reputation as "one of the most effective forces in the higher life of Seattle."[30] His congregation

41

ABOVE: Crews of construction workers continue site preparations for the new Carnegie library in this 1903 photograph looking south from Spring Street.

OPPOSITE, BOTTOM: The imposing edifice of the Carnegie library finally arises after a difficult birth plagued by financing and construction problems. This view is looking east across Fourth Avenue toward the building's columned façade.

doubled in size in just six years, rising from 500 members to 1,000, securing an eminent position among Episcopal churches on the West Coast. Llwyd, who later changed his last name to Lloyd, was esteemed as "a preacher of force and persuasiveness,"[31] qualities he was about to test in a difficult mission for the library board. Amid the serious budget shortage facing the Carnegie library, Llwyd offered to approach the benefactor himself for additional funds. The English-born minister said he would travel to Scotland and seek Carnegie's assistance; he offered to pay for his own Atlantic Ocean passage if the library board would finance his trip across the United States. That agreement was readily reached and the pastor set out from Seattle.

On a June day in 1904, Llwyd arrived at the Scottish railway station near Skibo Castle and immediately encountered the bearded philanthropist pacing along the railway platform. The visitor introduced himself and proceeded to outline the difficult situation facing the Seattle Public Library. It was readily apparent that the vacationing millionaire had no interest in this demonstration of "Seattle pluck" on his home turf. His indignation rose by the moment. "Why do you follow me to the ends of the earth?" Carnegie snapped. "I just come here for the purpose of getting away from such things as libraries."[32] But the minister persisted with his considerable powers of persuasion, and Carnegie finally did agree to contribute another $20,000 for furnishings in the Seattle Public Library.

That obstacle was overcome, at long last, but another cropped up several months later at the library construction site. Foundation work was well underway when it was suddenly halted by a startling discovery. The new Great Northern Railroad tunnel was being dug under downtown, using a route that passed directly underneath the library site. That major project was undermining the library's foundation and causing serious cracks. Activity on the Carnegie library moved from the construction site to the courthouse, as a three-month legal battle was waged with the railroad. The library lawsuit finally secured a damage settlement of $100,000 that paid for lost time on the project and also allowed construction on the library to proceed with improved shoring methods.

It took almost two more years for the Carnegie library to be completed, two more years of waiting

Four sidewalk superintendents (three human, one canine) assess what still needs to be done at the nearly completed Carnegie library.

TOP: Eager young readers throng the new Carnegie library's children's room, the largest in any American library at the time.

ABOVE: A grand atrium greeted those who made their way through the front doors of the new Carnegie library.

and watching as the edifice slowly rose along Fourth Avenue, a tantalizing presence. Seattle's library faithful endured one final setback in the spring of 1905. The Territorial University building had to be moved to a new site some blocks distant, which required the library to close its doors for several weeks. The relocation did considerable damage to the old building, forcing extensive repairs and extending the closure. When the library finally reopened in its threadbare temporary home, Smith and the library staff faced a significant decrease in patronage because, as Smith put it, the building was in "an almost absurdly inaccessible location ... surrounded by terrifying steam shovels and yawning excavations for several blocks."[33] This exile in downtown purgatory became one final reminder of what the Seattle Public Library had endured all too often in its itinerant early history.

Great excitement greeted the Carnegie library's opening when it was finally dedicated at a gala ceremony on the evening of December 19, 1906. Engraved invitations had been sent out, but these were intended only as souvenirs of the joyous occasion. This was a public event befitting a public institution, with only a few seats reserved for dignitaries among the 600 seats that filled the huge lecture hall on the building's south side, seats that were all taken long before the festivities began at 8:00 P.M. People kept pouring into the new library, perhaps an additional 400 people, some securing standing room spots in the crowded lecture hall, but many instead forced to wander through the Carnegie library and wonder at its grand entrance, its commodious spaces, its stylish furnishings. The early visitors marveled at the largest children's reading room in any American library; the first men's smoking and conversation room with its elegant leather couches and settees; the lavishly appointed women's reception room and parlor; the spacious reference room, with several fireplaces; the open-shelf circulation room with its towering twenty-foot ceilings, its massive oak tables, its collection of 15,000 books. Visitors were impressed by the iron stacks with their capacity to hold 200,000 books, the two electric elevators for passengers and freight, the interior telephone system, and the automatic heating plant that, as one newspaper put it, "does everything for itself but supply the coal."[34]

Little of that thoroughly modern heat was needed in the library's overflowing lecture hall during the dedication. Any warmth not provided by the crush of bodies was provided by the overheated verbiage. This glorious moment in the life of the city seemed as if it would never arrive, so relief mingled with elation and resulted in dedication speeches of unfettered grandiosity. Classical references were unleashed and the giants of literature were invoked, from Cicero and Homer to Dante and Shakespeare, from Samuel Johnson to Alfred, Lord Tennyson to Emily Dickinson. There were musical interludes too, provided by Wagner's Second Regiment Band and Orchestra of Seattle, with Theodore H. Wagner at the baton.

Charles Shepard of the library board opened the ceremony with a simple, yet eloquent statement that gave little hint of the rhetorical excesses to come: "The day of housing the Seattle Public Library in a fit and adequate building—so long looked for with deferred hope, but untiring efforts and unabated interest—has come at last."[35]

Shepard proceeded to give a history of the library; Mayor William Hickman Moore discussed the importance of education after receiving the ceremonial keys to the new building; librarian Smith provided a lofty verbal hymn to the role of libraries in society; and Benjamin Ide Wheeler, president of the University of California, propounded at ponderous length on the dismal state of American citizenship. Hovering throughout the speechifying was the bearded eminence of Andrew Carnegie, depicted as Seattle's Santa Claus in a cartoon on the front page of the morning's *Post-Intelligencer*. The press of business kept Carnegie from attending the dedication, but his name and his philanthropy were praised throughout the evening. Even the reading of a telegram from Carnegie's personal secretary prompted applause from the appreciative audience. The dedication closed with a benediction from the Right Reverend Frederick W. Keator, bishop of the Episcopal District of Olympia, who asked for God's blessing on the library building and those gathered to celebrate it, then concluded with a recitation of the Lord's Prayer.

Not long afterward, librarian Smith sat in his fine new office on the mezzanine level of the Carnegie library and composed his annual report to the library board and the citizens of Seattle. No person had endured more to arrive at this moment in the library's history. Smith had provided sure leadership through crisis after crisis: the devastating fire, the decimated collection, the daunting budget setbacks, the frustrating moves, the temporary quarters, the disappointed patrons, the

wrangling over the new site, the construction problems, the protracted delays. But now Seattle Public Library's promising future had finally arrived.

Smith may have paused a moment to ponder his own role in all that history and how, at the age of forty-one, he had done what he needed to do for Seattle Public Library and maybe should depart soon for the practice of law. But Smith wanted his annual message to capture what this new Carnegie library should mean to Seattle. So the librarian thought for a time, before recalling a quote from Robert Browning, and then he proceeded to write that it was "no extravagance now to say here must be one of the great public libraries of the world. The foundation is laid, the need exists, and it has a constituency who believe that tomorrow is theirs. Its destiny is manifest. 'Go boldly. Go serenely. Go augustly. Who can withstand thee now?'"[36]

Seattle's Xmas Present

The long-awaited dedication of the new Carnegie library on December 19, 1906, prompted the *Post-Intelligencer* to depict Andrew Carnegie as Seattle's Santa Claus, with the library stashed in his bag of presents, in a caricature that ran on that day's front page.

CHAPTER 4
Great Expectations

THE NEW CARNEGIE LIBRARY was jammed day and night. Crowds came to look from the first day and crowds decided to stay. The crush of people was so great in its first ten days that librarian Smith was already contemplating changes in the library's physical layout. The great lecture hall on the top floor, site of the gala opening festivities, was soon converted to a reading room for magazines and other periodicals. Out went the opera seats, in went tables and chairs and temporary stacks. In came the library patrons, too. There was no question any longer about the public being part of Seattle Public Library.

Use of the library soared. In the first full year of the new Carnegie era, the number of registered

ABOVE: In a rare moment of respite, a crew of Seattle librarians awaits the usual throng of patrons at the Carnegie library's expansive circulation desk. The number of books checked out increased by 50 percent in the first year of the new library's operation.

OPPOSITE: Seattle Public Library's varied offerings for readers were dramatized during the city's Fourth of July parades in the 1920s, with floats decorated and staffed by library employees.

borrowers jumped 94 percent, from 9,889 to 19,229. The number of books checked out of the library increased 50 percent, to 454,735. Many increases could be traced to the community excitement generated by the Carnegie building, but the library board had also taken an important step that made it much easier for all residents to avail themselves of the library's services. No longer were borrowers required to post a five-dollar deposit, as had been the case from the outset of Seattle Public Library's history. Instead, borrowers needed only to be known to the librarian or furnish two references in order to secure the privilege of taking out library books.

Librarian Smith expressed himself with the rarefied vocabulary of his university education, but he had an egalitarian heart. He constantly pushed, pulled, and prodded the library into extending services to anyone who might possibly benefit. "I believe," he once stated, "the public library should be the constant champion and exponent that the gates of knowledge should never be closed."[1] So Smith wanted Seattle Public Library to serve those who lived in the suburbs connected to Seattle by streetcars or ferryboats. Most important, Smith wanted Seattle Public Library to serve those who most needed its services, the newcomers to the city, the foreign born, the poor, and the working men and women who could use book education to make social progress and claim a better life. This was Smith's beneficent impulse from the outset, but it became a guiding principle for Seattle Public Library in the decades to come.

That principle led in 1905 to the opening of the new South Branch at Seventh Avenue South and Dearborn Street in a hardscrabble section of the city. Smith reflected on that branch deep inside the thirty-one-page annual report for that year. But some of his words deserved inscription on a bronze tablet at the Central Library because they so well described a cornerstone of the institution's philosophy.

"The phenomenal success of the year," Smith wrote, "is the South Branch.... Nobody asked for this branch. But it was established by the Board because it was believed to be needed by the people dwelling in that section of the city. Its popularity was instantaneous, first with the children, then with adults. It is open only four hours each weekday afternoon, but the daily home circulation has passed the 100 mark several times. Many of the residents have expressed their gratitude and even the policeman on the beat has been heard to remark that this branch library is a godsend to the neighborhood. It is work like this which furnishes incontestable reasons for the maintenance of libraries by public taxation whose value, nevertheless, can in no wise be measured by the comparative figures of the tax levy."[2]

Smith was not about to stop there. He wanted to make certain that no one could miss the lesson of South Branch, at this time or in the future either. So the librarian continued, "And such work must go on. The library deserves sympathy and support because it is of benefit, most of all, to the poor—the book supply of the bookless; the teacher of the untaught; a dispenser of the 'medicine of the soul' to those who have found no physician for their complaints. To such, the library must come with its supreme mission of equalizing opportunity. It must seek them out and bring them to its doors, or go where they are if need be.... It must establish branches wherever needed, so that the poor can use its treasures without paying what is to them the impossible tax of carfare. It must use every effort to attract and win the people by contact and trial to an appreciation of its riches and their great privilege."[3]

The urge to expand library service was a natural outgrowth of the long-awaited completion of Carnegie library and the changed world of Seattle in 1907. The city on Elliott Bay had reached almost 200,000 inhabitants, with an additional 25,000 people now residing in the surrounding area, and it was flexing its economic muscle on many fronts. Parks and boulevards were under construction, 120 miles of street railways were in place, and additional track was being laid at a rapid rate. Seattle boasted 17 banks with $45 million in deposits, 125 churches, and 1,000 students and 70 faculty members at the University of Washington. The city also had 30 miles of paved asphalt streets, 7 railroads, 4 daily newspapers, and its very first gasoline service station.[4] The first year of the Carnegie library also saw the birth of new institutions that would be linked forever with the city's good name; established in 1907 were Children's Orthopedic Hospital, the Pike Place Market, and the company that would later become known as United Parcel Service. Even the boundaries of the city expanded in 1907, with annexations of the communities of Ballard and West Seattle.

Seattle Public Library gained its first full-scale branch with the Ballard annexation, a two-story brick library that also had been built with funds provided by Carnegie. More Carnegie money was pledged for Seattle at the outset of 1908, with the philanthropist donating $105,000 for the construction of new branch libraries in Green Lake, West Seattle, and the University District. Sites for the libraries were donated by residents of those neighborhoods, a partnership that surely would have gladdened the expansive spirit of librarian Smith.

But the leader of Seattle Public Library through a pivotal time of great challenges had submitted his resignation in the spring of 1907, then left the post that fall on the twelfth anniversary of his appointment. Smith's departure, while "deeply regretted" by library supporters and staff,[5] came at a historic moment when most of his aspirations had been achieved. As he stated in his letter of resignation, "My object is fulfilled."[6] Unlike many leaders, Smith recognized the right moment to step down, leaving behind a record of accomplishment unsullied by advancing age or excessive tenure.

Smith also gave the library board a final gift—five months to find his replacement. The board was intent on a nationwide search in hopes of "securing applications for the position from desirable men,"[7] and it found what it was seeking in Judson T. Jennings, then assistant to the director of the New York State Library in Albany. The thirty-four-year-old native of Schenectady had already compiled a fine résumé in library service, working as a library page while he studied at the New York State Library School after graduation from Union College, then becoming librarian at the Carnegie Free Library in Duquesne, Pennsylvania. Jennings had been married a year after finishing library school, and he stayed in his Pennsylvania post for three years before returning to Albany in 1906 as assistant to the director. Jennings was lured west less than a year later by the chance to lead a growing city library that seemed on the cusp of greatness.

Jennings's assessment of the Seattle library was confirmed early in his tenure. In the annual report for his first full year on the job, Jennings was pleased to state that home circulation of books had increased more than 100,000 over the previous year to 555,374 volumes, that eight new positions brought the staff to eighty-two employees, and that "the library is now out of debt,"[8] although that encouraging pronouncement did not consider the $14,000 loan needed to pay the library's assessment for the dramatic change at its doorstep. Fourth Avenue was being widened and lowered, and that was going to require construction of an elaborate new entrance staircase to the downtown Carnegie building.

Alterations to the showplace library continued under the press of increasing patronage, with a women's newspaper room taking over the men's smoking room

Seattle's annexation of Ballard in 1907 brought the first full-scale branch to Seattle Public Library: this 1903 brick structure on NW Market Street, which had been built with funds provided by philanthropist Andrew Carnegie.

and with the reference room so overcrowded that the librarian was recommending the removal of partitions and a women's rest room in order to gain needed space. The reference room was enhanced by the addition of a special shelf devoted to books written by Seattle authors, as well as the acquisition of the first four volumes of *The North American Indian,* the monumental project by Seattle photographer Edward S. Curtis. "The magnificent plates in this work are made from actual photographs from life," Jennings wrote. "Such a valuable record of a race that is rapidly becoming extinct will be of great assistance to the future student and historian."⁹

Jennings's writings lacked the ruffles and flourishes of his predecessor, just one indication of the two librarians' marked differences in leadership style and personality. Jennings had an innate shyness and modesty that sometimes was mistaken for aloofness. In truth, he was a firm believer in actions speaking louder than words, yet actions that were taken only after a thorough pondering of alternatives. Go steady was his style, no matter what the situation, and those who came to know Jennings valued his kindness, integrity, and quiet strength. Those qualities were recognized early by the staff at Seattle Public Library but soon were also recognized by librarians around the state and around the nation, where this unassuming, square-jawed fellow from Seattle rose to a series of leadership positions that took advantage of his talent for organization.

Jennings had favorite areas of library emphasis. He was an early proponent of libraries assuming a leadership role in adult education, believing that schools only provided the building blocks for lifelong learning. "The schools teach the boy and girl how to read," Jennings wrote in 1911, a time when most students left school by the age of fourteen. "The library must continue their education by teaching them what to read and by providing the books."¹⁰

Jennings also had a keen interest in library architecture, which became an important asset in an era when Seattle Public Library embarked on its first period of branch building. An architectural competition was held to design three new Carnegie branches in the city, with entries limited to local firms. The winner, chosen from thirty-three applicants, was the flourishing partnership of W. Marbury Somervell and Joseph S. Coté, which provided branch designs of simple elegance in varying European styles. Then the library board dispatched Jennings on an extensive research mission through twenty-two eastern cities to study branch

The widening and lowering of Fourth Avenue in 1909 required the expenditure of $14,000 to construct a massive new staircase leading to the entrance of the Carnegie library (left).

libraries there and his enhanced expertise helped create branches in Seattle that won recognition as national models. Some Seattle designs, in a surprising twist, were copied in eastern cities and towns where Jennings had done his research.

New branch libraries were not the only evidence of Seattle Public Library's increasing maturity. Old library programs were refined and expanded; new programs sprouted like mushrooms in the Cascade Mountain forests. This was an era of promise fulfilled, not deferred.

The practice of answering the questions of patrons had started quietly in what soon became the library's Reference Department, that place where the heavy tomes resided, the dictionaries, encyclopedias, almanacs, atlases, and guides to periodicals. There quickly developed a Seattle library tradition, where no query from the public was considered too trivial or too tedious as the reference librarians went about their intrepid detective work. By 1907, questions were being answered by mail for people residing outside the city. By 1910, questions were being answered over the telephone. Students and debate club members were among the first to avail themselves of this handy reference service. But Charles H. Compton, an energetic library school graduate who took over as head of the Reference Department in 1910, tried to encourage more public queries for the department with a series of teasers in 1913: "Do you ever wish to locate a certain poem of which you know only the first line or title? Do you ever want novel ideas for parties or entertainments? Do you want to be intelligently informed on any political or economic question? Do you want to know what plays are really worth seeing?"[11]

Reference was a growth division. The library's sections for fine arts and periodicals were put under its control in 1911, and a new Technology Department was started in 1912. Its target audience of engineers and businessmen was alerted to the new department's existence by posters in many factories and shops around the city, and the dispatching of 3,000 personal postcards to those working men who could benefit from its collection, as many soon did. "Among the new users were some who were at first rather skeptical," reported Compton, "being of the opinion that technical books might be all right for theorists, but of little use to practical men like themselves. Some of these were moulders, plumbers, founders and house-movers who, receiving the desired information, went away with a new idea of what a public library could do for them."[12]

Personal postcards were also being dispatched in 1913 to all parents of new babies in Seattle, informing

Judson T. Jennings replaced Charles Wesley Smith as Seattle librarian in 1907 and brought a marked contrast in leadership style. Jennings was a modest, even shy man who believed that carefully considered actions spoke louder than words.

them of two helpful books on infant care available for borrowing. This parental outreach via the mails was no minor task, since Seattle (population 246,200) was seeing an average of 4,000 babies born every year. Community outreach had indeed become the guiding principle of Seattle Public Library. In 1913, the library was referring to itself as a "library system" and no wonder since it included 495 distribution points—from the Central Library and seven branches to deposit stations in twenty-four firehouses and six pharmacies, plus book collections in 443 school classrooms and at six playgrounds during the summers. There were also collection stations with books and magazines at the Jewish Settlement House, the streetcar barns for one of the city's electric railways, and the thriving Frederick & Nelson department store, a service for its employees. The days of downtown-only library service in Seattle seemed eons in the past, not a mere decade.

The new Carnegie branches were like gemstones added to the downtown Carnegie crown. The branches opened in one neighborhood after another, a steady progression that soon assumed an aura of inevitability. Three new branches opened in two triumphant weeks in the memorable summer of 1910—the West Seattle

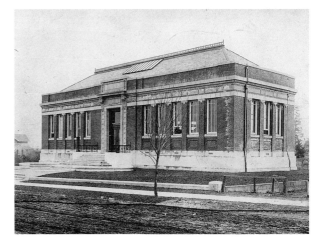

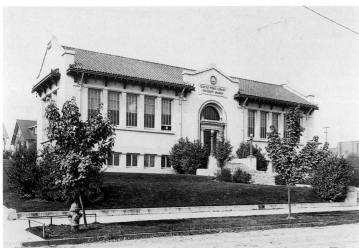

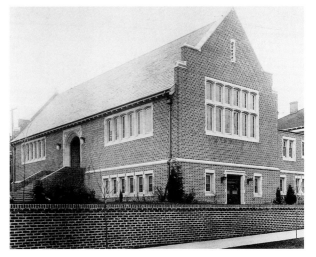

TOP LEFT: Green Lake was one of three new branches that opened in the summer of 1910, all paid for by a $105,000 donation from Andrew Carnegie and all designed by the flourishing Seattle architectural partnership of W. Marbury Somervell and Joseph S. Coté.

TOP RIGHT: The West Seattle Branch also opened in 1910.

BOTTOM LEFT: The University Branch also opened in 1910 (1925 photo).

BOTTOM RIGHT: The Queen Anne Branch, another new branch financed by Andrew Carnegie, opened on New Year's Day, 1914.

Branch (at a cost of $38,344) on July 25, the Green Lake Branch (at $37,749) on July 31, the University Branch (at $38,935) on August 6. All three branches were financed by Carnegie, as were two others from another $70,000 donation from the library philanthropist. The Queen Anne Branch opened its doors on New Year's Day in 1914, and the Columbia Branch opened on the next to the last day of 1915.

Between these two new branches came the opening of the first Seattle library not financed by Carnegie. Legal wrangling had ended at long last over the small parcel of downtown land donated for a library in 1889 by Henry Yesler. The park board finally bought the property, long considered unsuitable for a library, and the library used the resulting $15,000 to purchase a new parcel of land for a library at Twenty-third Avenue and Yesler Way. City funds of $40,000 paid for the construction of the new branch there, the first branch to carry a person's name, in recognition of the important library contribution made by the city's pioneering sawmill owner. The Henry L. Yesler Memorial Library opened on September 15, 1914, and soon became the busiest branch

of all. The Yesler Branch was often crowded with new-comers drawn to Seattle by the promise of a better life, just as Yesler himself had been.

This golden era of branch building prompted librarian Jennings to reflect, "Seattle people like books, they like the recreation and culture of reading, and though many of them will go to considerable inconvenience to patronize the library, others will not. The library is scarcely upon the same plane as the movies, vaudeville shows, poolrooms and other attractions of the kind, yet the library must compete with them for a share of the leisure of the people. That is why we extend library facilities to the more remote quarters of the city. It is to make reading easy."[13]

Dark clouds, though, were starting to appear. The library's finances took a turn for the worse in 1914,

TOP LEFT AND BOTTOM: The Columbia Branch, also financed by Andrew Carnegie, opened on the next to the last day of 1915 (1925 photo).

TOP RIGHT: The Henry L. Yesler Memorial Library opened on September 15, 1914, and represented several firsts for Seattle Public Library. It was the first branch built with city funds ($40,000) and the first branch to bear the name of an individual—the pioneering sawmill owner who played an important role in early attempts to start a library in Seattle. Yesler soon became the city's busiest branch library, serving many newcomers hoping to find a better life in Seattle, just as Yesler himself had done (1925 photo).

Soldiers catch up on their reading in the library at Camp Lewis, a growing military post outside Tacoma during World War I. The Camp Lewis library was aided greatly by the city to the north on Elliott Bay, with many of its volumes donated by Seattle citizens and its initial organization led by Seattle librarian Judson Jennings during a two-month leave of absence.

with deficits from the building of the Queen Anne and Yesler libraries leading to a decrease in 1915 library funding and "strict economies" right when home circulation of books had soared past 1 million volumes for the first time.[14] Far more ominous was the gathering storm in Europe. World War I's impact on the Seattle Public Library started with small matters—two bulletin boards at the Central Library used to display postcards and photos of towns in the war zone; a great increase in readership of foreign newspapers tracking the conflict; the sudden disappearance of new German periodicals from the library shelves, these subscriptions no longer fulfilled by their publishers.

America's 1917 entry into "The War to End All Wars" wrought major changes at the Seattle Public Library, as it did throughout the city. A massive parade through downtown came the day after the United States declared war against Germany and its allies. More than 50,000 people jammed the streets to watch a solemn patriotic procession that stretched for nineteen blocks and included groups of naval reservists, veterans of both the Civil War and Spanish-American War, the Seattle Bar Association, the Fraternal Order of Eagles, the American Red Cross Society, and 275 Japanese Americans, one of the largest contingents in the parade. Each member of that Asian community proudly carried a lit paper

lantern past the patriotic throng, such a dramatic contrast from what Japanese Americans would endure in Seattle during the next world conflict. The parade ended in the vicinity of the downtown library as 7,500 people crowded into the Arena on Fifth Avenue, where only eleven days before there had been wild cheering as the Seattle Metropolitans beat the Montreal Canadiens to win hockey's Stanley Cup, the first time that a team from outside Canada had claimed that coveted prize. The war crowd at the Arena was far more restrained, at least until the reading of a resolution that passed by acclamation and soon had everyone standing on their feet and cheering. The resolution said, in part, "The citizens of Seattle, in mass meeting assembled, resolve: That we pledge anew our loyalty and devotion to the government of the United States and . . . while expressing with vigor our abhorrence of war, we declare our unwavering and enthusiastic support . . . for bringing this conflict to a victorious termination."[15]

Seattle Public Library was soon doing its part in the war effort. The library quadrupled its book collection on shipbuilding in a single year, as Seattle shipyards on urgent war footing swelled to 40,000 workers. Seattle libraries collected 40,000 books for military libraries, many of the donated volumes destined for the growing Camp Lewis near Tacoma, where librarian Jennings spent two months on a leave of absence engaged in the organization of the post's library. Money for the military libraries was also collected in Seattle libraries, with more than $9,000 raised, including $500 contributed by schoolchildren who put their small change into classroom containers called "self-denial barrels."[16] Distant indeed seemed the innocent days of 1914 when the summer attention of Seattle boys in the city was riveted by the library's well-publicized model "aeroplane" contest with its host of prizes. The world war also saw auditoriums in branch libraries taken over by the Red Cross, with reading tables transformed into places where volunteers operated sewing machines and prepared surgical dressings for use in the war. Branches with many foreign-born patrons experienced a decline in use, due to a reduction in immigration during the war but also from the widespread perception that foreigners were no longer welcome in Seattle. The immigrants who did come to the libraries often had problems far beyond difficulties with language. They were, as library staffers noted, "lonely, depressed and bowed down with grief of losing relatives and friends in the war-ridden countries of their birth."[17]

Just when World War I started to grind to an end in the fall of 1918, with an Allied victory inevitable, an even greater threat gripped Seattle. An epidemic of Spanish influenza, already ravaging the East Coast and Midwest, arrived in Seattle aboard a troop train from Philadelphia filled with sick sailors destined for the University of Washington Naval Training Station. The city attempted to check the spread of disease through strict measures—dances were banned, streetcars and theaters were ordered to increase their ventilation, ordinances against spitting were rigidly enforced. The influenza still raged through the populace like wildfire, claiming scores of victims with its deadly pneumonia-like mix of high fever and choking fluid in the lungs. More stringent restrictions were soon imposed, as the virulent disease continued its rampage. Business was limited to two hours in the morning and three hours in the afternoon. Those who came in contact with the public had to don gauze masks, as did any member of the public who entered stores or restaurants. Funeral attendance was limited to immediate family members. And large places of public assembly were ordered to lock their doors. For the foreseeable future. Without exception. Closed were the schools, the churches, the theaters, and the Seattle Public Library and its branches.

The enforced closure lasted five long weeks, a strange and unsettling period when a nervous city watched and waited for more grim news. All hospitals were soon filled to overflowing and the old courthouse was converted to an emergency hospital for treatment of those with the most severe cases. The newspapers carried daily stories of the influenza's mounting death toll and its unfortunate victims. A six-year-old girl from North Bend was struck down while attending the funeral of her Seattle aunt, also a victim of influenza. A mother, a daughter, and a son in one family were killed by the disease, their deaths coming just a few hours apart and leaving behind a grieving father to care for a four-year-old boy and an eleven-month-old baby. Five passengers were fatally stricken after their steamship arrived in Seattle from Nome, Alaska, then four more passengers on another day, then three more on another day. The number of new cases of influenza peaked at 680 people stricken on October 12; the number of deaths peaked at 30 on October 21. The epidemic finally abated, but with maddening slowness. New flu cases declined from 5,653 in October to 3,317 in November.

The flu was receding as the end of the war arrived, a dual release for the battle-scarred citizenry. A throng of 100,000 celebrants filled Seattle streets with a cacophony of car horns and an outpouring of victory embraces as news of the armistice spread on November 11, 1918. Few donned their gauze masks amid the euphoria and the most stringent measures against the flu were lifted quickly, perhaps too quickly. There was great relief as public gathering places reopened, including schools, theaters, and libraries. Seattle Public Library's doors had been locked shut for the longest period in its history, a trying time that did not end with the return of its patrons. One of the library's own employees was struck down by influenza three weeks later. Ernestine Heslop, a twenty-nine-year-old member of the Circulation Department, was stricken in the prime of life, as so many flu victims were. Heslop was one of Seattle's 1,003 deaths in 1918 attributed to the Spanish flu, 24 percent of the deaths that year. Yet Seattle was said to have weathered the flu epidemic much better than many cities. The virulent scourge circled the globe and killed at least twice as many people as the 9.2 million who perished during World War I combat. Seattle and its public library were still left scarred by an epidemic that science writer Gina Kolata described decades later as "a macabre science fiction tale in which the mundane becomes the monstrous."[18]

The forced closure of Seattle Public Library during the influenza epidemic had a lingering impact, keeping circulation figures for 1918 from registering their normal increase, even though the library's collection had passed 300,000 volumes and registered borrowers had grown to 66,678 in a city with 293,820 residents. Nor did the long-awaited conclusion of World War I hostilities bring immediate closure to the war's impact on the library. Only weeks after the armistice, librarian Jennings was called to federal duty and was soon dispatched to Europe, where he spent five months organizing library service for the 300,000 American troops stationed in Germany. The irrepressible Compton of the Reference Department served as acting librarian.

Jennings's important overseas mission exemplified the growing stature of both the librarian himself and the Seattle Public Library. Another example of that status was the increasing number of staff members who came from other major libraries to Seattle, either as permanent employees or on one-year postings. Three members of the renowned New York Public Library joined Seattle Public Library in 1919, Grace Sigler as a permanent employee, Mary Rawlins and Josephine White on one-year stints. Josephine Taber's arrival at the library in 1903 had been heralded for her distinction as Seattle Public Library's first formally trained librarian; library training and library experience was now expected of new employees.

Jennings returned from Koblenz, Germany, in May of 1919 and soon was again sounding his call for the needed expansion of the Central Library. He had first made that plea in 1907, only a year after the library opened, then more of an alert than anything else: "The overcrowding of the reading rooms seems to indicate that the enlargement of the main building will be necessary in a very few years."[19] Jennings restated the case for a larger Central Library in stronger terms the following year and in many years after that; it became a kind of annual plea in the annual report. The Central Library finally received an addition in 1916, a two-story extension at the rear of the building that was taken over by the bindery on one floor and the Catalog Department on another. But this addition was a stopgap measure, far short of what the librarian had in mind, as he reiterated only months after his return from Europe.

Jennings devoted an entire page in the 1919 annual report to a detailed overview of the Central Library's shortcomings, including the need for expanded space for the Reference and Circulation Departments, the book stacks, and staff quarters. The librarian also argued that increasing demands and programs mandated new spaces—a room for the foreign books collection; a small reading room for the blind, who had been supplied with books in Braille by the library since 1907; a soundproof room to listen to phonograph recordings or play pieces on the piano from the library's collection of sheet music; an area for the telephone exchange; and an area for the Shipping Department so that it would no longer be operating out of a cramped passageway. Jennings stressed, "The building is now fourteen years old and is out of date when compared with newer library buildings. It is also inadequate for the library's growing book collection and increasing patronage."[20]

Jennings did not want this urgent matter to be considered as some library fantasy. He played on Seattle pride with a comparison to the newer library in Portland. The Rose City's 1913 library was of similar size, making it Seattle's only real municipal rival in the vast western territory stretching from Denver to San Francisco. Portland's new downtown central library had features that Seattle's lacked, including meeting rooms of varying size for public use. As the envious Jennings observed, "A surprisingly large number of the Portland organizations hold their meetings regularly at the library, making it something of a civic center. Such use should be encouraged and facilities for it should be provided here."[21]

The new decade of the 1920s opened with promise, as new decades often do. Several new programs blossomed at Seattle Public Library, reflecting the familiar goal of outreach in the community. The Circulation Department saw the start of a separate division to handle the special needs of foreign-born readers and help ease the path to "Americanization." Agnes Hansen was selected to head the new department in 1920 and she reported that 15,781 volumes were circulated among foreign readers that year. The Yesler Branch served the greatest number of foreign-born readers, with its concentration of Russian and Jewish immigrants, followed by the Georgetown Branch (Italians and Germans) and then the Ballard Branch (Scandinavians). Hansen noted that the department's social activities were aimed at helping immigrants increase their English skills, but she added that the library also maintained a collection of 6,377 volumes in various foreign languages so that the immigrants "might find in the literature of their own language temporary relief from the pangs of homesickness which, unalleviated too long, sap the mental and physical strength which often is the immigrant's only assets."[22]

The library also started extending a helpful hand to the sick, with deliveries of books to two city hospitals, a popular service from the outset. Each week, a librarian wheeled a cart of carefully selected books through the hospital wards where they found eager, if captive, readers. The library's Municipal Reference Division, established in 1919 at city hall, served as an important clearinghouse for city officials seeking up-to-date information on ordinances, zoning, and policing efforts in other cities around the country.

Fremont received its own new branch in 1922, the end of a long and winding road traversed by residents of that community. Fremont had been one of the early areas of the city served by a rented library space in its commercial district, with the quarters of the Fremont

Reading Room Association taken over by the library in 1902. Library service in Fremont was upgraded to branch status in 1903, yet residents there watched and waited as more affluent neighborhoods were awarded sparkling new branches financed by Carnegie largesse. The proud neighborhood rallied to its library cause after World War I, hosting a series of fund-raising events that ultimately paid $7,000 of the $10,000 needed to purchase a site for a new branch. There were rummage sales and dances, plus card parties and even street fairs, as Fremont steadily advanced toward its goal.

The new branch finally opened on July 27, a day of celebration surrounding a branch with a decidedly different architectural style. Architect Daniel R. Huntington said Fremont's red tile roof and white plaster exterior was intended to recall an Italian farmhouse, what must have seemed a curious choice in an area of the city with an industrial character from railroad and trolley car lines and mills. No one knew it at the time, but the opening of the Fremont Branch represented the end of an era. Fremont's $35,000 in Carnegie funds was the last money that the city would ever receive for a library building from the famed philanthropist. And no new branch of the Seattle Public Library would be erected for three more decades, a status quo period of stunning length, one of the greatest disappointments in the library's long history.

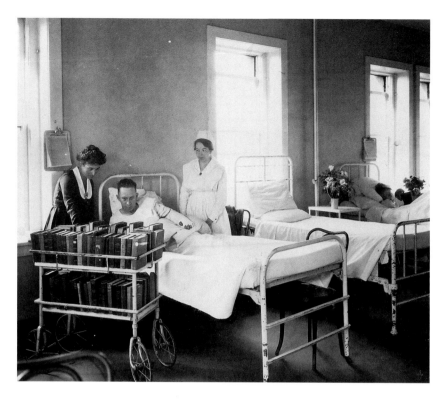

ABOVE: Seattle Public Library librarians started making rounds in two city hospitals after World War I. Library carts with carefully selected books promised hours of diversion for infirm readers.

BELOW: The Fremont Branch, designed to resemble an Italian farmhouse, opened in 1922 amid much community celebration after many years of efforts. Fremont represented the end of two eras for Seattle Public Library—it was the last branch financed by Andrew Carnegie and the last new branch built in the city for more than three decades.

The promise of the 1920s soon ground to a halt. The economy soured. Belts tightened. People left. Seattle actually lost residents in 1922, a population decline of 5,000 people to 319,324, only the third year of population decline in the city's remarkable record of robust growth. The circulation of books at Seattle Public Library did pass the 2 million mark for the first time in 1922, but there was little else to cheer. Another period of bust descended upon the library, with budget deficits forcing cuts in employees and book purchases. Expansive dreams were put on hold in favor of desperate attempts to maintain current programs. The library's 1923 expenditures of $274,432 registered the third straight year of decline and librarian Jennings was forced to make this gloomy admission: "The supply of new books became so inadequate that many regular borrowers stopped coming to the library, and for the first time in many years the circulation of books for home use showed an actual loss."[23]

The library's fortunes finally started to rebound in 1924, the same year that a national study showed that residents of Seattle and Portland took home more library books per capita than residents in any other large cities in America. The Northwest had started to forge its reputation as one of the country's prime reading territories, a region enamored of the printed word.

Jennings's own reputation reached new heights in 1923 with his election to a one-year term as president of the American Library Association (ALA). The soft-spoken Seattle librarian had already served twice as president of the Pacific Northwest Library Association, in 1909 (its first year of operation) and in 1921. Jennings's ascension to the prestigious national post was all the more noteworthy because he was the first librarian from the Pacific Coast to capture that honor since the pioneering professional group was organized in 1876 in Philadelphia.

Jennings delivered his presidential address at the 1924 annual convention in Saratoga Springs, New York, held over the Fourth of July weekend. There were not many fireworks in the lengthy speech by the Seattle librarian. It was a talk filled with sober common sense, much in keeping with Jennings's style. He urged his fellow librarians to focus on basics and forgo frills, to always remember that "library work deals primarily with books and reading—with print."[24] He told librarians to guard against surrendering to their natural impulses, the instincts of the "missionary" and the "welfare worker." He urged them to resist the temptation to add all sorts of programs that might satisfy someone's desires but could better be provided by some other

institution. Even Seattle Public Library, he conceded, was not immune to these seemingly laudable but misdirected appeals for additional programs.

"We have become too tender-hearted to deny them," Jennings stressed. "In my own library, I have at different times found exhibits of dolls, or embroidery, or bird houses, or even a collection of dead birds, each poor little carcass neatly labeled with its epitaph."[25]

Such comments might have made Jennings appear to be a library Luddite, an anti-change hard-liner favoring books and only books, but that was not the case. The Seattle president of the ALA supported expansion of library programming in one particular area where he was becoming a recognized national expert. Jennings continued to believe that the library could and should provide leadership in adult education. Jennings told the convention: "If we can persuade students when they leave school that their education has but just begun and that it is something that lasts through life, then we must also tell them that it must be acquired largely through reading. For the great majority, the books required for this reading must be obtained at the public library. Then why should not the librarian, a specialist in books, guide the reading and become the chief factor and agent in adult education?"[26]

Libraries would need new tools to accomplish this mission, in Jennings's view. He had some hopes that the latest innovation in books, something that he conceded might seem "visionary," could have some use in adult education.[27] That innovation was one southern printing plant's production of paperback books selling for only ten cents per volume. Amazing, but true. "Perhaps," Jennings speculated, "some such scheme for providing cheap books in quantities may be subsidized and utilized. Who can tell?"[28]

Jennings wanted every library to have a staff member or two designated as "readers' advisors," librarians who specialized in providing assistance to adults seeking to follow directed studies or readings. At the disposal of these readers' advisors should be a series of printed study courses provided by the ALA, a Jennings suggestion soon adapted with remarkable speed since the Seattle librarian was chairman of a special ALA commission studying the role of libraries in adult education. Just two years after Jennings's presidential address, the Seattle Public Library would boast twenty-eight "Reading with a Purpose" courses of study supplied by the ALA, including "Some Great American Books," "Ten Pivotal Figures in History," "Religion in Everyday Life," and "The Europe of Our Day." Some 5,000 copies of these courses were sold in that first year in Seattle and

360 residents signed up for directed studies, an early affirmation of the librarian's faith in adult education.

Jennings also had a more immediate goal in mind that Fourth of July weekend in Saratoga Springs. He had brought along a wealth of material about Seattle, photographs, brochures, and invitations from officials, all in hopes of convincing the ALA to hold its next annual convention in Seattle. It was an uphill struggle, since the group's preference was to hold meetings in hospitable smaller communities like Saratoga Springs. Yet Jennings was indeed successful and the following year's ALA conference convened in Seattle, with 2,000 delegates gathering at the grand Olympic Hotel, which had opened just seven months before. The convention-eers included 250 librarians who arrived in Seattle on a special train after touring through Glacier National Park in Montana, and they soon discovered a young, proud city in the Northwest of almost 350,000 inhabitants. Seattle's attributes were lavishly described in a seventeen-page welcome brochure with a back cover showing an aerial view that located the city's top twenty-two attractions, including six golf courses, perhaps a reflection of the librarian's own fondness for the game. The ALA welcome brochure was a fascinating snapshot of 1925 Seattle and the face that it wanted to present to the outside world.

"Seattle does not have the congestion of Eastern cities," the brochure proclaimed, "but is spread over 70 square miles, so that each house has light and air. There is little smoke from factories and in the winter the rain keeps the streets clean and shiny. The sense of space, the wonderful views, the flowers and gardens which grow so easily, endear it to home owners. The faith of its founders that it may become a second New York seems likely to be justified."[29]

The prognosis for Seattle Public Library was more guarded. Year after year, the library's annual reports in the 1920s stressed the urgent need for expansion of the Central Library. Year after year, nothing happened on the matter. In 1928, 10,000 of the library's less-used books were transferred into storage in the basement of the West Seattle Branch, just to create some breathing space at the Central Library. That same year, the library board hired an architect to complete preliminary plans for the long-delayed expansion of the Carnegie building, perhaps with the hope that architectural sketches might make expansion easier to envision, although the projected price tag of $1.2 million was not going to be an easy sell. A more comprehensive approach seemed imperative, something more persuasive than pleas in annual reports or statistics showing that 10,632

people were counted as they entered the library and its branches on a single day.

So the Seattle Public Library embarked on a land-mark effort. Nine committees were formed, each including a member of the library board, a library staff member, and Jennings himself. Statistics were compiled, research studies were completed, and what resulted after fourteen months of work carried the ambitious title "A Ten-Year Program for the Seattle Public Library." This report was a bold blueprint for the library's future, wide ranging, detailed, authoritative. The eighty-eight-page document argued that the Central Library needed to be expanded and that the required $1.2 million bond issue needed to be placed before Seattle voters "at the earliest opportunity."[30] But the ten-year plan had specific goals well beyond that, as it stressed in its introduction:

> If this proposed program can be carried out, the Seattle Public Library will find itself, in the year 1940, housed in a completed library building, with several additional branch libraries serving outlying districts, and with its service extended to all parts of King County. Its annual income will have increased with the growth in population and the growth in library service. Its employees will share the benefits of the municipal pension system. Its special service to city and county officials will be strengthened through a branch at the County-City building. Its service to the school libraries will be bringing forth fruit. And finally the Library will be in a position through endowment funds to develop special book collections and to extend and improve its service to the sick and to the blind.[31]

A Ten-Year Program for the Seattle Public Library was finally published in January 1930. The report received a positive review in the *Post-Intelligencer,* which praised its "careful thought and thoroughgoing investigation," as well as its "conservative" and "practical" proposals.[32] But all the work and thought that produced the landmark ten-year plan went mostly for naught when it was overshadowed by grim circumstances beyond the library doors. The forward-thinking report was released less than three months after the New York stock market crash signaled the onset of the Great Depression. The full impact of the national economic disaster took some months to arrive in the Pacific Northwest, but it did arrive—an unwelcome visitor in shabby clothes who descended on the city and then decided to stay for years. The Seattle Public Library's ambitious plans for its better future had been published at the worst possible time.

CHAPTER 5

Years of Depression

SOME MEN CAME FOR THE BOOKS. Some
men came for the job listings, crowding into the
newspaper reading room in such numbers that it
became known as "the sardine can."[1] Some men
came for the roof over their heads and a warm place
to sit for hour after hour, this welcome refuge from
their nighttime lodgings south of Pioneer Square in
the mudflat shantytown known as Hooverville. The
downtown library had always had its congregation
of down-and-out men with no better place to go. But
the Great Depression saw their numbers increase
dramatically, to include many who had never before
experienced the dejection of life without a job and
few prospects for finding one. Even a few women in

ABOVE: Men unemployed during the Great Depression
found refuge in the shantytown known as Hooverville,
south of downtown on the mudflats along Elliott Bay,
and also in the Seattle Public Library, where their numbers sometimes drove away other library patrons.

OPPOSITE: Many of the unemployed relied on soup
kitchens for meals and the Seattle Public Library for
daytime refuge.

62

ABOVE: Seattle Public Library's bookmobile, which debuted just two years before, makes a last visit to workers at Boeing in 1932 before being consigned to storage as a result of Depression budget cuts at the library.

RIGHT: Librarian Marjorie Bettinger (left) assists a patron in the Adult Education Department in 1930. This favored program of librarian Judson Jennings was discontinued in 1932, another victim of Depression budget cuts.

the same dire straits turned up at the library during the Depression, adding to the unprecedented crowds seeking whatever solace that Seattle Public Library could provide. "I've never read much in my life," an unemployed man told one library staffer, "but now that I'm without work, I'm going to read rather than hang around the streets."[2]

So inescapable was the growing crowd of jobless people at the library that regular patrons began to stay away for a variety of reasons, including discomfort with the situation, or sadness, or conscience. One female patron in the periodical room conceded, "I enjoy reading here, but I'm willing to do my reading at home if it will help these men."[3]

At the front lines, as always, were the librarians. Most had come to library work from a love of books and reading, but found in difficult times that their jobs involved so much more than the care and distribution of bound volumes of paper. They watched as swirling forces outside the library changed what happened inside their not-so-sheltered refuge.

"People had more time and less money than usual, and they turned to books as a means to escape from worry, as almost the only type of recreation they were able to afford," recalled librarian Natalie B. Notkin, who headed Seattle Public Library's Foreign Books Division. "Many of them could not take a card out, or had no place

to read in comparative comfort outside of the library, so old men and young men sat around the long tables and read from the minute the library opened till the dread moment when the lights blinked at night. For some reason, there were more men than women. Probably because, even during the business depression, women can always put in a full day's work at home, while men cannot bear the idea of staying home when they should be away working."[4]

The library had always had elements of a social agency, since it was an organization zealously devoted to the public good. But the nature of that social activism always changed in terrible economic times like the Depression. The library's role could no longer be focused mainly on helping knowledge triumph over ignorance or helping foster self-improvement, citizenship, or community. The library was, for many who came through its doors, the last refuge. The difficulties endured by many patrons led library employees to believe that dispensing a smile or words of encouragement was almost as important as dispensing books. The great irony of library work was that these added efforts always came during tough times when the library itself was also hurting. Its budgets shrank, its purchases of new books dwindled, its number of employees declined, and all that happened at the very moment the library was facing the greatest demands for its services.

The Depression year of 1932 elevated that dilemma to Shakespearean levels. Book circulation skyrocketed past 4 million volumes for the first time, all the way to 4,118,720, a high level of library usage that would not be reached again for more than four decades. Yet Seattle Public Library's 1932 budget was slashed 25 percent from the previous year, so that the library had to meet the great surge in demand with $114,234 less in its coffers. Drastic measures were soon instituted. The bookmobile, which debuted two years before amid much fanfare, was put in storage. The Adult Education Department, favorite outreach program of librarian Judson Jennings, was disbanded. Service to five hospitals was stopped. The small branch at Rainier Beach was closed. Hours at the Central Library were cut from eighty-six hours each week to seventy-three. Hours at all ten branches were also cut, with each branch now closed one day a week. Expenditures for new books plummeted from $68,935 to $26,489, the same amount spent on books way back in 1921. The number of library employees was reduced by 40 people, and the 174 who remained saw their work week increased to forty-four hours while their already low salaries were reduced by as much as 21 percent and their vacation hours were cut almost in half. In so many ways, it seemed the worst of times.

Then things got even worse, when a sad, sorry, and tragic occurrence at Seattle Public Library burst into public view. Readers of the Sunday edition of the *Post-Intelligencer* on February 21, 1932, awoke to the headline "Librarian, Discharged for 'Red' Books, Asks Hearing."[5] What followed was a basic news story about the dismissal of a public employee that would long be familiar to newspaper readers: the surfacing of a court case that brought the dismissal to light; the leader of the involved agency offering a sketchy outline of complaints and controversy that led to the employee's departure; and a stalwart profession of innocence by the employee, who insisted, "I am willing to stand on my record and reputation. I have done nothing I wish to conceal."[6]

But the newspaper story about the dismissal of librarian Natalie Notkin, head of the library's Foreign Books Division, also contained suggestions of extraordinary circumstances for those willing to read between the lines. There was the allegation that Notkin was involved in selecting "obscene and Communistic" books for the collection at the Central Library,[7] but those books turned out to be in the Russian language. There was the comment by John W. Efaw, president of the library board, that the complaints against Notkin were "grossly exaggerated,"[8] followed by his refusal to say anything more and then referring all questions to librarian Jennings. There was the revelation by Jennings that there were "many complaints of Mrs. Notkin's selection of Russian books and that she

SUNDAY, FEBRUARY 21, 1932.

Librarian, Discharged For 'Red' Books, Asks Hearing

A bitter controversy over alleged presence of "obscene and Communistic" books in the Central Library broke out last night with the revelation that the library board had summarily dismissed Mrs. Natalie Notkin, librarian of the foreign books department for more than six years.

Her discharge was discovered when she retained the law firm of Henry, Henry and Pierce to clear her of charges she branded as "maliciously false."

She declares she was dismissed by the board without hearing on February 10, "effective February 1," making her discharge take effect ten days before she was notified of it.

Chairman John W. Efaw, while declaring that the complaints against the librarian were "grossly exaggerated," refused to discuss the case and referred all inquiries to Librarian Judson T. Jennings.

Jennings refused to reveal the source of the alleged complaints and admitted that the objectionable books were still on the library shelves three weeks after the librarian who selected them was fired.

"The board had received many complaints of Mrs. Notkin's selection of Russian books and also that she was Communistic," Jennings said.

Attorney Hylas E. Henry, representing Mrs. Notkin, said his first step would probably be to demand a formal hearing before the board.

"We can prove that the policy Mrs. Notkin followed was one outlined by Jennings himself," Henry said.

Mrs. Notkin is the wife of James B. Notkin, a mechanical engineer, living at 4916 12th Ave. N. E. Both are American citizens and graduates of the University of Washington.

Mrs. Notkin's dismissal followed her refusal to sign a resignation penned by Jennings on the promise that the records would be stricken, Henry said.

"I am willing to stand on my record and reputation," Mrs. Notkin said last night. "I have done nothing I wish to conceal."

She said that she bought $1,500 worth of foreign books a year, largely on the recommendation of recognized reviewers or other libraries.

MRS. NATALIE NOTKIN
Denies Charge

Librarian Natalie Notkin, who headed Seattle Public Library's Foreign Books Division, was fired from the library in 1932 when it was alleged that she was a communist, a charge that Notkin vehemently denied.

Seattle Police Chief Louis J. Forbes submitted a letter to Congress in 1930 with what he said were the names of seventeen "prominent Communists" in Seattle, a list that included librarian Natalie Notkin.

was Communistic,"[9] although he declined to specify any source of the complaints, and that claim was accompanied by Jennings's admission that the suspect titles that led to Notkin's dismissal were still on the library's shelves three weeks after she was fired. There was the charge by Hylas E. Henry, Notkin's attorney, that the foreign-book librarian's book selections followed the policy "outlined by Jennings himself."[10] There was also the background of the librarian, the mention that she was the wife of an engineer and that both were "American citizens and graduates of the University of Washington,"[11] although left unsaid was perhaps the most intriguing element of her biography: Notkin had emigrated from Russia. Finally, there was the newspaper photograph of the thirty-one-year-old librarian, her face full but pretty, her dark hair cut fashionably short, her lips lightly pursed just short of a smile, her soulful eyes glancing slightly away from the camera lens, so that Notkin's look in the photograph managed to be both exotic and enigmatic.

Subsequent newspaper stories brought the Notkin case back into view throughout the year, stories that usually dealt with the disposition of legal proceedings, hearings granted or appeals denied. But files of documents being accumulated in the library and in lawyers' offices told a far more sordid tale than the brief news stories. What happened to Notkin became a classic case study of an organization's cowardice in the face of external pressures during a tense and trying time.

It was all the more disappointing because it showed the library violating one of its basic institutional tenets: that library shelves should be home to books of all perspectives and persuasions, even those that might offend some readers.

Notkin's problems at Seattle Public Library first surfaced, strangely enough, in Washington, D.C. A special committee of the House of Representatives, chaired by Representative Hamilton Fish Jr., had been charged with investigating communist activities in the United States. The Red Scare of 1919–20 had largely burned down to embers by the end of the 1920s, but the Fish committee showed that these embers could still generate heat when it held hearings around the country, including a visit to Seattle. That visit prompted Seattle Police Chief Louis J. Forbes to pursue his own investigation of communists in Seattle. The chief was a native of Oroville, California, a former blacksmith and shipyard worker who had steadily worked his way up the Seattle police ranks for twenty years before being named to lead the 600-man force just two years before. Forbes readily shared the results of his communist investigation in a letter to Congressman Fish on November 4, 1930, a letter that the representative from New York State made certain was read into the public record.

Forbes's letter was a chilling premonition of the excesses and slanders of the Joseph McCarthy era that would erupt two decades later and destroy many careers and reputations. For the chief's letter made no mention of the sources of his reports on communist activities, but did offer the assurance that he was "absolutely certain [the reports] are correct in every detail."[12] Then Forbes provided the names of seventeen "prominent Communists" in Seattle,[13] and not only names but also occupations and residences, along with bold-faced assertions offered as truth, yet without substantiation.

Notkin was the sixteenth person on the police chief's list of "prominent Communists" in Seattle. Her entry read: "Natalie Notkin (woman), member of Communist International, . . . Manager of foreign books in Seattle Public Library. Keeps and Distributes communist books among Russians (Soviet sympathizers) with propaganda purpose. These communist books are imported directly from Moscow or Berlin, Germany. Very active in propaganda among all classes, as she mingles and has contact with different society leaders. Residence: 1307 East Forty-first Street, Seattle."[14]

Forbes's damaging letter was included in its entirety when the special congressional committee published its official report of hearings in 1931. Notkin was the only public employee on the chief's list of communists

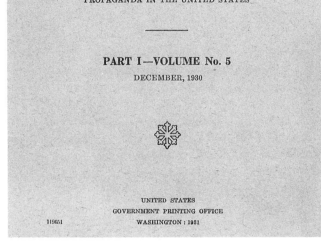

and word of that soon spread to Seattle, where it was brought to the attention of members of the city council and the library board. Notkin herself was "astonished" about the allegations and insisted in a notarized statement: "I am not a member of the Communist Party, have never attended any meetings of the Communist Party."[15] Notkin's assertions of her innocence, however, always seemed to fight a losing battle against the loaded punch of being smeared as Red.

Besides, two city institutions were already on high alert, seeking some way out of this communist embarrassment. Whether the allegations about this junior library staffer were true seemed to matter less to them than making a quick exit from this controversy. Because there had indeed been complaints about Notkin's handling of foreign books dating back almost to the day in 1927 when she started working at the Seattle Public Library after graduating from the library school at the University of Washington. Notkin was certainly

Forbes's list of alleged communists in Seattle was published in the *Congressional Record* and word soon spread to Seattle.

aware of the complaints, as were her superiors at the library, including Jennings. But the real issues in the case, ignored in the rush to exit the controversy, should have been: Who was making the complaints? And why?

Notkin's annual reports on the work of the foreign division were filled with hopeful optimism and cheery personal observations, except when it came to the Russian collection, the largest foreign collection at Seattle Public Library, which accounted for one-third of the foreign-language titles. In her 1928 annual report, Notkin conceded that the Russian collection "presents the greatest problem" because of political struggles over its content.[16] In her 1930 annual report, Notkin pointed out that those struggles continued, with a very vocal minority of Russian patrons objecting strenuously to any Russian-language books coming from the Soviet Union; they favored Russian-language books written and published by anticommunist Russian refugees who had resettled in such places as Paris. "The mere fact that a book is published in Soviet Russia is sufficient to condemn it," Notkin wrote of some Russian patrons. "As a matter of fact, they have little more upon which to base their judgement, for they seldom get beyond looking at the place of publication."[17] In her 1931 annual report, Notkin had clearly grown exasperated by the "sore spot produced by constant trouble with the Russian collection" and stressed, "The fact that I have been writing and talking about it for the last four years does in no way abate the trouble itself. The controversy over Russian books is purely political and is actuated by the same passionate and blind thrusting of political issues into every phase of Russian life, from church matters to dancing."[18]

Notkin's "great strain" over the controversy became so acute in 1931 that she decided to order no more books from the Soviet Union unless she could receive personal support for such purchases from Jennings.[19] A meeting was duly arranged and convened with the librarian. As Notkin recalled, "His statement was, as might be expected from any Librarian, that the Library was not taking sides in controversial questions and that the place of publication would neither recommend nor condemn a book."[20]

Jennings reiterated that point in a response to an angry letter about "the intolerable condition in the Russian Department of the Seattle Public Library,"[21] a letter that the library board received from the Seattle branch of the National League of Americans of Russian Origin. The conservative group's president, I. Panchenko, argued against the inclusion of any Soviet books in the library's collection, saying, "We are positively convinced

that the Bolshevik infection, depravity, contempt and spite to all mankind are so rapidly penetrating through these books, especially to young souls."[22] The league demanded the end of importation of any more Soviet books, as well as the immediate removal of any Soviet books then on the library's shelves.

Jennings responded to the letter in just four days, one measure of how much heat this affair had generated. The librarian's letter to the Russian organization was polite, but firm, and even asked the group to provide a list of Russian books that the library should acquire (a list never submitted). But Jennings also left no doubt about where the Seattle Public Library stood in this continuing controversy:

> We recognize the fact that there is a difference of opinion on the events taking place in Russia, and we have tried in this case to pursue our usual policy of having books on both sides of controversial questions. In collecting historical material, the library cannot base its choice on the pleasantness or unpleasantness of the facts, or else a large number of important historical documents would never be found in the library. What is now going on in Russia is part of the world's history, and surely books published in Soviet Russia form a part of this historical record. It should be the privilege of adult readers to acquaint themselves with different points of view and different theories, without necessarily agreeing with them or believing everything they see in print. We feel that our readers have a right to this privilege.[23]

Jennings's well-reasoned defense of the library's policy seemed unequivocal. It was never followed by any order from the librarian to withdraw Soviet books from the collection, so Notkin concluded "that the matter was closed."[24] She also believed that reason would prevail in the controversy if anyone took time to read the two-page analysis of the Russian collection that she had prepared in 1931. That report included the information that only one-tenth of the collection was books of Soviet origin and that more than half of those Soviet titles were "books of fiction of outstanding literary value," including works by Tolstoy and Gorky.[25] She also pointed out that the greatest number of Soviet publications had been selected, in both 1930 and 1931, directly from the *New York Public Library Bulletin*.

But Notkin's optimism about the controversy's conclusion was sadly misplaced. By the end of 1931, the city council and library board were grappling with where to make severe cuts in the library's budget for 1932. Included in the massive library reduction was $1,560 in salaries that would be saved by eliminating Notkin's position as head of the Foreign Books Division, a clever institutional maneuver that would not only reduce the budget, but also should end complaints over the Russian collection. Never mind that it would turn a loyal and conscientious library employee into a sacrificial offering to a fringe group with a censorship agenda that was antithetical to the library's mission. Never mind, either, what it would do to the American dream of a Russian émigré who had arrived in the United States in 1921 and had already contributed a decade of impressive accomplishment in her new country, including her undergraduate degree in 1924, her naturalization in 1928, and her leadership of a library program since 1927.

Notkin was offered the opportunity to resign in lieu of being fired, that so-called professional courtesy extended by Jennings himself, but she declined to resign for reasons enunciated in a powerful and impassioned letter to the library board. "I do not believe that any librarian of decent standing was ever accused of knowingly and consciously getting obscene books into the library," Notkin wrote. She continued:

Books are being continuously objected to on moral grounds, sometimes deservedly, sometimes not, and are taken care of by the Library. It happens even to English books, where the Library's source of information is considerably greater and the book reviewing force consists of the entire staff. It had happened to several foreign books, and whenever a book was called to my attention, it was treated accordingly....

As a citizen, I object against the implication that I was getting communist books, getting them, moreover, for propaganda purposes. I can truthfully say that, to my knowledge, the Russian collection has no communist propaganda. I did not believe, nor do I believe now, that a book of fiction describing life in Soviet Russia is a book of communist propaganda. On the contrary, most of the fiction books published in Russia, which were purchased by the library, present a picture of life so dreary, so horrible, that its effect would be rather the reverse of propaganda....

It has been rather a matter of pride to me that I was ordering books which, from the reviews, appeared to have literary value, impartiality or descriptive vividness, irrespective of the place of their publication, and have in every way been trying to follow the principle of librarianship: non-partisan fairness.

In spite of the fact, however, that I feel myself to be completely innocent in this matter, and the accusation to the Board unjustified, I would have signed my resig-

nation when requested to do so, moved by simple professional pride, should this be an isolated occurrence. But this appears to be part of a much larger thing, consisting of series of events, which I shall make an effort to stop.

At the time the first event took place, namely (police chief) Forbes' letter to the Hamilton Fish Jr. Committee, I had not taken legal action upon the recommendation of some of my friends, and of some members of the Library Board who assured me that such rumors die a natural death if left alone. For the sake of the institution with which I was connected, knowing the inevitable publicity that would be the result of any legal action, I have taken no steps to refute the libel. I now consider this to have been a mistake, and I feel that steps must be taken now, lest it should proceed any farther.

I must admit that I have no clear idea of what I can do, and that my accuser, being anonymous, is a difficult person to fight. I have no way of knowing that he is a creditable person, acting in good faith. I feel that the Board—in requesting my resignation at such a time and for such a reason—is withdrawing its support from me and, rather than combating the rumor which I hoped they knew to be false, lend it weight by their action.... In refusing to tender my resignation, I am not trying to defend my position with the Library, but my standing as a citizen of this city and this country.[26]

Notkin and her attorneys never succeeded in having the merits of her case heard in court; their legal efforts were brought to a halt by a superior court judge who ruled that the library board had the right to hire and fire library employees as it saw fit. But at least Notkin's library career did not come to an end with this sorry chapter in the history of Seattle Public Library. She went on to work for more than three decades as a librarian at the University of Washington's Suzzallo Library, serving in a variety of positions, including Russian specialist, before finally retiring at the age of sixty-nine because of illness. She died the following year.

Notkin's obituary headlined the staff newsletter of the University of Washington Libraries: "Her warm and lively reminiscences of her life in Russia . . . her several years in China en route to the United States, her time at the University of Washington where she earned a B.A. degree in English, followed by a degree from the School of Librarianship, have enriched the lives of all who have known her. She maintained a lively interest in the University Community, as well as an active participation in the affairs of the Russian colony in Seattle. Her deep affection for, and her keen

Mayor John F. Dore addresses a crowd of unemployed workers, many in business suits and hats, during a Seattle rally on his first day in office, June 6, 1932.

enjoyment of, the companionship of friends will long be remembered."[27]

Librarian Jennings made no more public comments about the Notkin case and offered no rationales or even excuses for his failure to defend her job amid external pressures. But the library's file on the Notkin case was found, decades later, hidden among Jennings's own personal files. It was tucked away from view, placed upside down and backwards, suggesting the hope that its bitter memories might remain buried there forever.

Jennings had plenty of other Depression worries to occupy his thoughts. The economic slide continued, with the library still scrambling to adjust to the diminished reality. Late in 1932, the library board instituted a new policy of replacing married female workers not dependent on their library paychecks with single women, in hopes of providing a better distribution of public funds. Eight married women ultimately were fired. Twenty-two more library employees were let go in 1933, as emergency budget cuts ordered by Mayor Frank Dore in April lopped another $43,000 from the library's budget, reducing it to $260,000. By the end of 1933, the library's annual budget had fallen so precipitously that it stood at only 55 percent of what it had been in 1931. Another round of cost-saving measures was again ordered. All deposit stations were closed. All headquarters staffers overseeing branches were let go. Book purchases were slashed by half and periodical purchases by a third. Even the Central Library's public rest rooms felt the Depression squeeze, as their entrances were locked and three comfort station attendants were fired. The national prohibition against alcoholic beverages ended on December 5, 1933, but there was precious little to celebrate at Seattle Public Library. "It is quite probable," Jennings conceded in his 1933 annual report, "that many of these curtailments may be continued indefinitely."[28] Alice Frost, who took over the schools division early in 1933, described the cuts and their impact in more graphic terms: "Sometimes the work has seemed like a three-ring circus."[29]

A few rays of hope did penetrate the gloom. The Boeing Airplane Company, a growing economic force in Seattle, continued its contributions to Seattle Public Library's outstanding aeronautics collection; the airplane manufacturer inaugurated that support with a $500 gift in 1929. The Albert S. Balch Autograph Collection was front-page news for the library in 1931 when it added a signed photographic portrait of Italian dictator Benito Mussolini. The collection was increased by another 53 signatures (to 481) in 1933 and was recognized as one of the leading autograph collections in

Adding a signed photograph of Italian dictator Benito Mussolini to the Balch collection was front-page news in Seattle in 1931, almost a decade before World War II changed Mussolini's image forever.

America. Balch started his collection as a young man when he traveled the country for a national college fraternity and continued his quirky pursuit once he settled in Seattle, where the mustachioed fellow with trusty pen and autograph book seemed to approach every notable who arrived in the city. He even continued autograph hunting after his career in radio advertising sales had given way to a career in real estate in 1935. Balch later became a key developer of such north-end Seattle neighborhoods as View Ridge and Wedgewood.

The federal government did come to the aid of the ailing Seattle Public Library at the end of 1933, providing forty workers from the Civil Works Administration, who performed many of the necessary maintenance and laborer tasks at the library that kept up appearances of normalcy. Some of the library's routine clerical duties were carried out in 1935 by more federal workers, fifty-five women and girls employed by the Works Progress Administration (WPA). The relentless hardships at the

A linoleum block print of a Seattle street scene by artist Vera Engel was one of the artworks donated to Seattle Public Library under a program of the federal Works Progress Administration.

library were having a real impact on the outlook of its leader, although Jennings did play the key role in winning passage of the landmark State Library Act in 1935, which aimed to extend free library service to all residents of Washington. At his home library, Jennings had no hopes of pioneering anything. No longer was he even making an annual plea for expansion of Seattle's Central Library. Basic survival was the sole focus of Depression days at a public institution suffering like so many of its patrons, who were decreasing in number year after year. "If dreams were permitted regarding the future," a chastened Jennings wrote, "they would include visions of former services resumed or restored."[30]

Similar dreams motivated the library's long-suffering employees, who in 1935 took their first step toward someday forming a union when they established the Seattle Public Library Staff Association, which represented members from all departments. The Depression's economic free fall increased the number of workers seeking the safety net of organized labor. Unions demonstrating new strength were much in the local and national news, including the sometimes violent 1934 dock strike on the West Coast that halted all Pacific port activities and the historic 1936 strike against the *Post-Intelligencer,* in which the fledgling Newspaper Guild scored a stunning success against the newspaper's famed antiunion owner, William Randolph Hearst, the titanic news baron in New York City.

Seattle Public Library employees may have been much less militant in their organizing approach, in keeping with the civility of their profession, but they had plenty of grievances of their own as the Depression ground on. They had witnessed scores of fellow library employees shown the door, unilateral decisions that sometimes seemed to defy reason. They had seen their hours increased while their pay was reduced; their vacation hours were decreased as well. They had also watched in frustration as every other class of worker on the municipal payroll was accorded pension benefits except those at the library, a galling situation that had continued since 1929.

So there was much impetus for the formation of the staff association. The new group soon organized a series of committees with a twofold goal of studying staff problems and working to promote and improve library service. The association's first significant success came in 1937 when library employees were added to the city pension system after passage of a city charter amendment. Its second significant success came in 1938 when studies by the staff association, the library board, and outside agencies resulted in the December adoption of a new staff classification system for library employees and higher pay, some of which started to appear in employee paychecks in 1939.

Seattle Public Library's rebound from the Depression's gloom started to show distinct progress in 1938, although a June burglary at the Fremont Branch demonstrated that hard times had hardly disappeared. The only thing taken in the burglary, reported the *Post-Intelligencer,* was "an undetermined amount of pennies, collected as fines on overdue books."[31] In 1938, the Boeing Airplane Company's contributions to the aeronautics collection resumed after several years' absence. Books borrowed by the library's patrons in 1938 registered an increase over the previous year, the first time that had happened in several years but the sort of annual increase that had once been an accepted fact of Seattle Public Library life.

The glimmers of a brighter future were best symbolized in 1938 by the fresh paint applied throughout the Central Library and all the branches, the interior work again performed by federal employees of the WPA. The WPA also commissioned Seattle artists to create individual works that were contributed to the library's collection, works that ranged from prints to paintings to watercolors. Among the WPA artists whose works graced library walls were Edgar Forkner, V. P. Shkurkin, Fokko Tadama, Vera Engel, and Eustace P. Ziegler. There was more brightness added to the Central Library when a new, improved method of illumination called "indirect lighting" was installed in the aging Carnegie building.

The decade of the 1930s produced much agony and very little ecstasy at Seattle Public Library. The library's budget in the decade's final year ($340,140) still fell short of the library budget in the decade's first year ($380,428). Seattle's population showed a similar stagnation, gaining just 2,700 residents during the Depression decade to stand at 368,302 in 1940. When the library's next ten-year plan was published in that same year, it included the admission that only two of the seven goals from its predecessor ten-year plan had been accomplished over the course of the 1930s. The establishment of a municipal reference service in 1931 and the extension of pension benefits to library employees in 1937 were hardly the heart of the library's once bold dreams.

Librarian Jennings had stayed at the helm throughout the library's most diminished decade and responded to its daunting challenges with only modest success. The Depression had produced a definite toll on both the man and the institution. Progress could no longer be seen as the Seattle Public Library's inevitable birthright. "Whatever the 1940s may have in store for us," Jennings wrote in the final month of the difficult decade, "the 1930s stripped from us many of the follies of the youth of the century and taught us so many hard lessons that we approach its fifth decade without illusion."[32]

Don't Let That Shadow Touch Them

Buy WAR BONDS

CIVILIAN DEFENSE

Books in the Seattle Public Library

DEFENSE PRECAUTIONS

Air defence and the civil population, by Hyde and Nuttal.	614.82
Air raid defense, by Wachtel.	614.82
Air raid safety manual, by Leyson.	614.82
A bibliography of air raid precautions and civil defense, by U.S. Works Projects Administration.	R
Bombs and bombing, by Ley.	623.4
Civil air defense, by Prentiss.	614.82
Civil defence, by Glover.	614.82(R)
Civilian defense.	Published each month
Civilian defense reference number, by Architectural Forum, January 1942 issue.	614.82

INCENDIARIES

Fire defense, by Bond.	614.84
Fire from the air, by Zanetti.	623.4
Training manual for auxiliary firemen.	614.84

WAR GASES

Gas warfare, by Waitt.	623.4
Manual of high explosives, incendiaries, poison gases, by Fairhurst.	623.4
War gases, by Jacobs.	623.4

CHAPTER 6

The War Effort

SEATTLE PUBLIC LIBRARY'S slashed budgets during the 1930s had made one thing frightfully clear: the starved library could no longer depend solely on its city financing. Finding extra sources of money was imperative if the Seattle Public Library were ever going to rise above a level of aching mediocrity. That had not been accomplished by annual pleas from the librarian, no matter how urgent or well reasoned. Nor had it been accomplished by a forward-thinking ten-year plan, which generated widespread praise but little action.

ABOVE: Seattle Public Library joined the war effort in countless ways, including displays of war-related books that carried this eagle logo on stickers inserted into the recommended volumes.

OPPOSITE: The uncertainty of war and its many fears hung over the home front during World War II, with Seattle Public Library publishing various war information booklets to aid worried residents during the conflict.

The fiftieth anniversary of Seattle Public Library was celebrated in April 1941 with flower-bedecked festivities at the Fremont Branch, just seven months before the attack on Pearl Harbor staggered residents of Seattle and the rest of the country.

As Seattle Public Library neared its fiftieth anniversary in 1941, concerned library supporters decided to take matters into their own hands. They understood how the library's ability to meet the community's needs was determined by its budget. Librarian Jennings made that case with simple eloquence: "More money means better facilities that result in greater use."[1] Yet the level of city funding for Seattle Public Library was usually so woeful that the library had received the minimum per capita expenditure suggested by the American Library Association in just five years during its first five decades.[2] No one was more aware of the dire consequences of that parsimony than the library's own employees. They dealt daily with the crowded facilities, the disappointing collection, the frustrated patrons.

The Seattle Public Library Staff Association aimed to change that. One of the group's founding principles had been to promote and improve library service and that worthy goal led to concrete action in 1939. The staff association pledged then to help create an organization that would become known as the Friends of

the Seattle Public Library. Friends groups had already demonstrated their value at dozens of libraries across the country, rallying community support and providing resources and assets that had not come from city funds. But the staff association did not just issue a public call for formation of a Friends group in Seattle; it slowly laid the foundation for such a group, lunch by lunch.

At the association's instigation, small groups of citizens were invited to a series of free luncheons at the Central Library where they heard from a member of the library board, a branch librarian, and two or three department heads, so that the library's needs could be discussed in an informal setting that allowed for questions, concerns, and answers. These regular gatherings continued for almost two years until all this luncheon persuasion led, at long last, to a dinner. More than ninety people turned out at the College Club on January 16, 1941, when a dinner meeting was held to organize the Friends of Seattle Public Library. Members of the staff association were among those in attendance, as were members of the library board, but the defining characteristic of the assembly that evening was its breadth. Those drawn to the new group included, as the *Post-Intelligencer* observed, "writers—of which the city has a number of no uncertain fame—civic leaders, teachers and just plain 'customers' of the Seattle Public Library."[3] Cebert Baillargeon, president of the chamber of commerce, presided over the meeting, which also saw librarian Jennings offer his thoughts on the library's needs and the new group's potential to help meet those needs. Then its first officers were elected, all by unanimous vote, with Mrs. H. N. Gridley chosen as president and George Mathieu as vice president, plus two more officers and three executive board members. This Seattle group joined 200 other Friends groups across the nation that had followed in the 1922 footsteps of the country's first Friends group at the Glen Ellyn Free Public Library in Illinois (the number of Friends groups would grow to more than 2,000 in the ensuing decades). Seattle's chapter, organized with such diligence and care, was still a pioneer among large cities on the West Coast, preceding San Francisco by eight years, Los Angeles by twenty-two years, and Portland by thirty-one years.

The fledgling Friends of the Seattle Public Library set about their business at a gallop. The group's initial priority was planning festivities to celebrate the library's fiftieth anniversary, which was only three months away. That April date soon arrived and the Friends managed to sponsor a host of anniversary events, which were all the more impressive because they extended far beyond the confines of the downtown Central Library. Each of the ten branch libraries had its own celebration, under the auspices of a district committee of Friends. A Pacific Northwest writer made a personal appearance at each branch, as did other speakers during a busy week of open houses and teas. The culmination of the anniversary festivities came on the evening of April 22, 1941, when more than 700 people gathered in the Metropolitan Theater to hear a lecture by writer Emil Ludwig. The recent German émigré—author of popular biographies of such historical figures as Napoleon, Michelangelo, and Goethe—spoke on "education and democracy," a topic of ever increasing urgency as the tornado of war continued to roar across Europe.

The Friends of the Seattle Public Library pressed forward, building on the momentum generated by the successful anniversary festivities. A committee was formed to solicit library gifts and donations, with much optimism about their prospects. New members were courted and continued to sign up at such a steady rate that the group soon passed 1,000 members. Everything

seemed poised for increasing success as the Friends planned their first annual meeting, which was set to take place on December 8, 1941.

Seattle awoke on the quiet Sunday morning of December 7, 1941, and residents soon heard the shocking radio bulletins about the Japanese surprise attack on the American naval base at Pearl Harbor in Hawaii. The U.S. Congress declared war against Japan the next afternoon, following the stirring "date of infamy" oration of President Franklin D. Roosevelt, yet the Friends of the Seattle Public Library still held their annual meeting only hours later. The group's vice president, George Mathieu, told the subdued and anxious gathering what was already on most everyone's mind—that the advent of war would no doubt mean curtailing many of the group's activities. Not many minutes later came a symbolic confirmation of Mathieu's prediction when word of an immediate blackout in Seattle brought an abrupt halt to the Friends' annual meeting.

Once again, catastrophe had descended and would doom the best-laid plans of the Seattle Public Library. Once again, the library's future promise would have to be deferred to face a current crisis. The Friends' encouraging momentum was stalled, as was any consideration of the library's second ten-year plan, a thirty-three-page report titled "The People's University," which had been issued at the start of the year. It had urged spending $1.2 million for an addition to the aging Carnegie library downtown, as well as $350,000 to construct five new branch libraries. Jennings's urgent arguments on the library's behalf in the ten-year document had a hollow ring eleven months later amid a world in flames. Contributing to the war effort took precedence over everything else, in homes, businesses, and institutions all across the country, including the Seattle Public Library.

World War II altered Seattle in profound and enduring ways. The war turned the Boeing Airplane Company into an economic colossus. The airplane maker's employment levels grew at a staggering rate, rising from 10,000 workers to 30,000 in just the last six months of 1941. Boeing's employment would crest at 50,000 workers in 1944.[4] It was a different workforce as well. The manufacture of Boeing's much needed bombers, first the B-17 Flying Fortress and later the B-29 Superfortress, was not the sole province of white males any longer. A small story in the March 28, 1942, edition of the *Post-Intelligencer* was headlined "7 Girl Riveters Start at Boeing." Hundreds more of these "Rosie the Riveters" followed in the pioneering footsteps of Mabel Stowe, Gertrude Wagner, Madge Tompkins, Leona Evans, Edna Peterson, Luella Poten, and Lila Baer.[5] As one female

library patron, seeking written materials on this momentous change, remarked to a Seattle librarian in 1942, "This is the greatest opportunity women have ever had. It will do more for women than anything has ever done."[6] Seattle's first significant influx of African Americans came to the city during World War II, more than doubling the city's black population to 10,000 by the war's end. These newcomers were drawn not only by work at Boeing, especially once a 1941 presidential executive order banned discrimination in companies receiving government contracts. They were also drawn by work at the many shipyards in the Puget Sound region, which employed even more people than Boeing and produced warships and merchant vessels of all shapes and sizes.

Pride in these "Made in Seattle" contributions to the war effort carried over to the combined annual report of the Seattle Public Library for 1940-41, where the azure cover featured artful sketches of a Boeing bomber in the clouds and an advancing line of merchant ships on the seas below. This was the first time that any image other than the downtown Carnegie library had ever graced the cover of the annual report, a small gesture that reflected the library's commitment to helping the war effort in whatever way it could.

But that effort was not led much longer by librarian Jennings. He reached the mandatory retirement age of seventy in 1942 and left the library in June of that year. Jennings's tenure as the library's leader lasted an astonishing thirty-five years. In directing the institution, he became an institution himself, the face of Seattle's library recognized locally, regionally, and nationally. Jennings was leader during a period marked by trying challenges on many fronts. He provided stability with his quiet-spoken leadership, but often fought a losing battle, or at least a holding action, as the library's fate was ruled by powerful economic forces well beyond its walls. Despite continuing appeals, Jennings could forge no progress in providing any major solution to the Seattle Public Library's greatest problem—the overcrowded, inadequate, and dated downtown Carnegie library. It had become an albatross.

TOP: The soaring demand for Boeing bombers prompted the manufacturer to triple its Puget Sound workforce to 30,000 employees during the last six months of 1941, and Seattle would never be the same.

ABOVE: Marjorie Bradley (left) and Evelyn Holt install equipment in the tail section of a B-17; these two Seattleites were among hundreds of "Rosie the Riveters" who redefined the notion of "woman's work" at Boeing during World War II.

John S. Richards came from the library at the University of Washington in 1942 to lead Seattle Public Library after its thirty-five years under librarian Judson Jennings. Richards had no doubt about his responsibility to Seattle library patrons, saying, "To give them the best war information is our first duty."

Seattle's new librarian came from across the city rather than across the country, another indication of the library's difficult circumstances. John S. Richards, fifty years old, was associate director of the library at the University of Washington, the school where he had been an undergraduate. He completed his postgraduate studies at the New York State Library School and the University of California before he embarked on a career in university libraries, institutions removed from the hurly-burly politics of city libraries. Richards had advanced steadily in his career, another quiet sort of leader, a sometime wearer of bow ties, a husband and father of two sons who had a fondness for an occasional detective story. He had few doubts about his primary mission as Seattle Public Library's first new leader in decades. Upon his appointment, Richards stressed, "I feel it is a great responsibility to carry on the work, especially this wartime year when the public wants to know the facts about war, defense, how to do the job better. To give them the best war information is our first duty."[7]

The library responded with a host of war-related services and programs, some major, others minor. From the outset, the library extended free service to all military personnel in the area and to those working in Seattle's war industries. A special shelf in the Technology Department was set aside for books on civil defense. Classes for Red Cross training and air-warden training were held in many libraries, classes that drew more than 14,500 participants in 1942. The Friends of the Seattle Public Library sponsored a series of popular forums in the branches on living in a world at war and preparing for peace. Technical books were circulated to war workers throughout the region, from Kirkland to Renton to Bremerton. The best-received books on the war itself were duplicated by the library in considerable quantities, set aside in special displays, and highlighted in book lists that received wide distribution.

Yet the Seattle Public Library soon encountered much evidence that it was operating in a drastically changed world. Girls had to be enlisted to replace boys in many of the library's junior positions. Orders for foreign books dwindled down to a trickle as a result of bombings in England and the sinking of merchant ships at sea. One unfortunate order of foreign books bound for Seattle was lost aboard a ship that was sunk by a torpedo, then its replacement order on another ship was lost the same way. Reading habits of the library's patrons turned more serious and often technical, as did their more than 50,000 reference questions submitted annually, although there were still frequent inquiries about what had happened to the animals at the London Zoo during the Nazi blitz. ("Answer: They are still there except for poisonous reptiles and spiders, which were destroyed purposefully. Polar bears, lions and tigers are locked in specially constructed underground rooms."[8])

The greatest change at the Seattle Public Library was a precipitous decline in book circulation, a slide of 18 percent in 1942 to 2,322,229 volumes, a slide of another 13 percent in 1943. This great drop was caused by many factors, all related to what librarian Richards called "the dislocations which the war has brought to every citizen of our democracy."[9] Gas rationing limited car trips to absolute necessities. Evening dimouts in Seattle, which mandated reduced lighting, prompted fewer children and young people to use the libraries. Those working in the full-tilt war industries, especially on late-night shifts, had little free time for reading. Just working and surviving was the order of these daunting wartime days and nights.

TOP: First stop for Japanese Americans forced from their homes in Seattle was the fairgrounds in Puyallup, which had been renamed Camp Harmony.

ABOVE: Clarence Arai, a prominent Seattle attorney, tends a vegetable garden during his internment at Camp Harmony in Puyallup only weeks after ending a five-year term of service on Seattle Public Library's board of trustees.

But one group of loyal library patrons was most noted in its absence. As the careful wording in the library's 1942 annual report related, "The evacuation of the Japanese removed some of the best patrons the library had."[10] The forced relocation of the Japanese Americans from their homes on the West Coast into internment camps in the interior West took place in two painful stages for the 9,600 Japanese living in Seattle and King County. In April 1942, notices were posted on light standards throughout the area with "Instructions to All Persons of Japanese Ancestry." They were ordered to evacuate their homes, with only a week's notice, and were sent to a temporary assembly center called Camp Harmony that had been hastily constructed amid the surreal setting of the western Washington fairgrounds in Puyallup. Four months later, most were transported by train with shuttered blinds to the permanent Minidoka Relocation Center in the high sagebrush desert of southeastern Idaho, a bleak incarceration camp that was still under construction upon their arrival, the electrified barbed-wire fence finally installed under the watchful gaze of the imprisoned Japanese.[11]

Seattle Public Library did manage several small gestures to show its former patrons that they were not forgotten in their camps. The library sent 300 discarded children's books and 200 adult books to Camp Harmony; this small collection was widely circulated through the four camp libraries run by a young internee named William Makino. The library sent a more sizable collection of books to the permanent camp at Minidoka, including many books in Japanese, a collection so heavily used that it registered an impressive circulation of 6,680 in 1943.[12] (The loaned books were returned to Seattle Public Library by the internees after the war.) The library also continued to respond to written requests from imprisoned Japanese American students seeking information about colleges and universities outside the forbidden "war zone" on the West Coast.

Among the imprisoned Japanese Americans at Minidoka was Clarence Arai, a prominent Seattle-born attorney who was serving on the Seattle Public Library's board of trustees at the time of Pearl Harbor. Arai was the son of the second Japanese man to settle in Seattle and became a familiar civic figure after his schooling at Franklin High School and the University of Washington, where he received his bachelor's and his law degrees. Arai was also a reserve army officer, having won a commission as an infantry lieutenant in 1923, and was active in local and state Republican politics. Despite the growing anti-Japanese sentiments in Seattle during the months after Pearl Harbor, Arai did serve out the remainder of his five-year term on the library board until April 1, 1942. Mayor Earl Millikin did not reappoint him and, only weeks after his last library board meeting, Arai was among those Japanese Americans forced to leave the city with only what they could carry, even though he was then a captain in the army reserve. At Camp Harmony, Arai served in the important role of judge advocate, handling all legal affairs for his imprisoned compatriots, but also found time to tend a small victory garden of radishes, beets, lettuce, and onions, the once powerful attorney photographed there by the *Post-Intelligencer*, a solitary figure stooped over to tend his rows of vegetables like a truck farmer. The sad newspaper photograph foreshadowed what was to come for Arai, as he and other organizers of the Japanese American Citizens League (JACL) fell out of favor among fellow internees over their aggressive cooperation with American authorities and their attempts at quashing dissent within their own ranks. The conservative, pro-America stance of the JACL leadership even extended to reporting potential subversive activities in their community to the Federal Bureau of Investigation under a special committee headed by Arai.[13] So the JACL leadership had almost no influence once the internees had been resettled at Minidoka. That meant that Arai, in

a matter of a few months, had lost prominent positions on the library board and within his own community, a fall from grace laced with bitter irony—one position lost because he was seen as not American enough, the other lost because he was seen as too American.

World War II's costs and sacrifices continued to be driven home to Seattle Public Library. Just two blocks north of the downtown Carnegie building was the wide plaza in front of the Olympic Hotel that was transformed into Victory Square. Starting with its dedication on May 2, 1942, this open area on University Street was where crowds gathered to support the war effort with civic rallies and drives to sell war bonds or collect scrap materials for the war effort. A partial replica of Thomas Jefferson's Monticello served as a speaker's stand at Victory Square's west end and a host of Hollywood stars made appearances there, including Bob Hope, Betty Grable, Bing Crosby, Lana Turner, Ginger Rogers. Battlefield triumphs brought thousands to Victory Square, but so did more solemn occasions, the times when the names of more war dead from King County were inscribed on the seventy-five-foot replica of the Washington Monument that stood at the square's east end. The first forty names of those killed in action were unveiled on July 17, 1942, along with a famed quotation from Abraham Lincoln's Gettysburg Address ("We Here Highly Resolve That These Dead Shall Not Have Died in Vain"). Victory Square resounded with a heartbreaking volley from eight riflemen that first "Hero's Day," plus moving words from Mrs. E. L. Caskey, who placed a bronze wreath at the foot of the monument bearing her son's name. The names of recent war dead continued to be added in the months and years ahead until thousands of names covered the temporary monument, so many fallen fathers, husbands, and sons who would never see Seattle again.

The poignancy of the war's toll was also underscored by a single overdue book at Seattle Public Library in 1943. The usual overdue notices were sent out by the library to an army air corps enlistee who had neglected to return a book, but those notices went unanswered, resulting in a standard warning being issued in June by the city's corporate counsel. That letter was forwarded from army post to army post, more than a dozen in the succeeding months, all in the vain attempt to catch up with the military addressee, until the letter was finally returned to the corporate counsel's office in Seattle from an overseas unit. The letter was covered with postmarks from various army destinations, along with one final handwritten notation: "Missing-in-action, 11-17-43."[14]

Seattle Public Library struggled to meet the new demands of its changed patronage. Use of the library by individuals declined, but use by institutions soared. Government agencies, military units, and local war industries all needed assistance from the library, often under the great pressure of impending deadlines. There was no more regular or insistent customer than the Boeing Airplane Company. The airplane maker's engineering library ran a daily messenger service to Seattle Public Library's Technology Department, ferrying 1,688 volumes between the two libraries in 1942; 3,820 volumes in 1943; 4,293 volumes in 1944. Seattle Public Library even altered its lending policies to serve Boeing, including the circulation of reference works that usually never left the library.

So crucial did Seattle Public Library's assistance become to Boeing that the company sent an unsolicited letter to the library in 1944 that read in part: "It is increasingly evident that the personnel of our organization regard the reference facilities of the Seattle Public Library as a prolific source of technical information. There is no criterion for estimating the enormous value derived from the many items borrowed daily by our company library. However, we are confident that the mass of material borrowed during the past several years has performed a very definite part in the technical development of the Boeing Flying Fortress and the Boeing Superfortress."[15]

Seattle Public Library's war efforts did not mean that it simply accepted the loss of individual patrons. Starting in 1942, the library established a new network of small stations to serve those in the community who found it difficult to get to its regular branches or the downtown library. The first such station opened in the High Point Housing Project in West Seattle, at the suggestion of the executive director of the Seattle Housing Authority. Five more stations were established by the end of 1943, circulating more than 75,000 volumes to 2,288 new borrowers. Librarian Richards had added the energetic Laura M. Eberlin to head the Branch Department in 1943 after a decade-long vacancy. Eberlin observed in 1943: "We are becoming more and more

aware of the fact that people are unable to go any great distance for library service and keenly appreciate the small neighborhood station stocked with up-to-date and popular titles."[16] Eight more stations were added in 1944, bringing station circulation that year to 133,413 volumes. Neighborhood stations were the primary reason why the war's precipitous drop in circulation at Seattle Public Library was finally arrested and there was an increase of 6 percent in the library's overall circulation in 1944. Two more stations were added in 1945, bringing the total to sixteen, their supply of new books provided by a welcome infusion of $11,171 in aid from the state.

There were other encouraging developments at Seattle Public Library during the difficult war years. The changed racial landscape in Seattle resulted in an increased interest in magazine articles on what the library's 1943 annual report called "race prejudice and the treatment of the Negro in the United States."[17] A similar increase in interest in books on that subject was noted the following year. These matters were no longer considered academic concerns in a changed city that now boasted more than 400,000 residents, including increased numbers of racial minorities.

Race riots elsewhere in the country, coupled with rising racial tensions in Seattle's workplaces and streets, prompted Mayor William F. Devin to form a Civic Unity Committee early in 1944. This group was patterned after similar groups in Detroit and New York, where there had been race riots, and it included prominent citizens from various walks of life in Seattle.[18] Their charge was to investigate complaints of racial mistreatment in Seattle and thereby diffuse tensions before they built into a powder keg.

But seven months later, a deadly night of what was described as racial violence erupted at Fort Lawton in Magnolia, where the garrison included hundreds of black soldiers in segregated units who had grown increasingly angry over their treatment both on post and in the community. Even the Italian prisoners of war at Fort Lawton, the black soldiers came to see, were treated better. On the night of August 14, 1944, more than fifty black soldiers rioted and attacked a barracks housing some Italian prisoners. Several of the Italians were seriously injured in the attack and one was hanged from a tree, his lynching leading to a mass court-martial where twenty-three of the black soldiers were found guilty on various charges.

The Civic Unity Committee had no power to investigate the riot itself, since it took place on a military post, but the group did examine local press coverage and found that much of it was inflammatory and rife

World War II changed many things in Seattle, but it could not dim the enthusiasm of young readers, as is shown by this group of children eagerly awaiting the opening of the new storefront library in Magnolia in 1945.

with racial stereotypes, a surprising wake-up call to a white community that had been smug about its assumed lack of prejudice. The Friends of the Seattle Public Library mounted programs aimed at educating the citizenry on race matters the next spring when it held a popular series of nine noontime book forums on "racial minorities and race relations," a timely demonstration that the library could be a catalyst for positive social change.

The world war ground to a victorious close, at long last, in 1945. Germany surrendered on May 7, the end of the war in Europe prompting muted celebrations in Seattle amid worries over the unfinished conflict in the Pacific. Japan surrendered three torturous months

later, the end coming after two atomic bombs killed 120,000 residents of Hiroshima and Nagasaki; this stunning weapon of new technology included a crucial ingredient that had been developed at the super secret Hanford Project in eastern Washington. The end of the Pacific war on August 14 set off delirious victory celebrations in Victory Square and the surrounding streets of Seattle, all the deferred emotions of the war spilling out in crowds, confetti, horns, sirens, whoops, embraces, and kisses. One newspaper said of the pandemonium, "Happy humans—utterly unable to check their emotions —laughed even when great tears rolled down their cheeks."[19] The terrible times and feared tomorrows had finally come to a close.

Celebrants fill the streets of downtown Seattle as victory over Japan on August 14, 1945, signals the long-awaited conclusion of World War II.

CHAPTER 7

Postwar Growing Pains

PATRONS SOON RETURNED in droves to the Seattle Public Library, especially in the final three months of 1945. New borrowers increased by an impressive 50 percent. Part of the cause was the immense sense of relief at the end of World War II; it was as if people had suddenly been given permission to grasp for any remnant of their former lives before the conflict. But part of the rush to

ABOVE: An outdated elevator often hauled both freight and passengers, just one of the many deficiencies of the aging Carnegie library downtown.

OPPOSITE: Problems continued to plague the downtown Carnegie library, turning what had once been a showplace into a worn albatross.

the library was also caused by the new demands of the altered postwar world. Thousands of young GIs arrived home, their focus now on education, careers, and family, while women could again concentrate on normal domestic life, even if many harbored regrets about the lost sense of purpose and worth from their wartime work. Great adjustments had to be made in this fast-paced new life and current information was crucial. That need sent many people straight to the library, where their arrival revived arguments for an "aggressive" program of adult education.

Librarian Richards had long supported adult education, as had his predecessor. Richards reflected on the challenges of the postwar world and stressed, "It is the diffusion of information rather than the collection of material which will determine whether the library is an educational institution in its own right or merely a storehouse for books. If the library is to assume the function of an educational institution, it must develop a leadership which will make the library's influence penetrate far beyond the approximate one-third of the population who use its resources more or less regularly of their own accord."[1]

Seattle Public Library was a changed institution in many ways. It had been tested by the war, but also strengthened. Richards instituted better statistical record keeping, with annual reference questions tabulated for the first time in 1944 and totaling 138,291. He also selected new leaders in program areas too long neglected: Laura Eberlin to oversee branches and stations in 1942 and Eleanor Kidder to direct work with young people in 1944, after eight years in a similar post at Rochester, New York. The library took an overdue stride forward into modern times in 1943 when the Friends of the Seattle Public Library purchased a phonograph that allowed patrons to listen to their favorite records, most donated in the early years by two generous Seattle men, Leslie Reamy and Clarence McKee. The library also ventured onto the airwaves in hopes of increasing interest, producing two weekly radio shows that debuted in 1942, one for adults, one for children.

The library benefited from institutional advances in the area—the formation of the Pacific Northwest Bibliographic Center at the University of Washington to act as a clearinghouse for library collections in the region (the result of a $35,000 grant from the Carnegie Corporation in 1940) and the establishment of the King County Library System in 1943, with close ties and fees to Seattle Public Library stipulated under contract, along with the provision that Seattle would open its library doors to all county residents. The relationship between the two public libraries was further cemented when Ella McDowell, who headed Seattle Public Library's Municipal Reference Division, was selected as the county system's first librarian.

Yet all these advances still did nothing to solve Seattle Public Library's greatest problem—the woefully inadequate Central Library. Stopgap improvements continued to be made, such as the 1945 conversion of the second-floor lobby into a browsing room to showcase copies of new books and magazines in the library's collection. The popular Library for the Blind, with its recorded books and books in braille, was relocated from its cramped quarters downtown to the basement of the Fremont Branch in a renovated space paid for by the Friends group. But there still seemed no way to carve out the much needed community meeting rooms or auditorium that the aging Carnegie structure lacked.

What was changing was the library's thinking. The inadequacies of the central building continued to be underscored by Richards in the library's annual reports, even during wartime, but with a subtle shift toward the need for "a new and modern library." There remained the long-delayed expansion plan outlined in now-dusty architectural renderings by the local firm of Bebb & Jones, but the Carnegie building began to be seen as part of an expanded structure that would consign the old structure to nonpublic uses, such as the bindery. Even the main entrance to the library would be transferred to Fifth Avenue, in hopes that the Carnegie structure could be turned into the back room of bad memories.

Postwar thoughts of the library's patrons were focused on other matters. Reference questions in 1946 centered on such suddenly prominent topics as atomic energy and juvenile delinquency, yet there was also great interest in two topics that had often been kept under wraps during the sacrifices of wartime: sex and humor. Both had a new impact on Seattle's reading habits, with forthrightness about sex prompting interest in such topics as psychoanalysis and psychiatry. The desire for laughter propelled a Seattle author's book to the height of popularity among readers at the city's libraries and also around the globe. Betty MacDonald's *The Egg and I,* a madcap account of her young married life on a bare-bones chicken farm outside Port Townsend, was the perfect antidote to the grim realities of the war years.

Young readers had their own reading tastes, as librarian Eleanor Kidder reported: "At one moment, it

A sleek new bookmobile began making rounds in 1947; it was the first mobile service offered by Seattle Public Library since Depression budget cuts.

may be selection of sound books on poise and popularity suitable for a 16-year-old girl who is taking a glamour course which the anxious mother cannot afford for her daughter. The mother, having married at 15, feels her daughter must not suffer the handicaps she endured. Next it may be the belligerent or indifferent demand for the shortest book in the library by a sullen boy who hates school and loathes the printed word in any form except comics or the sports page. Occasionally, as a special treat, it may be the librarian's delight, the rare and earnest reader with perception and ability to absorb the best. Each is equally important and must be met as an individual."[2]

A nationally known program of Great Books discussion groups was initiated in 1947 at Seattle Public Library, with much fanfare and even a live radio broadcast over KOMO, and it drew 600 enthusiastic participants, plus a waiting list of 100 more. But the library was no longer a place devoted solely to books. The popularity of other media was transforming the institution, turning it from, as librarian Richards put it, "a popular circulating library to an information center . . . a workshop rather than a storehouse."[3] The great-

est circulation gains, a hefty 36 percent in 1947, were registered by such nonbook materials as phonograph records, art works, and films. The library's collection of documentary films numbered over 100 titles, with favorites that included *Jet Propulsion, Peoples of the Potlatch,* and *Meeting the Emotional Needs of Childhood.* These films were circulated to 2,197 borrowers in 1947 and shown to audiences "conservatively estimated at more than 85,000 people,"[4] thus extending the library's reach far beyond its loyal book borrowers.

Seattle, a city remade by astounding growth during the war and afterward, was charging ahead. By 1949, the population stood at 460,589, an additional 100,000 residents over the number at the start of the tumultuous decade. Seattle Public Library struggled to keep pace with the changing demands and tastes of a rapidly growing city that boasted its first television station (KRSC, later KING) in 1948 and its first citywide television broadcast—a high school football championship game on a rainy Thanksgiving, featuring a 6-6 tie between West Seattle and Wenatchee—that produced grainy images on an estimated 1,000 television sets in the city. Seattle Public Library unveiled its own advance in 1947, a new bookmobile that traversed the city for the first time since the Depression, this branch library on wheels of such sleek design that it invited comparison with the beloved ferry *Kalakala.* The bookmobile carried 2,200 volumes, half for children and half for adults, and it proved so popular that it distributed 109,318 volumes in its first full year of operation, a circulation comparable to a medium-sized branch library made of bricks and mortar.

But the bright, shiny bookmobile conveyed a mistaken impression of the institution whose name was emblazoned on its side panels. Seattle Public Library continued to be hamstrung by budget constraints. Its librarians were consistently paid the lowest library salaries on the West Coast, so staff recruitment and retention was a recurrent problem. The city librarian did not fare much better in salary consideration. Richards had not had a pay raise during the first five years of his tenure and was earning an annual wage of $6,360 in 1947. That salary was $1,100 less than the librarian was paid during the Depression and $2,100 less than the average salary paid to the leaders of twenty-one of the country's largest libraries.[5]

Attempts to improve the library's staffing and salaries seemed to have no more success than the attempts to replace the aging Central Library. An additional eleven staffers (six professional, five clerical) were included in the librarian's 1948 budget but did not win city council approval. Richards's patience was wearing tissue-thin. He had taken to describing the library's situation as "critical" and was warning of "service curtailment" if the situation did not improve soon. "The Seattle Public Library is operating in buildings and with approximately the same staff which were considered barely adequate before the Depression cuts sixteen years ago," Richards argued. "In the meantime, the city has grown approximately 30 percent in population, and new services have been assumed by the library in response to community needs."[6]

Then, at long last, came a modest turning point toward progress at the Central Library, a turning point that arose out of yet another setback. Plans for remodeling of the Carnegie building and construction of a book stack addition had advanced to the letting of bids for the project, but the bid opening in April 1948 told a familiar sad story: there simply was not enough money. The lowest bid exceeded the $700,000 budget by more than a quarter of a million dollars, thus scuttling the bid process and sending the project back to the drawing board in the office of architect John Paul

Jones of Jones & Bindon. The Seattle architect, hardly an impartial observer, reexamined the entire project and arrived at a conclusion that should have come as no great shock.

The 1906 Carnegie structure, Jones advised, was simply too outmoded in too many respects to merit remodeling. A two-tier book stack could indeed be constructed along Fifth Avenue, but it should not be an addition to the Carnegie. Instead, Jones argued that the book stack should be the first unit for an entirely new library building, modern, advanced, spacious. The book stack designed by Jones's firm would be no panacea; its space for 200,000 volumes would be immediately filled to capacity upon its planned completion in 1949. Far more important was what reconsideration of the book stack project had accomplished: it convinced the library board and library administration that the Carnegie's days were finally numbered. The board decreed that it would put a library bond issue before Seattle voters in 1950, a bond issue to raise $6 million for a new downtown library and $500,000 for five much needed new branches. The sighs of relief from the library's administration and staff might have been audible near Mount Rainier.

Even the forces of nature seemed to align in support of the Carnegie decision. A massive earthquake struck the Puget Sound region at midday on April 13, 1949, causing widespread destruction and eight deaths. Initial news stories proclaimed that the 7.1 magnitude quake had done "no apparent damage" to the Central Library, even though the lengthy temblor tumbled books off the shelves and forced evacuation of the old building.[7] Subsequent inspections revealed that the sandstone structure, held together only by its mortar joints, had suffered damage so serious that another earthquake of similar magnitude could result in what Richards described as "ultimate complete failure of the building."[8] The only question remaining about the Carnegie's future seemed to be whether the building would be brought down first by the action of natural forces or by Seattle voters.

Most library focus soon shifted to the upcoming bond election, the first library-funding measure ever submitted to Seattle voters. Other library matters of importance still did occur, including the closure of the longtime branch in Georgetown because of changing demographics and declining patronage. Also, property was purchased near the Broadway commercial district on Capitol Hill for a new branch to be named in honor of Susan J. Henry, the funds raised by the sale of a

Librarian John S. Richards led Seattle Public Library through three bond-issue campaigns in the 1950s, as well as the building of the first new branches in more than three decades. But his tenure ended in controversy and rancor.

Capitol Hill residential site donated in 1934 by her family. But most library eyes were focused on the bond-issue prize.

The Friends of the Seattle Public Library marshaled their forces in support of the measure. Informational brochures were printed and distributed, community forums organized, and forty-two well-briefed speakers were dispatched to more than 200 social and civic clubs. Librarian Richards upped the volume in his continuing pleas for support, emphasizing how no new branch had been built in three decades in Seattle and how the library's woefully inadequate facilities frustrated its attempts to keep up with the current "communication revolution" and the growth of the "mass media." "The $5 million bond issue," Richards emphasized, "is perhaps the most important single event in the history of the library."[9]

Media coverage of the library measure was sympathetic but wary, especially as the 1950 ballot filled to overflowing with funding requests from the state, county, city, and schools. A whopping $91.5 million was being sought from Seattle voters in a single election.

Once again, timing was proving to be the greatest enemy of Seattle Public Library. As the *Seattle Times* editorialized, "The Seattle Public Library clearly needs a new central building. New branch libraries are needed no less. The question is, must this be done now? Can it wait for less parlous [perilous] and less uncertain times?"[10]

Seattle voters went to the polls that November after five months of increasingly grim headlines coming from the Korean War, and amid another Red Scare spreading suspicion and fear. The economy had also soured. The voters' mood, as might be expected, reflected the times. Library supporters had urged a "yes" vote on the library's Proposition B with a campaign slogan of "Long Past Due—It's Up to You," but voters left little doubt that they were not "up" for any such tax burden. The library's bond issue needed a 60 percent approval rate to pass, but it fell far short, garnering just 40 percent. The crushing defeat saw 72,863 votes cast against the library bond, 51,722 in favor. Librarian Richards tried to mask his great disappointment about how "the single most important event in the library's history" had turned into such rejection. He told reporters, "We are going ahead cheerfully to give the best service we can in the old building, as long as we have to be here."[11]

Richards's immediate post-election analysis blamed the bond issue's defeat on the crowded ballot and the difficult times. But the librarian offered a more insightful critique several months later in the important trade publication *Library Journal,* with a three-page article titled "On Losing a Bond Issue." Richards argued that the election revealed a profound misunderstanding of Seattle Public Library's mission and financing. One of the most frequent questions asked by citizens before the balloting, he reported, was why the new library buildings could not be paid for with Andrew Carnegie money, even though that philanthropy had dried up decades before. There were even those voters who mistakenly assumed that Carnegie money paid the library's annual budget. Perhaps even more disappointing was the discovery that, as Richards put it, "large numbers of people are not library-minded, [people] for whom the public library is a cultural agency primarily for the use of someone else."[12] Richards believed that such profound stumbling blocks could be overcome at bond issue time only when the Friends of the Seattle Public Library had been transformed into as potent a political force as the Parent Teacher Association had been for the public schools. "The next time we are on the ballot,"

Richards recommended, "we would like our organized Friends to number thousands instead of hundreds, and we hope that this membership will reach into every section and interest in the community."[13]

Guy R. Garrison, a librarian from Kansas City, Missouri, made much the same points in a 1960 article, "Seattle Voters and Their Public Library." Garrison's thorough research for his doctoral dissertation led to this cogently argued conclusion:

> Analysis of the Seattle Public Library bond issue elections confirms what librarians have known all along, that the public library, when it must seek financial support at the polls, is the victim not so much of opposition as of apathy. The number of persons who are active users and active supporters of the public library constitute such a small percentage of the city-wide electorate that their active support is not great enough to carry an election. Not that a large number of voters actively oppose the library . . . the library faces only the somewhat negative attitude of the many voters who, while they approve of the public library in a general way, seldom use it, and are much more concerned with reducing their tax bills than expanding public library service. Good will is not enough to assure a favorable vote.[14]

The bond issue's defeat meant that the Carnegie library was not about to be replaced anytime soon, so accommodation with the aging structure became the new imperative as sweet hopes gave way to bitter realities. Seattle Public Library did have the good fortune to have $156,000 left over from construction of the book stack and that money was soon poured into emergency repairs and remodeling at the Central Library, with the approval of the Seattle City Council. Completion of the book stack had already had one dramatic impact on the old building, since the added space meant that a long-sought goal was realized in the first month of 1950. The old newspaper room was converted into the Gallery-Auditorium, a large area for community forums and exhibitions. Four noon lectures on art by renowned painter Mark Tobey were just one of the reasons why the Gallery-Auditorium drew 8,000 people to its events during the first year of operation. The library was finally becoming the community center that had been envisioned long ago by Judson Jennings, the late librarian whose lengthy service was memorialized in a bronze tablet unveiled in the Gallery-Auditorium during one of its first events. That new space was soon hosting events for such disparate groups as Great Books, garden clubs, Planned Parenthood, P.T.A. committees, and the Mental Hygiene Association. Films and lectures brought some of the largest crowds to the library, including a talk on "What Is Modern Art?" which drew an overflow crowd that included, as librarian Grace Stevenson put it, "all segments of the city's life: artists, teachers, students, housewives, businessmen, skid roaders."[15]

Other improvements at the Central Library followed after the bond-issue defeat, with cracks repaired, leaks plugged, paint applied, lighting updated, all in hopes of making the Carnegie building seem, at least, well maintained. The death sentence still hovered over the once-grand building, so it would never again be viewed in quite the same way. But necessity forced the library to make the best of the bad situation, covering its long-time frustration with a coat of bright new paint.

Not all news about Seattle Public Library was so bright. For a long time, the library seemed to have a propensity for sparking short newspaper stories that linked the institution with moments of distress or strangeness. It was as if the library were Seattle's own maiden aunt, slightly frumpy, a little eccentric, prone to various foibles and mishaps that prompted knowing glances and suppressed chuckles. One of those short news accounts occurred in 1948 when George Sargent, a twenty-nine-year-old truck driver, was arrested in his Ballard home and taken to city jail for possession of two overdue library books, after having received repeated notices, including a registered letter and a personal call by a library janitor. Sargent showed up later in municipal court with the missing volumes— *Storming the Bastille* by Alexandre Dumas and *Hell on Ice* by Edward Ellsberg—and paid $15.00 in court costs and $2.27 in overdue fines after insisting that he had borrowed the books for a friend.[16]

The flooding of the Magnolia Branch library in 1952 was the subject of another short account. It occurred when vandals took a garden hose used to wash down the street and stuck it through the library's front mail chute and then left it running. Librarians arriving at the branch found several inches of water on the floor, plus many soggy books—damages totaling several hundred dollars, all the result of what branch superintendent Laura Eberlin described as "certainly a dirty trick."[17]

Even more serious library matters sometimes received the same news brief treatment, including the imposition of state-mandated loyalty oaths in 1951, a popular Red Scare requirement that led to the firing of a junior cataloguer at Seattle Public Library. The city's civil service department distributed 7,800 loyalty oath forms to city employees and all were returned with signatures, except for six. Four of those six employees later set aside their reservations and signed the forms. Two steadfastly refused to sign, a clerk in the fire department because of his religious beliefs, and Jean H. Huot, who had come to the library after graduating from the University of Washington in 1949. Huot stressed, "I am unhesitating and complete in my loyalty to the United States, its Constitution and its free institutions. I believe that 'loyalty' by coercion is a menace to the freedom it purports to protect. If signing with a protest is not to be permitted, and I must sign and like it or lose my position, then I prefer to join the growing ranks of those who have chosen to interrupt their careers rather than compromise their integrity and professional ethics."[18]

Huot's courageous stand went unsupported by Seattle Public Library, just as Natalie Notkin's had two decades earlier. Huot finally did sign the loyalty oath form under protest, then submitted a letter of resignation. But that action came too late. Huot had already been dropped from the employee rolls by the library's auditing committee because she failed to comply with the requirements of the loyalty oath form.[19] Some legal wrangling ensued and Huot's resignation was finally accepted by the library board a week later, the close of another sorry little chapter in an institution dedicated to upholding civil liberties. But this era of fear and cowardice also tarnished the reputation of the University of Washington, where three tenured professors were fired in 1949 after public hearings and questions about their suspected communist leanings. Red Scares claimed all sorts of victims, some intended, many not.

Seattle Public Library moved ahead with its long-delayed building plans. Another bond issue was submitted to the electorate on March 11, 1952, but with one crucial difference. Gone was the proposal to replace the Central Library; instead, the reduced $1.5 million bond issue concentrated solely on building new branch libraries, seven in all, and making additions to two existing branches. This proposal was a well-conceived, neighborhood-pleaser brand of bond issue that seemed guaranteed to receive enthusiastic support in areas of the city slated to receive new branches. The Friends also geared up another pass-the-bond effort, led by an ambitious telephone campaign ("Operation Library") that had a goal of reaching 50,000 residents. Strong support came from community newspapers and the city's dailies. The *Seattle Post-Intelligencer* described the bond issue as "rock-bottom minimum" and "desperately needed."[20] The *Seattle Times* abandoned its editorial fence-sitting from the previous library bond issue and strenuously urged a "yes" vote after proclaiming, "This city's neglect of its public library system has become almost notorious."[21]

All this persuasive reasoning still did not have the desired effect. The library's $1.5 million bond issue ran aground on the daunting shoals of the 60 percent plurality required for passage. The distance to that approval standard had been dramatically narrowed in 1952, more than cut in half over the election in 1950. But the 53.6 percent approval rate for the smaller bond issue was not 60 percent by any stretch of the imagination. Still, the library administration and board took great heart from the 58 percent support that the bond issue had garnered in several areas of the city with the greatest library needs. They vowed to reward such devotion and approached the Seattle City Council for assistance. The council responded by adding $492,000 to the library's budget in 1953 for the construction of three new branches in those supportive areas. Three different Seattle architectural firms (out of twenty-two applicants) were selected to design these first new branches for Seattle's library in more than three decades, new branches that librarian Richards described, with odd understatement, as "something of a milestone."[22]

There was much for Seattle Public Library to celebrate in 1954 as the three modern branches opened in steady succession to enthusiastic crowds: first the Greenwood Branch in a January rainstorm; then the North East Branch in June; and finally the Susan J. Henry Branch on Capitol Hill in August, that branch also offering fine new quarters for the Library for the Blind. A second bookmobile also debuted in 1954, all these new library presences helping increase circulation by a hefty 10 percent over the preceding year. The beautiful North East Branch—an airy, light-filled structure designed by noted Seattle architect Paul Thiry—soon enjoyed the heaviest use of any branch in the entire Seattle system and retained that distinction for many years.

Yet all these signs of encouraging progress came only after the library had weathered yet another crisis, as so often happened in its history. There were times when the Seattle Public Library seemed a star-crossed hero in a novel by Thomas Hardy, a protagonist incapable of taking more than a few steps forward without a step or two backward. Once again, the step backward was prompted by a sudden budget problem. Opening three new branch libraries delivered sorely needed progress at the library, but it happened at a time when the

TOP: The new North East Branch, designed by noted Seattle architect Paul Thiry, opened in June 1954 and soon became the busiest branch of Seattle Public Library.

ABOVE: The new Susan J. Henry Branch on Capitol Hill, named for a woman whose family had donated property elsewhere in that neighborhood for a branch, opened in August 1954 and offered modern facilities as well as a new home for the Library for the Blind.

LEFT: The Harry Hartman Memorial Room in the Henry Branch had the comfortable appointments of a residential living room.

The cramped conditions in the outdated Carnegie library downtown were highlighted in attempts to win voter approval of bond issues to replace it.

city's budget was strapped by inflation as well as costs from the annexation of new neighborhoods in the north end. So instead of receiving a larger budget in 1954 for its expanded library system, the library faced a $50,000 cut mandated by the city council. This reduction posed a painful dilemma: the $50,000 was too sizable to be absorbed throughout the library system, which meant that some library program would have to be drastically curtailed or eliminated—but what program?

As librarian Richards later recalled, "There were three alternatives: To eliminate some part of the extension service through the new branches; drastically cut the book fund or otherwise interfere with service to the public; or reduce the hours of the central building. After careful consideration, the Saturday and Sunday closing at Central was considered the least disruptive expedient. . . . The library staff has unhappy memories of what happened during the Depression years when the book fund was slashed by two-thirds and the

library's clientele dropped away because so few new books were purchased."[23]

The weekend closure of the Central Library did save money but caused many problems. It was a public relations nightmare, provoking widespread and continuing complaints from inconvenienced citizens. It penalized the have-nots in Seattle, working people and students, whose busy schedules mandated weekend use of the downtown library; it rewarded the haves, those in the prosperous north-end neighborhoods, who could visit their sparkling new branch libraries. The weekend closure also exacerbated the grim problems at the Central Library, as the weekday-only service put added stress on its overcrowded facilities. The telephone switchboard jammed, library staffers struggled for workspace, patrons scrambled for seats. Saturday service at the Central Library resumed at the start of 1955, amid much relief, but not before Mayor Allan Pomeroy had blasted the city council for ordering the $50,000 cut that led to the weekend closure. It was, the mayor charged, "a petty economy."[24]

The weekend closures at the Central Library did have one significant benefit. They focused attention on its grave deficiencies as library backers began laying the groundwork for a third bond issue in 1956. Even the 1955 ascension of librarian Richards to the presidency of the American Library Association became an occasion to point out the problems of the Central Library. Any Seattle pride in Richards's leadership of the national organization should be tempered, the *Post-Intelligencer* editorialized, by "another good look at the sorry ruin at Fourth and Madison, the ancient pile we call our public library."[25]

Richards followed in the footsteps of predecessor Judson Jennings as head of the professional organization that had grown to a membership of 20,000 librarians. Richards had long held national ambitions and had steadily worked his way up through a series of positions on ALA subcommittees and committees. So when his turn to lead finally came, Richards pursued his presidential duties with gusto, especially the opportunity for travel. In the fall of 1955, he flew off on a six-week transcontinental tour through libraries in the South and meetings there with fellow librarians. Richards returned to Seattle in November, invigorated by what he had discovered in what had long been derided as a backwater part of the country, but he was also disheartened by what he confronted when he resumed work at the Central Library. "Seattle is the last major city doing business in such an inadequate building," Richards stressed in a newspaper interview upon his return.[26] The observation may have been the truth, but it also displayed a certain political naïveté or perhaps hubris on the part of Richards. There was something unseemly about a city official coming back from a national tour, outside his real job responsibilities, and then telling his fellow Seattle residents just how shabby things were at home.

Just a week later, the Seattle City Council voted to put a $5 million library bond on the upcoming March ballot, with replacement of the Central Library as its main goal and any leftover money available to build new branches. The bond campaign soon began in earnest, strengthened by what had been learned in two previous elections. Support was widespread and influential. Key organizations not only endorsed Proposition 2, they also worked diligently for its passage, with support coming from the Municipal League, the Seattle Chamber of Commerce, the Central Labor Council, and the Seattle P.T.A. The newspapers trumpeted the library's case, both in repeated editorials and in elaborate photo spreads spotlighting the deplorable conditions at the Central Library. "Downtown Library in Danger of Falling Down," warned a front-page headline in the *Post-Intelligencer,* along with an inside page of photographs published less than two weeks before the election.[27] "Our Dilapidated Library,"[28] declared the *Seattle Times* in a headline accompanying its photo page just two days before the election. The newspaper photographs provided a pathetic portrait of the institution's centerpiece, with its overtaxed public elevator, its mail sacks delivered through an open window in the absence of a loading dock, and grim-faced library patrons and staff members looking as though they were being forced to serve life sentences in Alcatraz. Any Seattle resident daring to vote against the library bond, all this coverage implied, was guilty of gross civic negligence.

The voters finally did respond, with 86,509 votes cast in favor of the library bond, 49,139 votes against, part of the largest turnout ever for a municipal election in Seattle (180,000 votes cast). The difficult 60 percent standard required for passage of the library bond was surpassed in two-thirds of the city's census tracks, and the overall favorable vote registered 63.8 percent, a margin of victory that was thicker than a whisker, but much short of a landslide, despite all the high-profile pleas on the library's behalf.

Librarian Richards was relieved and gratified by the result, but wasted no time savoring the library's long-awaited victory. Only hours afterward, Richards took the first step toward building a new downtown library when he convened a special meeting of the library board to discuss the architectural plans for the structure. The 1950 plans prepared by the Seattle firm of Jones & Bindon were still on the table and those sketches of the exterior had been prominently displayed in two election campaigns, although Richards did voice some doubts about their current suitability: "They are good preliminary plans. But there have been advances in library architecture during the past six years and we want to be sure to have the best plans."[29]

This moment of singular triumph for Seattle Public Library soon turned into nine months of disaster and embarrassment for the institution. It readily became apparent that deciding on the "best plans" for building a new Central Library would be the subject of a bare-knuckled power struggle between the librarian and the library board, a struggle that started over the hiring of an architect for the new building but soon escalated way beyond that as many long-festering differences flared in full public view. Day after day, the bitter wran-

PLACE OF LEARNING, PLACE OF DREAMS

gling played out in the newspapers, often on the front pages, one startling development followed by another and then another. It was riveting drama, but verging on soap opera.

Librarian Richards set things in motion when he supported the hiring of Jones & Bindon as architects in recognition of their previous study and sketches for the Central Library. The library board did not immediately second his choice, and Richards was so miffed that he took his case to a closed-door meeting with the Seattle City Council and Mayor-elect Gordon S. Clinton. The library board was not pleased with the librarian's power play either. The board, in an executive session that very evening, met without Richards present to discuss policies. Much verbal sparring erupted. Board member Anne H. Goodfellow was Richards's fierce supporter and had accompanied him to the city council tête-à-tête. New board president Frank McCaffrey was Richards's prime critic, and he was joined by his board ally, J. Donald Sullivan. "I'm not here for an inquisition," Goodfellow snapped, before refusing to answer fellow board members' questions about Richards's meeting with the council. "If Richards is going to sulk and run off to City Council," countered Sullivan, "he's going to destroy his usefulness in helping to plan this library."[30]

Richards, in a written statement, contended that "the only point at issue between the board and the librarian has had to do with the method of interviewing architects."[31] McCaffrey, in a statement, heralded his discovery that Jones & Bindon had received $85,000 for its library design work over the past decade, plus the fact that the firm had an outstanding $7,064.02 memorandum of debt incurred for its work on the new Central Library. Goodfellow, in an interview, castigated unnamed board members for "confused thinking" caused by what she characterized as "excessive absenteeism" in recent years.[32]

The situation only became more contentious. The library board decided to have architect interviews conducted by an executive committee of two board members, then encountered criticism and instead decided to have all members present. The board began its first of more than twenty planned interviews with interested local architects, led off by Jones & Bindon in a closed executive session with Richards present, but reporters were barred from attendance and another flap ensued. The lame-duck mayor appointed a new member to replace Goodfellow, whose term had expired, only to have the appointee decline her appointment one day later, citing the board-librarian controversy, which she described as "a sickening thing."[33]

The Friends of the Seattle Public Library threw the group's moral weight into the fray, passing a resolution that urged the library board to "at all times seek the help and counsel of librarian Richards in all phases of the new library's planning and construction. His specialized training, his contact with other famous American libraries and his national standing as president of the American Library Association should not be ignored."[34]

Then came the real shocker of the controversy. The sixty-four-year-old Richards may have consulted on new libraries built in Denver, Milwaukee, and Minneapolis, but he was not going to bring that expertise to Seattle's new Central Library. Richards announced his intention to end his tenure in a few months, and he made his plans known in a blistering letter of resignation that delivered a series of body blows to the library board. He wrote:

> My decision to resign is based entirely on the complete breakdown of relationships between the Board and the Librarian. I refer, of course, to meetings being called without the knowledge of the librarian and his exclusion from meetings of the Board, on occasion. Furthermore, the librarian is not now being consulted as to what business should come before the Board. . . . We here feel that incalculable damage has been done the institution because of the controversy and the misrepresentations and misunderstandings which are circulating in the community. At this point, I am forced to conclude that the Board, as constituted, is not qualified to administer the affairs of the library. . . . Under these conditions, I can no longer continue the professional work for which I was employed fourteen years ago, nor could I perform my part in the planning of the new building.[35]

McCaffrey counterpunched, disputing Richards's contentions and also asserting that the board had no reason to go along with Richards's assumption that there had been a gentleman's agreement requiring that the Central Library design be awarded to Jones & Bindon because the firm had done some library work in 1948 for which it had not been paid. The battle was suddenly *mano a mano*, one bowtie-wearer versus another, as McCaffrey unloaded on Richards: "I was quite surprised that the librarian would lose his executive composure to such an extent as to lose all regard for truth and factual records. He has made recriminative accusations against the board, as individuals and as a group, that are utterly false and intended only to show himself as a deeply injured person. If the librarian were less emotional and more cooperative, most of his perplexities would not exist."[36]

The five new members of Seattle Public Library's board of trustees meet with librarian John S. Richards (back to camera) on July 9, 1956, in the wake of the bitter, nine-month controversy over the new Central Library that led to the replacement of their predecessors. The trustees are (from left) Arthur Gerbel Jr., Dorothy Bullitt, Wayne C. Booth, Harry L. Carr, and Ada W. Hartman.

A battle royal ensued, with many supporters rallying to Richards's cause, including Mayor-elect Clinton, the library staff association, the library department heads, the state library association, even the ALA. Richards, sensing momentum in his direction, suggested there was a definite possibility that he might withdraw his resignation—if a new library board were appointed. The library board, also sensing the momentum, declined to accept Richards's resignation and passed a McCaffrey motion pledging to work in harmony with the librarian in the future.

Then Richards responded by insisting that he would quit anyway. Then two members of the library board, Sullivan and John J. Eckhardt, resigned nine days later, with Eckhardt asserting, "The library system has become the personal property of Richards. . . . I bid fond farewell to the democratic processes of the public board in Seattle. It has ceased to exist except as a shadow."[37] A third member of the library board, Emil Lains, resigned two days later, leaving McCaffrey as the sole remaining member and under great pressure to resign himself, but he was resistant, even defiant. The city council fired McCaffrey on a unanimous vote and Mayor Clinton, in one of his first orders of his term, named a new library board with five replacements.

All this posturing and chaos had happened in just three months, so it was not surprising that the new library board followed a go-slow policy aimed at providing "a fresh, unemotional approach."[38] That motivated

one of the board's first actions, a postponement of any consideration of Richards's still-tendered resignation, allowing the librarian to continue his service beyond his announced departure date of August 1, 1956. The new board moved ahead, making a brief misstep when it stated that it would consider other sites for the downtown library, a startling move quickly rescinded after being overruled by the city council. Then the board steadied itself with the appointment of three outside experts to study the building plans. It also leased the former headquarters of Puget Sound Power and Light Company at Seventh and Olive to serve as a temporary library during the razing of the Carnegie structure and the construction of its replacement. In mid-December, in what must have seemed like a holiday gift to a library-battered city, the new board announced two dramatic decisions. It appointed assistant librarian Willard O. Youngs to replace Richards, with the librarian finally scheduled to retire thirteen months after his original date. The board selected Jones & Bindon as the architects of the new Central Library, assisted by associate architects Decker, Christenson, and Kitchin.

The nine-month nightmare at Seattle Public Library was finally over. It was difficult to conclude that the whole bitter controversy had been much more than, in Shakespeare's phrase, "sound and fury signifying nothing." Granted, the various verbal wounds had left some blood in the newspapers and a new library board installed in office. But the whole affair had produced stunningly little change. The choice of Jones & Bindon to design the new Central Library, the original source of the controversy, had been reaffirmed. Librarian Richards, who disclosed his plans to retire in three years in a little-noticed comment at the time of the bond-issue victory, ended up leaving his post just eighteen months earlier. And his successor turned out to be his forty-six-year-old deputy, who surely would have been a strong candidate to replace him whenever he departed.

The one real casualty in the controversy was Richards's once-sterling reputation. He did achieve his long-standing goal of national stature and respect, but his fifteen-year tenure at his home library was forever sullied by a high-profile battle with the library board. Richards's wishes for the new Central Library would be followed ultimately, but his method of achieving his goals ("rule-or-ruin," in McCaffrey's apt phrase[39]) had proved painful and divisive for the community. Richards's britches had gotten too big for Seattle, it seemed, and that led to several climactic months when the librarian's actions ran roughshod over important tenets of public service.

ABOVE: The former headquarters of Puget Sound Power & Light Company was leased to provide temporary quarters for the downtown library during demolition and replacement of the old Carnegie structure.

BELOW: Voter approval to finally replace the downtown Carnegie library prompted this banner of gratitude over its front entrance.

CHAPTER 8

Celebration and Tumult

QUIET PURSUITS appealed to Willard O. Youngs, Seattle Public Library's new leader. He was a dedicated librarian and a dedicated sailor, too. The forty-six-year-old native of Berkeley, California, had advanced through a progression of posts at West Coast libraries, from Berkeley to Stanford to San Diego, and finally to Seattle Public Library in 1948, where he headed the Reference Department before becoming assistant librarian in 1950. Sailing was another constant in his life. He was a navy

ABOVE: Willard O. Youngs took over as the head of Seattle Public Library in 1957 and brought a smooth-the-waters approach to the job after the hurricane of controversy that had ensnarled his predecessor.

OPPOSITE: An early drawing of the new Central Library by the Seattle architectural firm of Bindon & Wright showed that the structure would represent a total departure from the Carnegie.

from 4th Ave.

officer serving aboard the battleship *Oklahoma,* based in Honolulu, and he continued that pursuit in civilian life. Sailing suited the temperament of the man widely known as "Bill." Youngs was steady handed, unflappable, conservative, and polite—a popular, well-groomed figure with professorial glasses who was described in a 1955 issue of the library's staff newsletter as a "combination of scholar and a sailor...a man of understanding, good humor, patience and erudition."[1]

These were qualities that the Seattle Public Library needed in a leader after the bitter public controversy over Richards and the new Central Library. Youngs demonstrated that in his first comments after taking over as librarian on August 1, 1957, displaying a much needed confidence and calm-the-waters approach. "When you've spent your life in the library field and have had as good a chance to get acquainted with this library as I have," Youngs commented, "there isn't much to worry about."[2]

Richards had still been in his post to supervise the move to the temporary library at Seventh and Olive, a massive, five-week undertaking that was performed mostly at night and on weekends. The library's book collection was split roughly in half, with 350,000 volumes moved to the temporary library site, along with all usable shelving and furniture, and 300,000 volumes remaining in the new book stack addition at the old library. The staff took much pride in providing normal library service throughout the momentous move, with no public department closed down for more than a day. The well-planned library move went more smoothly than many home moves, with just one problem popping up into public view. The snake-bit Richards was forced to defend the use of reject Olympia Beer cartons to transport books in the move ("it meant a saving of $360," he said after complaints[3]) before he trundled off into the sunset of retirement and his planned rendezvous with *Tom Sawyer, Huckleberry Finn,* and *20,000 Leagues Under the Sea.*

The walls of the old Carnegie library soon came tumbling down, as the 1906 structure was demolished, its once imposing facade razed into a pile of sandstone rubble along Fourth Avenue. The $52,400 demolition project proceeded with relentless attacks on the structure, exposing the massive front pillars as nothing more than ornamentation, enveloping the area in a cloud of deconstruction haze. But the old, earthquake-wounded edifice still proved a hearty foe for steel wrecking bars wielded by an army of well-muscled men in hard hats. Few tears were shed as the long-derided library was turned to dust, its grand rooms and stately staircase

consigned to memory, much like the long-dead philanthropist who had stunned Seattle with this fortuitous gift. The prevailing sentiment of 1957 was: gone at last was this place of civic pride turned to civic embarrassment. A reporter with the poet's name of Robert Browning was assigned to write the old building's obituary for the *Post-Intelligencer,* and he responded with something approaching poetry, although he could not resist referring to the historic structure one last time as "a moldy barn."[4]

Browning went on to sing the praises of the modern library to come on the old library site as he peered into his reportorial crystal ball: "The people will use it as they used the old one—to read for fun, to read to forget, to read to learn—the young children and the old men, the bright and the dull and the middling and the sweethearts in the quiet reading rooms who write each other eager little notes when they should be taking notes instead. Then 50 or 60 or 70 years from now, someone will decide the hideous old library should be replaced."[5]

Youngs had more immediate concerns. He had started his tenure with a generous $10,000 annual salary granted by the library board, but he soon found himself required to perform a balancing act worthy of a circus acrobat. His administrative attention had to be divided between the functioning of the current downtown library, split between two operating sites, and the planning for the new downtown library. Revised plans for the new library were submitted by Bindon & Wright (successor to Jones & Bindon) in the first weeks of Youngs's leadership, with space for books increased from 750,000 volumes to 970,000, but three planned floors were deleted from the design long displayed in public. The revised building of 175,000 square feet had more style, with a greater use of windows and more welcoming entrances, yet it was also a less imposing structure that did indeed look as though some missing ingredient could have provided more graceful proportions. That imbalance could be rectified with the addition of the deleted three floors when the space might be needed, perhaps in twenty years, as Youngs estimated.

The temporary library presented its own challenges. The most popular titles in the library's collection had been relocated to the temporary library, but other requested titles had to be fetched and ferried from the book stacks blocks away. Seattle Public Library's newspaper reading room, one of its more popular features, had remained open at the book stacks, causing some confusion and also depriving the temporary location of many potential visitors. The lack of meeting rooms or an auditorium in the temporary library forced popular

programs to be suspended or relocated to the branches, further eroding its use. There was also the frustrating matter of public knowledge about the temporary site. As Blanche Smyth, head of the General Reading Department, admitted, "It was evident that although the address of the new location was widely advertised, both before and after moving, the public seemed completely unaware of the change."[6] Circulation, as a result, plummeted through most of the year.

Youngs soon put his leadership stamp on Seattle Public Library with a series of decisions. An early Youngs appointment was Robert Gilkeson as the library's coordinator of television and radio. This new position recognized the library's enthusiasm for working with new media and its unstinting efforts to expand the reach of adult education programs. The library had premiered a television show (*The Challenge*

Two workers tear into the ornamental front pillars of the downtown Carnegie library during its demolition in 1957.

Attendance at the temporary downtown library was hampered by the fact that much of the collection remained in stacks at the old library site and had to be ferried back and forth between two locations.

Seattle Mayor Gordon S. Clinton (right) gets an assist from Wayne C. Booth, library board president, during the traditional groundbreaking ceremony for the new Central Library, while librarian Willard Youngs watches their joint attempt to turn the hard ground.

of Books), a weekly half-hour discussion focusing on a single title, in the fall of 1954 on KING-TV, such an innovative idea that it merited a grant from the American Library Association. The library also played a signal role in the early years of KCTS-TV, acting as one of the coordinating agencies during the 1955 start-up of the local public television station and producing a popular series on Great Books. There was angry finger-pointing in 1957 at laggard American institutions in the wake of the shocking launch of *Sputnik,* the Soviet space satellite that first circled the globe. But Seattle Public Library was not among the guilty public agencies, having long demonstrated its willingness to utilize new technology.

Excitement about the new Central Library continued to build, as the Carnegie structure disappeared in truckload after truckload of Tenino sandstone rubble (asking price: $20.00). Ground was broken for the new Central Library on June 17, 1958, with Mayor Gordon S. Clinton requiring the assistance of Wayne C. Booth, library board president, in order to get the traditional shovel to finally loosen some of the hardpack earth. This semi-embarrassing moment with two men laboring over one shovel seemed another symbol of the new library's difficult birth. The shovel struggle was depicted in a newspaper photo on the same day that teen heartthrob Ricky Nelson performed two evening shows at Seattle's Orpheum Theatre, riding the crest of his new number

one hit, "Poor Little Fool." Soon, the newspapers were tracking the new library's construction progress with headlines heralding percentage of completion—35 percent, 65 percent. What had long been described as a $2.9 million library was soon pumped up to a $4.5 million library, the larger figure reflecting the inclusion of costs for demolition of the Carnegie structure, the move to the temporary library, and other fees, including that of the architects.

Some setbacks did bedevil the new library's construction, setbacks of a strangely elemental nature, including earth (a thirty-foot cave-in during excavations), water (a shipping strike in Italy that imperiled delivery of decorative mosaics), and fire (a blaze that gutted the home of James FitzGerald, sculptor for one of the library's four new signature artworks, badly damaged in the fire). But the library's cornerstone was installed without incident in a public ceremony on September 22, 1959, after a contest sponsored by the Friends that awarded $10.00 to the Society of Women Engineers for their winning suggestions of what to enshrine in the traditional cornerstone box, contents that included $2.91 in change, a photograph of a Boeing 707 passenger jet, reports from the library itself and the upcoming Century 21 Exposition, and photographs of the Alaskan Way Viaduct and the Seafair Parade. Plans for the gala luncheon at the Olympic Hotel during the grand-opening festivities were in the capable hands of seventy-four-year-old Josephine Quigley, a legendary library figure in Seattle. She helped found the University of Washington's library school early in the century and later served nearly two decades on the Seattle Public Library's board, including fourteen years as its president. Quigley finally left the board in 1953, after compiling a record of service so exemplary that she was the first Seattle resident to receive the national Citation of Merit for board trustees from the ALA.

The long-awaited day for Seattle Public Library finally arrived. The grand opening festivities on March 26, 1960, began with the Friends' Olympic luncheon, which drew nearly 1,000 local dignitaries and library supporters to hear an address by Professor Giovanni Costigan of the University of Washington. Then, with full stomachs and unsated curiosity, celebrants marched two blocks to the library, where dedication ceremonies were scheduled at 1:45 P.M. The day's first library visitors had already ventured inside. Fifth and sixth graders from two Seattle schools were given a tour of the new building before squaring off in the auditorium for the 260th edition of the popular school quiz show *Quizdown*, sponsored by the *Post-Intelligencer* and KOMO-TV. The students' tour and quiz show (won by West Queen Anne Elementary) were broadcast live as part of an hour-long KOMO show that employed four cameras to capture the grand opening from the wide-eyed perspective of schoolchildren.

The public's turn came at 2:00 P.M. after a mercifully short dedication ceremony, a stark contrast to the marathon night of speech making that had opened the library's Carnegie predecessor on the same site. There were just fifteen minutes of brief comments

Work progresses on the new Central Library in this view from across Fourth Avenue.

LEFT: Bright and spacious places to sit, read, and, yes, smoke were provided when the new Central Library opened in 1960.

BELOW: Glen Alps's abstract metal screen greeted visitors near the auditorium of the new Central Library.

and stylized gestures, with Mayor Clinton praising the library as "a symbol that people can work together,"[7] then handing a gold key to board president Booth, who presented it to librarian Youngs, who then performed the ceremonial unlocking of the library doors. That action came none too soon, since the waiting crowd had grown to hundreds of people starting to press forward toward the doors with, as one newspaper reported, "an almost solid mass of squashed noses against the clear glass."[8]

Then the throng rushed in to inspect what twenty-one months of construction had produced. Many people were stunned by the library's striking ultra-modern design, the broad expanses of solar glass, the colorful mosaics, the sleek furniture, the earth-tone accents, the spacious open areas, the recessed fluorescent lighting, the exterior terraces, and the first escalator ever installed in a public library, a cause of noise concerns for some librarians until it was discovered that the moving stairs made "little more noise than the fluttering pages of an oversize book."[9]

The new Central Library's design would not go on to win many plaudits from architectural critics or prizes from architectural organizations, who found this early Seattle expression of the International Style to be functional, yet undistinguished.[10] But to those in Seattle used to the library's well-worn Carnegie predecessor, it was as though they had suddenly been transported

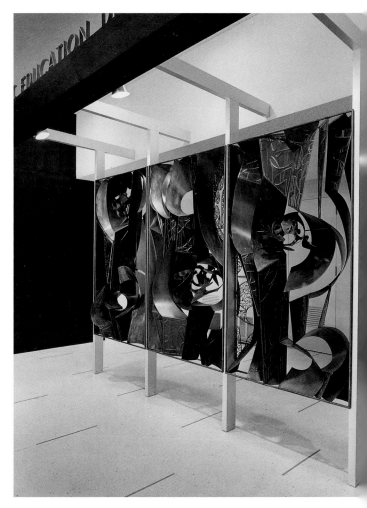

into the Tomorrowland section of Disneyland, which had opened five years before in Southern California.

They gawked, they pointed, and they paused in their tracks, and nowhere did that happen with greater frequency than at the library's four commissioned art pieces. This public art was one of the new library's true innovations, the first extensive use of art to complement a new public building in Seattle. The library board's bold commitment to public art came fifteen years before a Seattle ordinance began to require such art in new public structures. The library's four major works of modern art by Seattle artists were placed strategically throughout the glistening new building. Glen Alps's metal screen, *Activity in Growth,* was near the entrance to the auditorium; James FitzGerald's twenty-seven-foot glass-and-metal screen, severely damaged in the fire at his studio but reconstructed, was opposite the library's main entrance off Fourth Avenue; Ray Jensen's bronze sculpture of three fused hurdlers, *Pursuit of Knowledge,* was atop a pedestal on the third-floor rooftop terrace outside the children's department; and George Tsutakawa's twelve-foot *Fountain of Wisdom* was just outside the library's secondary entrance off Fifth Avenue.

Grand opening visitors streamed into the library past Tsutakawa's fountain on the breezy afternoon, with few taking much time to experience the soothing cascades of water over its shapes of bronze. They would not discover

until later how much pressure the fifty-year-old sculptor felt with this $18,000 library commission or what it would mean to his future career.

Tsutakawa was a Washington native son, born in the family's home on Capitol Hill on February 22, 1910, his first name a result of being born on the birthday of George Washington. He started his schooling in Seattle, then continued it for a decade in Japan, the two countries of his formative years influencing his art for decades to come. Tsutakawa returned to Seattle late in his teens and studied at Broadway High School and the University of Washington's Department of Art. His own career as an artist endured a series of detours caused by financial, familial, and societal obligations.

None presented a greater challenge than World War II. Tsutakawa was drafted into the army as an American-born citizen, while many others in his family were shipped off to internment camps, his uncles and their families to the Minidoka camp in Idaho, his sister to the Tule Lake camp in California. He did manage to visit his sister there during the war years, experiencing that disorienting schism endured by many Japanese American families, with some of the family members in uniform to defend the very country that was imprisoning other members of the family. During his visit to the internment camp, Tsutakawa found his family "living in meager but decent surroundings, and not as demoralized as he expected."[11] He also found, during his visit to Tule Lake, the woman who would become his wife, Ayame Iwasa.

Tsutakawa was fortunate to spend his entire army service within the United States, spared from shipment overseas with a combat unit at one point because of minor surgery and his advanced age. At the war's conclusion, he returned to Seattle, where he began graduate studies in art at the University of Washington, using his veteran's entitlements from the G.I. Bill, as did so many returning servicemen. His career soon was advancing on a dual track, as he taught art at the university and created his own art in a variety of media—drawing, painting, and sculpture.

Crucial to Tsutakawa's artistic development was an unlikely source—a gift copy of William O. Douglas's 1952 book, *Beyond the High Himalayas.* The U.S. Supreme Court justice from Washington described the Tibetan stone towers known as *obos,* which were created by travelers who placed a stone or two on these rock piles in order to mark a successful mountain passage or honor a place of beauty or of sacred significance.[12] The elemental nature of *obos* resonated in Tsutakawa's soul. He was taken by the way in which, as he said, "they honor the earth and point to heaven."[13] There followed a series of successful Tsutakawa sculptures based on *obos,* a series that produced much notice and many purchases by museums and influential collectors. It also brought him to the attention of the Seattle Public Library board of trustees as they made plans for the new Central Library.

The board envisioned a small fountain for the library's auditorium, but Tsutakawa soon balked at that concept. He instead proposed a fountain for the plaza entrance off Fifth Avenue, which was already under construction. The artist won over the building's architects and the library board with his hurried charcoal sketches for the plaza fountain. Then, problems arose. Tsutakawa had no doubts about the artistic concept behind the fountain; it would be an *obos* sculpture with the addition of water, what he described as "the most mysterious and elusive element in the natural world."[14] But creating his first fountain had its own mysterious and elusive elements for Tsutakawa, who grappled with a series of technical problems, adding new pressure to his awareness that Seattle had not seen a new fountain in more than a quarter century.

"It was a big gamble and I was it," Tsutakawa recalled a decade later. "I knew all the time that if I did this fountain right, it would be the beginning of a fountain revival in Seattle. If I failed, there might be no more fountains for another 25 years."[15] But Tsutakawa did not fail, although a pesky leak did limit the fountain's operation during the new library's opening weeks. The Seattle sculptor went on to become world-renowned for his fountains, creating an unmatched output of seventy-five fountains around the globe, fountains of varying sizes and Asian-influenced shapes but all derivative of Tsutakawa's first fountain, which resulted from the bold opportunity presented by Seattle Public Library.

The grand-opening throngs continued to pour into the new building until an estimated 5,000 people had passed through its doors, toured through its floors, heard live chamber music, drunk free cups of coffee, exchanged pleasantries with librarians wearing corsages. The crowds kept coming after the library officially opened for business, with its first Monday resulting in the loan of almost 5,000 books and the

Seattle sculptor George Tsutakawa faced great risk when building his *Fountain of Wisdom* for the Central Library's Fifth Avenue entrance, but his first such artwork led to the creation of scores of fountains around the globe.

The new Central Library seemed the essence of sleek modernity in three views showcased on a postcard.

issuance of 363 new library cards. Librarian Youngs likened the festive and crowded atmosphere at the new library to a department store during the Christmas season and, by the end of the year, he reported, "The overwhelming use of the new facility during the first nine months of operation exceeded the most optimistic predictions of those who had a hand in its planning."[16] The new Central Library saw almost a million volumes checked out during its first nine months, a 31 percent increase in circulation over the preceding year. Children's books, displayed on shelves that were readily accessible to young library patrons, showed a phenomenal increase of 88 percent. The new library quickly became the city's favorite gathering place, hosting 579 meetings that drew 18,749 people by the end of the year.

But all this popularity came with a price. The library's *Biennial Report for 1959-1960* opened with a glossy photograph of the new building, along with pages displaying architectural plans for floor after floor, plus Youngs's proud assertion that the opening of the new Central Library was "the single most important event in the history of Seattle Public Library."[17] The report's subsequent pages, however, contained surprisingly frank references to a gathering storm of problems. Amid all the excitement, Seattle's library was still following its frustrating pattern of two steps forward, one step back. Helen Wright of the personnel office warned, "Unless the Seattle Public Library can meet the salary scale of other libraries comparable in size, Seattle cannot hope to interest qualified librarians. The problem involves not only recruitment, but also retention of experienced personnel."[18] Phoebe Harris, head of the History, Government and Biography Department (formerly Reference), worried, "Our adult patrons had short shrift. Book budgets, unfortunately, never show the same increase percentage-wise that circulation does and our book stock needs additions and replacements for which there have been no funds."[19] Edith Fry, head of the Technology Department, admitted, "Intensive use of the library by the army of students periodically left the shelves a shambles and whole subject areas depleted. It is alarming that irresponsible and selfish borrowers stole reference books which are irreplaceable."[20] Roman Mostar, superintendent of branches, bemoaned the great demands placed on the library by its student users and "the frequent problem of discipline."[21]

A different decade had dawned with a new emphasis on youth, and nothing better symbolized that change than the country's new president, John F. Kennedy. It was a late autumn day of unlikely sunny skies on November 16, 1961, when Kennedy arrived at Boeing Field and took a seat in the open Lincoln Continental convertible that soon led a twenty-car motorcade through the streets of downtown Seattle, as tens of thousands stood on the sidewalks and cheered. The forty-four-year-old chief executive went without an overcoat in the open car despite the brisk temperature, the Kennedy magnetism much on display, just as it would be in a similar November motorcade in Dallas two years later. A portion of the excited Seattle crowd even surged from the sidewalk and surrounded the president's limousine at Fourth Avenue and University Street, to the utter surprise of police and Secret Service officers. Kennedy, unharmed during the unscheduled stop, then proceeded to the Olympic Hotel for a brief respite before heading to the University of Washington to celebrate the school's centennial with the delivery of a major Cold War foreign policy address before an enthusiastic crowd of 11,000 people in Clarence "Hec" Edmundson Pavilion.

The success of the Kennedy visit filled pages of the Seattle newspapers on the next day, muscling other news out of the way, including a wire service story that began, "President Kennedy has decided on the measures that the United States is prepared to take in order to strengthen the capacity of South Vietnam to withstand the communist-led assault on its independence. . . . The U.S. plans do not include the dispatch now of combat units. They do call for sending several hundred specialists in guerrilla warfare, logistics, communications, engineering and intelligence to train the forces of President Ngo Dinh Diem."[22] Kennedy's Seattle visit also dominated the national news, providing much fodder for the leading columnists of the day. The Puget Sound city of 558,000 residents was still basking in the afterglow of the president's visit three days later when Seattle Public Library appeared on the front page because of a startling development: six branch libraries were going to be closed in the evenings because of rowdyism by teenagers.

Librarian Youngs reported that the closures were in response to increasing discipline problems in recent weeks, although he hoped the closures of the North East, Lake City, Green Lake, Greenwood, Yesler, and Susan J. Henry Branches would prove to be "very temporary."[23] Branch superintendent Mostar conceded that most of the problems involved instances of noise and minor misbehavior, but added that a recent evening in the Greenwood Branch saw a gathering of 200 young people who "milled about, waiting for something to happen."[24] Mostar stressed, "Rude and insolent behavior is a constant source of harassment to branch librarians, who spend their entire evenings trying to maintain order when they should be helping persons who are seeking information."[25]

The public response was instantaneous and unanimous. The local P.T.A. leader was shocked and the newspaper editorialists were outraged, with the *Post-Intelligencer* describing the situation as "shameful,"[26] and the *Seattle Times* charging that "library officials acted hastily" in ordering closures that "will result in serious inconvenience to an incalculable number of persons."[27] A minister from a Lutheran church near the Greenwood Branch penned a letter to the editor in which he said his own observations of Greenwood "made one realize that 'gangism' was as rampant in Seattle as in some areas of New York City."[28] Mayor Clinton soon entered the fray, sounding as if Seattle itself were under attack from marauding teen armies. He promised that the "entire resources of the city" would be brought to bear on the problem, including police officers. "It is unthinkable," Clinton emphasized, "that a small number of out-of-hand youngsters can be allowed to disrupt our libraries like this."[29]

Within a week, the forces of order had regrouped and the six branch libraries were set to reopen, even without the imposition of martial law. Youngs credited increased public awareness and an outpouring of support for the libraries as the reasons why the evening-closure order was rescinded. The drastic measure may or may not have been warranted, but it did prove to be a brilliant political ploy on the librarian's part, turning an annoying discipline problem in some library branches into a matter of citywide concern and action, garnering much citizen support for a new no-tolerance campaign toward library disruptions by young people. No extended debates by the library board or city council were required, no extra funding requests were submitted, and no librarian pleas were repeated time and again. Even some high school students enlisted in the campaign to restore library order, including six

Four students relax in the "living room" of the new Central Library, which featured carpeting and lounge chairs. Enjoying this area designed for young adult readers are Sid McFarland, Roberta Smith (foreground); Bonnie Steever, Gary Anderson (background).

from Roosevelt High School who volunteered to ride herd over their compatriots at the North East Branch. When the six libraries did reopen on the evening of November 28, they were under intense media scrutiny that ensured swift action at the first signs of trouble, which was indeed what happened at Green Lake, the only branch where the sounds of silence did not prevail. Branch superintendent Mostar was on an inspection tour when he spied three non-studying students at Green Lake who were whispering loudly. He asked them to leave the library. They did, but not before the superintendent had his ears blistered by "a steady stream of profanity" from the mouth of a thirteen-year-old girl,[30] an early salvo fired across what would soon become known as "the generation gap."

Seattle's focus soon turned to the Century 21 Exposition, the first World's Fair of the decade. It opened on April 21, 1962, in the shadow of the city's futuristic new landmark, the Space Needle. The World's Fair ran for six exhilarating months and Seattle Public Library shared in the excitement. The town was alive with tourists and many stopped by the new Central Library, including such notables as Secretary of State Dean Rusk. The

library became such a prime tourist attraction that volunteers began giving daily tours of the building.

Then there was the World's Fair itself, Seattle's coming-out party. One of the most remarked upon exhibits at the fair was the *Library of the Future* at the new Washington State Coliseum, which was designed by Paul Thiry (the same prominent Seattle architect for the library's much praised North East Branch). *Library of the Future* was sponsored by the ALA and dazzled visitors with technological wonders that were expected to impact library service in the next century. There was a $1 million UNIVAC computer, a mammoth machine that occupied more than 100 square feet of the exhibit and produced three megahertz of computing power. The amazing UNIVAC was capable of answering questions submitted to it on subjects stored on its magnetic tapes. There was closed-circuit television for interlibrary communication. There were also facsimile machines that, as one admiring news account explained, "will permit libraries far apart to send, by reproduction, the actual material wanted by another library in a matter of minutes. . . . The machines not only will speed transmittal of information, but with their use, the material does not need to leave the home library as it does with today's inter-library loan procedures."[31]

These wonders of the *Library of the Future* were explained to visitors by librarians from some of the country's leading libraries, including the Seattle Public Library, where Dorothy J. Anderson and Janice S. Roberts were among the eighty-nine American librarians who did six-week work stints at the exhibits. The World's Fair had many positive effects on Seattle, bringing the city unprecedented national attention and many out-of-town visitors among the nearly 10 million fairgoers. But the World's Fair did have one negative impact on Seattle Public Library. So intense was the interest in the festivities that book circulation declined significantly during the fair's six-month run. Library books had a hard time competing with Century 21's Bubbleator, Monorail, and Space Needle, and appearances by real live celebrities that included John Glenn, Lyndon Johnson, Carol Channing, John Wayne, Richard Nixon, Roy Rogers, Louis Armstrong, Walt Disney, Lassie, and Elvis Presley.

Seattle emerged from the World's Fair with a new-found confidence, its self-image bolstered by the praise of outsiders, and so did Seattle Public Library. The library was entering a rare expansive phase. Shortly after the World's Fair ended, a librarian catalogued *Democracy Speaks Many Tongues* by Richard Poston, bringing Seattle's collection to 2 million volumes for

The new Southwest Branch opened in 1961 and later received an award from the American Institute of Architects.

the first time. The library soon was receiving 1,000 annual donations and one of two adults in the city possessed a library card. The library was freed in 1962 from any responsibility for running the libraries in public schools, and that allowed it to concentrate its efforts for younger readers on offerings in the downtown library and the branches.

Completion of the long-awaited Central Library had both psychological and financial benefits for the institution. It liberated the library from its perennial holding pattern with the frustrating sense of suspended dreams, dashed hopes, and making the best of bad circumstances. Seattle Public Library's defining refrain stopped being "if only." Completion of the building also provided $500,000 remaining from the 1956 bond issue, which was used to build three new branches and purchase the site for a fourth.

The first new branch built with those funds was the Southwest Branch, which opened in 1961. The pleasing structure, designed by the Seattle architectural firm of Durham, Anderson and Freed, won a local design award and in 1964 was one of just five libraries in the country to receive a national Award of Merit from the American Institute of Architects. The new Ballard Branch followed in 1963, its solid design and strong natural materials influenced by the Scandinavian heritage of that neighborhood.

Magnolia Branch followed in 1964, perhaps the most distinctive branch ever added to the library system. Noted Seattle architect Paul Hayden Kirk nestled the library on a hillside amid native madrona trees, using much glass, open wood beams, and red cedar shake siding in a quintessential Northwest design with distinct influences of Japan, including furniture designed by recognized master George Nakashima. Magnolia residents had long suffered through library service offered in a series of stations and leased quarters, so they were ecstatic about the new branch and raised more than $2,000 in donations to purchase two large pieces of art for the branch under a project sponsored by the Magnolia Community Club. The Magnolia Branch went on to win a top national honor award for library architecture in 1966 and also won praise in the prestigious *Architectural Record* magazine for "the modesty of its architectural solution, the unaffected scale appropriate to the area it serves, and the delightful use it makes of its wooded hill site."[32]

Not all branches were so fortunate. Declining circulation spelled doom for the small Aloha Branch in

ABOVE: The design for the new Magnolia Branch by Paul Hayden Kirk, noted Seattle architect, resulted in perhaps the most distinctive branch added by Seattle Public Library. The much praised branch, with its quintessential Northwest design, opened in 1964.

OPPOSITE: Closure of the small Aloha Branch in 1960 ignited a public outcry in the surrounding Capitol Hill neighborhood.

late 1960, a closure ordered by the library board that set off a firestorm of criticism in the east Capitol Hill neighborhood. More than 300 people descended on a library board meeting a month later and forced a brief reconsideration of the closure of the branch with Seattle's lowest circulation. Aloha's circulation was so low, supporters countered, because the branch had so few books and was open so few hours. But the library board decided to keep Aloha closed because adequate service could be provided at less cost by the newer Susan J. Henry Branch, just one mile west.

Declining circulation and many other problems continued to threaten the Yesler Branch, Seattle's most urban library. The branch named for the library's pioneer benefactor was buffeted by a gale force of shifting demographics and changing demands from the day it opened in 1914. For its first seven years, Yesler was the busiest branch in the Seattle Public Library system, crowded with foreign-born immigrants often bewildered by their first encounters with a library and naturalization classes that promised citizenship in their new land. In the decades that followed, Yesler's

neighborhood saw a shift to residents of Jewish descent, then Japanese descent, each with their own foreign-language demands that shaped the branch's collections, although that shifted again with the onset of World War II and the departure of faithful Japanese patrons to internment camps. Boarded-up Japanese businesses were an open wound in the Yesler neighborhood during the war years, a constant reminder of a community ripped apart, and the war years were followed by an exodus of Jewish residents to more desirable neighborhoods. The Yesler Branch continued to be the entry station, the place to start out and then, hopefully, leave behind.

So it was for blacks who started arriving in the Yesler neighborhood during World War II and whose numbers greatly increased after the war. The nearby Horace Mann Elementary School testified to this seismic demographic shift, with its enrollment of black students increasing from 19.7 percent in 1944 to 47.65 percent in 1950, and with Jewish students decreasing from 39.5 percent in 1944 to 18.4 percent in 1950. By 1953, Horace Mann's black enrollment had grown to 75 percent and was still rising. The Yesler Branch's patrons were no longer foreign born, but American success was just as foreign to these residents of what sociologist Michael Harrington would soon describe as "the other America."

Children and young adults made the most use of the Yesler Branch, which was one reason why overdue books and lost books were a never-ending problem, although Yesler librarian Jean H. Glafke attempted to rationalize the loss of more than 300 books in 1962 by saying, "More than half of the books were ready for discard anyway."[33] Yesler was a second-class branch heading steadily downhill, with little being done to stop the decline. Even the branch's basement meeting room had been commandeered in 1957 to hold book stock for the library system's bookmobiles and other branches. This change carried an implicit message that the downstairs area of Yesler Branch could be better utilized as a storage space for library patrons elsewhere in the city than as a meeting place for patrons in its own neighborhood. The Yesler Branch, an outpost of white culture and white values in a black neighborhood, seemed to be nearing its final gasp.

Enter two unlikely branch saviors, one white and the other black, librarian James A. Welsh and activist Millie Russell. Welsh had been offered the chance to lead the branch in 1964, what seemed a promotion from his lieutenancy at the prospering North East Branch until he made a brief inspection visit to Yesler and could not help but burst out laughing.[34] Yesler was an unmitigated disaster, Welsh observed, where black students ruled the room and terrified white librarians cowered behind their desks. Welsh watched that chaotic drama play out for about a half hour, before calling Mostar, superintendent of branches, and announcing that he would take the Yesler post, but only if he could do things his way.

Welsh soon set about his task of bringing some semblance of order out of Yesler's anarchy, a task that might have daunted many other whites at the time, but not this one. Several significant life experiences had shaped his character and suggested that this thirty-six-year-old librarian might be a good match for the dire situation at Yesler. Welsh had grown up in a large family, so he was no stranger to conflicting demands and chaos. He also had spent a half-dozen years of his adult life in Korea, so he was familiar with being an outsider in foreign territory. And Welsh's empathy for the poor and the dispossessed had been strengthened greatly by his recent reading of Hubert Selby Jr.'s gripping social novel *Last Exit to Brooklyn,* which the librarian considered "one of the most powerful things I read up to that point in my life."[35]

The new librarian tried a host of tactics to revive the moribund branch. Foremost was his practice of leaving the branch and venturing into the neighborhood to meet community leaders and average citizens, too. This was no time for retreat, he believed, into a library ivory tower. As Welsh recalled, "I have been out at least two days a week meeting and talking to people who are leaders in this community, in an attempt to know what the community is doing and what they might want from a library. This has produced some interesting insights, not the least of which is that, on the whole, the community as presently constituted does not really know that the library is here."[36]

Solving Yesler's discipline problems was another priority for the new librarian. Welsh tried a radical tactic, one that caused some nervous stomachs among downtown library administrators. He went straight to the parents of the young people causing the most trouble at the branch. In many cases, the parents were simply letting their sons and daughters go to the library after school, with the best of intentions, and were appalled when Welsh informed them of the result. Soon, the librarian's personal calls to the parents of troublemakers were producing a once unthinkable result—those same students, accompanied by their parents, walked back into the branch and apologized for their previous behavior. "These kids, by and large, came from very respectful and very disciplined families,"[37] Welsh observed, as the chaos receded and order descended on Yesler Branch in the space of six months.

Bringing more people inside the Yesler Branch was another priority for the new librarian and that resulted in a series of programs designed to interest the surrounding black community. First was the February 1965 celebration of Negro History Week, which brought 265 people to the branch and reaped a promising new harvest of neighborhood goodwill, what Welsh described at the end of the year as "our greatest single achievement."[38] Children's movies on Monday evenings proved another popular branch program, as did a May 1965 cultural forum on "The History of Negro Church Music," which drew 230 people. These programs brought people into the Yesler Branch and started to change community attitudes about the library, but they had one notable shortcoming: they were not producing much interest in the branch's book collection.

Timing had often been an enemy of Seattle Public Library during its history, but timing smiled on the Yesler Branch at this moment. Millie Russell had befriended Welsh during her frequent visits to the branch, and it was not long before the librarian let this lifelong Yesler patron know that the branch was being threatened with closure. Russell soon conveyed that distressing message to Roberta Byrd and other members of the local chapter of Alpha Kappa Alpha, a national sorority of black college women founded in 1908 at Howard University. The local chapter soon approached Welsh with an offer of assistance for the branch.

The librarian searched his mind for the most relevant project to involve the sorority and he kept coming back to what he had learned during his two-week visit to the Countee Cullen library in Harlem. That visit was part of a Seattle library-sponsored research trip to two libraries serving black communities back East that Welsh had taken prior to becoming librarian at Yesler. The pride of the Countee Cullen library (renamed after a beloved black poet and teacher) was the Schomburg Collection, the country's most extensive selection of black literature and history. Perhaps the sorority could help Yesler start a similar collection, Welsh thought, and thus spark some interest in the neighborhood.

The sorority readily agreed and its first gift to Yesler's new Negro Life and History Collection came on November 28, 1965, with the donation of forty-five volumes of *The Journal of Negro History*. More gift titles followed over the next few years, funded by small donations from individual sorority members and from the group's highly successful fund-raising teas, elegant affairs with silver service. Welsh also played a pivotal role, urging the downtown library administration to purchase additional black titles, with some success, and refocusing many efforts at Yesler to increase its black collection. Magazine subscriptions at the branch were changed to reflect community interests, photographs of prominent African and African American personages were gathered and displayed, and relevant pamphlets and other visual materials were tracked down, too. The black collection grew steadily at Yesler, with 352 titles by 1966, as did community interest and pride.

But the Yesler Branch still was waging an uphill struggle on many fronts. As Welsh stressed in his 1967 annual report: "The time has come to do something about staff facilities at Yesler Branch. As things stand, we very neatly fit anybody's stereotype of ghetto accommodations. We have rodents. Our kitchen facilities dare not use the name. Four staff members must try to make one of their major meals for the day on what

Librarian James Welsh's tireless efforts to revive the imperiled Yesler Branch include this meeting with neighborhood women helping to plan library events during a Negro History Week celebration. This photo from *The Facts* newspaper includes (from left): Mrs. Gloria Henderson, Mrs. James W. Johnson, Mrs. Mikki Frye, Welsh, Mrs. Sicille Marie Tielson, and Mrs. Leroy McMillon.

certainly must be the first hotplate ever made—this in a day when portable meals are designed for an oven. We only ask, as the ICBM's [intercontinental ballistic missiles] fly overhead and space exploration goes on apace, that we be given a kitchen circa 1950."[39]

The black collection was now accounting for one-third of the adult circulation at the Yesler Branch and that circulation was finally starting to rise. But it was happening so slowly that the branch was still threatened with closure, to the continuing dismay of the Alpha Kappa Alpha sorority sisters, including Russell, who first started visiting the branch in the 1930s. She was a young girl then, brought to the branch by her mother on Friday evenings along with her brothers and sisters, these regular family library outings infused with a sense of wonder and purpose because, as Russell recalled decades later, "we knew that library service was not always open to our ancestors, so that made us even more determined to be good library patrons."[40] Threatened closure of Yesler was not the only frustration for Russell and other branch supporters. The growing neighborhood prominence of the Yesler Branch increased the urgency of returning its basement space to a community meeting area—Welsh had first argued for that change in his initial annual report back in 1965—but repeated entreaties to downtown library administration produced no positive results. The book-mobiles remained in their nighttime parking spots outside Yesler, while their book collection remained in the Yesler basement, a galling neighborhood reminder of the branch's second-class status.

Direct-action politics were transforming the nation in these tumultuous 1960s days, with the Civil Rights movement blazing an impressive trail of hard-won success that was starting to be followed by those opposed to the escalating war in Vietnam. Concerted pressure with nonviolent tactics was working against entrenched power in many arenas of American life, and Russell soon adopted that approach in efforts to fend off closure of the Yesler Branch and return its meeting room to the people. First came the 1968 formation of a branch support group, Black Friends of Yesler Library, which was not associated with the Friends of the Seattle Public Library. Then came pressure politics by this self-described "militant" group and organizer Russell, who was then working as director of technical education for the Puget Sound Blood Center.

Russell and her Yesler compatriots were finished with quiet appeals to librarian Youngs and his continuing rebuffs. They had in mind a different sort of Yesler tea party, one without the usual hats and gloves and silver, one more reminiscent of the famed tea party in Boston. "I told Willard Youngs," Russell remembered, "that if he would not help us remove the books from the basement, then we would wait for a rainy day and throw them out onto the lawn, where he would have to deal with them."[41]

Russell had an important new ally in Sam Smith, her former schoolmate who had served five terms in the state legislature before becoming, in 1967, the first black elected to the Seattle City Council. Smith was a Louisiana preacher's son who prided himself on solving his constituents' problems, and Smith's efforts helped secure $30,000 in reserve library funds for the renovation of the Yesler basement. That appropriation came only two months after riots in the surrounding Central Area and in other cities followed the Memphis assassination of the Reverend Martin Luther King Jr., the nation's leading civil rights leader.

The downtown library administration could stall at Yesler no longer. The bookmobiles were dispatched to the Green Lake Branch and the Yesler basement was returned to its original use as an auditorium in May 1969. The reclaimed space was mostly used for children's events at the outset, but was the site of two extraordinary events with writer Alex Haley. The first

night was a champagne reception for the writer who was best known then as coauthor of *The Autobiography of Malcolm X*. The second was a public talk about his work, including an upcoming novel based on his family's history, a novel that would carry the title *Roots*.

Yesler Branch was hardly the only institution buffeted by the seismic shifts of the 1960s in Seattle. Everything had changed from those giddy days of the World's Fair, which scarcely seemed part of the same decade. Even the research questions that came into the Seattle Public Library, more than half of them via telephone, were shockingly different. As its biennial report for 1966–67 recounted, "The hippie influence is evident in questions about narcotics laws, light shows, psychedelic art, metaphysical religions, horoscopes, how to play the guitar and the pros and cons of drug usage. One young man asked for evidence with which to counter a friend's suggestion that he try marijuana. The straight world seems eager for information, abundantly supplied by periodicals, about its detractors. New attitudes about sex are reflected in the assignment to young students of term papers on prostitution, birth control, homosexuality and other topics generally taboo only a decade ago."[42]

The downtown Central Library was often ensnarled in street protests, since many demonstrations against the Vietnam War focused on the U.S. federal courthouse directly across Fifth Avenue. Police authorities sometimes positioned themselves inside the library to spy on protestors outside, and protestors sometimes took refuge in the library. Stones in the pool surrounding the Tsutakawa fountain were removed in order to prevent their use as missiles in the growing confrontations that swept across Seattle.

A bomb went off in the administration building at the University of Washington, the Naval ROTC offices were set afire, and thousands of demonstrators blocked traffic on Interstate 5. The most violent protests at the federal courthouse broke out on February 17, 1970, leading to the injury of twenty people and the arrest of seventy-six, including members of the short-lived Seattle Liberation Front, later known as the Seattle Seven.

Society's foundation was being shaken, and so was Seattle Public Library's, not only by great societal change but also by the new Seattle-First National Bank Building across Fourth Avenue. Excavation for the fifty-story skyscraper undermined the Central Library's foundation, just as excavation of the Great Northern Railroad tunnel had done to its Carnegie predecessor.

Four pillars supporting the new Central Library's third, fourth, and fifth stories shifted more than an inch during the skyscraper's construction and cracks appeared in several parts of the building, structural damages prompting a city lawsuit and requiring repairs estimated at $20,000.

There were challenges within the library as well. In 1969 and 1970, outbreaks of sexual harassment in the downtown library required police patrols and decoy operations to nab offenders, including eleven in one week, six of those on a single Saturday. The offenses of those described by the newspapers as "degenerates" ranged from exposing themselves to touching young girls in the library elevators. "It is difficult," summarized one police detective, "for the women working there, as well as the public."[43]

The library's staff also felt the impact of women's liberation, the third major social movement of the tumultuous decade. Most of the library's staff was female and the administration was male, so the Seattle Public Library was a fertile ground for feminist consciousness-raising and its challenges to entrenched male-dominated organizations. Librarian Youngs responded by 1970 with what he considered important concessions to female members of the library's staff: "A married woman may use her own name on her library card instead of her husband's, and the female staff may wear pants suits to work."[44]

Far more significant changes were sought by employees. A year of labor-organizing spadework paid off in late 1970 when the library's professional staff members voted to form a union affiliated with the Washington State Council of County and City Employees, AFL-CIO. Seattle Public Library's long-standing low pay helped fuel the organizing drive, remembered union activist Elke Boettcher, but even more crucial was "frustration in not having a say in how the library was run; we had a sense we might be able to do something about that with a union."[45] Sixty-seven library staffers voted in favor of forming a union, forty-four voted against. The new employee union at Seattle Public Library stood as one more testament to the altered order in these changing times, as did the liberated basement in the Yesler Branch, where speakers included members of the radical Students for a Democratic Society and the militant Black Panther Party.

The tumult of the late 1960s helped fuel the successful drive to organize Seattle Public Library's professional employees into a labor union in 1970.

CHAPTER 9

Tight Budgets, Tough Decisions

IT WAS TIME TO CELEBRATE Seattle Public Library's decade in the new Central Library, and what the celebration should involve was the question. Anniversary cake was an obvious option, traditional but trite, and would leave little behind other than a scattering of crumbs. An anniversary speech was another option, and indeed one would be delivered by the University of Washington's beloved

ABOVE: The tenth anniversary of the new Central Library was celebrated in 1970 with a one-day amnesty for overdue books, what was billed then as a one-time-only event.

OPPOSITE: Volunteer Ina Bray pauses from her sorting duties in preparation for the 1978 used-book sale by the Friends of the Seattle Public Library, which created that popular community event in the early 1970s.

professor Giovanni Costigan, just as he had done on the library's dedication day. But something more innovative seemed in order, something with more lasting benefits than pastry or praise, and thus was born the library's first-ever Amnesty Day on March 26, 1970, a one-time chance for negligent borrowers and sometime thieves to return missing library property with no questions asked and no fines incurred.

King County Library had already sponsored several such events with some success, but Seattle's response was uncertain, although the library was taking no chances that patrons might abuse the anniversary largesse. No word of the unprecedented amnesty was supposed to appear in the press until four days before the event, in hopes of preventing undue hoarding of overdue books and other materials. Word of the amnesty did finally spread in news reports and in libraries themselves, and the appointed March morning dawned with a steady stream of people returning missing volumes. "Some patrons arrived with sheepish grins and large shopping bags," reported the *Seattle Times.* "One gentleman, unloading a dozen books on loan since 1968, said he just could not afford to pay the fine [which would have amounted to about twenty-five dollars]."[1]

The gentleman voiced a widespread perception—that the library's fine meter was ringing up new totals for an overdue book with each passing day—and his comment pointed up the delicate policy dilemma posed by late books. In fact, library fines were capped at a small maximum amount (two dollars for an adult book, one dollar for a children's book). But publicizing that could convey the mistaken impression that the library did not care about the continuing problem of missing materials, thereby encouraging even greater numbers of overlooked returns and also outright thefts. Seattle Public Library had a similar dilemma with its first Amnesty Day. To declare it a huge success could create the impression that it should be repeated, causing more hoarding. So day-after reports to the press were restrained, pegging the number of returns at "about 2,000," and also warning the public again that the amnesty day would not be repeated.

The returns were actually four times greater than the number given in initial news reports, which had deflected most attention toward the library's most overdue volume—a copy of Henry Herbert Kibbs's *Sundown Slim,* a popular Western yarn due for return in 1927. Seattle Public Library was losing 7,000 books annually by 1970 and the amnesty resulted in the return of 8,505, so it was a significant success, even if it turned up few of the library's rarest missing volumes. Among the amnesty's returnees were 471 books that had been stolen and 87 books belonging to other libraries, which were forwarded via the mail. Verda Hansberry, head of circulation services, still felt compelled to include in her year-end report a warning against holding another Amnesty Day ("it shouldn't be repeated or the public will save books to return on fine-free day").[2] Hansberry's admonition carried weight for a time, although the amnesty idea continued to have supporters among library staffers and the public. Seattle Public Library's amnesty would be repeated again in 1980 and again in 1988, a time when it would be expanded to an entire week. Although still described as "one-time-only," the amnesty was becoming a library tradition of sorts.

Another library tradition was also born in the early 1970s. After many months of discussion, the Friends of the Seattle Public Library began seeking used books in the summer of 1971 for a public sale to be held in October. Collection barrels were distributed to most libraries, donated books were sorted by Friends volunteers, and posters announcing the sale were placed all over town. The Friends' sale finally took place on October 2 and 3 in the Lake City Community Center, with 20,000 volumes available for purchase at nominal prices. That first sale netted a surprising $2,634, along with the determination to hold additional sales on an annual or even semiannual basis. Proceeds from each Friends' sale continued to increase steadily—topping $10,000 only six years later and $20,000 within a decade. The used-book sale soon became a mandatory date on the Seattle book lover's calendar, plus an excellent opportunity to enroll new Friends.

The Friends' new source of library funding could not have come at a more propitious time. The Seattle economy was in a serious nosedive as the fortunes of the city's leading employer, the Boeing Company, took hit after hit. The most serious blow came in the last month of 1970, when the U.S. Senate withdrew federal support for Boeing's plan to build an American supersonic airliner (SST). A layoff of 7,500 Boeing workers soon followed, a staggering head shot to the local economy, but the "Boeing Bust" had been worsening for many years. Long gone were the heydays of the World's Fair, when it seemed that anything was possible in Seattle. Boeing had slashed more than 60,000 jobs from its payroll from 1967 to 1971 and Seattle's population felt the chill. The city's population peaked at 591,000 in 1969, then lost 60,000 in the following year and another 5,000 in the year after that. The rest of King County had more people than Seattle by that time, a dramatic shift to the suburbs that would never be reversed. Unemployment continued to climb to double the national average, to 12 percent and beyond, the worst unemployment of any metropolitan area in the country, unemployment at levels not seen in any city since the Depression.[3] Things got so bad that a billboard near Sea-Tac International Airport suggested, "Will the last person leaving Seattle turn out the lights." The leased billboard was a $160 attempt at gallows humor by two local real estate men (Bob McDonald, Jim Youngren)—their humorous intent underscored by its unveiling on April Fools' Day, 1971. But the sentiment cut too close to the sad truth to prompt much laughter.

Seattle Public Library's fortunes plummeted along with the city's, as had happened in the past. The early years of the 1970s were so unrelentingly grim for the library that newspapers could easily have recycled the same news story, with updated bad numbers, underneath the same headline—"Budget Blows Batter Seattle's Library."[4] Tens of thousands of dollars were axed from library budget requests, operating hours were reduced at the Central Library and the branches, staff members were fired. Federal funding for city services, which had become an increasingly important source of library money, was also imperiled. That prompted a one-day protest in 1973, when candles were placed on desks in libraries all across the country, including those in Seattle and King County, in a symbolic gesture to suggest that the federal cuts could "dim the lights" in libraries.

Then came prominent criticism of Seattle Public Library for having a "plush service structure."[5] That red-flag phrase was well buried in the appendix of a 509-page analysis of Seattle Public Library prepared by an outside consulting firm, Public Affairs Counseling of San Francisco. The phrase may have been buried in the $100,000 report, but it did not escape the notice of James Hornell, budget director for the city's Office of Management and Budget. He was prepared to use that word weapon during deliberations on the library's 1975 funding, which the budget office had proposed to slash by $154,931 from the previous year, an unkind cut that would come in a year when the library was also slated to lose $127,918 in federal money.

Verda Hansberry, promoted to assistant librarian, attempted to persuade the city council budget committee that cuts of that magnitude in the library's $4,784,381 budget would require distinct program reductions, especially at the Central Library. "There will be," Hansberry warned, "hurried service by a harried staff."[6]

Hornell, in response, unloaded his ammunition, quoting not just that one critical phrase from the consultant's report but also the entire surrounding passage. A reporter from the *Post-Intelligencer* took notes as Hornell intoned the consultant's verdict: "Put bluntly, the Seattle Public Library has a plush service structure, and extra staff is needed to maintain the structure. So firmly rooted is this structure and the personnel in it that the budget has been adjusted year by year upward for staff but downward for materials, thus retaining the body of the organization while starving it for nourishment."[7]

Hornell's budget office wanted to start correcting that imbalance with the library's next budget. No longer would 83.5 percent of the budget be devoted to staff and only 9 percent to books and other reference materials. Instead, the budget office sought to increase spending on books and materials to 12.8 percent of the budget, while also reducing staff expenditures through the elimination of thirty-three positions by attrition. But that intent was nowhere near as prominent in news coverage as the consultant's conclusion about the library's structure. As a large headline on the front page of the *Post-Intelligencer* blared, "Public Library Hit for 'Plush' Service Setup."[8]

The use of "plush" was strange—it seemed to imply that Seattle Public Library was a place with expensive leather chairs, Oriental rugs, and afternoon tea in tiny china cups. But it was a damning charge about a public institution, especially in a time of austere budgets. It was little wonder then that the leader of the Public Affairs Counseling study team soon voiced regret that the phrase had not been removed during the final editing of their report. "That phrase," commented Roger Malek, the firm's associate director, "does not really represent the whole scope, thrust and depth of the report."[9]

Malek's point was well taken, but too late. The "plush" label had been already affixed to Seattle Public Library, with its taint of mistaken elitism and misplaced priorities. A follow-up story two weeks later in the *Post-Intelligencer* summed up the charges with blunt headlines: "Seattle's Libraries: The Facts & the Fiction. Are They Really That Bad?"[10] The accompanying story by reporter Lee Moriwaki turned out to be a journalism rarity, a thorough and serious-minded attempt to place a local institution in a national context. Moriwaki gathered relevant information from public libraries in cities that included Boston, San Francisco, Sacramento, Portland, Baltimore, and Los Angeles. He reported that Seattle's allocation of 83.5 percent of its budget for staffing did top that allocation at other libraries, which ranged from 62 percent in Sacramento and 73 percent in

Boston to 79 percent in Portland and 80 percent in San Francisco. He also reported that Seattle's budget allocation of 9 percent on books and other reference materials did lag behind that allocation at other libraries, which ranged from 10.7 percent in Boston and 12 percent in Portland to 15 percent in San Francisco and 20 percent in Sacramento. Seattle's library funding did seem skewed toward staff costs in these comparisons, but not at great variance with national norms, and certainly not so skewed that it should be described as "a plush service structure." Moriwaki also pointed out that Seattle Public Library's circulation of 3.9 million volumes was greater than that of almost all libraries in cities with similar populations; such heavy library usage in Seattle offered a strong argument in favor of greater staffing needs. Moriwaki's report answered the headline's question about Seattle libraries, "Are They Really That Bad?" with its findings of "No, Probably Not."

Still, changes did need to be made at Seattle Public Library, as was revealed in the exhaustive analysis of Public Affairs Counseling. Beyond its much quoted "plush" charge, the firm's report on the library was packed with well-documented conclusions and well-argued steps for improvement: reorganization of the library's staff and administration, installation of automated systems for record keeping and book security (soon to follow), distribution of staff and materials throughout the library system in a more equitable manner, strictures to insure effective budget accountability, established priorities to focus the library's collection, and measures to counter low staff morale caused by poor internal communications, inadequate staff development programs, and a lack of confidence in the library's leadership. Never before in the library's long history had there been such a detailed look at its programs, policies, and budgeting by an outside agency. What Public Affairs Counseling discovered took on added urgency in difficult budget times. A report with the cumbersome title "Imperatives for Change: A Management Improvement Analysis of the Seattle Public Library" was a startling rebuke of continued business as usual. It was, above all, a public cry to get current.

Malek told the *Post-Intelligencer* that Seattle Public Library did have its commendable attributes, but added, "There's a tendency for the library to say, 'Well, look, we've been doing very well. We don't want to question what to change.' But the point is: They really have to rethink it through, given the fact that money isn't as plentiful as it used to be."[11]

Ten task forces of library staffers soon set off on their own studies of the consultant's report and how to implement its recommendations. But their reports would not be delivered to librarian Youngs. The deliberate sailor opted for early retirement at the end of 1974 after seventeen years of service, and perhaps none too soon since his leadership and administration received much criticism in the Public Affairs Counseling report (one staffer likened the library to "a bus without a driver").[12] A nationwide search was mounted to find Youngs's successor, a new librarian with the daunting task of implementing a mandate for change while wearing an economic straitjacket.

Positive library news was in short supply during the rough 1970s, which is why the drive to build the new Broadview Branch was such a heartening development. What happened in the quiet neighborhood in northwest Seattle, a place with dazzling panoramas of Puget Sound and the Olympic Mountains, was a story with the elements of an uplifting Sunday sermon—a story of government injustice, citizen protest and activism, and a lingering wrong finally being righted. It was hailed as the triumph of the "world's greatest naggers."[13]

All these Broadview residents wanted was a branch library to call their own, saving countless trips of a couple miles to other branches, and it seemed that their wish would be fulfilled in 1967 when Broadview property was purchased for a branch library and the city appropriated money for its construction. Enter an unlikely villain, a team of major league baseball players. The newly organized Seattle Pilots were coming to town in 1969, and Sick's Stadium required expansion in order to bring it up to some semblance of big league snuff. City money was needed for this project and city money was found. The funding for Broadview's library was snatched away, like some late-inning swipe of home plate, and transferred instead to the old ballpark in the Rainier Valley.

Broadview residents were justifiably outraged, their indignation further increased when the Pilots abandoned ship after one pitiful losing season, lured away to Milwaukee by a car dealer named Bud Selig. Broadview residents vowed to never forget their loss and never let the Seattle City Council forget it either. Every year at budget hearing time, as regular as November rain, citizens from "Broadview Library Now" showed up to remind the city council about their misappropriated appropriation. Often in the lead was Mrs. Alfred (Elsie) Von Stubbe, who would sometimes have to remind reporters that she was "a housewife, not a houseperson."[14] All manner of tactics were employed by her insistent community group, from phone calls to council members and library staff, to petition drives, to

Mrs. Elsie Von Stubbe wields the ceremonial shovel during groundbreaking for the new Broadview Branch, an unlikely triumph of neighborhood activism by what she called "the world's greatest naggers."

a protest action that drew 200 well-mannered support-ers to a "read-in" on the Broadview Branch's vacant lot.

Mrs. Von Stubbe, who had first described the group as the "world's greatest naggers," even stated the case for the branch library in a letter to the editor of the *Seattle Times*. "My darling husband says keep quiet," she wrote, "it will come eventually and they (whoever They are) are doing their best. But he wasn't quite so complacent when I explained we have lived in Broadview 25 years and with hundreds of apartments now lining Greenwood Avenue North, and retirement homes and nursing homes and junior highs and the largest elemen-tary school in the city, we in Broadview have the poorest of library services in the entire King County. We've been pleasant and patient long enough . . . I get madder and madder, the more I think about it."[15]

Eventually, Broadview Library Now found an influ-ential friend in city council member Tim Hill, who engineered a successful strategy to pay for the long-overdue branch library with $350,000 in federal revenue sharing money and $250,000 in city funds. Groundbreaking was finally held on March 10, 1975, with the Broadview activists reflecting on their long battle. ("It was low-key and a lot of fun," Mrs. Von Stubbe said the day before. "But, at times, it was terribly frustrating

The new Broadview Branch was dedicated on January 25, 1976.

125

because the city wheels turn so slowly ... but I guess we've won now, so I shouldn't say anything nasty.")[16] What arose on the site was a low-slung structure of brick and cedar reminiscent of a Native American longhouse, featuring murals and wood carvings in North-west Coast style by Native artist Marvin Oliver. The branch's Native American references were surely appropriate, since the Broadview citizens had waged a tireless campaign that seemed worthy of the legendary Chief Joseph and his band of Nez Perce. Dedication of the new branch took place on January 25, 1976, with Mayor Wes Uhlman and library leaders in attendance, but was directed instead by a mistress of ceremonies who needed no introduction in the neighborhood—none other than Mrs. Von Stubbe, leading things at Broadview one last time after her eight years of labors.

Another demonstration of "people power" at the library was taking place at the Yesler Branch, where the continued growth of the African American collection led to dreams of a new name for the branch that would better reflect that neighborhood. A public contest was held to rename the library to honor black history and the branch's growing collection. Receiving top votes were the names of two former slaves who played important roles in nineteenth-century American history, a man and a woman, both writers of important autobiographies, and both receiving about the same number of votes—Frederick Douglass (1817–95) and Sojourner Truth (1797–1883). A proclamation by Mayor Uhlman made the name change official in 1975, the Yesler Branch transformed into the Douglass-Truth Branch, with murals of the two activists soon completed there by artist Eddie Walker. The name change was another triumph for the black neighborhood that had rescued its own library, but this triumph also had an unfortunate consequence for the city. It erased any reminder of the crucial role played in the library's early history by the pioneer sawmill owner. No other Seattle Public Library facility, not even a meeting room, honored the name of Henry Yesler.

More immediate concerns were on the mind of Seattle's new librarian, Ronald A. Dubberly. He had arrived in town full of youthful vigor, and no wonder. At thirty-two, Dubberly had been selected for the top library job in Seattle with its $34,128 salary, besting four other finalists despite the fact that he had worked

The Yesler Branch was renamed Douglass-Truth Branch to honor black activists Frederick Douglass and Sojourner Truth, another triumph for community activism. At the renaming ceremony on December 5, 1976, are (from left) Robert Maxie, vice president of the library board; Cheryl Watson, branch librarian; Millie Russell, influential activist from Friends of Douglass-Truth; and Mayor Wes Uhlman.

at only two libraries since graduate school at Florida State University. Dubberly's résumé was limited to four years at the library in Baltimore County, Maryland, then six years as director of the library system in Sioux City, Iowa. He was a young man in a hurry, an energetic, personable fellow with no shortage of self-confidence. Change was needed at Seattle Public Library and he planned to lead it. The future was so much of Dubberly's focus that, after two months on the job, he still had not bothered to pay a courtesy call on his retired predecessor, despite Youngs's decades of experience in Seattle. The new librarian seemed to know what he wanted to know. As Dubberly told a reporter, "When a library has the reputation Seattle's has, serving 38 percent of the people compared to 25 or less in many cities, and when it has built the kind of staff Seattle has, somebody had to be doing something right."[17]

Dubberly's first two years at the helm turned out to be a baptism by inferno. Budget battles continued, with the library often forced to fight desperate holding actions against the sharp knives wielded by the Office of Management and Budget and the city council. The situation went from bad to worse when the library's requested 1977 budget was slashed by almost $1 million by city budgeteers. Their proposed amount was 3.1 percent less than the library had received the year before and came when the library was experiencing increased usage and was also under continued pressure to increase its spending on books.

Something had to give and that something was the library's staff, already reduced 9 percent (thirty-seven staffers) in the past three years and slated to be reduced further. The cut in staff was not made through attrition any longer, but through layoffs—of thirty librarians or twenty-four librarians or twenty-three librarians, or some number fewer than that, as some reports said. It was all very confusing as it played out in the media, and all very contentious. Dubberly huddled with Mayor Uhlman in hopes of heading off the layoff; the librarians' union filed a formal protest and urged that reductions instead be made in administrative costs; 100 angry citizens packed a special library board hearing and vented their outrage about imperiled library services ("the erosion of this valuable asset must stop and, in fact, be turned around," said one).[18] All this Sturm und Drang prompted the library board to cut the layoffs in half at one meeting, then rescind them altogether at another. The board made the cuts instead in the lagging book budget, as the librarian suggested.

Dubberly was definitely not in Iowa anymore. Negotiations for the second contract with the librarians'

Librarian Ronald Dubberly was just thirty-two years old when he was picked to become Seattle Public Library's new leader.

union had broken down in 1976, forcing mediation and prompting a week of informational picketing by librarians (a decision reached "with great trepidation" by union members who instead found themselves heartened by public support).[19] The settlement was finally reached with the librarians, although not without rancor, and Dubberly also encountered staff resistance to his plans to regionalize the branch system. Regionalization was an innovation driven by savings in staffing costs but was controversial because it ended the long-time stability of librarians being assigned to specific branches; that policy was replaced with mandatory rotation through several branches in a geographic sector. Marion, the familiar branch librarian, was suddenly on the move, an itinerant professional without a home anymore, whether she wanted that or not.

All this turmoil was only increased by another public relations debacle for the library. The *Post-Intelligencer* broke a copyrighted story on its front page, along with a photo of Charles Rose cradling an armload of books

ABOVE: Construction supervisor Charles Rose cradles some of the discarded Seattle Public Library books that he rescued from the Midway landfill. Rose's discovery, revealed on the front page of the *Post-Intelligencer*, led to a revision in the way that the library disposed of used volumes.

that he had rescued from the Midway landfill, books from what were discovered to be 1,000 volumes dumped there by Seattle Public Library. The discards rescued by Rose, a construction supervisor from Kent, included two copies of John F. Kennedy's *Profiles in Courage,* the 1957 Pulitzer Prize winner. They were still enclosed in the library's plastic covers and in excellent condition. "It seemed to me that what I was seeing," Rose commented, "was almost unpatriotic."[20] The newspaper's own digging revealed even more book dumping: 4,250 library volumes discarded in 1976, 12,000 library volumes in 1975.

Librarian Dubberly, required to respond, assumed the bureaucrat's classic defensive posture—blame others, blame regulations, too. The library had been storing up 9,000 volumes that year with hopes of finding other means of disposal, Dubberly said, if only the city's legal office would provide a requested opinion on this matter. The library was willing to resell the discarded volumes to the public rather than dump them in the landfill, Dubberly added, but that would seem to be in violation of state law on property disposal by government agencies. The president of the library board, Robert Maxie, disagreed with the librarian's retreat into legalisms and the *Post-Intelligencer* editorialized, "Seattle City Librarian Ron Dubberly seemed to be suffering from a terrible case of timidity. . . . He should sell unneeded books or give them away and worry about lawsuits when—if ever—one arises."[21] Even that dim possibility was quickly dismissed when it was discovered that the state attorney general's office had advised the library three years before that it had the authority to sell its discarded books, an opinion that somehow had not prompted any change in the library's book-dumping policy. That policy was indeed changed only days after the *Post-Intelligencer*'s revelations about landfill disposal (a practice mentioned five years earlier in the *Queen Anne News* with no apparent controversy). Although the 1977 book-dumping imbroglio lasted just a few days, Dubberly did manage to stub his toe in public a couple more times, including this truthful, yet callous-sounding assertion: "People tend to feel books last forever. We have to look at them as stock and therefore some must be discarded."[22]

These were such sorry days for Seattle Public Library that its best news was provided by Robert Charles Bunn, who had been dead for six years. The Yakima native had died in Seattle at age fifty-three, a lifelong bachelor who still lived with his mother at the time of his death. Bunn had been working as a shipyard electrician in 1943 when he was surprised to inherit $500,000 from his great-aunt. The windfall allowed the University

New technology instituted dramatic changes at Seattle Public Library with its switch from card catalog to a microfilm catalog searchable by push button, a two-year project partially financed by Bunn Funds.

of Washington botany graduate to devote his life to favored pursuits—stock market investments that parlayed his inheritance into millions of dollars; hiking and climbing around the Northwest as a lifetime member of the Mountaineers; and the dedicated study of botany and geology, much of the indoor research conducted during his frequent visits to Seattle Public Library. Friends and family described Bunn as a quiet and brilliant fellow, with an eccentric streak, but also a committed book lover who belonged to several antique-book collecting clubs. His love of books and libraries earned the Seattle Public Library a prominent place in Bunn's will, but that bequest did not take effect until after his mother's death in 1976. The library received a $5,000 check from the Bunn estate soon after the death of Carrie Bunn, and officials assumed that was the extent of her son's bequest. But a year later, it was learned that Bunn had actually donated the largest sum that the library had yet received—$3.5 million. That staggering largesse, especially in a time of starved library budgets, was going to result in annual interest payments totaling over $130,000. "We're still in a pleasant state of shock," commented Nancy Wright, the library's public spokeswoman.[23]

Bunn Funds, as they became known, soon were put to work by Seattle Public Library and provided a crucial supplement to the library's annual budget. Improvements and innovations that would have been beyond the reach of the library instead became reality through the steady infusion of unrestricted Bunn Funds, including the inauguration of computer-assisted information

services in 1978; the new Dial-a-Story telephone program, which reached an estimated 200,000 listeners in its first year; the purchase of 16-mm film projectors for public loan; partial funding of the two-year project to convert the library's paper card catalog to microfilm records searchable by the push of a button; and the purchase of a compact pickup dubbed the Rainbow Truck that provided information about the library and its programs during stops at various community events and celebrations. In 1981, the library established the Robert Charles Bunn Prize, which initially conferred $3,000 on a distinguished person of letters or science

Robert Charles Bunn, shown in his graduation photo from the University of Washington, left a $3.5 million bequest to Seattle Public Library in 1976. It was the largest donation that the library had ever received and provided much needed support in a time of strapped library budgets.

129

ABOVE: Seattle Public Library's new Rainbow Truck provided library information at community events and was just one of the many programs supported by the historic bequest of Robert Charles Bunn.

BELOW: Virginia Burnside capped her important civic contributions in Seattle with the formation of the Seattle Public Library Foundation in 1980, when she was serving as president of the library board.

and brought the winner to Seattle for a free address that attracted large audiences. The first winners of the Bunn Prize were a veritable honor roll of American historians—Daniel J. Boorstin, Barbara Tuchman, Theodore H. White, and John Hope Franklin.

Awarding the Bunn Prize was a new library support group, the Seattle Public Library Foundation. The organization was founded in 1980 by Virginia Burnside, then president of the library board. She had grown weary of watching the library suffer so many budget wounds and had become convinced that Seattle Public Library was "an under-appreciated, under-valued resource . . . a neglected child in Seattle's giving."[24] So the sixty-one-year-old dynamo summoned up a little help from a few of her influential friends (Robert Block, Norman MacLeod, Betty Jane Narver, Emilie Schwabacher, David Sprague) and formed one of the earliest library foundations in the United States. It was the first in the Northwest, established seven years before a similar foundation in San Francisco and fifteen years before one in Portland. The Seattle Public Library Foundation supplemented the long-running efforts of the Friends of the Seattle Public Library, since a private organization has greater freedom in using donations from individuals and organizations. The new group garnered $50,644 in its inaugural year of operation, although that impressive amount was not reached again for another six years.

The establishment of the library foundation was the capstone of Burnside's fascinating career in public and private life, the legacy of a love affair with books that began in childhood when the young Seattle native liked nothing better than sitting and reading the dictionary. Burnside became an exemplary student, earning Phi Beta Kappa honors at the University of Washington, married an army colonel and raised two sons. She kicked off a long career in journalism when she started writing about state government for the *Post-Intelligencer* (introduced to readers under the headline "Housewife to Write Series"),[25] and she later wrote a weekly column on politics that was published for many years in community newspapers across the state. Burnside also hosted an early political talk show on local television in the 1950s *(Question Before the House)*, wrote speeches for prominent democratic officeholders, and publicized the Seattle World's Fair. She was an outspoken, forceful person with a journalist's dry wit that was sometimes unveiled even when she presided at the library board. During one meeting, Burnside listened to the reading of a letter from a ninety-five-year-old library patron who said that "the arrival of the bookmobile makes me feel like a girl waiting for her lover," which prompted the board president to quip, "Romance comes to the library."[26]

The romance soon dissipated, replaced by the usual *Perils of Pauline* existence of Seattle Public Library, although occasional glimmers of hope did break through the gloom of the late 1970s and early 1980s. The downtown Central Library underwent a nineteen-month renovation that was a remodeling nightmare of dust and disorder for staff and patrons, but it produced a much improved facility in 1979. It then featured 62 percent more shelving, 16 percent more tables and chairs, and 14 percent more space with the fourth floor opened to public use, plus new paint and carpets to brighten the fading decor. All these improvements were the result of a $2.3 million economic development grant from the federal government. Another federal grant paid for construction of the Rainier Beach Branch library, a 9,000-square-foot facility with a $1.2 million price tag that opened in 1981 and soon registered three times the usage of the small station that it replaced. The year 1981 also saw the library complete its first-ever overhaul of its policy manual for branch libraries, a thankless but necessary task, ending its longtime reliance on an assemblage of outdated policies that board chair Burnside described as "a rambling wreck."[27]

There was little time to savor advances, since the library continued to be threatened by an ever tightening budget noose, with dire consequences that were untenable or unpopular or both. The frustrations of these recession times boiled over in July of 1981 when Mayor Charles Royer mandated a $211,000 additional cut in the library's budget at midyear as part of his $3.6 million reduction in city funding. The library board's response included the likely closure of three small stations, two of which were in low-income housing projects (Holly Park, High Point), while the third was in the middle-class district of Wallingford (Wilmot). A fusillade of criticism followed and set off a five-month tug-of-war between the city council and the library board over where the library's cuts should indeed be made. When the often bitter battle of verbal posturing and closed-door maneuverings was finally concluded, the library board abandoned the station closure plan and opted instead to close all other branches one day a week and to close the Central Library one morning a week, plus lay off between six and ten library employees. It also slashed another 15 percent from the library's book budget, that ever vulnerable expenditure.

No party emerged unscathed during these budget travails. Librarian Dubberly was put under the media

microscope in a way that none of his predecessors ever had been when an influential alternative newspaper, *Seattle Weekly*, examined the library's condition in a lengthy article late in 1981. The highly critical analysis began under a huge headline ("Dubious about Dubberly: The Seattle Public Library Is Sinking under the Weight of Budget Cuts, Ill-Advised Reforms, and Poor Morale") and beside a large photograph that showed the librarian wearing a natty three-piece suit and a Cheshire cat grin, seemingly unaware of the article's tack.[28] Writer Rebecca Boren rounded up many of Dubberly's critics for the pointed analysis, which took a scalpel to the librarian's fondness for technological innovations, his penchant for administration building during a time of budget cuts, his strained relations with library staff, and his inability to restore needed spending on the library's book collection. "The library's worst problems aren't caused by the budget," Boren concluded. "The deepest wounds have been self-inflicted, caused by the library's own management, which seems to have forgotten the library's basic mission."[29]

Even the sunny countenance of the library's annual reports, which were becoming glossy public relations tools, turned glum. Dubberly looked back over 1982 and described it as "a troubled year" in the annual report, while the main narrative conceded, "Major adjustments in services and hours haunted downtown library staff and users alike."[30]

The Seattle Public Library finally seemed to be slowly emerging from its decade-plus of budget crises by the fall of 1984, even benefiting from the September passage of a citywide capital improvement levy to renovate the city's seven historic Carnegie libraries over the next four years. But that same month, the library suddenly found itself confronting the divisive issue of censorship for the first time since some black activists tried unsuccessfully to convince the library to remove *Little Black Sambo* from its shelves almost two decades before.

This time, the removal target was more contemporary —*Playboy,* the popular men's magazine known for its liberal politics, but known even more for its liberal use of photographs of nude women. Andrea Vangor, a Kirkland homemaker leading an ad hoc group called Together against Pornography, had persuaded several area supermarket chains and drugstores to stop selling adult magazines, including *Playboy.* Vangor's next objective was removing *Playboy* from three libraries in Seattle and six libraries in King County. She and her supporters argued their case in a joint meeting with librarians Dubberly of Seattle and Herb Mutschler of the King County Library System. Vangor recounted the meeting to a *Post-Intelligencer* reporter: "This type of literature, we told them, is linked to crimes and abuse against women. The pornographic stereotypes in *Playboy* are the same as in other adult magazines. It's porno that says women like to be raped."[31]

Such bold assertions by Vangor were persuasive with retail chain managers, skittish about anything that might offend any customers, but her complaints to the two librarians fell on deaf ears. Both Dubberly and Mutschler said they would keep *Playboy* on their library shelves, since there were patrons who wanted to read the adults-only publication there. Vangor and others in her Eastside-based group were unsatisfied by that response and pressed their case a week later at the regular meeting of the Seattle library board. "Taxpayer money," the Kirkland woman stressed, "should not be spent on promoting hate literature."[32] Vangor supported her argument with citations of various studies linking male violence against women to abusive pornography, and showed a scrapbook, prepared by supporter Tasha Ballou, that included clipped *Playboy* photos and verbiage on such subjects as bondage and bestiality, plus what they saw as jokes about rape and child molestation. Ballou told the board that *Playboy*'s content had changed in recent years to hard-core pornography, as a result of its declining sales in the competitive adult market, and she added, "We're not against erotic, beautiful portrayals of women. We're against violence and hatred directed at women."[33]

Together against Pornography happened to be raising its objections to *Playboy* at the very time when Seattle Public Library had its annual display for Banned Books Week on the third floor of the Central Library. Roberta Stock, president of the librarians' union, suggested that the anti-pornography crusaders ought to visit the exhibit, which included such banned works as *Gulliver's Travels,* plays by Shakespeare, and even the Bible. Stock insisted that the real issue before the library board was censorship, not *Playboy* magazine: "There are many materials at the public library that many groups and individuals find objectionable. Once we begin removing materials, where do we stop?"[34]

The library board responded that it would consider the objections of Together against Pornography, and the board's operations committee did begin a review of the library's policy for selecting materials in light of the complaints about *Playboy*. Editorial comment in the city's newspapers lined up squarely in support of the library's retention of the men's magazine. A cartoon by Brian Basset in the *Seattle Times* depicted members of Together against Pornography as "termites" trying to gnaw their way through the library's foundation,[35] while the *Post-Intelligencer* responded with a laudatory editorial (headlined "Librarians defend principle") that concluded: "Even though librarians probably would rather fight for the freedom to read Shakespeare than be forced to defend *Playboy,* we honor them for having the courage to do both."[36]

That the library board would retain *Playboy* seemed a foregone conclusion, and indeed it was. At a board meeting four months later, Macon Cummings, chair of its operations committee, said that the group had reviewed the library's policy on materials selection and recommended no change. The board concurred. Case closed, or so it seemed. But Vangor, whose group had not attended the board meeting despite expectations, offered an ominous-sounding comment when contacted by a reporter. "We'll get back to them," she promised, then declined to elaborate.[37]

Only six days later, Vangor and her group were back in the headlines with a new campaign. The target this time was *Show Me! A Picture Book of Sex for Children and Parents,* a 1975 sex education volume. Vanger's objections would be raised not with the library board but instead would be directed to Norm Maleng, King County prosecutor, with the hope that he would take action against the library for stocking a book that she described as "child pornography."[38] The *Playboy* roundabout would soon seem a mere overture. *Show Me!* was about to become a full-force Wagnerian opera, with a huge cast of characters, many twists and turns of plot, much sound, much fury, much grandstanding, much buck passing, all building in a fortissimo crescendo toward an uncertain climax.

This was not debating *Playboy* anymore—that much was certain from the outset. Dubberly did reiterate that the library would review *Show Me!* as a result of the complaints, but he also conceded that this case was a "new situation" because of recent changes in federal and state laws regarding sexually explicit depictions of children.[39] Those changes had been set in motion when the U.S. Supreme Court ruled in 1982 that states did have the right to ban almost all forms of child pornography. In the immediate aftermath of the Court's ruling, St. Martin's Press in New York City announced that it was ceasing publication of *Show Me!,* with the company president telling booksellers that the Court's decision will result in "the loss of a superb and enlightened work."[40] But the publisher's jettisoning of the sex education volume also could be interpreted as a de facto admission that *Show Me!,* however enlightened, was also

likely illegal under the new rules, a red cape waved in the face of the book's bullish foes.

Show Me! was already an inviting target for would-be censors. The large-format volume (9½ by 13½ inches) was bold, aggressive, graphic, and distinctly European in its approach to sexuality. First published in Germany in 1974, the book also had the aura of 1960s sexual permissiveness. American photographer Will McBride had worked with Swiss child psychologist Helga Fleischhauer-Hardt to produce a book of large-scale photographs of nude children and adults in a variety of sexual and nonsexual activities, plus accompanying comments by children and parents on what the photographs depicted. The narrative portions also included an "explanatory text" and appendix that, while informative on sexual matters, also tended toward the didactic with such pronouncements as: "Parents who feel that the book is good, but hesitate to show it to their 7 or 8-year-old, do so almost certainly because they fear they might impart to their children anxieties about their own sexual feelings or behavior patterns."[41]

The explicit photographs were clearly the defining feature of *Show Me!* and they left little to the imagination. The arty, black-and-white photographs showed everything from a mother breast-feeding an infant to nude parents and children embracing; from a sexually aroused young boy touching the breasts of a young girl to close-ups of female and male genitals during masturbation (including an erect penis that measured eight inches in one photograph) to another close-up of genitals during sexual intercourse purportedly between two teenagers. As Fleischhauer-Hardt underscored, "The photos show most of the usual forms of sexual activity."[42] That *Show Me!* was destined to prompt some controversy about its young subjects and their involvement in the book seemed to be conceded by McBride in a photographer's note at the end of the book that said, "The models were all friends. Except for the coitus scenes, mothers and fathers of the children were present and helpful during the photographic sessions."[43]

Controversy about *Show Me!* did not take long to develop in Seattle after the public complaint, even though the library had stocked four copies for almost a decade with the only real problems being occasional pages torn from the book and two of the four copies apparently stolen (as also happened to King County Library's two copies). In fact, Seattle library patrons were already precluded from using the book in the manner intended–showing *Show Me!* to their children at home and having frank parent-child discussions of its contents. The book could only be viewed in the library itself.

Such subtleties did not seem to come into play during Seattle's controversy over *Show Me!* Only a month after the complaint was raised by Vangor's group, the office of prosecutor Norm Maleng decreed that the book should not be on the shelves of Seattle Public Library because it was "not appropriate."[44] Yet Maleng declined to elaborate further or declare whether he considered the book to be illegal under a new state law that prohibited possession or distribution of child pornography. It was debatable indeed whether the county prosecutor should be determining "appropriate" material for the city's library to stock, but there was no debating that Maleng's willingness to jump into the discussion and his equivocations about the legality of *Show Me!* only served to raise the ante in the controversy. Duck-and-cover soon became the preferred posture of most people caught up in the gathering hurricane.

The prosecutor's office said it would take more time to evaluate the legality of *Show Me!* The library said it would hear testimony on the book in closed meeting, then backed off from that stance after criticism, then announced it would seek written public comment on the book. City attorney Doug Jewett, who was responsible for providing legal advice to the library board, decided that the board needed outside counsel and hired William Dwyer, a respected Seattle attorney with expertise in constitutional law. Librarian Dubberly tried to have it both ways by offering a public comment that "the library stands for ... open access to ideas and information" but also "has a responsibility to act within the law."[45]

The *Post-Intelligencer* was one of the few voices of reason cutting through all the *Show Me!* obfuscation. In an editorial, Seattle's oldest daily zeroed in on "local public officials who have allowed a legal question to escalate into an emotional and pointless community-wide debate."[46] The editorial continued:

> Dubberly did not take a strong stand, at least publicly, one way or the other. Maleng, while saying there are "very serious concerns" as to whether the book violates a law which he helped draft, declines to say if he thinks the book does in fact violate the law.... The [library] board first had the wrongheaded notion of holding a secret meeting to hear Maleng's experts. Now it has gone overboard on the other side by announcing it will seek written public comment on whether *Show Me!* should be in the library's collection. How citizens can say anything meaningful about a book most of them have never seen (even Maleng does not have a copy) is not explained.... More delay and attempts to hide behind a screen of public comment only will compound the earlier errors."[47]

No such expeditious conclusion was forthcoming. Two months later, the library had received 295 letters from citizens on the issue of *Show Me!*, with those seeking removal of the book outnumbering those supporting its retention by a 60 to 40 margin. The American Civil Liberties Union, a longstanding foe of censorship, had weighed in with its opinion that *Show Me!* was "a serious and thoughtful educational work" and argued that the library board should continue to stock it "until a court holds that possession of the book is illegal."[48] Opponent Vangor had continued to assert that the book had been used by child molesters to convince young people to engage in sexual acts, a position also affirmed by local talk show host Jennifer James. Prosecutor Maleng had finally offered a written memorandum that seemed to tack off onto another tangent, this time asserting that *Show Me!* should be judged not by its impact on the viewer but rather "from the enlightened viewpoint of its impact on the children used in its production."[49]

How that would be determined from a continent and a decade away seemed as elusive as how Seattle citizens were to assess a book that most had never seen. The *Seattle Times* at least tried to come up with an answer about the book's impact on its subjects, telephoning the photographer of *Show Me!* in Germany and one of its subjects, then a twenty-eight-year-old man living in South Africa. Both asserted that no coercion was used with the book's subjects. Michael Kurz, who was sixteen when he posed for McBride's camera, said his parents were present during the session and that both his brother and sister also were models for the book. "Why not pose nude?" Kurz said. "The book had a good purpose. I wasn't harmed."[50]

The *Show Me!* spotlight finally fell on the Seattle Public Library's board. It was time for its decision. The board met on May 2, 1985, in closed session to listen to attorney Dwyer and city attorney Jewett and consider its options and their legal ramifications. Then, the following day, the board met in public session and voted unanimously to retain *Show Me!* in the library's collection, basing that decision on the belief that the book was educational in intent and not child pornography.

Dwyer's legal advice to the board had proved instrumental in its decision and he restated that advice during the public meeting: "The courts would clearly hold that this book is serious in its purpose and that it has real, legitimate, substantial value as an educational resource. I don't believe there is sufficient legal basis, under either the federal law or state statute, to justify removing the book from the collection of the library."[51]

In retaining *Show Me!,* the library board took the strongest stand against censorship in its long history, defending principle and asserting its independence despite bitter controversy and veiled threats of possible prosecution. As board member Frank Greif asserted in the much watched public session, "We, the body that makes the policy decisions, cannot let the radical rhetoric of the right or the limitless liberal left cajole us into those kinds of decisions."[52]

The *Show Me!* controversy dragged on toward conclusion, with aftershocks felt in the days and weeks and even years ahead. Bitter opponents of the sex education volume vowed that the library board would live to "regret" its decision.[53] Newspaper editorialists saluted the library board's "correct" and "courageous"[54] stand. Prosecutor Maleng, in another retreat into legalisms, decided not to file charges against the library board—not because the board's ruling was correct, but rather because it would be difficult to convince a jury "beyond a reasonable doubt" that the library retained *Show Me!* "for the purpose of sexual stimulation of the viewer," as the state statute would require.[55] Columnist John De Younge of the *Post-Intelligencer* was just one of the prosecutor's critics who took him to task for his final pronouncement: "Maleng could have said that weeks ago and spared the city a broil over censorship."[56]

The aftershocks of *Show Me!* still lingered, especially for two of the principals in the controversy. Dwyer's 1986 nomination to become a federal district court judge was delayed for twenty months in Washington, D.C., in part because of conservative opposition led by Senator Strom Thurmond. In public hearings, the South Carolina lawmaker grilled the Seattle attorney about his advice to the Seattle Public Library regarding the controversial sex education volume. Librarian Dubberly—more outspoken in defense of *Show Me!* in a private staff memo after the library board's decision than he had been in public comments during the controversy—leaped at the chance to put Seattle and its

bitter battles behind him. Dubberly resigned his position a year after the *Show Me!* imbroglio and departed for more placid southern climes to serve as director of the Atlanta-Fulton County Library in Georgia. Dubberly's tenure at Seattle Public Library, eleven years of constriction and contentiousness, was finished, with few tears shed.

CHAPTER 10

Gathering Promise

SEATTLE WAS CHANGING in dramatic fashion in the late 1980s, its downtown transformed by major construction projects that often left the streets torn up and its skyline dotted with construction cranes. Downtown was sometimes derided for resembling Beirut, with all the rubble and ruckus. But this messy work-in-progress on Elliott Bay was the city assuming its long-sought position as the Northwest's dominant American city, its stature recognized beyond the borders of the region and the country. Nothing symbolized that new Seattle more than the seventy-six-story Columbia Center, a cold, black skyscraper that arose from the dreams of Seattle developer Martin Selig and dominated the city's skyline from its completion in 1985.

ABOVE: Seattle Public Library's move to a system of computerized circulation, called Project Quest, was symbolized by the Q.Card required of all borrowers after the changeover was completed in 1988.

OPPOSITE: Spencer Shaw, an expert on children's literature from the University of Washington graduate library school, enthralls a group of young readers and one older clown during a storytelling appearance at the Central Library, just one of the many outreach efforts that characterized Seattle Public Library during the late 1980s and early 1990s.

137

Librarian Elizabeth F. Stroup, long an administrator at the Library of Congress, took over as leader of Seattle Public Library in 1988 and soon proved to be a gale force of new energy and ideas.

The Space Needle had been a perfect symbol of the city in its time, a tourist magnet that said "Hey, look at us," a fun place from which to gasp at Seattle's blessed geography while watching the sunset in its revolving restaurant. The Columbia Center was the perfect symbol of the new Seattle, a serious business edifice that was the tallest skyscraper on the West Coast, its best views owned by a private club at the top and with scores of floors below "stuffed with enough lawyers to replace nearly half the attorneys in Japan," as Seattle writer Timothy Egan observed.[1]

The population of the metropolitan Seattle area had also been expanding, with 2 million inhabitants sprawling into the once forested countryside and 40,000 new arrivals every year looking for their own piece of "America's most livable city."[2] Even the population of the city itself had started to grow again, rebounding past 500,000 residents after two decades of decline and stagnation. Seattle Public Library harbored hopes of similar rebound in these increasingly prosperous times. Annual budget battles over dwindling city resources had hardly been conducive to much forward thinking during an unbroken string of trying years, but 1985 produced the first steps toward formulating a new ten-year plan for the library's direction. The 1986 annual report even dared mention "a library system designed for the 21st century."[3]

The most visible aspect of the library's move toward the future carried a title that seemed borrowed from a National Geographic television special. Project Quest was the library's move to a computerized circulation system, a massive five-year undertaking to launch the library into the electronic bar code age and provide more accurate tracking of materials and record keeping. It also provided each of the library's 125,000 users with a piece of red library plastic known as the "Q.Card" to be presented at the checkout desk. This was hardly the stuff of most patrons' library dreams, but laborious efforts by staff members and volunteers did indeed deliver "state-of-the-art library technology to the people of Seattle," a crucial modernization finally completed in 1988.[4]

Elizabeth F. Stroup roared into town early that same year. Seattle Public Library's new librarian was a forty-eight-year-old gale force of personality, quotations, and ideas. A spark plug of a person with large spectacles, the woman soon known throughout the city as "Liz" was the antithesis of her predecessors as the city's chief librarian, and not just on the basis of her gender. "Feisty" was not a word applied to previous Seattle librarians, but it seemed to be a mandatory adjective in any description of Stroup. She was also outgoing, outspoken, and just plain out there. She preferred to be referred to as "coach," although she also liked to be described in library materials as "chief executive officer," this melding of terms from athletics and business reflective of Stroup's approach to leadership. After two decades at the Library of Congress, the Oklahoma native returned to claim an annual salary of $75,000 and embrace the city where she had received both her bachelor's and her master's degrees in library science at the University of Washington. Stroup was soon energizing a long-strapped organization that had seen nothing quite like her, especially at the helm. "My dream," the new librarian remarked in one of her first media interviews, "is

The Library Equal Access Project (LEAP) aimed to make library use easier for those with disabilities and was one of several such outreach programs instituted under Stroup's leadership.

to make the Seattle Public Library the indispensable resource for every person in Seattle."[5]

Stroup described her new post as "the job I've been preparing for all my life."[6] Her initial actions in Seattle displayed elements of her previous work—from extension programs for small community libraries in north-central Washington to her various positions at the mammoth Library of Congress, including programs for the blind and handicapped, as well as outreach programs in states across the country. Stroup had become a master of both timeless small-town folksiness (her first message in a library annual report began, "Dear Friends") and the latest trends and buzzwords of the organizational elite ("empowerment" was a favorite).[7] Stroup, who grew up in Richland, even knew how to play the ever-effective trump card of Northwest chauvinism. She bowed to a local retail institution revered for its customer service and pledged that the Seattle Public Library would "become the Nordstrom of public libraries."[8]

The Stroup administration started at a sprint. Her initial year on the job resulted in the first reorganization of the library in fifteen years. It also produced a new, 420-word mission statement after what was described as a "visioning process" that involved members of the public and the library staff, administration, and board.[9] But the feel-good verbiage that emerged bore the unmistakable hand of Stroup herself, from its opening pledge ("our mission is to become the best public library in the world") to its closing suggestion ("both staff and patrons are encouraged to laugh often and out loud").[10] The new mission statement had enough fuzzy-wuzzy words to fill a sampler ("love," "nurture,"

"enrich," "collegial," "caring," "sensitive," "accessible," "supportive," "welcoming," "inviting," "valued").[11] But it also pledged that Seattle Public Library would stress such precepts as intellectual freedom, employment diversity, borrower confidentiality, appropriate use of technology, and respect for the different needs of its varied patrons.

A series of well-publicized new programs soon demonstrated that the library under its new leader was not just going to be talking the right talk. Stroup was no ivory-tower librarian; she was a relentless proponent of program initiatives, especially those extending services to society's less fortunate. "The library is the great equalizer," the new librarian stressed from her bully pulpit. "Knowledge is power and the library is the source of that."[12]

Community outreach had been a tradition at Seattle Public Library, but outreach had never been pursued with such fervor as it was under Stroup. The establishment of the Community Outreach Office in 1989 was a sign of this intensified priority. The library pledged to pursue "a barrier-free environment" a year before passage of the landmark Americans with Disabilities Act in 1990 started to mandate changes in accommodations and facilities.[13] The new Library Equal Access Project coordinated those efforts at the downtown library. Adult literacy centers were established in the Rainier Beach and Greenwood Branch libraries, the first new programs designed to reach the estimated 60,000 adults in Seattle (1 in 7) who were considered "functionally illiterate." This long-overlooked societal problem posed a particular threat to the library and its ability to serve the citizenry. After-school homework centers

Green Lake Branch became a construction zone during the extensive renovation of Seattle's seven landmark Carnegie branch libraries, a project that went on to win a prestigious national award in 1989.

Preservation in Washington, D.C. The five-year project returned the luster to these historic structures, with $4.6 million from a bond issue spent to upgrade mechanical systems, earthquake reinforcement, and handicapped access, plus $500,000 in donations from foundations and individuals spent to provide period-style furnishings. A $1,000 donation came from eighty-five-year-old May Freeman, who had been making weekly visits to the Fremont Branch for most of her life. "That was one place," she said, "that I was happy to give. I've had the use of it for 60 years and that's a long time."[14]

Hundreds of other Carnegie jewels had been turned to dust and memories across the United States, including Seattle's once magnificent Central Library, so the continued use of Carnegie buildings in the late twentieth century was fraught with increasing peril in a country where the latest thing is usually prized above all. As a feature story in the *Seattle Times* observed, "The Seattle Public Library could have abandoned the dowdy old gals with good reason. Roofs leaked. Solid oak front doors, fronted with intricate metal grillwork, had been replaced by tacky aluminum. Skylights were removed or painted over from the days of World War II blackouts. The interior workings—electrical, heating and plumbing—were woefully out of code. An earthquake could have crumbled the structures like cookies. Instead of tearing them down, the community decided to breathe new life into a legacy. It took a cast of characters: the library board of trustees and its foundation, citizens, private donors, architects, artisans, contractors."[15]

By the time the remarkable restoration was completed, Seattle's remaining Carnegie libraries sparkled with period-inspired details and furnishings. They included rosettes on the new handicap ramp at the West Seattle Branch that matched the rosettes on the original entrance railings through the meticulous efforts of a metalsmith, and copies of Fremont's beloved Gustav Stickley lounge chairs that had been fashioned from original Craftsman designs by state convicts at the McNeil Island Corrections Center. Carnegie's presence in seven Seattle neighborhoods had been assured for future generations of library users who could read, study, or just relax amid the

were established in several branch libraries to provide a study environment for children whose parents worked and who often did not have that option elsewhere. Seattle Public Library's After School Happenings, otherwise known as SPLASH, joined the growing series of new programs (LEAP, HELP, etc.) during a time when it seemed as though the library was competing in a contest to make the greatest use of cutesy acronyms.

A prestigious national honor was bestowed upon Seattle Public Library early in the Stroup administration. The recently completed restoration of Seattle Public Library's seven landmark Carnegie branch libraries received one of fifteen National Preservation Awards in 1989 from the National Trust for Historic

stately grace and sturdy furnishings of these classic structures.

But the chance to bask in past accomplishments never seemed to last long at Seattle Public Library, as Stroup soon learned. Present challenges, often from unexpected quarters, always seemed to intrude. That happened again in late February 1989, when Ayatollah Ruholla Khomeini, leader of Iran's 50 million Shia Muslims, proclaimed a *fatwa* death sentence against writer Salman Rushdie for "blasphemies" against the Islamic religion in his novel *The Satanic Verses*. Not only was a five-million-dollar bounty placed on Rushdie's head, sending the Anglo-Indian writer into hiding under armed British guard, but the death sentence was extended to others involved in the novel's distribution, presumably including publishers, translators, librarians, and booksellers. Protests over *The Satanic Verses* erupted around the globe, including ritual book burnings, plus riots in India and Pakistan that killed more than twenty people. Paranoia over the death sentence was soon racing past borders and across oceans, all the way to the United States, where the country's two largest bookstore chains (Waldenbooks, B. Dalton) removed the new American edition of the novel from their stores out of concerns for the safety of their bookselling staff.

The frigid chill of the death sentence was felt even in Seattle, where Rushdie had been scheduled to read from *The Satanic Verses* in early March. His American book tour was abruptly cancelled. Area booksellers faced both worries over security and rising public demand for the book, which soon claimed all their stock. Seattle Public Library grappled with the same problem and librarian Stroup swung into action. There would be no *Show Me!* debates and equivocations in this crisis over a controversial book, just as the library's new mission statement had promised. Its tenet of "active support and defense of intellectual freedom" was translated into the library affirming its commitment to circulating the novel.[16] It also led the library to attempt to purchase any copies of *The Satanic Verses* still left in Seattle, plus request the donation of copies from any readers finished with their own. And when the Washington State Coalition against Censorship mounted a protest reading in support of the Rushdie novel by local writers and artists, it was held in the plaza outside Seattle Public Library's Fifth Avenue entrance, drawing a crowd of 200 people, many wearing buttons that proclaimed, "I am Salman Rushdie."

Stroup was steadfast from the outset of the controversy, saying, "The library subscribes to the freedom to read. We believe it's very important to fight for that freedom, even if the reading material is unpopular, controversial or disturbing." "But don't you fear for the librarians?" asked Jean Godden, then a columnist for the *Post-Intelligencer*. "Of course," the librarian replied. "There's only one thing we're more concerned about. And that's the freedom to read. If any terrorists come, I'd hope that they'd ask for Liz. . . . A public library is a dangerous place."[17]

Seattle Public Library was also a busy place. Circulation soared past 5 million books and materials for the second straight year in 1989, keeping pace with the library in Toledo, Ohio, Seattle's usual challenger for bragging rights as the country's most used public library on a per capita basis. But Seattle's circulation of 5,271,252 also displayed a disappointing, if thoroughly modern trend: use of adult books, backbone of the collection, declined by almost 1 percent, while use of films, recordings, and videotapes ("media") jumped by 21 percent.

Public questions asked of reference librarians, another measure of the Seattle library's intense usage, surged 25 percent in 1990 to almost 2 million inquiries, many prompted by the city's hosting that summer of the Goodwill Games. This international athletic competition was originated by Ted Turner, an Atlanta cable television magnate who had grown frustrated with the superpower boycotts and national chest thumping that marred the Olympics in what was turning out to be the last decade of the Cold War. Civic boosters were aching then for Seattle to be considered a "world-class city" and it did bask in some world attention during the seventeen-day Goodwill Games. But many questions beyond athletics lingered long after the games' closing ceremonies in Husky Stadium at the University of Washington, questions about the Goodwill Games' promises, staging, finances, and impact that eluded answers even by Seattle Public Library's intrepid researchers providing its much praised Quick Information Service.

Program changes and initiatives continued apace at Seattle Public Library, many with the unmistakable Stroup stamp. Overdue fines for children's books were eliminated in 1990 because the librarian believed such fines might discourage lower-income parents from having their children use the library. Two-day training workshops on appreciating social and cultural diversity were attended by all of the library's 550 full-time and part-time employees in 1990. The policy of rotating staff members through branch libraries was ended that same year after more than a decade of continuing criticism; the policy was replaced with permanent branch assignments as part of the library's effort to

A crowd watches the latest developments in the 1991 Gulf War against Iraq unfold on a television monitor in the Central Library.

decentralize operations and provide knowledgeable outreach to various communities. Another outreach effort was started by the Washington State Center for the Book, which was established at the library in 1989 under charter from the Library of Congress. The center began modestly with a compilation of local book clubs.

The year of Seattle Public Library's official centennial finally arrived in 1991, but it was a letdown to those who dared hope that the library might coast through months of celebration and congratulation. This was no anniversary cakewalk. The centennial year instead provided a startling microcosm of Seattle Public Library's entire history, with its turbulent ebb and flow between accomplishments and disappointments, plus noble plans swamped by bitter realities. Seattle Public Library, during its 100th anniversary, faced a stern reality check.

January led off the year with war, as multinational forces under United States command attacked Iraq after its invasion of Kuwait. The Persian Gulf War proved mercifully short, a six-week campaign conducted primarily with airpower, but thousands of protestors turned out in the streets of Seattle in what seemed like an eerie reprise of the Vietnam era. There were also widespread expressions of patriotism in support of the troops in the war zone, many from Puget Sound

military bases. Seattle was gripped by intense anxiety as the conflict unfolded live on television sets, many set up in public places, including Seattle Public Library, which had also gathered materials on the conflict in special war-information displays. An open microphone was provided in the Central Library's auditorium for anyone wishing to express their views on the war. The Gulf War concluded with the expected triumph over Iraq, a triumph that cost the lives of ten military personnel from Washington State, but the war's aftershocks continued for many months, especially in the American economy, which soon plunged into recession.

The three-day celebration of Seattle Public Library's 100th anniversary took place in April during the brief respite between two powerful events, the war and the recession. The anniversary festivities included an ice cream social, library tours, musical performances by the Total Experience Gospel Choir and a navy brass band, readings from favorite children's books by local celebrities, including writers Tom Robbins and Charles Johnson and Mayor Norm Rice (the city's first black chief executive, elected in 1989). *Seattle Times* columnist Mindy Cameron visited librarian Stroup on the eve of the centennial festivities and came away much impressed, even by Stroup's often-stated intention to turn Seattle's library into "the best public library in the

TOP: Seattle Mayor Norm Rice reads aloud from a favorite children's book during the 100th anniversary festivities.

LEFT: Seattle Public Library's 100th anniversary in 1991 was celebrated with three days of activities for library users of all ages.

ABOVE: Young readers take part in the Centennial celebration.

world," a lofty goal adopted in the library's new mission statement, but one considered hyperbole by many skeptics. "It takes no more than 60 seconds with Stroup to realize she actually believes she can do that," Cameron reported. "Spend a half-hour with her, and she'll have you believing it, too."[18]

That belief was tested in the following weeks when the recession deepened and declining Seattle city revenues resulted in sudden budget cuts, including a $559,000 reduction at Seattle Public Library. Stroup had largely avoided the budget travails that ensnarled her predecessor, but there was no way for her to skate past the pitfalls caused by this 3 percent slash in the library's budget. Drastic measures resulted. Some staff positions were eliminated and a hiring freeze was instituted. The library's in-house bindery, a source of craftsmanship and pride for decades, was shut down, its two staff members let go, because the bindery had become "a luxury we can no longer afford" in the view of Stroup.[19] She promised a $120,000 annual savings from sending the library's well-worn volumes to a commercial bindery. The library's information center for local government in the Municipal Building was also shuttered, its services returned to the Central Library. Separate library phone lines for directory assistance and for stock and securities information were eliminated. Even the general information desk at the Central Library was shut down, a dubious approach to savings in an institution that had been trumpeting its commitment to customer service, but one that did convey a public message that all was not well with Seattle Public Library in its centennial year. The usually ebullient Stroup was forced to admit the obvious: "It's a tough time."[20]

The increasing support of the Friends of the Seattle Public Library and the Seattle Public Library Foundation was even more crucial in these periods of budget troubles. The Friends, which was celebrating its fiftieth anniversary in 1991, had turned its semiannual book sales into sterling fund-raisers that produced more than $40,000 annually to support library materials and projects. The Foundation's annual donors had increased more than ten times in the past five years, to 2,783 individuals and groups in 1991. The donations to the Foundation registered a similar increase, with more than a half million dollars donated during the centennial year. Foundation money purchased two new bookmobiles to serve homebound seniors and day-care children and provided "Raise a Reader" information packets to nearly 1,500 new mothers at two area hospitals, along with a first book and a "Read to Me" T-shirt for their newborns (an updated version of outreach to

new mothers that began at the Seattle Public Library in 1913).

The Foundation money added greatly to the centennial celebration, with $30,000 spent on related events that the library could not fund itself. The Foundation hosted a series of centennial breakfasts and luncheons that brought many community leaders to the Central Library throughout the year in hopes of building support for the institution, especially during the budget downturn. It also paid much of the cost of a candlelit centennial dinner at the downtown library in November, a lively gala that drew 250 guests from among the city's notables and featured a participatory mystery drama that centered on solving a "murder" staged on the library escalator. Solving the library's past shortcomings in fund-raising was the dinner's real objective.

The centennial dinner was the inspiration of Frank V. Greif, president of the library board. As he recalled later, "I saw the library as an institution that should be revered in the community. But a library is a lot like good health—it's assumed it's there, until it goes away. We needed more understanding of just how vital Seattle Public Library is. There had long been big support in this community for the Seattle Symphony Orchestra, Seattle Opera and the Seattle Repertory Theatre. The dinner was a way to begin that kind of approach to important donors. We wanted to create the feel of a place that people with deep pockets would not only feel comfortable. We wanted to show them a place they should contribute. We wanted to make them feel a civic responsibility to the library."[21]

The centennial dinner on Veterans Day came at a difficult time for the library board. A long-simmering dispute among its members had suddenly boiled over in full public view, the second time in the library's history when board discord erupted into headlines. The final straw this time was the awarding of a $417,400 contract for new carpet in the Central Library. Joseph C. "Bill" Baillargeon, who had been appointed to the board two years before, demanded that a task force investigate how and why the contract had been awarded to a firm that was not the low bidder on the hurried project. The sixty-one-year-old retired banker also demanded that librarian Stroup and two fellow board members (president Greif and Macon H. Simmonds) be suspended pending the outcome of the investigation because of their possible roles in the carpet affair.

The suspensions were not approved by the board, but it did direct the two attorneys on the board (Wallace Loh, O. Yale Lewis) to investigate the matter. They found "no credible basis" for Baillargeon's "accusa-

Frank V. Greif, president of Seattle Public Library's board of trustees, spearheaded a successful Centennial fund-raising dinner but later came under fire over his business connections during a bitter campaign waged by board member Joseph C. Baillargeon.

tions against the Seattle Public Library personnel and the trustees who were involved on the (now finished) recarpeting project or his assertions that the contract was manipulated for somebody or other's benefit."[22] The city's law department had reached a similar verdict about possible unethical conduct, although *Seattle Weekly*'s examination of what it called "Carpetgate" did reveal a series of bungles by the city and the library in the awarding of the contract to a firm that was supposed to include minority subcontractors but did not.[23]

Nothing mollified Baillargeon, who had gone from tweedy gadfly on the library board to self-righteous avenger. When his two fellow trustees presented their findings of "no credible basis" for his accusations, Baillargeon launched into an uninterrupted twenty-two-minute tirade replete with conspiracy theories and personal charges. Loh, dean of the University of Washington Law School, had been trying to serve as a

mediator between Baillargeon and his fellow trustees, but no longer. Loh introduced a motion for Baillargeon's dismissal two weeks later, declaring himself "saddened" by Baillargeon's "almost guerrilla warfare" against the library board and library staff.[24] The dismissal motion passed 4 to 0, with Baillargeon abstaining. Mayor Rice ordered his own investigation into the dispute on the library's governing body. Ten days later, the mayor demanded that Baillargeon resign, and he did, but not before compiling a three-page letter of resignation that repeated many of his allegations.

What had happened was nothing less than "a tragedy" in the views of board president Greif and librarian Stroup.[25] That assessment might have been overstated, but not by much. Baillargeon, a cum laude graduate from Princeton University who was a member of a long-prominent Seattle family, had come to the board with great potential. He knew Seattle, loved books, was even in the process of writing a doctoral dissertation on poet T. S. Eliot at the University of Washington. Baillargeon campaigned for a seat on the library board, a rare occurrence, with his candidacy supported by written recommendations from the city's elite. What no one mentioned about Baillargeon to representatives of Mayor Charles Royer, as Eric Scigliano of *Seattle Weekly* reported, was that this well-connected candidate had "shaken up other boards and pilloried their members,"[26] especially during his board service at the Seattle Foundation, a non-profit charity usually considered a model of decorum and accountability. So the clueless mayor went ahead and appointed the campaigning Baillargeon to the library board.

Fireworks were not long in coming. Baillargeon, a scholarly fellow, was soon raising hackles with his erudite but acute approach to library matters. He was a bulldog with the tiniest scraps of information, requesting this, insinuating that, questioning everything. Boards of trustees often need an in-house critic to avoid operating on autopilot, but Baillargeon charged right past that role to become a vituperative spinner of library conspiracy theories and conflict-of-interest scenarios. Baillargeon zeroed in on the possible relocation of the Central Library, recently made the subject of a study by a national firm. He concluded that powerful downtown forces were conspiring to move the library to a vacant block at Second and University adjacent to property owned by the Wright Runstad development company. Wright Runstad's vice president of commercial leasing, Frank Greif, also happened to be president of the library board. Baillargeon spun this connection into a supposed web of deceit. Possible relocation of the downtown library was an issue of public import, but Scigliano's exhaustive article examined Baillargeon's complaints and concluded, "His charges against library 'insiders' are complicated, shifting from target to target, from elusive speculation to outright assertion and back to speculation. . . . Baillargeon has a point—to a point. . . . As board member Loh says, 'There's a ring of plausibility in *everything* Bill alleges. He does a service in raising these issues. But having raised them, he won't let go.'"[27] Carpetgate became the inevitable last dispute in the short, unhappy career of a library trustee whose considerable potential was squandered by an abrasive style that so alienated others that they finally forced him to resign.

Baillargeon's reputation was not the only one besmirched in this ugly fray. Slung mud covered the library and many other library figures, including Stroup. Baillargeon's accusations against the librarian may have stretched credulity, but they did focus attention on her leadership after three years at the library. Honeymoon glow had given way to dented luster. Scigliano's article was the first major acknowledgment of that change when it stated, "Even supporters concede that Stroup's whirlwind style of managing tends to be more inspirational than methodical . . . until the city budget crisis hit, they had hoped to install a deputy to look after the details."[28]

Eight months later, a critical article in the *Seattle Times* went even further, depicting Seattle Public Library as "a sorely stressed place" bedeviled by lagging budgets, rising demands, low morale, internal strife, and anguished leadership.[29] It was difficult to imagine that this newspaper was the very same one that, just fifteen months before, had published columnist Mindy Cameron's paean to Stroup and her infectious vision of leading "the best public library in the world." But reporter Mary Ann Gwinn had dug much deeper, producing a more convincing portrait of the institution displayed on the *Times*'s front page.

Stroup's high-profile outreach programs still merited some praise, but they were depicted as coming with a price, especially to traditional programs and priorities (maintenance of the collection, book purchases) in a time of crimped budgets. It was one thing for board president Greif to trumpet how Seattle Public Library was handling a workload that had increased 260 percent since 1971 and managing that with four fewer staff members ("that's service!"),[30] but quite another to be a library staffer trying to work under the crush of such demands. Reference librarian Eric Cisney, a longtime union activist, minced no words when he told a March

1992 board meeting, "I've never seen morale as low as it is now. There is increasing stress and tension due to inadequate staffing and to conflicting demands from public and administration. People are discouraged, disillusioned and indignant at policies that are tearing away the fabric that has made this institution strong."[31]

Such criticisms did not sit well with Stroup, who had a distinct tendency to shoot from the lip. Gwinn recounted how the librarian had told managers during a staff retreat that she did not want any more hiring of "wimps, victims or loners,"[32] a disparaging remark that received much play in the office gossip mill. Nor was the once sunny librarian in a more charitable mood in her meeting with Gwinn. Stroup groused, "I felt I was very patient the first three years I was here. I'm now less patient with people who want to cling to the safe operating modes of the past in a world that's totally changed. I'm pissed. I'm so tired. I worked 20 hours a day trying to save our budget and nobody lost their jobs. Not only was there no appreciation, people don't even want to be (transferred to another position)."[33] The honeymoon with Liz Stroup was over, RIP.

Seattle Public Library soldiered on, as it always had done. The library continued to march smartly into the electronic age, going on-line for computer use late in 1992 and replacing its microfilm catalog, which had once seemed so advanced. The move to computerized record keeping was not without its difficulties or its glitches. As the library's 1992 annual report conceded, "Transferring the records of two million items in our collections to a new system took more than three months, during which time more than 80,000 titles were temporarily lost. For weeks, it was impossible to process the public's requests for best-sellers."[34] The new system did finally provide a stunning new world of public access, allowing a person with the right computer equipment to browse through the library's entire collection; to discover what books were available by author, title, or subject; to make book reservations; and to have all this without leaving the comforts of home. Seattle Public Library was not in the national forefront of computer access, having installed a Dynix system already in use at 450 libraries around the country, but this form of library service had not even been envisioned three decades before in the futuristic *Library of Tomorrow* at the Seattle World's Fair.

The library's move on-line also spelled the death knell for what had once been the heart and soul of the library's reference service, the card catalog. This imposing bank of wooden cabinetry, its file drawers packed with small cards, was intimidating to those first seeking access to its seeming secrets, but it was invaluable to those who had mastered its sometimes arcane methods of tracking subjects and books in the collection. Its intricacies meant that the card catalog often enhanced the authority and stature of librarians, who, for decades, unlocked its mysteries for the uninitiated, the unsuspecting, or the just plain mystified. Librarians were the only ones granted access to the card catalog during its final years. Its once busy file drawers were sequestered in a back room, as if hoping against hope that its whiz-bang technological replacements might prove unsuitable and it would be drafted back into service. No such call ever came, and instead the card catalog's cards, more than a half million pieces of the library's history, were dumped into bins and carted off to recycling in August 1992. This jettisoning of the card catalog, once utterly unthinkable, merited only the briefest of public obituaries. "It was, sob, the end of an era at the downtown Seattle Public Library last week," wrote columnist Jean Godden of the *Seattle Times.* "No more crumbling edges to finger. No more cross references in faded, Spenserian script."[35]

The eventful year headed to a close with Seattle Public Library in the spotlight again over another book on sex—a book actually titled *Sex,* filled with the erotic musings and posings of a pop star named Madonna. This glossy volume had 128 pages filled with Madonna's stark erotic fantasies as captured by fashion photographer Steven Meisel, and it was a brilliant expression of the calculated marketing and packaging so prevalent in the hype-filled 1990s. *Sex* was wrapped in Mylar to prevent bookstore perusal, was priced at $49.95 to suggest its art-book intentions, and was launched with enough weighty news articles and social commentaries to sink the *Titanic.*

Of course, the book was an instant number one bestseller, with libraries across America suddenly confronting demands that the Madonna book be included in their collections, or excluded. A two-week review of *Sex* was undertaken at Seattle Public Library after it received a copy from a donor who preferred to remain anonymous (a big secret indeed since it turned out to be none other than Stroup herself). The library review concluded that Madonna's book was "representative of ideas that are unique, alternative, experimental or controversial,"[36] and it was decided to put the library's copy on reserve in the Fine and Performing Arts Department, the only place where patrons could view the copy since home borrowing was prohibited. The library braced for a reprise of the *Show Me!* controversy, but the response to *Sex* never approached that level, perhaps because librarian Stroup

had already demonstrated such a fervent defense of intellectual freedom. The library's copy of *Sex* did receive a steady succession of viewers, so many that assorted pages soon separated from its ineffective spiral notebook–style binding, so many that the table where patrons examined the book was long described by departmental librarians as "the Madonna desk."

Two seemingly unrelated events a year apart—the closure of a downtown department store and the issuance of a library facilities report—soon dominated discussions, actions, and energies at Seattle Public Library for many months to come. The closure of the bankrupt Frederick & Nelson department store in May 1992 delivered a blow to the city's psyche, since the 101-year-old retail institution had been *the* place to shop for generations of Seattle families. The closure of the landmark ten-story structure left a gaping wound in the city's retail core that suggested Seattle's downtown might be headed for the same death throes that had occurred in countless other American downtowns, where crucial retailers had all fled to the climate-controlled refuges of suburban shopping malls.

A year after the Frederick & Nelson closure, Seattle Public Library released a facilities master plan drafted by a team of consultants who studied each of the library's buildings in the city and also conducted three public hearings seeking suggestions on the library's future needs and direction. The consultants' wide-ranging report concluded that one-third of the library's facilities did not meet seismic standards and that two-thirds did not meet current mechanical or design standards, nor had they kept up with patron demand. The downtown Central Library had the most shortcomings, some so serious that its improvement or expansion would not be a wise investment of money. Replacing it with a new downtown "anchor," carrying a possible price tag of $125 million, was the 1993 report's most noticed recommendation and what soon linked it with the closure of Frederick & Nelson.

Seattle Public Library, Seattle Symphony Orchestra, and the Nordstrom fashion retailer all became major players in a deadly serious game of civic musical chairs with the fate of downtown Seattle hanging on the outcome. Whose facility should go where in downtown fostered public debates and backroom maneuverings that lasted more than a year. Seldom had so many possible courses of action in downtown Seattle tantalized so many policy makers, retail developers, and would-be shoppers. Should the symphony's new concert hall be placed on the largely vacant hillside block just east of the new downtown Seattle Art Museum, bringing a new

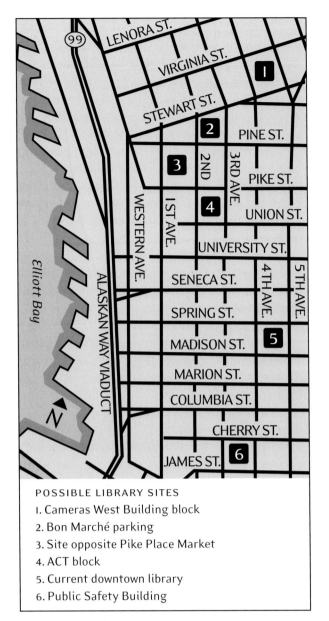

POSENTE LIBRARY SITES

POSSIBLE LIBRARY SITES
1. Cameras West Building block
2. Bon Marché parking
3. Site opposite Pike Place Market
4. ACT block
5. Current downtown library
6. Public Safety Building

Consideration of a new Central Library produced a plethora of possible sites, each with its proponents, and turned Seattle Public Library into a major downtown player.

cultural emphasis to the urban core? Or should the symphony move to a renovated Paramount Theatre? Should the Seattle Public Library move into the Frederick & Nelson building, leasing the first floor for retail, in hopes of bringing the crowds back to that long-visited site? Or should the library move to the urban crossroads of First and Pike, across from the fabled Pike Place Market? What if Nordstrom, the specialty retailer becoming a national name with a string of grandiose stores elsewhere, could be convinced, with some city incentives, to transform the boarded-up Frederick & Nelson into its flagship? And whither the library then?

One unexpected result of all this plotting was that the library finally did rebound from the treading-water era under librarian Dubberly. Stroup had put an activist face on Seattle Public Library, her ability to lead the library's charge forward in the community enhanced with the 1992 hiring of Craig Buthod to handle administrative duties in the new position of deputy librarian. But the library's possible construction of a new Central Library changed its image even more than having a gung ho librarian. It suddenly transformed Seattle Public Library from quirky maiden aunt into a major downtown player, a force earning added respect because of Seattle's legions of book-loving citizens, including more than 6,000 donors to the Seattle Public Library Foundation who were contributing more than $500,000 annually to support the library.

The downtown musical chairs continued, an agonizing slow waltz toward denouement. Jockeying for prime real estate positions finally started to yield prohibitive favorites. The symphony would build on the site by the art museum. Nordstrom would revitalize Frederick & Nelson and gain a 1,600-stall underground parking garage financed by the city on property across Sixth Avenue. That left the library lurching for a vacant site, with Stroup still hoping that the deal for her favored option, Frederick & Nelson, might yet fall through. Then came word of a January 1994 meeting with Deputy Mayor Bob Watt, who was set to inform the librarian that the mayor and civic honcho James Ellis had shaken hands on a deal that would put the library in the bottom four floors of the expanded state convention center on the eastern fringe of downtown. The next sound heard in Watt's office was a loud clash of wills.

As *Seattle Weekly* reported, "The bespectacled Stroup, who has a reputation for single-minded tenacity, said no way. Well, responded Watt, a man with a social-work background who's not inclined to play enforcer, perhaps Mayor Norm Rice needed to call in Stroup's superiors, the possibly more malleable library board, to rubber-stamp the deal. Fine, Stroup replied, but if more than two members were present, Hizzoner had better be prepared to air his plans in a public meeting. Gulp. Never mind, said a frustrated Watt, who had spent months working quietly on a downtown-rescue plan."[37]

The library regrouped and set off on its own course with Stroup providing spirited rebuttal to any suggestions that the library was a suitable fit with the convention center. There was a dizzying selection of possible downtown sites for a stand-alone Central Library, thirteen in all, hopefully capable of being narrowed in time to submit a library bond issue to voters in the fall of 1994. A citizens committee recommended that the library select the site by the Seattle Art Museum or demolish its current library and rebuild on that traditional library site. The library board took a different tack, choosing three other sites before finally settling on the property across from the Pike Place Market, a decision reached just two months before the impending election.

The library and its supporters quickly switched gears from site selection to passage of the library's proposed $155 million bond issue, with the Friends contributing $15,000 to help persuade voters. But the brief time before the election did not offer much room for assuaging doubts about the Pike Place Market site, which had definite drawbacks in many people's minds, including its scarcity of parking and its reputation as a gathering spot for downtown's down-and-out denizens. The library also found itself ballot partners with Seattle Public Schools and Seattle Police Department, which also sought approval of bond issues, $322 million for schools, $122 million for public safety. That situation meant that Seattle voters were going to the polls to consider a whopping total of $600 million in bond-issue improvements at one time, not a most promising prospect for any of the measures, even with the campaign's appeal for "Kids, Books, and Cops."

The library's chances were not helped either when the city's two daily newspapers were split in their recommendations on the bond issue. The *Post-Intelligencer* supported passage of the library bond, with its provisions to build a new downtown library and three new magnet libraries, and rebuild or renovate eight branches. "If anything, the library project is overdue," editorialized the morning newspaper. "Not only has the need for additional space fallen short of citizen demand, new technology has left our libraries in the dust."[38] The *Seattle Times* argued against passage of both the public safety and library bond issues, saying more time

was needed to refine the proposals because of "many remaining questions."[39]

Both the public safety and library bond issues were rejected by voters, while the school measure won passage, just as the *Seattle Times* had urged. But library supporters were greatly heartened by the impressive showing of the library's bond issue, which registered 57 percent support with voters, a near miss just 3 percent short of passage. "Our library," stressed William Golding, president of the library foundation, "finds itself standing on the threshold of greatness."[40] That opinion was shared by increasing numbers of people as the library board began to consider changes in its building plans to garner the needed additional support to pass a new bond issue at some future date. The figure of 3 percent danced in supporters' heads like some holiday sugarplum as 1994 drew to a close. Seattle Public Library's bold remaking seemed an attainable prize, not a fantasy anymore.

There were other indications that the library was indeed on the threshold of greatness. The library may not have been a leader in providing computer access to its collections, but it soon made up for lost time with a series of computer initiatives that attracted much notice. In February 1994, it started offering free classes on use of the Internet titled "Drivers' Education on the Information Superhighway." The ninety-minute classes proved so popular that they were soon offered several times a week, with more than 1,000 new Internet users trained at the library by year's end. Similar classes for the sightless were also offered at the renamed Washington Talking Book and Braille Library. Seattle Public Library also became the first library in the country to offer free access to U.S. government databases in October 1994, the very same month it became one of only eleven libraries in the country to offer interactive electronic access to White House information. These efforts earned a national prize for the library—the 1995 James Madison Award as "a champion for the public's right to know" from the Coalition on Government Information. The group recognized Seattle Public Library's "pioneering efforts to promote broad public access to computerized local, state and federal government information."[41]

The library also saw the flowering of three program-based initiatives. The Center for Literacy Advocacy and the Center for Technology in Public Libraries were established in 1993 and joined a reconstituted Washington Center for the Book. Nancy Pearl was recruited to direct the Center for the Book from her position as head of acquisition and collection development at the Tulsa

City-County Library Association. Pearl, another spark plug with short hair and outsized glasses, soon proved to be one of the few Seattle library staffers with an internal combustion engine that ran at similar revs as the librarian's. The new executive director of the Center for the Book was a tireless book lover willing to go anywhere and talk to anyone about the delights of reading, including her most recent book discovery, sometimes a novel finished only hours before. "My mission," Pearl related, "is to talk about the wonderful books that are available to read in libraries and I'd almost rather do that than anything."[42]

Pearl was everywhere, on radio, on television, in the newspaper, in front of groups small and large as Seattle Public Library's new public face. New programming also flourished under Pearl and associate director Chris Higashi, with the Center for the Book sponsoring fifty-eight events in 1994 attended by 2,500 book lovers. There was a noon book review series, a poetry discussion series, the new C. K. Poe Fratt Writers' Room for working authors in the downtown library that was funded with $60,000 in donations, plus a monthly meeting for authors called Writers' Salon that *Seattle Weekly* described as "one of the most important ongoing literary events in the city."[43] The center even sponsored an annual statewide photo contest that focused on capturing Washington's avid readers in a host of creative settings, from candlelight to wheat field.

A less romanticized view was provided in 1994 by a consultant hired by the Seattle Public Library Foundation to evaluate the library's collection with an eye toward securing federal assistance, although few other libraries had undertaken a similar study so comparisons would prove problematic.[44] The ninety-page report by Brenda P. Tirrell from Houston did paint a dreary picture of the library's collection, revealing inconsistencies and shortcomings exacerbated by years of inadequate funding. But the primary impression left by Tirrell's examination of 13,181 books at the library was the collection's age, especially at the Central Library. As the consultant stressed, "The collection on the shelf at the downtown library is old and worn. The initial visual impression as one approaches the shelves is that the library houses a tired and outdated collection. One staff member expressed this by describing the collection as 'gray.' Many damaged volumes are still on the shelf and there is an overall insufficiency of current materials. . . . In many subject areas, readers simply would not be able to find recent books on a topic of interest. The collection requires a major investment in both new

titles and replacement copies to enhance the quality of the collection available to the public."[45]

A new centralized program of book ordering was in the process of being implemented at the time of the report's publication, with three-quarters of the purchases being made in the downtown office of Jean Cobberly, collection services coordinator, in order to avoid the sort of collection gaps that Tirrell had found. More collection help came just four months later when the library's Foundation received a $250,000 gift from Mrs. Eulalie Bloedel Schneider through the R. D. Merrill Foundation. This timely donation, the largest to the library since Robert Bunn's, was divided in two, with one-half going toward purchase of "best books" and one-half going toward purchase of "books on tape," two areas of the collection receiving pointed criticism in Tirrell's report.

Another welcome donation was announced late in 1995 when the Redmond-based Microsoft Corporation unveiled a one-year pilot program to help libraries provide on-line access to their patrons. Seattle Public Library received the largest grant ($680,000 in cash and software) among the nine recipient libraries across the country. Seattle's portion was destined to establish community computer labs at the Central Library, Rainier Beach Branch, High Point Branch, and the library at West Seattle High School. "We will also be setting up community-based classes for all age groups," promised Willem Scholten, director of the Center for Technology at the Public Library, which was administering the Microsoft grant and providing operational support to the eight other recipients.[46] That arrangement underscored Seattle Public Library's national prominence in the use of on-line technology, just as the grant itself underscored the national prominence of Microsoft. It had become a software colossus in the years since its unlikely founding in 1975 by two former students at Seattle's exclusive Lakeside School, Bill Gates and Paul Allen, who were becoming two of the world's wealthiest billionaires as a result of their Microsoft stock holdings.

Much seemed to be going well for Seattle Public Library as 1995 headed toward 1996. Annual circulation of library materials continued to soar past 5 million items, the library Foundation's annual donations topped $1 million for the first time ($1,413,177), and the library's new home page had spent several months posted on the World Wide Web with detailed information on library services. But all was not so rosy behind the scenes at the library. Growing disenchantment with librarian Stroup was rippling through the library staff, the library board, and city officials. There were no doubts

A tearful Liz Stroup attempts to restrain her emotions during a standing ovation that followed her surprise resignation on August 30, 1996. Joining the standing ovation (at left) were members of the Seattle Public Library's board of trustees, who forced the librarian's departure because of problems with her leadership.

the long-term interest of the library, then I become a mother bear").[48]

So anticipation built for the trustees' meeting, with many Stroup supporters, library staff members, and other interested parties expecting Seattle Public Library's very own version of the Gunfight at the O.K. Corral, prompting 100 people to show up for the meeting and force its move from the boardroom to the main auditorium.

But a series of executive sessions that day had averted the potential firefight. A last-minute agreement had been hammered out between the board and the librarian, with Stroup agreeing to resign and drop her discrimination lawsuit in exchange for six months of severance pay ($45,000). Still, Stroup did get her chance to address the crowd after the board announced its unanimous acceptance of what was described as her "voluntary resignation." The fifty-seven-year-old librarian, wearing a button that proclaimed "Kids Who Read Succeed," assumed the unaccustomed role of diplomat in her farewell to eight years at the library's helm.[49]

about Stroup's energetic commitment to the library or her tireless advocacy of new programs, but there were increasing inside criticisms of her abilities as manager of an institution with 380 employees and an annual budget of $23.4 million. Deputy librarian Buthod had been hired to provide direction in that area, but relations between the two were often frosty and occasionally contentious. Other negatives began to surround Stroup as well. Her outspokenness, so refreshing at the outset, had turned as tiresome as a record stuck in the same groove. Her public stand against including the new Central Library in the state convention center had earned the distrust, if not the animus, of Mayor Rice. Even some of Stroup's personal habits were the subject of criticisms and rumors in the gathering private storm against her.

It all came to a head in a dramatic meeting with the board of trustees on August 30, 1996. That day's *Seattle Times* had shocked many readers with its headline "City Librarian Expects She'll Be Fired Today."[47] The accompanying story provided its jolts too—that Stroup had recently filed a lawsuit against the board and the mayor, alleging sex and age discrimination in her likely firing; that Stroup was making $1,400 less in annual salary than Buthod; and that Stroup had no intention of going quietly ("if I think something's going to hurt

Stroup said that it was in the library's best interest, and her own best interest as well, to resign at this time. What she had done at Seattle Public Library had been a "labor of love," but now "it's time for new leadership to raise this library to new levels."[50] The library should move on, Stroup added, and she would move on too, taking time for herself to drive around the country in her camper van and visit libraries, large and small. She would do "some serious stock-taking" about her future during her meanderings,[51] but she promised to still return to Seattle as her home and always remain a "passionate advocate" for Seattle Public Library.

There were tears in many eyes as Stroup concluded her remarks and the crowd quickly rose for a loud standing ovation. All five library board members (Lazelle Johnson, O. Yale Lewis, John Mangels, Gordon McHenry Jr., Betty Jane Narver) also stood and applauded Stroup, but none of the board members offered public comments afterward, their tense mission accomplished. The meeting quickly adjourned, with many faces in the crowd still registering shock at what had just transpired. A nationwide search would begin soon for someone other than Stroup to lead Seattle Public Library across the threshold of greatness and into the twenty-first century.

CHAPTER 11

Libraries for All

THE NATIONWIDE SEARCH for a new librarian for Seattle Public Library was taking far longer than had been anticipated as it continued under the direction of a Los Angeles–based search firm and a twenty-one-member search committee. Months passed with Craig Buthod serving as the interim librarian, the suspicion growing that his long-rumored ascendancy to permanent head of the library was becoming a forgone conclusion. More months passed without any public sign of progress toward a new librarian; the start of 1997 arrived and passed with the same result. Seven months after Liz Stroup's resignation, a sense of unease had settled

ABOVE: Librarian Deborah Jacobs and architect Rem Koolhaas (at right) were long-shot candidates when hired by the board of trustees of Seattle Public Library. The two formed a fine working partnership, cemented by much mutual kidding, that paid dividends as construction progressed on the new Central Library.

OPPOSITE: A power shovel claws away at the skeleton of the downtown Central Library, part of the dramatic changes wrought by the Libraries for All program.

Deborah L. Jacobs had been named national librarian of the year for her leadership of the public library in Corvallis, Oregon, but the move to the helm of the Seattle Public Library represented a huge leap in responsibilities.

over the institution that seemed to be waiting for a new librarian named Godot.

The library's next chance to seek voter approval for its crucial bond issue was being held hostage by the librarian search. Or it was progressing without the guidance of a permanent librarian. Both troubling scenarios had their supporters. Tina Podlodowski of the Seattle City Council raised the issue of missing leadership in public comments, as did Eric Cisney, president of the AFSCME Local 2083, which represented three-quarters of the library's union employees. In April, Cisney wrote to the *Post-Intelligencer:* "We are also concerned that irrevocable decisions regarding a new Central Library and improvements to the branches are being made without the involvement of the new director."[1]

More months passed, including May and June, the target months that board president O. Yale Lewis had predicted would yield a list of finalists for the vacant position. That finalist list did not surface until September, more than a year after Stroup had announced her departure. The three announced finalists did not include Buthod, as had been widely anticipated. The

protracted search produced two male librarians running libraries similar in size to Seattle's, although Sacramento and Buffalo, New York, were hardly cities with the flourishing book culture of Seattle. The third candidate seemed the long shot, younger than the other candidates by at least five years and running a Northwest college-town library dwarfed by Seattle's library, with only one-seventh of its budget and its number of branches. The third candidate was also the only woman, although it was difficult to assess whether that was an advantage or a disadvantage, given the library board's soured relationship with Stroup.

But the long shot left the strongest impressions during the round of community meetings and board presentations by the three librarian candidates competing in a very public audition process. Deborah Jacobs, head of the city-county library in Corvallis, Oregon, demonstrated the best speaking talents of the three finalists, the strongest vision, the greatest energy and empathy. She also seemed to arrive with the least baggage of the three finalists, unencumbered with significant criticisms of her administrative talents or policies in past jobs. Then there was the matter of courage, not the usual trait associated with leadership of a library, but one that Jacobs had shown she possessed during a bruising electoral battle in Oregon. A 1992 ballot measure called Proposition 9 sought to impose restrictions on government "promotion or endorsement" of homosexuality and could have led to the banning of some library books and materials. Jacobs, then serving as president of the state library association, took a leadership role in the efforts to defeat Proposition 9, despite considerable personal risks. The Corvallis librarian, her partner, and her twelve-year-old son received hate mail and death threats left on her home answering machine as a result of her highly visible activism against the measure. Gay and lesbian materials in the Corvallis library were also vandalized. Proposition 9 was finally defeated, with a key contribution made by Jacobs's rallying of library forces, a campaign that the American Library Association honored as the most effective defense of intellectual freedom in the United States that year. Jacobs's efforts to defeat Proposition 9 also played a significant part in her being named 1994 national Librarian of the Year by *Library Journal* magazine in an issue with the editor-in-chief's admiring profile saluting Jacobs for her "warmth, intelligence, gentle humor and soft-spoken leadership."[2]

Still, it was one thing for a national magazine to honor a college-town librarian who had made good. It was quite another for one of the country's major urban library systems to elevate that college-town librarian to its helm without the benefit of big-city seasoning as a prerequisite. So Seattle Public Library's board did not have an easy time in finally selecting the new librarian. The board met in closed executive session on Sunday, September 28, with the five members weighing their own impressions along with the flood of citizen phone calls, letters, and e-mails on the finalists that left board member John Mangels "surprised by the strength of the views people expressed, and at times taken aback."[3] An hour passed in board debate, then another, then another. Four hours of discussion occurred before the board could reach a unanimous decision announced in public a day later: the new Seattle librarian would be the forty-five-year-old long shot from Corvallis, the Los Angeles native who had received degrees from Mills College in California and the University of Oregon and had first worked as a children's librarian in Bend, Oregon.

The selection of such a long shot is not the usual result of lengthy public leadership searches, especially by controversy-shy citizen boards, so library leaders in Seattle were quick to defend their selection of Jacobs for the $100,000 post. Betty Jane Narver, the board's increasingly influential president, stressed, "There's no question that it's a leap in terms of the size of the institution, but the total picture for us was more complete with Deborah."[4] Barbara Duffy, president of the Friends of the Seattle Public Library, argued that Jacobs's talents were exactly what was needed to lead the campaign to pass the library's upcoming bond issue and build support for a site for the new Central Library, the contentious issue that had done so much to derail Stroup. "One of her [Jacobs's] greatest strengths," summarized Duffy, "was her ability to develop consensus and her leadership from the grass-roots up. I believe she will apply those same skills, look forward and, frankly, not spend a lot of time on the history."[5]

Jacobs arrived in Seattle that November and indeed never cast a glance back. She soon proved to be a library dynamo, short in stature, but unlimited in energy, enthusiasm, and dimpled smiles, as she demonstrated during public assemblies in meeting rooms and community halls, night after night after night. Jacobs's stated mission was familiarizing herself with Seattle and gathering community suggestions for the crucial bond issue that loomed less than a year away, but her real goal was enflaming citizens with a love of libraries commensurate with her own. Stroup's feistiness had been replaced by Jacobs's passion. Here was a seemingly guileless public official who had no compunction about getting misty-eyed over the dedication of library employees or how she had started out as a children's librarian because of her long-held belief that "if I could help one child as a librarian, I'd forever affect the quality of life for everybody in the universe."[6] Here was an avid reader who was proud to admit that "one of my most cherished 'decadences' is reading in a bubble bath."[7] And here was a stylish woman who changed her hair color, eyeglasses, and apparel with such regularity that she came across as a constant work-in-progress, as if always in search of the right combination to suit both her sense of professionalism and her sense of fun.

Those who assumed that Jacobs was merely a combination of sap and velvet soon learned there was steel to her as well. She was one of those savvy professional women who know that employing a traditional male approach to leadership would undercut her own strengths, including the ability to listen and project compassion. Paul Schell, an urban developer and planning activist, became mayor of Seattle at about the same time that Jacobs started to lead the library. The two new civic leaders quickly developed a strong working relationship. Schell came to admire Jacobs's approach to getting things done. "When she speaks, it's not just words that happen," the mayor said. "It transcends conversation. It's not an imposing physical presence, more an intellectual and spiritual presence. She listens with both the mind and the heart at the same time."[8]

Jacobs needed all those talents in the months ahead as the bond issue was reshaped to better suit the community's needs and the sticky issue of a location for the new Central Library arose once again. But there was a crucial difference this time. No longer were a dozen potential sites under consideration by the library board, producing a confusion of competing possibilities. Nor was the favorite any longer the site near the Pike Place Market, which possessed as many negatives as positives. The new front-runner, boosted by the public support of Jacobs, was the current library site, familiar to Seattle Public Library users for ninety years. The main argument against the current site was that it would require two moves of the downtown library's extensive collections, one out of the building before demolition of the old library, then another back into the building after construction of the new library. But much reduced figures for the cost of those moves—down from an estimated $18 million to $11.5 million through a faster timetable and other revisions—had dissipated the opposition to the current site that had led to the board's adoption of the Pike Place Market site for the previous bond issue. Familiarity started to breed support, not contempt. The current library site had history, had excellent pedestrian traffic and public transport, and had the decided advantage of a deed already owned by the library. There also happened to be only one holdover on the library board from the days of its Pike Place Market site selection.

The *Seattle Times* editorialized in favor of the current site, describing it as "a proven success.... the right choice for almost a century, and will be for the next."[9] Meade Emory, an iconoclastic University of Washington law professor whose seven-year tenure on the library board ended in 1989, also threw his support behind the current site with a well-argued op-ed piece in the *Post-Intelligencer* that concluded with a prescient prediction: "Using a world-class architect at what almost everyone agrees is the optimal site would excite this city, and its philanthropists as well, beyond all expectation. It could result in something so grand that the memory of any hardship associated with its realization will quickly fade."[10]

Seattle had an often sorry history of marathon go-arounds, especially over new public facilities. It often seemed as though Rome was built in fewer days than, for example, Westlake Center shopping mall in downtown Seattle, which produced two decades of ink and acrimony before its compromised birth. But support for the current library site soon reached such a crescendo that a decision was made in its favor after only one month's debate, perhaps a civic record.

Decisiveness became the 1998 hallmark of an energized Seattle Public Library under Jacobs's new leadership, with definite momentum building support for passage of the library's historic bond issue in the November election. One measure of that momentum was the first public hearing on the revised "Libraries for All" bond issue on April 22. Members of the city council and library board braced themselves for an encounter with critics, complainers, and snipers at the $195.5 million bond issue, a massive expenditure even during boom times in Seattle. They instead found themselves presiding over a library lovefest, with speaker after speaker lavishing praise on the bond issue. "A good library system is not a luxury," stressed Wilma Bishop, one of the fifty speakers at the hearing. "It's a necessity."[11]

Jacobs's expeditions into Seattle neighborhoods to gather suggestions and requests had paid great dividends. But the revamping of the bond issue had also been carefully calculated to engender support. "Libraries for All" may have had a ring of public relations sloganeering to it, but even a cursory look at the bond issue revealed that this was truly a measure that delivered on its promise of something for everyone. No Seattle neighborhood was left untouched by the bond issue's proposed largesse, from southwest to northeast, from southeast to northwest.

The ambition and scope of "Libraries for All" were staggering, especially for a city library system that had been forced to tread turbulent waters through so much of its history. Seven libraries were to be replaced with entirely new structures under "Libraries for All" (Central Library, Ballard, Beacon Hill, Capitol Hill, Greenwood, High Point, Montlake). Seven libraries were to receive major expansions (Broadview, Columbia, Douglass-Truth, Lake City, North East, Rainier Beach, Southwest). Five libraries were to receive major renovations (Green Lake, Madrona–Sally Goldmark, Magnolia, Queen Anne, University). Five new libraries were to be built in unserved areas of the city (Delridge, International District, Northgate, Sand Point, South Park). Two libraries were to receive both renovation and an addition (Fremont, West Seattle). And two small libraries were to be relocated (New Holly, Wallingford-Wilmot).

But the voter appeal of the "Libraries for All" campaign was not limited to new and renovated library buildings. The Seattle Public Library Foundation, under president Jack Faris, pledged its intention to supplement the bond issue with a whopping $40 million in donations from private individuals, corporations, and foundations that would be used to improve the expanded library's book collection and its technological assets. New recruits were rallying to the library's cause, doubling the foundation's number of donors in a single year to more than 8,500 in 1998. The library Foundation's goal of raising $40 million reflected a wildly optimistic time when any goal seemed attainable and the future seemed limitless. Seattle's economy was riding a high-technology high, with stock market paper fortunes being made on the rise of such Seattle-based firms as Microsoft. An influx of new money was transforming the Seattle landscape, from waterfront mega-mansions along Lake Washington that replaced "tear-down" abodes to condominium and apartment towers that turned the seedy Regrade into the trendy Belltown. Fancy restaurants sprouted overnight, filled with flush young "foodies" in search of the best new use of goat cheese. Packs of limousines cruised the streets. Euphoria reigned.

In March 1997, the Seattle Public Library Foundation had announced a "Books, Bytes & Believers" campaign to raise a hefty $5 million to revitalize the library's collections, both at the Central Library and at the branches. Less than a year later, the foundation had reached half of its $5 million goal on the strength of a single donation, the largest ever received by Seattle Public Library.

The charitable foundation of Paul Allen, Microsoft co-founder, contributed $2.5 million to boost the library's collection, an amount so sizable it could purchase an estimated 100,000 books. Allen's well-publicized donation was even more significant because of its timing. It conveyed the local billionaire's philanthropic seal of approval on the library at the very moment when the Foundation was upping its fund-raising ante with its stunning pledge to raise eight times the amount sought for "Books, Bytes and Believers." Allen set off a signal and a challenge to other potential donors to Seattle Public Library: Get on board now.

Timing had often proved to be Seattle Public Library's greatest enemy during its history, with various grand plans and bold initiatives announced just as the economy started to sour, or a war broke out, or an election ballot was crowded with other funding measures, or the library's own leadership turned timid or contentious. But, finally, as if by some law of probability or some sudden outpouring of poetic justice or some karmic something, Seattle Public Library was proceeding with the largest bond issue ever proposed for an American library at what was turning out to be the absolutely perfect moment in its history. Timing had suddenly become Seattle Public Library's brand-new best friend.

The campaign "Libraries for All," called Proposition 1 on the November ballot, charged ahead. A campaign committee spearheaded the efforts to secure passage, providing many of the 1,115 volunteers who supplemented an ad campaign that cost $477,000. Token opposition did emerge, but with too little, too late; it was out-muscled by the library's exhaustive outreach efforts. Newspaper editorialists praised the plan's boldness, including the *Seattle Times,* which had often been critical of past library bond measures. "The need is clear," the *Times* proclaimed in urging passage of Proposition 1. "The plan is sound. . . . The plan leverages with private dollars. . . . The plan keeps faith with neighborhoods."[12] Most important of all, voters responded favorably at the polls, casting "yes" votes at a rate seldom achieved in any democracy—a dazzling 69 percent. No city measure in Seattle history had ever received such support at the polls.

The good news did not end on election night. Just three weeks later, Faris of the library Foundation presided over a press conference in the library's packed Lee Auditorium to announce receipt of the largest donation ever given to any American library. Seattle residents' enthusiastic support for "Libraries for All" had convinced Bill and Melinda Gates to donate $20 million to the Seattle Public Library, with $15 million going to branch libraries, $4 million to the book collection, and $1 million to special programs. The Microsoft cofounder told the assembled crowd of dignitaries, public officials, library supporters, and media: "It's really more a celebration of the bond measure than anything else. It says a lot about this city and how we believe in creating equal opportunity."[13] Added Melinda Gates, "Libraries help level the playing field by giving everyone—no matter what their economic situation—access to the same tools and information. This gift will ensure that the Seattle Public Library continues to connect people with the information they need."[14]

The Gateses' donation could have propelled the library Foundation to the halfway point in its $40 million campaign, but Faris announced that the Foundation would instead seek to raise an additional $20 million, another indicator of Seattle Public Library's surging confidence amid the greatest moment of triumph in its history. Librarian Stroup's often repeated goal that Seattle would boast "the best public library in the world," once easy to dismiss as a feel-good fantasy, was starting to assume an air of distinct possibility.

But there was no pause to savor the library's increasing good fortune. Even Seattle Public Library's annual report for 1999 described the activity of the following months as "feverish,"[15] an adjective rarely applied to library efforts, but accurate. The "Libraries for All" undertaking was so massive that it soon required creation of a new and complementary infrastructure, what would become a kind of shadow library with its own administration, own policies and procedures, own citizen outreach, own finances. Alexandra Harris, an architect and veteran administrator for the City of Bellevue and the City of Seattle, was hired to direct the library's capital projects program, her astute political sense soon teamed with the budget savvy of Robert Goldstein, the library's chief financial officer, who took on added responsibilities with his genial good nature.

Seven years initially sounded like a distant deadline for completion of the library's $256 million makeover, but any such notion quickly vanished amid the vast demands of a building campaign that would almost double the square footage of Seattle Public Library's branch system. Each branch required the recruitment and appointment of a citizen review panel; selection of an architect and often a new site from multiple possibilities; establishment of a timetable leading toward completion; designation of a project manager, a library board liaison, a local Friends representative; and selection of artists to create work to enhance the branch.

These complex demands only intensified with the new Central Library, expected showpiece of "Libraries for All" with its construction budget of $90 million. The 362,987-square-foot structure presented great opportunities as well as great risks. It would be *the* Seattle Public Library in many people's minds, its downtown headquarters, its symbol, its heart, plus it would be heir to the legacy of two other libraries on the same site that had once been the source of great civic pride and memory, their big-budget successor standing on what librarian Jacobs described as "sacred soil."[16] Architect Peter Steinbrueck, a member of the Seattle City Council, also was inspired to use a religious metaphor, likening construction of the new downtown library to the construction of a cathedral centuries before in the cities and towns of Europe. Yet the new Central Library would be the result of a high-profile process where various visions, needs, agendas, and egos all competed in the public arena until some consensus could be reached. Consensus usually represented the committee mentality, seldom the breeding ground for innovation and creativity. The likely result was a building of common-denominator mediocrity, the least offensive approach to the greatest number of people, especially in Seattle where there was no tradition of inspiring civic architecture.

Seattle Public Library was under great pressure to do much better, to set a new standard, to pioneer a new path. After all, 69 percent of voters had given an unprecedented mandate to the library, a mandate that it could fulfill, or that it could squander. Crucial to the project was selection of the new Central Library's architect, under a process that revved into action only four months after voters left their polling places. February 1999 saw the hiring of two Seattle veterans of architecture and construction (Gordon Walker and Dan Dingfield) to advise the library during the architect selection process. The same month also saw the appointment of a fourteen-member citizens' panel to screen the architectural firms applying for the important commission, compile a short list of finalists, and then provide a recommendation to the library board.

The large committee represented many segments of the community with an interest in architecture and the library project, including developers, architects, the library staff, the library Foundation, the library Friends, the city design commission, a venture capitalist, a software executive, a visual artist, a downtown attorney, and a literary novelist. Librarian Jacobs served as one of the group's four advisors. The Architect Selection Advisory Panel's acronym (ASAP) said as much about the group

as its diverse membership, since it was supposed to reach its momentous decision on a very fast track, no more than three months.

The committee's responsibility was even more daunting once applications for the commission arrived at Seattle Public Library. The library project prompted proposals from twenty-nine architectural firms from across the country and around the world. The applicants included many names from the global elite of architecture: Arthur Erickson and Moshe Safdie of Canada; Norman Foster of Great Britain; Cesar Pelli, I. M. Pei, Michael Graves, and Richard Meier of the United States. The committee commenced its winnowing work, rating the applicants through the use of a five-page evaluation score sheet that included such standard architectural criteria as "experience with large public sector projects," "record of building designs illustrating functional excellence," and "evidence of collaborative skills."[17] These criteria had added weight since the architect selection process at Seattle Public Library would not result in competition between actual designs for the Central Library from the finalists; rather, the Seattle selection would hinge on which firm demonstrated the greatest spirit of creativity and collaboration during interactions with its prospective client.

The citizens' committee conducted its deliberations with an air of collegiality and purposefulness. Five finalist firms were selected near the end of April—an intriguing mix of established architectural stars (Cesar Pelli and Associates, Foster & Partners), rising talents on the international stage (Steven Holl Architects of New York, Office for Metropolitan Architecture from the Netherlands, led by Rem Koolhaas), and a respected Northwest firm based in Portland (Zimmer Gunsul Frasca Partnership). Things seemed to be proceeding right on schedule when, only weeks later, there was a major setback. The two most stellar finalists withdrew from the competition, Pelli because the library was requiring architects to pay their way to Seattle in the second phase of the competition, and Foster because of a scheduling conflict with another major commission he had just received. The loss of Foster was probably the most disappointing, since the London architect had been selected only the week before to receive the prestigious Pritzker Prize, architecture's highest honor.

The selection process proceeded with the three remaining architects, but with a definite loss of luster. Gone, too, were the important benchmarks that were expected to be set by the established architectural luminaries. Even before the in-person portion of the competition, the architect choice had been reduced to a selection between two rising international talents (Holl, Koolhaas) and one safer choice based in the region. Holl seemed to be the leading candidate, in part because he was a native of Bremerton, but also because his starkly beautiful Chapel of Saint Ignatius at Seattle University had cast a mesmerizing spell on the city since its opening in 1997. Zimmer Gunsul Frasca also had support from its increasing work in the Seattle area, including the well-liked Bellevue Regional Library. That left Koolhaas as the wild card in the competition, the only architect without a local presence or, for that matter, a presence in the United States.

The stage was set for the architects' visit to Seattle, at their own expense, during three days in May. What transpired was a decathlon of activities, both public and private, presentations of recent architectural work, interviews by the citizens committee, consultations with library staff, media questions, and a social reception, all leading up to the competition's climax—a design exercise in which the three firms had to demonstrate their creative approach under the tight deadline of just forty-eight hours.

The content of the design exercise was a closely guarded secret, even from the citizens committee charged with evaluating the results. But it was quite straightforward. Under the headline "Introduce Us to Your Design Perspective" were these directions: "Please prepare a set of visual images offering your ideas, impressions and observations to design the Central Library. These ought to include, but not be limited to, such aspects as natural light, site characteristics, context, major program imperatives, the entry sequence, the relationship between interior and exterior, technology, and building flexibility. The number of drawings is only limited by the time you have to present them, which is one half hour of a 45-minute allotment per firm, allowing time for questions by the Library Board or Architect Selection Advisory Panel. The sketches should be hand drawn on the paper provided. You may use the pens provided, pencils, or watercolor."[18]

The final competition, moved to the Sheraton hotel because of intent public interest, opened with librarian Jacobs describing the past two days as "electrifying" and then offering a festive exhortation to "let the wild rumpus begin."[19] What followed was less rumpus than grad school lecture, at least as the first two architects took their turns at the podium. Holl went first, expounding at length about fifteen different issues that would influence the library's design. Robert Frasca followed, outlining the "approach and process" that would be followed by his firm in formulating the library's

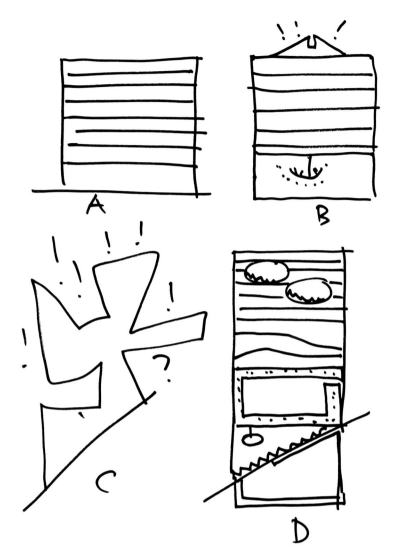

The Seattle competition between three architectural firms to design the new Central Library was marked by the creative and sometimes whimsical solutions from the Office for Metropolitan Architecture, Rotterdam.

design. Koolhaas closed, the only architect in the threesome who seemed energized by the intellectual challenges of this final face-off. The globe-trotting Dutch architect had been attending his daughter's college graduation in New York City on the previous day, but was soon peppering his comments with a series of wry wisecracks that prompted much laughter in the audience. Koolhaas also unveiled a creative pièce de résistance to the competition—design concepts for the Central Library using the library's provided paper as mandated, but with stand-up cutouts of neighboring skyscrapers to offer site context and some pieces of paper actually folded and shaped by the architect himself to present other concepts, as the fascinated audience watched this sly end run around the competition's

OMA's creative pièce de résistance during the design competition is delivered when Koolhaas takes the presentation paper required by the library, then folds and shapes it into a three-dimensional representation of the firm's design approach, a clever end run around the rules which prompts applause from the crowd.

rules. "Architecture is three-dimensional," Koolhaas deadpanned, "and this is our ploy to be both polite and architectural."[20] The crowd applauded.

Koolhaas, the Euro wild card, had stormed into contention for the Central Library commission, at least with those in the audience. He had proved to be a master of the public review process, just as Jacobs had been during her job interviews in Seattle. He was charming, glib, rigorous, intellectual, comfortable in the spotlight, and adroit at conveying understanding for the needs of the institution. Yet Koolhaas still came with one major handicap, the equivalent of Jacobs's lack of big-city administrative experience. The architect's handicap was the unfamiliarity of his work, almost all of it in distant Europe and "experienced" in Seattle only via photos and slides. Holl had the Saint Ignatius chapel in Seattle, Frasca had the Bellevue library, but Koolhaas had no similar building anywhere on the North American continent. Whether the citizens committee would make an architect recommendation based on such a transoceanic leap of faith seemed an open question.

The fourteen-member citizens committee proved profoundly split during its deliberations after the architects' presentations. Although no formal vote was taken, it was obvious from discussions that half of the committee members favored Holl, half favored Koolhaas. The deadlock seemed as solid as concrete.

Matthew Stadler, the literary writer on the citizens committee, was one of the few library people who had actually walked through some of Koolhaas's buildings. He had gravitated to the Koolhaas camp during the architects' presentations, although he still found much to admire in Holl's work. Stadler cogently described the committee's dilemma in a lengthy analysis sent via e-mail to Jacobs and subsequently shared with library board members. Stadler wrote:

> Now we've met the two design firms who could guide us toward the conclusion of this shared inquiry: Steven Holl Associates and the Office for Metropolitan Architecture. They made brilliant presentations of their past work and design philosophies. They made clear how radically

different they are from each other. Our options could not be more distinct.

Steven Holl demonstrated his commitment to what he called "artistic intensity," consistently reading design challenges as aesthetic problems to be solved by a visionary sensibility. . . . This is Holl's strength. He is unwavering in his commitment to a unified artistic vision. His buildings have great power and presence. This strength was echoed in every part of his presentation. He bristled against constraints and against any notion of compromise of his vision. He promised us a beautiful building, a historically important building, if we join him and support this artistic quest. . . .

By contrast, OMA left us hanging in a world of uncertainty. We were given no way to picture the building we would get. OMA took us on our word that we are interested in collaborating with an architect to find the design of our new library. They took our call for collaboration seriously, and forced us to ask: Are we serious about what we set out to do? . . . Koolhaas said architecture was not something holy or sacred, but a set of choices that could be understood by anyone. He displayed a limitless curiosity about the possibilities of the building, offering us an inventory of possible shapes and strategies, rather than a set of pre-determined designs. Faced with constraints, he accepted and then capitalized on them. . . .

I believe that if we hire Steven Holl we are announcing that the public process is over. We have found our visionary and he will give us our library. . . . If it is fear of the unknown which keeps us from embracing OMA—and I think it is—let's find out all we can about them, to allay our fears and relieve our worries, and then let's recognize that we set out to discover something unknown. OMA is the only firm to see that, rise to that challenge, and take us on our word. I think it's notable that public reaction, and reaction among staff and librarians, in the wake of meeting and engaging with the architects, was very strongly enthusiastic about OMA. Clearly the city is ready and serious about what we set out to do with this unique project. It would be a terrible failure and a betrayal of that process to turn our backs on that.[21]

Stadler's analysis closed with a kernel of an idea that was seized upon by the citizens committee. Its deadlock meant that the committee could not produce a recommendation that the library board hire Holl over Koolhaas, or Koolhaas over Holl, either. But, in a spirit of compromise, the committee could indeed recommend that the library board make its choice from those two architects. The committee could also add another recommendation that might help break any similar library board deadlock over Holl versus Koolhaas. It strongly urged the library board to travel to Europe and visit buildings designed by both Holl and Koolhaas. At the least, the visit could help remove what Stadler called the "fear of the unknown" with Koolhaas.

The library board began its brief visit to Europe less than a week later. The entire board (president Betty Jane Narver, Gordon McHenry, Linda Larson, Gilbert Anderson, Greg Maffei) traveled on the hurriedly arranged expedition, their way paid by a donor to the library Foundation. Also joining the group were librarian Jacobs, advisor Dingfield, and several members of the citizens committee.

Their first European stop took place on May 20 and was a visit to Holl's Kiasma Museum of Contemporary Art in Helsinki, the visit coming only hours after the group arrived at the airport in the Finnish capital. Whether the trip was even necessary had been on the board members' minds as they made their way across the Atlantic. There was some grousing that all this effort and all this money was being expended when the end result was already known. As Anderson, the retired president of a medical technology company, later recalled, "If the trustees had been forced to take a vote on the airplane, it would have been in favor of Holl."[22] That support had been echoed in a *Seattle Times* editorial published on the eve of the group's departure ("Holl seems right") and was the legacy of his wondrous Chapel of Saint Ignatius in Seattle.[23] But the board members' support for Holl began to unravel at Kiasma. The 130,000-square-foot museum turned out to be a boldly modern structure that dwarfed the Seattle chapel in size and lacked its immediate appeal. Kiasma was a stark symphony of cool white and dramatic shapes, but without the chapel's welcoming grace. Even more crucial was the discovery that the museum, which had opened only a year before, did not seem to have aged well. Finishes and materials appeared worn and tired to the board members, perhaps as a result of its heavy usage, but also perhaps from the finishes used. "That new building looked 10 years old." Anderson remembered. "The finishes just didn't seem right."[24] Holl had triumphed over 515 other architects in winning the Kiasma commission and it represented a significant advance in his career, but seeing the building sowed doubts about the architect among the visitors from Seattle.

The next day in the board's whirlwind trip was spent in the Netherlands, ferried about from one Koolhaas site to the next. The first stop was the Educatorium in Utrecht, a combination student and classroom center

that was part of a new university campus on the outskirts of the old city. The OMA-coined name for the building, created to suggest a "factory of learning," typified the firm's creative and entertaining approach to the building, which had opened two years before. This was architecture with a visual jazz of unexpected touches and materials—an upper stairway landing of plywood that curved out and up to the ceiling like some interior skateboard platform, support structures nakedly exposed, a cafeteria for 1,000 people that had the feel of a glass-sided spaceship. Two large auditoriums (dubbed "Theatron" and "Megatron") displayed high dramatics from contrasting colors, shapes, and materials. Glass surrounding a staircase was etched with enigmatic phrases in English ("The truth would be nothing but the shadow of the image"). A massive exterior ramp to the second floor was shielded by an overhang and provided a covered place where small groups of students gathered between classes, some sprawled on the steeply sloped concrete, others seated on what looked like giant plastic teardrops. The Educatorium seemed to reflect a questing intellect with a wry sense of humor, much how Koolhaas had come across in Seattle, and the visiting board members could not help but be impressed.

Next stop was the Kunsthal in Rotterdam, a home to changing art exhibitions that had opened seven years

before. Again, the Seattle visitors encountered a bold entrance ramp; a startling mix of materials from expensive to prosaic; and another brilliantly rendered auditorium, this one brightened by a wall of floor-to-ceiling windows on one side and featuring concrete support beams and a concrete floor topped with plywood risers where sat individual chairs, each displaying a bright color from a ten-hue palette. The Kunsthal auditorium was another visual jazz number, with a fascinating interplay of creative details and surprising effects, the very antithesis of the ho-hum assembly hall. Koolhaas's dazzling auditoriums were "very important" to the Seattle visitors, as Anderson later stressed, since one of the key elements of the new Central Library was an auditorium that would host many of the library's public events.[25] It would be Seattle Public Library's gathering place.

The Seattle visitors moved on to OMA itself on the top floor of an anonymous office block in downtown Rotterdam. The firm's multinational staff of sixty young architects and support personnel worked in large open areas with clusters of crowded tables and bookshelves. The office gave little immediate sense of the intense pressure-cooker atmosphere that often ramped up amid the long hours on the firm's complex projects and the exacting requests of Koolhaas delivered at any hour of the day or night via fax from some distant corner of the globe. The next morning, all but three of the Seattle visitors were driven to their final Koolhaas stop, the Congrexpo, or Grand Palais, in Lille, France—an oblong-shaped multiuse facility that held a concert hall seating 6,000 people, plus convention center auditoriums and meeting rooms. Again, there were contrasting elements and surprising dramatics that the Seattle visitors had now come to recognize as signatures of OMA buildings. And again, there were testimonials that Koolhaas had managed these effects despite low building costs ($95 per square foot in the Congrexpo). "It showed," recalled board member Linda Larson, "that he could live within a budget."[26]

The Seattle visitors returned to the Netherlands. Final arguments in Koolhaas's favor were offered by three members of the party who, at Koolhaas's invitation, spent a day traveling with him to Maison a Bordeaux, his most praised structure. Anderson of the library board and Val Thomas and Janet Ketcham from the citizens committee toured the remarkable residence created by Koolhaas for a newspaper executive who was wheelchair-bound after being severely injured in an auto accident. The Seattle threesome shared what they had seen and heard on the Bordeaux trip when they rejoined the rest of the group in Amsterdam on the night before their return to Seattle. In addition, Thomas, an architect and a developer, provided a written account of that Bordeaux trip in a memo to board members and librarian Jacobs.

Thomas was greatly impressed by the Bordeaux house, a brilliant Koolhaas testament to the concept of accessibility that *Time* magazine had praised as the best design of 1998. Thomas reported in his memo: "The house is spectacular, serene, beautiful. It is a thoughtful minimalist vision. Shows extreme attention to detail. The house works. It creates, or rather interacts with, several quite different environments. The owners love it. RK has a wonderful relationship with Bordeaux clients."[27]

Thomas's memo was peppered with telling personal observations about the architect, from how he "experiences and sees life on a global scale" to how he "is a likable, sincere person—strongly interested in many things, and his mind always seems to be on several of them at once" to how he had had a severe reaction to a yellow fever inoculation the year before that turned into viral meningitis, which cost him twenty pounds on his lanky frame, required three months' rest to recover, and "changed his perspective on life and the world."[28]

Thomas's two-page memo also included his recounting of Koolhaas's thoughts on the Seattle Public Library commission and what he could bring to the project, a matter of acute interest to the board members charged with selecting its architect. Thomas wrote, "He is strongly interested in this job. Believes he can create beauty with an adequate budget and good clear client. Says Seattle's budget is sufficient to do so. . . . Has strong respect for Deborah [Jacobs]. Regarding the question of responsiveness, I believe he can be. He sees the design process as beginning with a strong analysis and then being cyclical with the client to approach and solve program issues. The design emerges from this process. He will be strong, I believe, in his design viewpoint, but open to give and take on how things work. Likes to work directly with the client."[29]

Only a few days later, the board of trustees of Seattle Public Library reassembled in the Central Library's auditorium, where they faced a standing-room-only crowd gathered to hear one of the most momentous decisions in the library's history. The board's vote was unanimous: Seattle's new Central Library would be designed by the Office for Metropolitan Architecture, in partnership with the Seattle firm of Loschky Marquardt & Nesholm Architects (LMN). The library board's visits to Koolhaas's buildings in Europe had produced a dramatic turnaround in his favor and the Dutch architect had won OMA's most significant American commission.

Board members explained their rationales for selecting Koolhaas, both in the public meeting and in media questioning afterward. These five Seattle citizens, with not an architect or a design professional in their group, appeared enthusiastic about their stunning selection of the long shot architect with the avant-garde credentials, but they still appeared a bit shell-shocked by how their made-up minds had been unmade and then remade during their brief trip to Europe. So board member Larson, an attorney, praised Koolhaas's work for possessing "a joy and exuberance and a range of expression that I just found compelling,"[30] while board member McHenry, a lawyer who worked as a senior manager at the Boeing Company, observed that Koolhaas's structures "also felt like successful buildings that would withstand the test of time."[31] Board member Maffei, a Microsoft executive, stressed Koolhaas's analytical methods and predicted that "the intellectual approach to the library of the future that Rem brings will be seminal."[32] But it was board president Narver, a public policy expert at the University of Washington, who best summed up the visit to Europe and what it had wrought. "It was a wonderful experience," she emphasized. "But we are entering scary ground."[33] Maffei added a final coda with these blunt words: "I'm for Rem, but I think we will need to manage him."[34]

The board's daring selection of Koolhaas startled many people in Seattle, and perhaps none more than Norie Sato, a respected visual artist who served on the citizens committee on architect selection but held out little hope that the challenging Dutch architect would emerge as the final choice of the library board. Sato was "dumbfounded,"[35] but greatly heartened, when Koolhaas was named as the unanimous winner. "For once in Seattle," she emphasized, "we've made a leap."[36]

It was the second such leap for the library board in less than two years, a reprise of the boldness that had resulted in the selection of Jacobs to lead the library. The board's hirings of the Corvallis librarian and the Dutch architect were rare acts of institutional courage in an era of calculated governance when public decisions usually followed the safest path and produced middling results.

Seattle Public Library was emboldened by its leadership and its public support as the weeks and months

Under Nancy Pearl's leadership, Seattle Public Library's Center for the Book rose to new prominence, with a host of public programs including its innovative "If All of Seattle Read the Same Book," which was promoted with buttons bearing the name of the featured author.

ticked down toward the dawning of a new century. Never before in its history had the library experienced such fortuitous synergy. Innovation bred more innovation. Support bred more support. As the library's 1999 annual report proclaimed with justifiable pride, "The extraordinary has become the norm at Seattle Public Library."[37]

Often in the public forefront was the library's Center for the Book, under the leadership of the omnipresent Nancy Pearl. When a loss of funding imperiled the Washington State Library's longtime program honoring the best books by the state's writers, Pearl and the Center for the Book stepped up to rescue the program. Pearl pledged an infusion of grant money to reinvigorate the program, soon renamed the Washington State Book Awards. She also pledged efforts to restore credibility to a selection process that faced criticism for its failure to convey awards on several noteworthy books by state authors who had been much honored in the national literary arena, a reflection of the state's burgeoning literary culture. Those overlooked books included Charles Johnson's *Middle Passage,* winner of the National Book Award; David Guterson's *Snow Falling on Cedars,* winner of the PEN/Faulkner Award; and Jon Krakauer's *Into Thin Air,* a critically acclaimed account of a fatal mountaineering disaster on Mount Everest and a book that became a towering best-seller.

One of its own program initiatives earned the most notice for the Center for the Book. The idea was hatched in 1996 when Pearl, associate director Chris Higashi, and arts consultant Nancy Stillger met to suggest new ways to assist the hundreds of local book groups that held regular meetings to discuss a specific title. The trio came up with the creation of what would be, in essence, a citywide book group. One book would be selected for study by interested Seattle residents, then the author would come to town for a series of gatherings with those readers. The hope was that this new program—dubbed "If All of Seattle Read the Same

Writer Ernest Gaines speaks and teen readers provide an appreciative audience during his Seattle visit for the second edition of "If All of Seattle Read the Same Book." The Seattle Public Library program was soon copied in the New York State cities of Rochester and Buffalo; both also featured Gaines's novel of the South, *A Lesson Before Dying.*

Book" on Stillger's suggestion—would enhance the spirit of community and forge an increased appreciation for literature.

"If All Seattle Read" did that, and much more. Grants of $190,000 from the Lila Wallace-Reader's Digest Fund paid for planning of the program and its first three years of operation. It debuted in 1998 with Russell Banks's powerful novel of a small town's response to tragedy, *The Sweet Hereafter,* a discussion-worthy work that would be unfamiliar to most readers. The program was supported with thousands of free study guides and lapel buttons ("I'm Reading Russell Banks"), complemented by several hundred posters around town. Banks arrived in Seattle and drew hundreds of readers during a series of public events of varying size, including several held in libraries. The response to the Center's program was enthusiastic, if not exactly galvanizing, since Seattle already boasted one of the country's most active calendars of author appearances through the vital efforts of The Elliott Bay Book Company, the University Book Store, and Seattle Arts & Lectures. "The foundation of our program," Pearl conceded, "has always been book groups."[38]

Then the whole process was repeated a year later with Ernest Gaines's novel of southern injustice, *A Lesson Before Dying.* Other cities soon began to copy the Seattle program, first two in New York State, Rochester in 2000 and Buffalo in 2001, programs of such faithful adaptation that they even used the same cumbersome title with their own city's name and selected the same

Gaines novel. The program also spread to Kentucky and Arkansas.

National publicity followed, first on National Public Radio and later in the *New York Times,* especially in 2001 when Chicago launched its much ballyhooed "One Book, One Chicago" program with Harper Lee's Pulitzer Prize-winning classic, *To Kill a Mockingbird.* So many inquiries about the program poured into Seattle's Center for the Book that Higashi was prompted to write a four-page booklet, "Building a Citywide Book Club," to answer such questions. Some controversy even started to shadow the little Seattle program that could, especially when book selections elsewhere seemed motivated less by literary merit than by political correctness, to Pearl's chagrin. "You're never going to please everyone," she stressed. "We don't even try."[39] The Seattle program continued to spread to more cities, counties, and states—from the state of Alaska to Palm Beach, Florida; from Bangor, Maine, to the island of Maui, Hawaii. The number of such community reading programs topped 120 and showed no sign of slowing. No program born in Seattle had prompted such widespread emulation since owner Warren McPherson first banned workplace smoking at Radar Electric in 1977 after his mother died of lung cancer.

Seattle Public Library also continued to blaze an impressive trail in its fund-raising efforts. The library's Friends numbered 8,000 members in 1999 and raised $71,000 that year, much of it through its popular semi-annual book sales, which had found a welcome home

A full range of services were offered downtown in Seattle Public Library's temporary new home in the Washington State Convention & Trade Center during construction of the new Central Library. The temporary library, designed by LMN Architects of Seattle, won a national design award in 2003.

at the former naval base at Sand Point. The following year, the library's Foundation passed the $65 million mark toward its ambitious goal of raising $75 million in private donations to supplement the "Libraries for All" program. Among the landmark donations received by the library were a 1999 gift of $4 million from the heirs of attorney A. Scott Bullitt to improve programs in history and biography and a gift of $20 million from Microsoft billionaire Paul Allen in 2000 to improve the library's book collections. That donation also established Allen as the library's most generous benefactor, at $22.5 million, among a multitude of contributors that had swelled to an astonishing 10,000 individuals, corporations, foundations, and organizations.

Allen's second major gift was a testament to his youthful visits to Seattle Public Library's North East Branch, where the son of a librarian at the University of Washington whiled away many enjoyable hours, as did his sister, Jody. In announcing the $20 million donation, Jody Allen Patton said that it was given so that future generations of library users "can have those same positive experiences."[40] The North East Branch also produced fine memories for the Seattle Public Library's other $20 million contributor, Bill Gates, years before he and Allen founded Microsoft.

The "Libraries for All" program continued its forward march on many fronts. Citizen oversight panels were appointed, architects selected, plans formulated, branches closed for remodeling or demolition. The

final days of the 1960 vintage Central Library were commemorated in 2001 with a series of festivities, including the compilation of a memory book that included patron H. M. Nelson's recounting of how he cooled his bare feet in the library's fountain on a hot summer's day during his youth. "I will miss this library," Nelson wrote, "because it's one of the last places holding memories from growing up in Seattle."[41] The last patrons walked out of the tired old library on the afternoon of Friday, June 8. The doors were then locked, signaling final doom for the sluggish elevators' chances of ever stopping at floors six, seven, and eight, missing floors displayed on the elevators' control panels in expectation of an expansion that never came.

A temporary Central Library opened a month later in a new portion of the Washington State Convention & Trade Center. The library's temporary space of 130,000 square feet was just several blocks away on Pike Street and was large enough to hold two-thirds of the downtown collection after a complex transfer operation that compiled a book-moving bill of $459,000. One hundred marchers celebrated the opening of the temporary library with a short parade destined to be dwarfed by the festivities surrounding the much anticipated opening of Koolhaas's new Central Library two years later.

Demolition of the old Central Library proceeded through the fall of 2001 and the Koolhaas structure started to rise in its place, Seattle's third library on the same downtown block, each representing a remarkable

What was once the pride of Seattle Public Library turns to wasteland as demolition proceeds on the second library to occupy the downtown site.

advance over its predecessor. But one of the people most responsible for the latest architectural leap forward would not get to see it take final form. Betty Jane Narver, an important member of the library board for a decade, suffered a stroke and died on December 9, 2001, her sudden loss devastating the library community and many Seattleites whose lives she had touched with her energy, her intellect, and her commitment to service. Narver, sixty-seven, had retired a year before from her position as director of the Institute for Public Policy and Management at the University of Washington, but her retirement only meant that she "slowed down to 110 miles per hour,"[42] recalled Congressman Jim McDermott, a longtime friend. Narver's last week of life included a typical host of activities, a dinner party for 100 people in her home, plus attendance at meetings in Atlanta and New Orleans. The esteemed civic leader, who played a pivotal role in the board's hiring of both Jacobs and Koolhaas, had served as a mentor to the new Seattle librarian (both were Mills College graduates) and many other Northwest leaders brought together for spirited discussions around her kitchen table.

Koolhaas, now a figure of world architectural renown, made repeated visits to Seattle as the new library proj-

ABOVE: A computer-generated image by the Office of Metropolitan Architecture depicts the "mixing chamber" in the new Central Library where patrons will be able to do research from print and electronic resources.

OPPOSITE (ABOVE): Patrons in the mixing chamber overlook the new Central Library's grand "living room."

OPPOSITE (BELOW): The children's area in the new Central Library.

ect advanced, the OMA design work under the leadership of Joshua Ramos, a native of Bainbridge Island. Relations between OMA and the library had their stresses, as happens with any project of such complexity. Strong wills on both sides led to intense debates, much give-and-take, and compromises that sometimes pleased neither party. At issue were matters that included the location of the building's prime entrance, the distribution of public art, the organization of its innovative book spiral, and the building's glass exterior, which was dramatically upgraded at Koolhaas's request, with an additional $4.3 million in private donations. The greatest loss in the process may have been book shelving that Koolhaas wanted to design for the library and have custom manufactured, a proposal

Another OMA image captures the high dramatics and soaring space of the "living room" in the new Central Library, off the Fifth Avenue entrance.

that the architect tried to save in a personal last-ditch mission to Seattle that ultimately failed because of uncertainty about how long it would take to produce the shelving. Its omission left Jacobs and many others feeling, at the time, "heartbroken."[43]

A work session with the library board and Koolhaas on April 11, 2002, mirrored both the strengths and tensions in the relationship between client and architect. The subject of the afternoon meeting in the offices of LMN Architects was interior materials and colors to be used in the new Central Library. But the meeting's subtext was who would make the final selections, whether the architect's sometimes flamboyant choices would be accepted by library board members or compromise options would have to be formulated. Much verbal jousting resulted, with Koolhaas presenting his rationales for various choices and librarian Jacobs presenting the concerns of the library board and staff. The mutual respect between Koolhaas and Jacobs was evident, as was their fondness for exchanging sarcastic jabs.

"Are you fond of pink?" Jacobs asked the architect at one point during a discussion of the floors in the teen section of the library, which carried a color closely resembling Pepto-Bismol.

"I am," Koolhaas conceded.

"Pink," the librarian stated flatly, "is a no-go."

"Let's test it," he countered. "I would be really interested to know what people think then."

"We can have a focus group, Rem, or you can go with the orange instead. . . . You know, Rem, everything you learn from this project will help you in the future."

"It will help me . . . to design prisons," Koolhaas quipped, before breaking up in laughter.[44]

More give-and-take followed in the ensuing minutes. Koolhaas explained that distinct colors were intended to give different character to different rooms in the library. Board member Linda Larson countered that the pink color was simply "too much" and board member Greg Maffei stressed that he just didn't "get it."[45] Amid the standoff, Koolhaas finally proposed a reconsideration of the floor color, with black as a possibility to replace pink. The discussion then moved on to other, less contentious, matters.

Smoothing over differences in client-architect opinions was seldom too difficult, since excitement over the new Central Library coursed through those involved in the project like a river running high with spring snowmelt. The bold Koolhaas design went from blueprint to steel with surprisingly few major changes, its most

The top of the new Central Library's innovative book spiral (at left) and an adjacent reading room is suffused with light from the building's exterior wall of windows in its distinctive diamond-shaped patterns.

dazzling features still intact. Perhaps the most anticipated was the great "living room" on the library's third level, a towering interior space with ceilings as high as fifty feet and 360-degree views of the Seattle cityscape beyond. This room seemed destined to become Seattle's secular cathedral, a place of inspiration and awe. There was also much anticipation about the library's distinctive exterior walls with their dramatic diamond-shaped patterning; the children's area with its unusual sloping columns; the reading room on the tenth level with its infusion of light; the auditorium that, when not in use, would offer a kind of terraced hill climb between the library's first and third levels. Providing added drama throughout the building was to be Koolhaas's arsenal of hyper-colors, provocative, unexpected, sometimes verging toward strange. There were to be curving walls in resplendent red, flashes of happy yellow and pink in the children's section. Nowhere to be found in the new library was the muted palette of earth tones that often made Seattle seem one great gray city. Koolhaas's Central Library would earn many adjectives in upcoming attempts to describe or critique it, but those adjectives would never include "muted." Nor would they include that proverbial put-down of Seattle's youth culture—"boring."

Just when the new Central Library started to rise from the ground in 2002, a vexing problem arose at Seattle Public Library. The high-tech and Internet boom—the expected foundation for an ever more prosperous twenty-first-century future—instead collapsed like a house of straw. Internet companies disappeared in a dot-com implosion, billions of dollars were lost in a stock market nosedive, capital investments and donations turned to vapors almost overnight. Seattle and much of the Northwest reeled into recession as one of the country's hardest-hit regions.

Huge deficits loomed in the City of Seattle's budget, and all city departments were required to make emergency budget cuts, including the library. But so much of the library's budget was still tied up in personnel costs that significant savings could only be made with cuts there. Layoffs seemed a distinct possibility, posing a grave threat to the library's diverse recent hires with low seniority, until a more palatable compromise was reached with the reluctant approval of the library's unions.

The compromise still had drastic effect: the entire Seattle Public Library was closed down for two periods in 2002 (August 26–September 1 and December 17–23). Staff members received no pay during those shutdown

171

This OMA depiction of the new Central Library's exterior (a southwest view from Fourth Avenue and Madison Street) became the most frequently used public image of the daring Rem Koolhaas design.

periods, the longest at the library since the influenza quarantine of 1918; nor did staff members accrue any vacation or retirement benefits. Even the library's book-collection boxes and web site were rendered inoperative, as the library virtually disappeared from civic life. But layoffs had indeed been avoided.

Librarian Jacobs stressed, "It was a risky bold move to take. When my chief financial officer first thought this up, I was personally opposed to it. But I came to understand that it was not grandstanding before the public, not blackmailing the city government; it was the fiscally correct thing to do. Because we chose to close during weeks with low library use, that meant the numbers of people affected, although not trivial, were

PLACE OF LEARNING, PLACE OF DREAMS

Ironworkers steady the final piece of structural steel for the new Central Library during the traditional topping-off ceremony in May 2003.

not as great as they would have been other weeks in the year."[46]

The system-wide library shutdowns still shocked and outraged some citizens, especially since the closures came during Seattle Public Library's heralded building boom (funded by money approved not long before the recession descended). Tania Hill was one of the library's disappointed patrons, voicing her upset in a letter to the editor at the *Post-Intelligencer.* "How is it that my city government can bar me from the services that my local library offers?" Hill wrote. "How is this fair, especially to the low-income people of the Seattle area? Where are they supposed to go for books, movies and to use the Internet?"[47]

Even more library budget cuts loomed in 2003, with a $4.8 million cut (11.4 percent) from its annual budget to reach a final operating figure of $32.6 million. Two more weeklong shutdowns were ordered, prompting more criticism. The book budget was reduced, as were library operating hours. The bold optimism of just two years before started to fade into bittersweet memory. The Seattle Public Library's long history of boom and bust seemed to be cycling back to bust once again.

But there was a crucial difference this time. Seattle Public Library's resources were no longer limited to revenues from the city. The Friends of the Seattle Public Library had first started to supplement city funding. The Seattle Public Library Foundation had altered the library's resources in ever more dramatic fashion, amassing an endowment of $20 million that was in the top rank of all American libraries. The Foundation's millions in private funds could not be used to offset city budget cuts at the library, but did provide a constant source of programs, acquisitions, and improvements at the library. "Libraries for All" had provided an unprecedented brick-and-mortar expansion that would shape Seattle Public Library for decades into the future.

Librarian Charles Wesley Smith, sitting in his office in the imposing new Carnegie library downtown, had predicted in 1906 that Seattle Public Library's great future was now "manifest." His prediction proved overly optimistic for the library through many of the ensuing decades, as challenge followed challenge, budgets stagnated or shrank, and disappointments mounted.

That manifest future had finally arrived almost 100 years after Smith's rosy prediction, thanks to the tireless good works of the Friends, thanks to the Foundation's financial muscle from its contributors, thanks to the landmark "Libraries for All" program approved in a landslide by Seattle voters. There would be setbacks at the library still, frustrations too, but a perennial goal was elusive no longer. Sustained progress was finally assured at The Seattle Public Library.

Notes

CHAPTER 1. THE DAWNING OF KOOLHAAS

1. "Bequest Is Accepted by Library," *Seattle Post-Intelligencer,* 10 March 1959, hereafter cited as *P-I.*

2. Deborah L. Jacobs, interview by author.

3. Ibid.

4. Deborah L. Jacobs and Rem Koolhaas, *Benaroya Hall Public Presentation of Architect's Plans on 3 May 2000,* #2.

5. Jacobs, interview.

6. Jacobs and Koolhaas, *Benaroya 2000,* 2.

7. Pritzker Architecture Prize 2000 Laureate Citation, Hyatt Foundation, Purchase, N.Y., 29 May 2000.

8. J. Carter Brown, statement released on the awarding of the Pritzker Architecture Prize 2000, Hyatt Foundation, Purchase, N.Y., 29 May 2000.

9. *Benaroya 2000,* 2.

10. Ibid.

11. Ibid., 2-3.

12. Arthur Lubow, "Rem Koolhaas Builds."

13. Rem Koolhaas, *Delirious New York,* 9.

14. Ibid., 290.

15. Rem Koolhaas and Bruce Mau, *S,M,L,XL,* xix.

16. Ibid., 1094.

17. Office for Metropolitan Architecture (OMA), *The New Seattle Public Library Research.*

18. Jacobs and Koolhaas, *Benaroya Hall Public Presentation of Architect's Plans on 15 December 1999,* 10.

19. Jacobs and Koolhaas, *Benaroya 2000,* 4.

20. Ibid., 5.

21. Ibid., 6.

22. Ibid., 7.

23. Jacobs and Koolhaas, *Benaroya 2000,* 8.

24. Jacobs and Koolhaas, *Benaroya 1999,* 8.

25. Susan Buckingham Reilly, letter to Alexandra Harris.

26. Jacobs and Koolhaas, *Benaroya 2000,* 9.

27. Ibid.

28. Charlie Cunniff, letter to the editor, *Seattle Times,* 19 January 2000.

29. Matthew Stadler, "Koolhaas, Library Design Deserve Kudos," op-ed article, *Seattle Times,* 8 February 2000, hereafter cited as *Times.*

30. O. Casey Corr, "The Hiring of Rem Koolhaas and the Shock of the Shoes," editorial column, *Times,* 16 June 1999.

31. Jacobs and Koolhaas, *Benaroya 2000,* 10.

CHAPTER 2. SEEKING A LIBRARY

1. Emily J. Carkeek, "Historical Sketch of the Seattle Public Library."

2. Thomas W. Prosch, *A Chronological History of Seattle, from 1850 to 1897,* 182-83.

3. *Weekly Intelligencer,* 10 August 1868.

4. Prosch, *A Chronological History of Seattle,* 189.

5. Linda Peavy and Ursula Smith, "Sarah Burgert Yesler," 144.

6. Ibid., 159.

7. "Henry Yesler's Native American daughter, Julia, is born on June 12, 1855," HistoryLink.org.

8. Roberta Frye Watt, *Four Wagons West: The Story of Seattle,* 145.

9. Jalmar Johnson, *Builders of the Northwest,* 110.

10. J. Willis Sayre, *This City of Ours,* 120.

11. Prosch, *A Chronological History of Seattle,* 256.

12. C. T. Conover, *Mirrors of Seattle,* 256.

13. Peavy and Smith, "Sarah Burgert Yesler," 175.

14. *P-I,* 30 August 1887.

15. *P-I,* 14 April 1889.

16. *P-I,* 25 May 1889.

17. Murray Morgan, *Skid Road: An Informal Portrait of Seattle,* 110.

18. Library Commission, City of Seattle, *Report for the Year Ending December 31, 1891,* 1.

19. Library Commission, City of Seattle, *Report for the Year Ending December 31, 1892*, 9.

20. *P-I,* 16 December 1892.

21. Ibid.

22. *P-I,* 17 December 1892.

23. *P-I,* 18 December 1892.

24. Ibid.

25. Library Commission, *Report for the Year Ending December 31, 1894*, 2.

26. Library Commission, *Report for the Year Ending December 31, 1895*, 13.

27. Library Commission, *Annual Report for 1895*, 9-10.

28. Seattle Public Library, *Annual Report for 1896*, 6-7, hereafter cited as SPL.

29. SPL, *Annual Report for 1898*, 12.

30. Ibid.

31. SPL, *Annual Report for 1897*, 10.

32. SPL, *Annual Report for 1899*, 2.

33. Ibid., 14.

34. Ibid., 15.

35. Ibid.

CHAPTER 3. FROM THE ASHES

1. *P-I,* 25 December 1950.

2. *P-I,* 2 January 1901.

3. Ibid.

4. *P-I,* 25 December 1950.

5. *P-I,* 3 January 1901.

6. Ibid.

7. *P-I,* 6 January 1901.

8. *P-I,* 7 January 1901.

9. *P-I,* 8 January 1901.

10. *P-I,* 6 January 1901.

11. Theodor Schuchat, *The Library Book,* 6.

12. Ibid., 5.

13. Stuart H. Holbrook, *Far Corner: A Personal View of the Pacific Northwest,* 107.

14. *P-I,* 6 January 1901.

15. Ibid.

16. Ibid.

17. Ibid.

18. Ibid.

19. Ibid.

20. Ibid.

21. *P-I,* 8 January 1901.

22. Ibid; *P-I,* 7 January 1901; ibid.; *P-I,* 8 January 1901.

23. *P-I,* 8 January 1901.

24. Ibid.

25. Ibid.

26. *P-I,* 15 January 1901.

27. SPL, *Annual Report for 1903,* 5.

28. Ibid., 7.

29. Ibid., 5-6.

30. Col. William Farrard Prosser, *A History of the Puget Sound Country,* 2:14.

31. Ibid.

32. Clarence B. Bagley, *History of Seattle,* 1:288.

33. SPL, *Annual Report for 1905,* 20.

34. *P-I,* 20 December 1906.

35. SPL, *Opening of the Seattle Public Library Building,* 2.

36. SPL, *Annual Report for 1906,* 12.

CHAPTER 4. GREAT EXPECTATIONS

1. SPL, *Annual Report for 1906,* 16.

2. SPL, *Annual Report for 1905,* 14.

3. Ibid.

4. *Sketches of Washingtonians,* 44-48.

5. SPL, *Annual Report for 1907*, 5.

6. SPL, *Minutes of Meeting of Seattle Public Library Board*.

7. Ibid.

8. SPL, *Annual Report for 1908*, 7.

9. Ibid., 12.

10. Judson T. Jennings, "Public Libraries for Public Service," 22.

11. SPL, *Annual Report for 1913*, 12.

12. Ibid., 13.

13. SPL, *Annual Report for 1915*, 41.

14. SPL, *Annual Report for 1914*, 12.

15. *P-I*, 8 April 1917.

16. SPL, *Annual Report for 1917*, 4.

17. SPL, *Annual Report for 1918*, 6.

18. Gina Kolata, *Flu: The Story of the Great Influenza Pandemic of 1918 and the Search for the Virus That Caused It*, 6.

19. SPL, *Annual Report for 1907*, 16.

20. SPL, *Annual Report for 1919*, 8.

21. Ibid.

22. SPL, *Annual Report for 1920*, 10.

23. SPL, *Annual Report for 1923*, 1.

24. Jennings, "Sticking to Our Last," n.p.

25. Ibid.

26. Ibid.

27. Ibid.

28. Ibid.

29. *Seattle Welcomes the American Library Association*, 2.

30. SPL, *A Ten-Year Program for the Seattle Public Library*, 24.

31. Ibid., 7.

32. *P-I*, 28 February 1930.

CHAPTER 5. YEARS OF DEPRESSION

1. Judy Anderson, Gail Lee Dubrow, and John Koval, *The Library Book*, 46.

2. SPL, *Annual Report for 1931*, 11.

3. Ibid.

4. Natalie B. Notkin, *Report for the Year Ending December 31, 1931*, 1.

5. *P-I*, 21 February 1932.

6. Ibid.

7. Ibid.

8. Ibid.

9. Ibid.

10. Ibid.

11. Ibid.

12. U.S. House Special Committee to Investigate Communist Activities in the United States, *Investigation of Communist Propaganda*, 154.

13. Ibid., 155.

14. Ibid., 156.

15. Notkin, sworn statement taken in deposition.

16. Notkin, *Report for the Year Ending December 31, 1928*, 3.

17. Notkin, *Report for the Year Ending December 31, 1930*, 3.

18. Notkin, *Report for the Year Ending December 31, 1931*, 3-4.

19. Ibid.

20. Ibid.

21. I. Panchenko, letter to Board of Directors, Seattle Public Library.

22. Ibid.

23. Jennings, letter to I. Panchenko, 2.

24. Notkin, *Report for the Year Ending December 31, 1931*, 4.

25. Notkin [presumed], *Analysis of Russian Collection*.

26. Notkin, letter to Library Board, Seattle Public Library, 2-3.

27. "Natalie Brodskaya Notkin, 1900-1970," *Washington Library Letter*.

28. SPL, *Annual Report for 1933*, 5.

29. Ibid., 10.

30. SPL, *Annual Report for 1934*, 10.

31. *P-I*, 13 June 1938.

32. SPL, *Annual Report for 1939*, 4.

CHAPTER 6. THE WAR EFFORT

1. Jennings, *The People's University: A Ten-Year Program for Seattle Public Library*, 31.

2. Ibid.

3. *P-I*, 17 January 1941.

4. Roger Sale, *Seattle, Past to Present*, 181.

5. *P-I*, 28 March 1942.

6. SPL, *Annual Report for 1942*, 32.

7. *P-I*, 8 April 1942.

8. SPL, *Annual Report for 1940-41*, 19.

9. SPL, *Annual Report for 1942*, 6.

10. Ibid.

111. David A. Takami, *Divided Destiny: A History of Japanese Americans in Seattle*, 60.

12. SPL, *Annual Report for 1943*, 17.

13. Takami, *Divided Destiny*, 56.

14. *P-I*, 31 December 1943.

15. SPL, *Annual Report for 1944*, 7-8.

16. SPL, *Annual Report for 1943*, 37.

17. Ibid.

18. Quintard Taylor, *The Forging of Black Community: Seattle's Central District, from 1870 through the Civil Rights Era*, 168.

19. *P-I*, 15 August 1945.

CHAPTER 7. POSTWAR GROWING PAINS

1. SPL, *Annual Report for 1945*, 4.

2. SPL, *Annual Report for 1947*, 8.

3. SPL, *Annual Report for 1949*, 12-13.

4. SPL, *Annual Report for 1947*, 3.

5. *P-I*, 25 January 1947.

6. SPL, *Annual Report for 1947*, 21.

7. *P-I*, 14 April 1949.

8. SPL, *Annual Report for 1949*, 6.

9. Ibid.

10. *Times*, 15 October 1950.

11. *P-I*, 9 November 1950.

12. John S. Richards, "On Losing a Bond Issue," 250.

13. Ibid.

14. Guy G. Garrison, "Seattle Voters and Their Public Library," 77.

15. SPL, *Annual Report for 1950*, 12.

16. *P-I*, 28 April 1948.

17. *P-I*, 1 December 1952.

18. *Times*, 8 September 1951.

19. *Times*, 12 September 1951.

20. *P-I*, 28 February 1952.

21. *Times*, 18 February 1952.

22. SPL, *Annual Report for 1954*, 4.

23. SPL, *Annual Report for 1953*, 6.

24. *P-I*, 9 December 1954.

25. *P-I*, 5 July 1955.

26. *P-I*, 16 November 1955.

27. *P-I*, 15 March 1956.

28. *Times*, 11 March 1956.

28. *Times*, 11 March 1956.

29. *P-I*, 15 March 1956.

30. *P-I*, 10 April 1956.

31. *Times*, 10 April 1956.

31. *Times*, 10 April 1956.

32. Ibid.

33. *Times*, 11 April 1956.

34. *P-I*, 25 April 1956.

35. Richards, letter to Library Board, Seattle Public Library.

36. *Times*, 3 May 1956.

37. *P-I*, 17 June 1956.

38. *Times*, 4 July 1956.

39. *P-I*, 6 July 1956.

CHAPTER 8. CELEBRATION AND TUMULT

1. SPL, *Flash*, 1.

2. *P-I*, 12 December 1957.

3. *P-I*, 28 February 1957.

4. *P-I*, 11 September 1957.

5. Ibid.

6. SPL, *Annual Report for 1957*, 11.

7. *P-I*, 27 March 1960.

8. Ibid.

9. Ibid.

10. BOLA Architecture + Planning, *Report on Landmark Nomination of the Central Library for Seattle Public Library*, 14, 24.

11. Deloris Tarzan Ament, *Iridescent Light: The Emergence of Northwest Art*, 139.

12. Ibid., 141.

13. *P-I*, 17 August 1971.

14. Ibid.

15. Ibid.

16. SPL, *Biennial Report for 1959-1960*, 3.

17. Ibid.

18. Ibid., 20.

19. Ibid., 17.

20. Ibid., 19.

21. Ibid., 15.

22. *P-I*, 17 November 1961.

23. *P-I*, 19 November 1961.

24. Ibid.

25. Ibid.

26. *P-I*, 21 November 1961.

27. *Times*, 20 November 1961.

28. *Times*, 24 November 1961.

29. *P-I*, 29 November 1961.

30. *P-I*, 29 November 1961.

31. *Times*, 8 April 1962.

32. "Four Public Libraries," *Architectural Record*, 182.

33. SPL, *Yesler Branch Library Annual Report for 1962*, 1.

34. Kathryn Harper, interview with James R. Welsh, 3.

35. Ibid.

36. SPL, *Yesler Branch Library Annual Report for 1964*, 1.

37. Harper, interview with Welsh, 2.

38. SPL, *Yesler Branch Library Annual Report for 1965*, 1.

39. SPL, *Yesler Branch Library Annual Report for 1967*, 2–3.

40. Harper, interview with Millie Russell, 1.

41. Ibid., 4.

42. SPL, *Biennial Report for 1966–1967*, 6.

43. *P-I*, 1 May 1970.

44. SPL, *Biennial Report for 1969–1970*, 8.

45. Elke Boettcher, interview by author.

CHAPTER 9. TIGHT BUDGETS, TOUGH DECISIONS

1. *Times*, 27 March 1970.

2. SPL, *Annual Report for Circulation Services for 1970*, 1.

3. Sale, *Seattle Past to Present*, 232.

4. *Times*, 8 November 1974.

5. Public Affairs Counseling, *Imperatives for Change: A Management Improvement Analysis for the Seattle Public Library*, B-167.

6. *P-I*, 8 November 1974.

7. Ibid.

8. Ibid.

9. *P-I*, 25 November 1974.

10. Ibid.

11. Ibid.

12. Public Affairs Counseling, B-177.

13. *P-I*, 9 March 1975.

14. Ibid.

15. *Times*, 1 June 1972.

16. *P-I*, 9 March 1975.

17. *Times*, 10 August 1975.

18. *P-I*, 18 November 1976.

19. Boettcher, *Local 2083, 1970–1990*, 2.

20. *P-I*, 3 March 1977.

21. *P-I*, 4 March 1977.

22. Ibid.

23. *P-I*, 14 January 1977.

24. *Times*, 26 March 1982.

25. *P-I*, 18 November 2000.

26. *Times*, 20 December 1980.

27. Ibid.

28. *Seattle Weekly*, 18 November 1981.

29. Ibid.

30. SPL, *Annual Report for 1982*, 4; ibid, 1.

31. *P-I*, 14 September 1984.

32. *P-I*, 21 September 1984.

33. Ibid.

34. Ibid.

35. *Times*, 27 September 1984.

36. *P-I*, 24 January 1984.

37. *P-I*, 25 January 1985.

38. *P-I*, 31 January 1985.

39. Ibid.

40. Ibid.

41. Will McBride and Helga Fleischhauer-Hardt, *Show Me! A Picture Book of Sex for Children and Parents*, 143.

42. Ibid., 171.

43. Ibid., 176.

44. *P-I*, 2 March 1985.

45. *P-I*, 5 March 1985.

46. *P-I*, 8 March 1985.

47. Ibid.

48. *P-I*, 6 April 1985.

49. Ibid.

50. *Times*, 2 May 1985.

51. *P-I*, 4 May 1985.

52. Ibid.

53. Ibid.

54. *P-I*, 7 May 1985.

55. *Times*, 7 May 1985.

56. *P-I*, 7 May 1985; 10 May 1985.

CHAPTER 10. GATHERING PROMISE

1. Timothy Egan, *The Good Rain: Across Time and Terrain in the Pacific Northwest*, 88.

2. Ibid., 98.

3. SPL, *Annual Report for 1986*, 2.

4. SPL, *Annual Report for 1987*, 1.

5. *Times*, 14 March 1988.

6. Ibid.

7. SPL, *Annual Report for 1988*, 2; ibid.

8. Ibid.

9. SPL, *Annual Report for 1989*, 2.

10. Ibid.

11. Ibid., 3.

12. *P-I*, 23 February 1989.

13. SPL, *Annual Report for 1989*, 3.

14. *Times*, 26 September 1989.

15. Ibid.

16. SPL, *Annual Report for 1989*, 2.

17. *P-I*, 23 February 1989.

18. *Times*, 7 April 1991.

19. *Times*, 20 June 1991.

20. Ibid.

21. Frank W. Greif, interview by author.

22. *P-I,* 30 November 1991.

23. *Seattle Weekly,* 4 December 1991.

24. Ibid.

25. Ibid.

26. Ibid.

27. Ibid.

28. Ibid.

29. *Times,* 17 July 1992.

30. SPL, *Annual Report for 1991,* 2.

31. *Times,* 17 July 1992.

32. Ibid.

33. Ibid.

34. SPL, *Annual Report for 1992,* 6.

35. *Times,* 26 August 1992.

36. *P-I,* 7 November 1992.

37. *Seattle Weekly,* 9 February 1994.

38. *P-I,* 2 November 1994.

39. *Times,* 23 October 1994.

40. SPL, *Annual Report for 1994,* 8.

41. SPL, *Annual Report for 1995,* 2.

42. SPL, *Annual Report for 1994,* 2.

43. Ibid., 3.

44. *Seattle Weekly,* 15 June 1994, 13.

45. Brenda P. Tirrell, *Collection Evaluation: Seattle Public Library,* 4.

46. *P-I,* 24 November 1995.

47. *Times,* 30 August 1996.

48. Ibid.

49. *P-I,* 31 August 1996.

50. Ibid.

51. Ibid.

CHAPTER II. LIBRARIES FOR ALL

1. *P-I,* 19 April 1997.

2. John Berry, "Deborah Jacobs," 41.

3. *P-I,* 30 September 1997.

4. Ibid.

5. *Times,* 1 October 1997.

6. *Times,* 7 February 1997.

7. *P-I,* 10 October 1997.

8. *Times,* 7 February 1999.

9. *Times,* 8 March 1998.

10. *P-I,* 3 March 1998.

11. *Times,* 23 April 1998.

12. *Times,* 15 October 1998.

13. *Times,* 24 November 1998.

14. Bill and Melinda Gates Foundation, press release.

15. SPL, *Annual Report for 1999,* 3.

16. *Times,* 9 June 2001.

17. SPL, *Score Sheet for Architect Selection Advisory Panel,* 4 March 1999.

18. SPL, *Directions to Finalist Architecture Firms.*

19. SPL, *Architect Selection Competition.*

20. Ibid.

21. Stadler, e-mail to Deborah Jacobs.

22. Gilbert W. Anderson, interview by author.

23. *Times,* 18 May 1999.

24. Anderson, interview.

25. Ibid.

26. *Times,* 9 April 2000.

27. Val Thomas, memo to Seattle Public Library Board of Trustees and Librarian Deborah Jacobs.

28. Ibid.

29. Ibid.

30. *P-I,* 27 May 1999.

31. SPL, press release on the Board of Trustees' choice of Office for Metropolitan Architecture to design New Central Library, 26 May 1999.

32. *Times,* 27 May 1999.

33. *P-I,* 27 May 1999.

34. *Times,* 27 May 1999.

35. Norie Sato, interview by author.

36. *P-I,* 27 May 1999.

37. SPL, *Annual Report for 1999,* 4.

38. *P-I,* 29 August 2001.

39. *Times,* 24 March 2002.

40. *Times,* 30 August 2000.

41. *Times,* 9 June 2001.

42. *P-I,* 11 December 2001.

43. Jacobs, interview.

44. Notes taken by author during meeting between Seattle Public Library Board of Trustees and representatives of Office for Metropolitan Architecture in offices of LMN Architects in Seattle, 11 April 2002.

45. Ibid.

46. Jacobs, interview.

47. *P-I,* 14 August 2002.

Bibliography

Ament, Deloris Tarzan. *Iridescent Light: The Emergence of Northwest Art.* Seattle: University of Washington Press; La Conner, Wash.: Museum of Northwest Art, 2002.

Ames, William E., and Roger A. Simpson. *Unionism or Hearst: The Seattle Post-Intelligencer Strike of 1936.* Seattle: Pacific Northwest Labor History Association, 1978.

Anderson, Gilbert W. Interview by author. Seattle, 13 January 2003.

Anderson, Judy, Gail Lee Dubrow, and John Koval. *The Library Book.* Seattle: Seattle Arts Commission, 1991.

Bagley, Clarence B. *History of Seattle.* Vol. 1. Chicago: S. J. Clarke Publishing, 1916.

Berner, Richard C. *Seattle Transformed: World War II to Cold War.* Seattle: Charles Press, 1999.

Berry, John. "Deborah Jacobs." *Library Journal,* January 1995.

Bill and Melinda Gates Foundation. Press release, 24 October 1998.

Blair, Karen J., ed. *Women in Pacific Northwest History.* Seattle: University of Washington Press, 2001.

Boettcher, Elke. Interview by author. Seattle, 19 September 2002.

——. *Local 2083, 1970-1990.* Seattle: Local 2083, November 1990.

BOLA Architecture + Planning. *Report on Landmark Nomination of the Central Library for Seattle Public Library.* Seattle: BOLA Architecture + Planning, September 2000.

Carkeek, Emily J. "Historical Sketch of the Seattle Public Library." Seattle Public Library, 1919.

Churchill, Bonnie. "Dutch Maverick Wins Architectural Award." *Christian Science Monitor,* 20 April 2000.

Conover, C. T. *Mirrors of Seattle.* Seattle: Lowman & Hanford, 1923.

Crowley, Walt. *Rites of Passage: A Memoir of the Sixties in Seattle.* Seattle: University of Washington Press, 1995.

Crowley, Walt, and HistoryLink Staff. *Seattle & King County Timeline.* Seattle: HistoryLink and University of Washington Press, 2001.

Cuito, Aurora. *Rem Koolhaas/OMA.* Barcelona: LOFT Publications, 2002.

Egan, Timothy. *The Good Rain: Across Time and Terrain in the Pacific Northwest.* New York: Alfred A. Knopf, 1990.

Forgey, Benjamin. "Rem Koolhaas, Master Planner: Dutch Architect Wins the Pritzker Prize." *Washington Post,* 17 April 2000.

"Four Public Libraries." *Architectural Record,* September 1967.

Garrison, Guy G. "Seattle Voters and Their Public Library." *Illinois State Library Research Series,* no. 2. Illinois State Library, Springfield, Ill.: September 1961.

Goldberger, Paul. "High-Tech Emporiums: Prada and Toys 'R' Us Have Much in Common." *New Yorker,* 25 March 2002.

Greif, Frank W. Interview by author. Seattle, 9 December 2002.

Harper, Kathryn. Transcript of interview with James R. Welsh on 28 July 1999. Addendum to "Truth at the Crossroads," independent study research project. Antioch University, Seattle, 1999.

——. Transcript of interview with Millie Russell on 22 July 1999. Addendum to "Truth at the Crossroads," independent study research project. Antioch University, Seattle, 1999.

Heron, Katrina. "From Bauhaus to Koolhaas." *Wired,* July 1996.

HistoryLink.org. Selected on-line articles, 1998-2003.

Holbrook, Stuart H. *Far Corner: A Personal View of the Pacific Northwest.* New York: Ballantine, 1973.

Jacobs, Deborah L. Interview by author. Seattle, 12 March 2002.

Jacobs, Deborah L. and Rem Koolhaas. *Benaroya Hall Public Presentation of Architect's Plans on 15 December 1999.* Seattle Public Library. Videotape transcript.

——. *Benaroya Hall Public Presentation of Architect's Plans on 3 May 2000.* Seattle Public Library. Videotape transcript.

Jennings, Judson T. Letter from Librarian, Seattle Public Library, to I. Panchenko, National League of Americans of Russian Origin, 2 September 1931. Seattle Public Library. Photocopy.

——. *The People's University: A Ten-Year Program for Seattle Public Library.* Seattle: Seattle Public Library, 1940.

——. "Public Libraries for Public Service." *Pacific Northwest Commerce,* May 1911.

——. "Sticking to Our Last." *Library Journal,* July 1924.

Johnson, Jalmar. *Builders of the Northwest.* New York: Dodd, Mead, 1963.

Kirsner, Scott. "Seattle Reboots Its Future." FastCompany.com, May 2001.

Kolata, Gina. *Flu: The Story of the Great Influenza Pandemic of 1918 and the Search for the Virus That Caused It.* New York: Farrar, Straus & Giroux, 1999.

Koolhaas, Rem. *Delirious New York.* New York: Monacelli Press, 1994.

Koolhaas, Rem, and Bruce Mau. *S,M,L,XL.* New York: Monacelli Press, 1995.

Library Commission, City of Seattle. *Report.* Seattle: Library Commission, 1891-95.

Lubow, Arthur. "Rem Koolhaas Builds." *New York Times Magazine,* 9 July 2000.

Luscombe, Brenda. "The Rem Movement." *Time Europe,* 24 April 2000.

McBride, Will, and Helga Fleischhauer-Hardt. *Show Me! A Picture Book of Sex for Children and Parents.* New York: St. Martin's, 1975.

Mcguigan, Cathleen. "How Kool Is Rem." *Newsweek,* 28 June 2002.

Morgan, Murray. *Skid Road: An Informal Portrait of Seattle.* Seattle: University of Washington Press, 1995.

Muschamp, Herbert. "Koolhaas, a Guiding Force in Modern Theory, Gets the Pritzker." *New York Times,* 17 April 2000.

"Natalie Brodskaya Notkin, 1900-1970." *Washington Library Letter* 11, no. 14 (15 July 1970).

Notkin, Natalie B. Letter to Library Board, Seattle Public Library, 8 February 1932. Seattle Public Library. Photocopy.

——. *Report for the Year Ending December 31, 1928.* Seattle: Seattle Public Library, Circulation Department, Foreign Division, 1929.

——. *Report for the Year Ending December 31, 1930.* Seattle: Seattle Public Library, Circulation Department, Foreign Division, 1931.

——. *Report for the Year Ending December 31, 1931.* Seattle: Seattle Public Library, Circulation Department, Foreign Division, 1932.

——. Sworn statement taken in deposition, 5 September 1931. Seattle Public Library. Photocopy.

——. [presumed]. *Analysis of Russian Collection.* Seattle: Seattle Public Library, Circulation Department, Foreign Division, 31 December 1931. Photocopy.

Office for Metropolitan Architecture (OMA). *The New Seattle Public Library Proposal.* Rotterdam, Netherlands: OMA, October 1999.

——. *The New Seattle Public Library Research.* Rotterdam, Netherlands, October 1999.

Olson, Sheri. "How Seattle Learned to Stop Worrying and Love Rem Koolhaas' Plans for a New Central Library." *Architectural Record,* September 2000.

Panchenko, I. Letter from Seattle Branch, National League of Americans of Russian Origin, to Board of Directors, Seattle Public Library, 27 August 1931. Seattle Public Library. Photocopy.

Pearman, Hugh. "Prophet Sharing." *Sunday Times* (London), 25 July 1999.

Peavy, Linda, and Ursula Smith. "Sarah Burgert Yesler." In *Women in Waiting in the Westward Movement.* Norman: University of Oklahoma Press, 1994.

Prosch, Thomas W. *A Chronological History of Seattle, from 1850 to 1897.* Northwest Collection, University of Washington, Seattle, 1900-1901. Typescript.

Prosser, Col. William Farrard. *A History of the Puget Sound Country,* Vol. 2. New York: Lewis Publishing, 1903.

Public Affairs Counseling. *Imperatives for Change: A Management Improvement Analysis of the Seattle Public Library.* San Francisco: Public Affairs Counseling, 1974.

Reilly, Susan Buckingham. Letter to Alexander Harris, Capital Projects Director, Seattle Public Library, 2 April 2001.

"Rem Koolhaas, Architect and Designer, Office for Metropolitan Architecture." *Business Week,* 11 June 2001.

Richards, John S. Letter to Library Board, Seattle Public Library, 3 May 1956. Seattle Public Library. Photocopy.

——. "On Losing a Bond Issue." *Library Journal,* 15 February 1951.

Ritz, Richard E. *Central Library: Portland's Crown Jewel.* Portland, Ore.: Library Foundation Inc., 2000.

Rupp, James M. *Art in Seattle's Public Places: An Illustrated Guide.* Seattle: University of Washington Press, 1992.

Sale, Roger. *Seattle: Past to Present.* Seattle: University of Washington Press, 1994.

Sandler, Linda. "Dutch Architect Takes Starring Role— Koolhaas Is Revered by Many, but Too Hip for Some." *Wall Street Journal,* 12 May 1999.

Sato, Norie. Interview by author. Seattle, 12 January 2003.

Sayre, J. Willis. *This City of Ours.* Seattle: Seattle School Board, 1936.

Schuchat, Theodor. *The Library Book.* Seattle: Madrona Publishers, 1985.

Seattle Post-Intelligencer. Selected issues, 1881-2003.

Seattle Public Library. Annual reports. Seattle: Seattle Public Library, 1891-2001.

——. Architecture Selection Competition, 11 May 1999. Seattle Public Library. Videotape.

——. *Biennial Report for 1959-1960.* Seattle: Seattle Public Library, 1961.

——. *Biennial Report for 1966-1967.* Seattle: Seattle Public Library, 1968.

——. *Biennial Report for 1969-1970.* Seattle: Seattle Public Library, 1971.

——. "Directions to Finalist Architecture Firms." Seattle Public Library, 9 May 1999.

——. *Flash* (staff newsletter) 13, no. 2 (February 1955).

——. *Minutes of Meeting of Seattle Library Board.* Seattle Public Library, 24 May 1907.

——. *Opening of the Seattle Public Library Building.* Seattle: Seattle Public Library, Ivy Press, 1907.

——. Press release on the Board of Trustees' choice of Office for Metropolitan Architecture to design new Central Library. Seattle Public Library, 26 May 1999.

——. *Score Sheet for Architect Selection Advisory Panel.* Seattle Public Library, 4 March 1999.

——. *A Ten-Year Program for the Seattle Public Library.* Seattle Public Library, 1930.

——. *Yesler Branch Library Annual Report for 1962.* Seattle Public Library, 1963.

——. *Yesler Branch Library Annual Report for 1964.* Seattle Public Library, 1965.

——. *Yesler Branch Library Annual Report for 1965.* Seattle Public Library, 1966.

——. *Yesler Branch Library Annual Report for 1967.* Seattle Public Library, 1968.

Seattle Times. Selected issues, 1898-2003.

Seattle Weekly. Selected issues, 1981-2001.

Seattle Weekly Intelligencer. Selected issues, 1868-81.

Seattle Welcomes the American Library Association: Handbook of Information for Conference in Seattle, July 6-11, 1925. Seattle: Seattle Chamber of Commerce, Argus Press, 1925.

Sketches of Washingtonians. Seattle: Wellington C. Wolfe, 1907, 44-48.

Stadler, Matthew. E-mail to Librarian Deborah Jacobs of Seattle Public Library, 13 May 1999.

Stone, Elizabeth W. *American Library Development, 1600-1899.* New York: H. W. Wilson, 1977.

Sudjic, Deyan. "He Likes Brutality and Shopping. He's Going to Be the Next Big Thing." *Observer,* 26 November 2000.

Takami, David A. *Divided Destiny: A History of Japanese Americans in Seattle.* Seattle: University of Washington Press, Wing Luke Asian Museum, 1998.

Taylor, Quintard. *The Forging of a Black Community: Seattle's Central District from 1870 through the Civil Rights Era.* Seattle: University of Washington Press, 1999.

Thomas, Val. Memorandum to Seattle Library Board of Trustees and Librarian Deborah Jacobs, 22 May 1999.

Tirrell, Brenda P. *Collection Evaluation: Seattle Public Library.* B. Tirrell, Houston, January 1994.

U.S. House Special Committee to Investigate Communist Activities in the United States. *Investigation of Communist Propaganda: Hearings Pursuant to H. Res. 220.* Washington, D.C.: 71st Cong., 3rd sess., Part I, Vol. No. 5, December 1930.

Warren, James R. *The War Years: A Chronicle of Washington State in World War II.* Seattle: History Ink, University of Washington Press, 2001.

Watt, Roberta Frye. *Four Wagons West: The Story of Seattle.* Portland: Binford & Mort Publishing, 1993.

Wiley, Peter Booth. *A Free Library in This City: The Illustrated History of the San Francisco Public Library.* San Francisco: Weldon Owen Inc., The Library Foundation of San Francisco, 1996.

Winger, Howard W., ed. *Library Trends: American Library History, 1876-1976.* Urbana-Champaign, Ill.: University of Illinois Graduate School of Library Science, 1976.

Wolf, Gary. "Exploring the Unmaterial World." *Wired,* June 2000.

Yaeger, Lynn. "Retail Space: The Final Frontier." *New Yorker,* 28 January 2002.

Index

Illustrations are indicated in boldface type.

PLACE OF LEARNING, PLACE OF DREAMS